fun with the family

Northern California

hundreds of ideas for day trips with the kids

Eighth Edition

Karen Misuraca

travel

Guilford, Connecticut

All the information in this guidebook is subject to change. We recommend that you call ahead to obtain current information before traveling.

To buy books in quantity for corporate use or incentives, call **(800) 962-0973** or e-mail **premiums@GlobePequot.com.**

Copyright © 2011 by Karen Misuraca

ALL RIGHTS RESERVED. No part of this book may be reproduced or transmitted in any form by any means, electronic or mechanical, including photocopying and recording, or by any information storage and retrieval system, except as may be expressly permitted in writing from the publisher. Requests for permission should be addressed to Globe Pequot Press, Attn: Rights and Permissions Department, P.O. Box 480, Guilford, CT 06437.

Editor: Amy Lyons
Project Editor: Heather Santiago
Layout: Joanna Beyer
Text Design: Nancy Freeborn and Linda R. Loiewski
Maps: Rusty Nelson © Morris Book Publishing, LLC
Spot photography throughout © Photodisc and © RubberBall Productions

ISSN 1540-305X
ISBN 978-0-7627-5719-0

Printed in the United States of America
10 9 8 7 6 5 4 3 2 1

Contents

NORTHERN CALIFORNIA

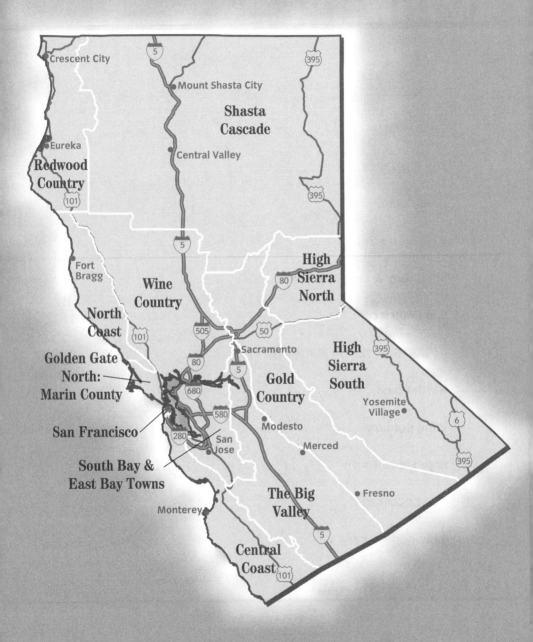

For Rachel, Wyatt, Melati, Melanie, Izzie, and Acacia, our rising stars

About the Author

A native Northern Californian who lives in Sonoma in the heart of the Wine Country, **Karen Misuraca** is the author of several guidebooks and travel literature, including *Quick Escapes from San Francisco: The Best Weekend Getaways, Backroads of the California Coast, The California Coast, Backroads of the California Wine Country, Insiders' Guide to Yosemite, Our San Francisco*, and *The 100 Best Golf Resorts of the World*.

She specializes in writing about golf travel and luxury resorts, California, and international travel, contributing to in-flight magazines and other publications. She is the international golf travel columnist for Examiner.com, and the founder and editor of www.BestGolfResortsoftheWorld.com.

Misuraca is also the author of the iPhone apps California Coast North and California Coast Central.

She and her husband, Michael Capp, explore Northern California's outdoors with her three daughters, five granddaughters, and grandson.

Introduction

C alifornia is for the young, no doubt, especially for the under-18 set. From theme parks to ocean beaches, from aquariums to ski resorts and museums that kids actually like, from cable cars to canoeing down the river and fishing in a mountain lake—it may take your family a lifetime of vacations to see and do it all.

Anchored by America's favorite city by the bay, San Francisco, and by the capital city of Sacramento with its charming gold rush–era riverfront, the northern half of the state is a different world than the more densely populated Southern California. The dramatic, rugged northern coastline is dotted with small coves and dashed by foaming surf. Nineteenth-century towns and villages look just as they did more than a century ago, and when the snow flies in the Sierras, skiing and winter play is the best in the West.

Fun with the Family Northern California will help you choose destinations that are perfectly suited to the ages of your children or grandchildren, and the activities that your family enjoys.

This book is divided into 12 geographic regions. The major towns in each region are featured, together with information on nearby attractions, family friendly restaurants, and places to stay that welcome and provide for children.

Does your family like water sports and camping? Consider spending a few days in California's Central Valley, at one of its many lakes and reservoirs, or on the inland Delta waterways, a paradise for families who love to fish, water-ski, houseboat, and camp out.

In the mountains of the Sierra Nevada, pitch a tent in a pine forest or settle into a rustic lakeside resort. Head for Redwood Country and park your RV beneath the tallest trees in the world, or hit the beach with your boogie boards in Santa Cruz.

Near the waterfront in San Francisco, your young scientists will enjoy one of the world's largest hands-on science museums. Shake hands with a robot at the Tech Museum of Innovation in San Jose, the birthplace of the personal computer.

Fancy accommodations can be hard on the family budget, so you'll find suggestions for comfortable, reasonably priced motels, inns, campgrounds, and hostels with amenities such as coin laundries, sofa beds, swimming pools, playgrounds, and game rooms; some offer supervised "kids' camps."

You'll find a strong focus on recreation, nature, and the environment. Many state parks and nature preserves are recommended as places to get close to wildlife and to see a tremendous variety of native flora and dramatic landscapes—images that stay with children for the rest of their lives. In the northernmost reaches of California, in the Shasta Cascade region and around Lassen Volcanic National Park, the trails and roads are lightly used, a key advantage if one of your vacation goals is to spend quiet time together in the wilderness.

Learning about the history of California is something that just happens in many of the towns and villages you will visit. In the perfectly preserved gold rush settlement of

Top California **Campgrounds**

A leading campground reservation company, ReserveAmerica (www .reserveamerica.com) recognized these Northern California parks as among the "Top 100 Family Campgrounds" for 2010 (nearly 4,000 parks were reviewed). State park campground reservations can be made by phone (800-444-7275) or online (www.parks.ca.gov).

- Anthony Chabot Regional Park, Castro Valley
- Del Valle Regional Park, Livermore
- Donner Memorial State Park, Truckee
- Folsom Lake State Recreation Area, Folsom
- Meeks Bay-Lake Tahoe Basin National Forest, Meeks Bay
- The campground at Pinnacles National Monument

Additional nods from ReserveAmerica:

- "Top 25 Amazing Locations": D.L. Bliss State Park near Emerald Bay and Pinnacles National Monument
- "Top 25 Kid-Friendly Parks": Donner Memorial State Park and Pinnacles National Monument

Columbia, shopkeepers and blacksmiths dress and work just as their forebears did a century ago, and you can still get a sarsaparilla and have your tintype taken. On the plaza in the Spanish mission town of San Juan Bautista, step into the stables to have a look at horse-drawn carriages and wagons from the 1860s, when a dozen coaches a day arrived with travelers from the East, bound for the boomtown of San Francisco.

Amusement parks, playgrounds, rest stops, and easy hiking trails are described in every region. On driving trips, it's good to take fresh-air breaks frequently so kids can let off steam.

TRIP PLANNING & RESOURCES

Go to www.visitcwc.com to locate California Welcome Centers and roadside rest areas throughout the state. The centers are stocked with brochures, maps, and the latest information for travelers, and you can check your e-mail there, make hotel reservations, and enjoy the picnic grounds.

If wildlife is your family's passion, the website www.cawatchablewildlife.org offers excellent driving itineraries focusing on more than 200 places where you can get up close to birds, mammals, and other wildlife; animal- and bird-related festivals are described, too.

Karen's Tips for **Traveling with Kids**

- **Toys.** In restaurants and other public places, I dip into my bag of tricks for younger children—a set of tiny wooden farm animals, a miniature deck of cards, colored pencils (colored pens can be dangerous) and paper, beads, and trinkets. Put the goodie bag away between trips so the toys don't get boring.

- **Where Are We Going?** As soon they learn to read, let the children be the trip navigators. With a highlighter pen, help them mark the route before you leave, and keep track of where you are during the day. In advance, present your young passengers with brochures, maps, and a blank notebook for stories and notes of the trip. Encourage them to keep their eyes out for postcards along the way to paste into the family album at home.

- **Don't Hurry, Be Happy.** The younger the child, the more important are frequent R&R stops. In advance, locate parks and other public places where they can run around, take a nap, and have a snack or a picnic (when the weather is crummy, an indoor shopping mall may not be a bad choice). The younger the child, the more the whole family will benefit from breaking the day into small segments of traveling, resting, sightseeing, restaurant stops, and outdoor recreation.

- **Preteens Can Be Happy Campers.** I can tell you from (vast) experience that your chances of a good time with younger teens are greatly increased if you allot them the following:
  - some time alone each day
  - some money each day to spend as they wish
  - permission to make a few phone calls or e-mails to friends at home
  - input and some decisions about destinations and activities

- **Hi-Tech Surrender.** For school-age kids and up, headphones, DVDs, iPods, video games, cell phones—give in to it. At the risk of creating havoc, limit the number of electronically enhanced hours, and check out their choices of entertainment before they descend into the abyss.

- **Snacks.** Have healthy snacks on hand at all times. You just don't know when you'll be waiting for a restaurant table, for your orders to come, or when your child just doesn't want what's on the menu or gets hungry 2 miles down the trail or 5 minutes before the plane takes off.

California's state park system is the largest in the lower 48 states—with nearly 300 parks, more than 15,000 campsites, 280 miles of coastline, and more than 3,000 miles of trails. An annual pass to the parks, which admits everyone in your vehicle, is $125. The Golden Poppy Pass saves money by the carful on admission to 95 of the state parks ($90 annually). There is also an annual boat-use pass ($75), a sno-park pass ($25), a Golden Bear Poppy Pass for seniors ($5), and passes for the disabled and for veterans. Apply online at www.parks.ca.gov or by calling (800) 777-0369. For campsite reservations call (916) 638-5883 or (800) 444-PARK. Good news (or is this bad news?)! Many state parks now have Wi-Fi at picnic tables, tents, RV spaces, cabins, and other sites; see the website for the list of participating parks.

The State of California's website for travelers, www.visitcalifornia.com, will keep you occupied for hours, browsing for theme parks, new attractions in each region, state and national parks, recreation and sports, driving tours, and much more. The **free** *California Visitor's Guide* is full of information about things to do, see, and enjoy throughout the state, and you get a large, pull-out map. You might also ask for the annual *California Celebrations* booklet, containing an extensive calendar of events, and another booklet, *The Best of California Driving Tours* (916-322-2881).

ACCOMMODATIONS, RESTAURANTS & ATTRACTIONS RATES

Dollar signs indicate general price ranges for meals, lodging, and attractions, when appropriate. For meals, the prices are for individual dinner entrees. For lodging, the rates are for a double room, with no meals, unless otherwise indicated; rates for lodging may be higher during peak vacation seasons and holidays. Always inquire about family and group rates and package deals that may include amusement park tickets, ski area tickets, and tickets for concerts and other performing arts events. Visitor bureaus can steer you to lodging with family packages. Rates for attractions are a general guide to what you can expect to pay in admission fees. We note when attraction fees differ for adults and children, and we point out with the **free** icon when something is free.

Rates for Accommodations

$	Less than $80
$$	$80 to $110
$$$	$110 to $170
$$$$	More than $170

Rates for Attractions

$	Less than $5
$$	$5 to $10
$$$	$10 to $20
$$$$	More than $20

Rates for Restaurants

$	up to $10
$$	$11 to $15
$$$	$15 to $20
$$$$	More than $20

Attractions Key

The following is a key to the icons found throughout the text.

SWIMMING		FOOD	
BOATING / BOAT TOUR		LODGING	
HISTORIC SITE		CAMPING	
HIKING / WALKING		MUSEUM	
FISHING		PERFORMING ARTS	
BIKING		SPORTS/ATHLETICS	
AMUSEMENT PARK		PICNICKING	
HORSEBACK RIDING		PLAYGROUND	
SKIING/WINTER SPORTS		SHOPPING	
PARK		PLANTS/GARDENS/NATURE TRAILS	
ANIMAL VIEWING		FARM	

Central Coast

racing the coastline south from San Francisco to Big Sur, Highway 1 is one of the most spectacular and diverse scenic highways in the world. Sandy beaches, rocky promontories, coves and harbors, dramatic mountain ranges, and farmlands create a rich geography. Along the way are a scattering of fishermen's villages and historic mission-era towns, the honky-tonk of a vintage seaside amusement boardwalk, the sophistication of European-style cafes, and state-of-the-art museums. Take time to stop frequently and make discoveries. Stroll on the beach; peer into tide pools; load up on veggies and fruit at a produce stand.

Whale-watching and beachcombing attract weekenders to Half Moon Bay, the Pumpkin Capital of the World. South along the coast from here to Santa Cruz are a chain of redwood parks, dozens of tide-pooly beaches, and tiny seacoast hamlets. At Año Nuevo State Reserve, thousands of elephant seals pose an unforgettable sight.

Fringed with 20 miles of wide sandy beaches, the classic beach towns of Santa Cruz and neighboring Capitola Village offer surfing, boating, seafood restaurants, and a boardwalk extravaganza of rides and games. Just inland from Highway 1, the Santa Cruz Mountains are crisscrossed by country roads meandering through ancient redwood groves and along the banks of the San Lorenzo River. Kids like the campgrounds and Roaring Camp, an 1880s logging settlement with a steam train.

Farther south the rich heritage of Spain is alive in the thick-walled adobes and colonial haciendas of Monterey. Museums and restored buildings from the days of the conquistadors are found on the "Path of History." The largest in the world, the Monterey Bay Aquarium is the most popular destination on the Central Coast.

The fairy-tale village of Carmel-by-the-Sea is chockablock with hundreds of shops. The glorious Carmel Mission and a jewel of a town beach are not to be missed. Carmel Valley is a good choice for a family vacation headquarters in the area because of dependably warm, dry weather and less-expensive lodgings.

CENTRAL COAST

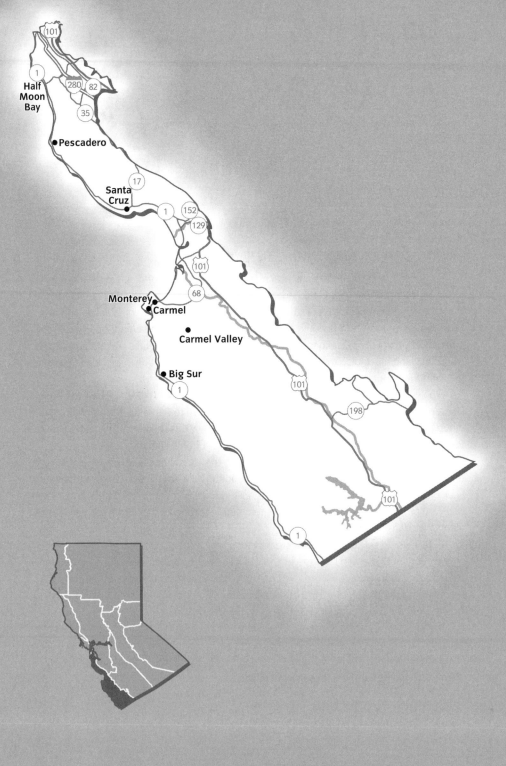

Running 90 miles south from Carmel, Highway 1 threads along the Big Sur coast between high cliffs and river valleys above a coastline legendary for its wild beauty. A national forest and four state parks and rocky beaches are worth exploring here.

Half Moon Bay

Good weather, sea air, and lots of outdoor fun near the harbor town of Half Moon Bay lure weekenders from the Bay Area in great numbers. It's worth the drive for a day on a sandy beach or a walk in a silent redwood forest.

Besides commercial ocean fishing and tourism, the main activities in the area are flower and vegetable growing. Within huge greenhouses and in the fields around them, flowers such as carnations, roses, tulips, and irises are grown for shipment all over the world. You can buy plants and produce—and Christmas trees—at several places along the highway. Colorful flower markets take place on third Saturdays, May through September, outside on Kelly Avenue, and November through April, inside at La Piazza, downtown.

A stroll through this small Victorian town turns up Western saloons, country stores, and 100-year-old hotels and homes, many on the National Register of Historic Places. Trendy galleries and shops abound. On the north end of town in Princeton, at the harbor, Harbor Village is a brand new atrium mall of about two dozen shops and cafes, many locally owned, anchored by the luxurious Ocean Hotel.

In October families come to the Art and Pumpkin Festival for pumpkin carving, pie eating, a haunted house, an exhibition of a 1,000-pound-plus winner of the Great Pumpkin Weigh-Off, and entertainment galore, plus 250 vendors (www.miramarevents.com). You can meet locals at the pancake breakfast and the Halloween costume competition. Come early to avoid the huge crowds.

Pillar Point Harbor (all ages)

At Princeton, 5 minutes north of Half Moon Bay on Highway 1; (650) 726-4382.

Watch a fleet of more than 200 fishing boats and yachts go in and out of the marina, fish from the wharf, go shelling on the little beach west of the jetty, rent kayaks and canoes, and hike or bike for miles. Tiny cafes, bars, and fish markets at the harbor are frequented by the locals. Whale-watching tours depart from the wharf. From December through April you are almost guaranteed to see California gray whales on their 4,000-mile migration from the Arctic to Baja. Surfers from around the world come to Mavericks off Pillar Point, where 30-foot waves breaking over a rocky reef up the ante; some say these are the biggest waves in the world. (Hang out with the Maverick surfers on the ocean-view deck at the Half Moon Bay Brewing Company here.) There's boat launch ramps, public restrooms, and RV parking. Near the harbor is a new atrium mall of shops and cafes.

Pillar Point Marsh and Shoreline (all ages)

On Capistrano Road at Princeton (pass the Pillar Point Harbor, going left on Prospect Way; turn right onto Broadway, left onto Harvard to the end; go right on West Point, then 0.5 mile to the parking lot); (650) 728-3582.

A 0.5-mile easy walk, perfect for toddlers, where you will see great blue herons, snowy egrets, and red-winged blackbirds, as well as a variety of other sea- and shorebirds. Follow the trail to the breakwater and tide pools on the far side, and watch for sea lions on the offshore rocks. Restrooms, wheelchair accessible.

Half Moon Bay State Beach (all ages)

Just south of Half Moon Bay, west on Kelly Avenue; (650) 726-8820.

Buy a kite at Lunar Wind Inventions in town, and head for these 3 miles of adjacent sandy beaches. At Francis Beach, the most popular, are developed RV and tent camp-sites, cold showers, BBQs, picnic sites, and the ranger station. If the campground is full, try the nice Pelican Point RV Park on Miramontes Point Road (650-726-9100). Notice the skateboard park on the highway at Kelly Avenue. Water temperature is chilly, even in summer, and the surf can be treacherous, so plan to dip your toes and play on the sand.

Cowell Ranch Beach (all ages)

Highway 1, Half Moon Bay; (650) 726-8819; www.sanmateocoastnha.org. Free.

About 3.3 miles south of town, by way of an easy, flat, 0.5-mile trail and steep stairs, there is a secluded, sandy beach. From the bluff, through a permanent telescope, you can see the seal preserve, where animals can be spotted from February through April on the beach or near the shoreline. A half mile south of Miramonte Point Road, look for the yellow gate. No dogs.

Coastside Trail (all ages)

From the coastal/west end of Poplar Avenue, 4.2 miles south of Pillar Point; (650) 726-8297.

This flat, easy, 7-mile paved biking and walking trail along the coastline, with access to several beaches, is beautiful! There is a parking lot, picnic area, and a bridge to the southern coastal trail here. A horse trail parallels the Coastside Trail from Roosevelt Beach to Francis Beach.

Fitzgerald Marine Reserve (all ages)

California Avenue off Highway 1, about 10 minutes north of Half Moon Bay, in Moss Beach; (650) 728-3584.

A 0.5-mile easy trail loops through the tangled garden of an old estate, a spooky forest of Monterey cypress, and along a bluff above some of the richest tide pools on the Pacific Coast. At low tide a kaleidoscope of sponges, sea anemones, starfish, crabs, mollusks, and fish emerge. A California sea lion may be watching you, and you can see gray whales offshore December through April.

Top Shops in **Half Moon Bay**

- **Quail Run.** 412 Main St.; (650) 726-0312. A nature-oriented emporium with elaborate bird mansions for the feathered few and butterfly gardens for kids.

- **Harbor Seal Company.** 406 Main St.; (650) 726-7418. This marine and wildlife shop sells sea- and birdlife toys, puzzles, soft animals, educational toys, books, and games.

- **Paper Crane.** 315 Main St.; (650) 726-0722. In the Tin Palace, among myriad gifts and cards are baby blankets, musical stuffed animals, and tchotchkes (small toys/knickknacks) for little kids.

- **Half Moon Bay Feed and Fuel.** 331 Main St.; (650) 726-4814. A warehouse sort of space chock-full of everything for hamsters to horses. Western- and farm-themed gifts, toys, clothing and more for cowboys and cowgirls.

- **Half Moon Bay Salt Water Taffy.** 270 Capistrano Rd. at Harbor Village; (650) 200-8526. Two dozen flavors of handmade taffy and other old-fashioned barrel candy, plus wooden toys and handcrafted pine furniture.

- **Surf Factory.** 270 Capistrano Rd. at Harbor Village; (650) 726-1476. Cool, casual clothes for the family, from Maui Jim to Billabong and UGG boots, plus sunglasses, shoes, surf stuff and more. The main store, Half Moon Bay Board Shop at 3032 North Cabrillo Hwy., has board rentals, repairs, and a huge array of surf gear.

- **Cunha's.** 448 Main St.; (650) 726-4071. A country store out of the Old West, with wooden floors, cowboy boots, hardware, and hardtack. After browsing the scrumptious gourmet picnic foods, look for the nice picnic table area on the corner across from the store.

With a special fishing license, try your hand at rock fishing. For the best tide pooling, call ahead to find out when the low tides are expected. Docent tours are available. Restrooms, picnic tables, interpretive center.

Mavericks Surf Competition (all ages)

Pillar Point Harbor, Half Moon Bay; (415) 462-6200; www.maverickssurf.com.

Your crazy-about-surfing kid already knows about Mavericks Surf Competition, the world-famous annual surfing contest that takes place a half mile off the coast near Pillar Point Harbor. Alerted with just 24-hours notice, elite surfers flock to Half Moon Bay sometime between November 1 and March 31 (depending on wave patterns) to compete for a

$150,000 prize purse. To catch the action up close, book a spot on one of the boat tours, or watch it on a big screen at AT&T Park in San Francisco. Watch it live on the website; check on the site about viewing from the shoreline, which may change in condition and location from year to year, due to huge crowds.

Half Moon Bay Nursery (all ages)

11691 San Mateo Rd., 3 miles east of Half Moon Bay off Highway 92; (650) 726-5392.

Keep a sharp eye out for the turn into the nursery. This is a rambling, gorgeous kingdom of blooming plants for the home and garden, from orchids and ferns to thousands of geraniums, herbs, azaleas, camellias, climbing vines, hanging baskets, and seasonal bulbs—a veritable flower show. In the wintertime it's cozy in the main greenhouse by the woodstove.

Just west, across the highway, Lemos Pumpkin Patch is popular with little kids, offering weekend pony rides and a play area.

Where to Eat

Barbara's Fish Trap. 281 Capistrano Rd. at Pillar Point Harbor; (650) 728-7366. A fun, noisy, casual place full of families, overlooking the harbor. Oilcloth-covered tables and a covered patio with outdoor heaters. Try the daily fresh fish specials; chowder, burgers, thick-cut fries. Cash only. $–$$

Cafe Classique. 107 Sevilla Ave., Half Moon Bay; (650) 726-9775. At the north end of town near Pillar Point, a casual place that's been here forever, serving giant omelets, sourdough French toast, and hotcakes for breakfast; steak hoagies and other unique sandwiches for lunch; and homemade soup and desserts. Children's portions available. Open from 4 a.m. $

Cameron's Pub. 1410 South Cabrillo Hwy., Half Moon Bay; (650) 726-5705; www.cameronsinn.com. Just south of town, watch for the red phone booth and the double-decker buses, just like in London. One of the buses serves as a game room for kids and there are arts, games, and volleyball out back of this pub and restaurant. From the warm welcome and hearty pub food to the handcrafted boat/dining booth made from Chinese relics, this funky British outpost is like no other. On the menu are fish-and-chips, bangers and mash, chili, steak, clam chowder, pizza, and more comfort food, with European brews on tap. With small kids, you may wish to avoid weekend evenings: open mic night on Thurs, Coyote Night on Fri, and karaoke on Sat night. $–$$

Half Moon Bay Coffee Company. 20A Stone Pine Rd. at the north end of Main Street, Half Moon Bay; (650) 726-3664. A casual place busy with locals and tourists digging into homemade pies and pastries, pancakes, burgers, sandwiches, and simple, hearty entrees. Breakfast, lunch, dinner. $

Ketch Joanne. Pillar Point Harbor, Princeton; (650) 728-3747; www.ketchjoanne restaurant.com. Big breakfasts, clam chowder, and fresh seafood in a booth by the potbelly stove. It's like a ship inside, with hatch covers, old photos, and paintings of sea creatures—and seagoing mateys at the bar. Breakfast, lunch, and dinner. $–$$

Main Street Grill. 547 Main at Miramontes, Half Moon Bay; (650) 726-5300; www.main stgrillhmb.com. Cajun sausage, homemade waffles and muffins, grilled sandwiches, thick shakes, microbrewed beer, and a jukebox. Breakfast and lunch. $

Miramar Beach Restaurant. 131 Mirada Rd., Half Moon Bay; (650) 726-9053. Formerly a circa-1918 Prohibition roadhouse, this joint jumps on the weekends with live music. Kids like watching the surfers off Miramar Beach. Fresh seafood and steaks, and a kid's menu. Lunch, dinner, and weekend brunch. $$–$$$

Where to Stay

Half Moon Bay Lodge. 2400 South Cabrillo Hwy. (Highway 1), south end of Half Moon Bay; (650) 726-9000 or (800) 368-2468; www.halfmoonbaylodge.com. Eighty spacious rooms with small patios or balconies overlooking gardens; some fireplaces; refrigerators, microwaves on request. Large swimming pool, enclosed oversize spa in a glass house, fitness center, sauna, complimentary continental breakfast, child care. Ask about the Family Picnic package that includes a beach blanket, beach toys, a kite, and gourmet treats. Less than 5 minutes from here starts a coastal walking trail. $$$

Harbor View Inn. 51 Avenue Alhambra, El Granada; (650) 726-2329; www.harbor viewinn.net. A Cape Cod–style motel near Pillar Point Harbor; large rooms with 2 queen beds, bay windows; cribs available. Walking distance to beaches, harbor, restaurants, walking trails. $$

Oceano Hotel and Spa. 280 Capistrano Rd., Half Moon Bay; (888) 623-2661; www .oceanohalfmoonbay.com. Brand new upscale hotel located in a shopping mall on the harbor has spacious king and double rooms, and extended-stay villas with loft bedrooms, kitchens and living/dining areas, and fireplaces. Luxurious throughout, right on the water, with fitness venue, day spa, restaurant and bar, in-room dining. $$$$

For More Information

Half Moon Bay Coastside Chamber of Commerce. 520 Kelly Ave., Half Moon Bay; (650) 726-8380; www.halfmoonbaychamber .org.

Pescadero

South of Half Moon Bay along Highway 1 are a string of beautiful beaches, several wildlife preserves, and two tiny historic towns. The town of Pescadero is a block or so of clapboard buildings and steepled churches, circa 1850. Peek into a few antiques boutiques and stop at Arcangeli Grocery, where the irresistible aroma of warm artichoke and garlic-cheese bread wafts out the door; some of the 24 kinds of bread are "half-baked," to take home, stow in the freezer, and bake later (650-879-0147). You'll find picnic supplies and locally produced gourmet items here, too, to take or to ship.

Just south of Pescadero near Año Nuevo State Reserve, the circa-1870, 10-stories-tall Pigeon Point Lighthouse is open for tours on weekends (650-879-2120). The Pigeon Point Hostel has inexpensive private and shared rooms, and marvelous views (www.norcal hostels.org).

Pescadero State Beach (all ages)

Fifteen miles south of Half Moon Bay, on Highway 1; (650) 879-0227.

Two miles of sheltered beach, with tide pools, huge dunes, and trails. The sea lions and the seagulls like it here, as do the fishermen who catch steelhead and salmon at spawning time in Pescadero Creek. Kids love investigating the big tide pools and sliding down the dunes. Restrooms, picnic tables, barbecues.

Just across the highway, Pescadero Marsh is 600 acres of uplands and wetlands, an important stop on the Pacific Flyway and a must for avid birders or for anyone who likes to walk on nature trails. Fall and spring are the best times to see thousands of birds nesting and feeding. An underpass provides safe access to and from the beach; no pets.

Duarte's Tavern (all ages)

202 Stage Rd., Pescadero; (650) 879-0464. $$.

Crowded on sunny weekends but worth the wait, for more than 50 years Duarte's has been a family restaurant serving cioppino, seafood specialties with a Portuguese accent, artichoke soup, deep-fried calamari, and olallieberry pie. Local ranchers belly up to the Old West–style bar. Daily breakfast, lunch, and dinner.

Costanoa Coastal Lodge and Camp (all ages)

2001 Rossi Rd., P.O. Box 842, Pescadero 94060; (650) 879-1100; www.costanoa.com. $–$$$$.

A new idea in upscale camping—luxury wood cabins, tent cabins, and lodge rooms; some sleep 3 or more. All 40 lodge rooms have 2 double beds, refrigerator, Bose stereo, coffee-maker, and patio or deck, and some have fireplaces; includes breakfast. Tent bungalows and cabins have nice amenities like down comforters and skylights; they share "comfort stations" that include restrooms, indoor hot showers, heated concrete floors, a dry sauna, and outdoor fireplaces. RV and tent sites include breakfast, too. You can sign up for guided hikes, horseback riding, and bike rides (rentals available); take a yoga class; or go kayaking. Shop the well-stocked general store for gourmet and deli foods to take out or enjoy at picnic tables. Walk to Gazos Creek Beach, a sheltered curve of sand with shallow tide pools. During the summer, the Kids Camp for ages 5 to 12 offers supervised games, nature walks, tide pooling, storytelling, and crafts for $35 per child per day.

Phipps Country Store and Farm (all ages)

2700 Pescadero Rd., off Highway 1, 0.5 mile east of town; (650) 879-0787; www.phipps country.com. Free admission Oct through Mar; otherwise $.

A combination produce market, farm, plant nursery, and menagerie of exotic birds and farm animals, just made for kids. Among the cacophony of sounds are parrots' squawks, green and orange canaries' songs, and peacocks' trumpetings. There are fancy chickens, big fat pigs, a variety of bunnies, and antique farm equipment. You can pick your own strawberries, raspberries, and olallieberries, and eat them at a picnic table in the middle of a flower-filled greenhouse. Restrooms are available.

Año Nuevo State Reserve (all ages)
Highway 1 at New Year's Creek Road, Pescadero; (650) 879-2025 or (800) 444-4445; www .anonuevo.org. Parking $; admission $; kids 3 and under are free.

On 1,200 acres of dunes and beaches, the largest groups of elephant seals in the world come to breed from December through April. A moderately strenuous, 3-mile round-trip walk through grassy dunes brings you to an unforgettable sight: dozens of 2-ton animals lounging, arguing, mating, cavorting in the sea, and wiggling around on the beach. As many as 2,500 seals spend their honeymoons here, and there's lots of other wildlife to see, too. During the mating season it is necessary to reserve spaces in 3-hour, guided interpretive tours (800-444-7275). At other times you can wander around on your own; smaller herds remain all year. The boardwalk enables wheelchair access. Affording great views of the coastline, the 1.5-mile Whitehouse Ridge Trail connects Año Nuevo with Big Basin State Park.

Purisima Creek Redwoods Open Space Preserve (all ages)
Off Highway 1, 4.5 miles south of Half Moon Bay, west on Higgins-Purisma Road.

A beautiful path winds up Whittemore Gulch through redwoods along lovely fern grottos for a mile, then climbs out of the canyon into open foothills; take a short ramble or hike the whole way, 2.2 miles to Skyline Boulevard on the ridge.

Santa Cruz

The summer resort town of Santa Cruz is known for a 20-mile string of wide, sandy, warm-water beaches and an old-fashioned waterfront boardwalk with rides and concessions. Here at the top end of Monterey Bay, the climate is mild, and surf's up every month of the year.

The town is composed of hundreds of fanciful Victorian homes. The main street, Pacific Avenue—called the Pacific Garden Mall—is a pleasantly tree-shaded boulevard with outdoor cafes and dozens of shops. Musical performances and festivals take place on Pacific all summer long. In this artists' town, notice the many sidewalk sculptures, and watch for building-size murals on side streets.

From the Santa Cruz waterfront to Natural Bridges, a road winds above the ocean for several miles. Popular for walking and jogging, the West Cliff section runs north from Light-house Point.

In the Santa Cruz Mountains are ancient redwood groves, sunny riverbanks, quiet little resort towns, and a rollicking steam train.

Virtually every resident of Santa Cruz County lives within walking distance of a state park or beach. A water shuttle provides seagoing transport between Santa Cruz Harbor, Santa Cruz Wharf, and Capitola Wharf. A bus shuttle also runs to Big Basin State Park on weekends. You can stay overnight, hike back down on the 10-mile trail, or just shuttle back at the end of the day.

Santa Cruz Beach Boardwalk (all ages)

400 Beach St., Santa Cruz; (831) 426-7433; www.beachboardwalk.com. Free admission; individual rides $; day pass $$$$.

The only beachside amusement park on the West Coast. The classic 1911 carousel and the Giant Dipper roller coaster are National Historic Landmarks. You'll need a whole afternoon for more than three dozen rides, an old-time arcade, shops, and restaurants. At Neptune's Kingdom, the indoor mini-golf course, volcanoes erupt, pirates threaten, and cannons fire. If you hear screaming, it's probably coming from the Hurricane and the Astro Canyon Virtual Coaster. Video arcade, pool tables, air hockey, laser tag, virtual reality, shooting gallery, and bowling are other attractions. The Fright Walk is for ages 13 and older. Get ready for the Cave Train, a spooky prehistoric journey; the Pepsi Convoy; Tornado thrill ride; the Sea Serpent family roller coaster; and Space Race bumper cars. The new Haunted Castle ride under the board-walk is a scary one, where you glide through dimly lit rooms filled with spooky special effects.

Crowds gather all summer for Friday Night Bands shows; check the website for other free shows, such as the Chinese Acrobats.

Across from the boardwalk is the Santa Cruz Wharf, lined with seafood restaurants and souvenir stores, fishermen, crabbers, and sea views galore. Look for Marini's Candies, the place for fresh saltwater taffy, caramel corn, candy apples, and handmade chocolates and fudge since 1915 (866-MARINIS; www.mariniscandies.com).

The Fun Spot skateboarding park is nearby at the corner of Washington and Beach, with more than a dozen obstacles for intermediate to advanced skaters, including a halfpipe, quarterpipes, and steel rails. Beginners can try the 3-foot halfpipe.

Surfin' Safari (all ages)

Surfers have been riding the waves in Santa Cruz since the early 1920s. Surfers and surf-kayakers from around the world congregate here for annual contests on the consistently big waves, and it's still one of the best places in the world to learn to surf—Monterey Bay provides a variety of facing beaches and types of breaks. The main beach at the board-walk, Cowell, is best for beginners, with a sheltered point break, long gentle waves, and a sandy bottom. The other top surfing beaches are Pleasure Point in Capitola and Steamers Lane, just north of the boardwalk; north a few miles, surfers also flock to Natural Bridges State Beach.

On Cowell Beach, Club Ed Surf School is the place for lessons and rentals of surf- and sailboards, kayaks, and more beach stuff (831-464-0177; www.club-ed.com). The other long-established, top-rated headquarters for lessons and surf camp is Richard Schmidt Surf School (831-423-0928; www.richardschmidt.com).

Above Steamers Lane in the Mark Abbott Memorial Lighthouse on West Cliff Drive, it's free to cruise through a hundred years of surfing history at the Surfing Museum; look for the Shark Attack surfboard.

Bookshop Santa Cruz (all ages)
Pacific and Front Streets, Santa Cruz; (831) 423-0900; www.bookshopsantacruz.com.

One of the largest bookstores in Northern California, a gathering place for locals and visitors. Throughout the store are benches, stools, and armchairs, cozy spots to peruse the books and the huge variety of domestic and international magazines and newspapers. The children's books-and-toys department is comfortable.

Pacific Edge Climbing Gym (ages 6 and up)
104 Bronson St., Santa Cruz; (831) 454-9254; www.pacificedgeclimbinggym.com. Day pass: adults $$$; kids 11 and under $.

At one of the largest indoor climbing gyms in the world, you can take an introductory class with 2 hours of instruction, equipment, and a pass for the day for about $30, with discounts for more than one climber; kids can take an introductory class for about $15, and there are **free** clinics.

Forest of Nisene Marks State Park (all ages)
Aptos Creek Road, Aptos; (831) 763-7064. Day-use fee $$.

A cool, green place to take a walk in the highlands inland of Santa Cruz. This densely forested, 10,000-acre wilderness on Aptos Creek is popular with runners, bikers, horseback riders, hikers, and picnickers. In elevations from 100 to 2,600 feet, unpaved roads and trails lead to a wide variety of mixed evergreen woods and creekside willows and ferns. Walk-in camping is permitted, as is horseback riding.

Capitola-by-the-Sea (all ages)
Three miles south of Santa Cruz, off Highway 1; (831) 475-6522; www.capitolachamber.com.

Located on the edge of a small, protected beach where Soquel Creek enters the sea, Capitola is a few short blocks of boutiques, art galleries, and beachwear shops—a quaint art colony that has welcomed vacationers since 1861.

Restaurants with outdoor patios are lined up on the waterfront. The shops and galleries are touristy but fun. Check out the charming Capitola Museum in a little red house (831-464-0322), rent a kayak for a paddle around the quiet cove (831-462-2208), amble along the river trail, and take a blufftop walk at sunset on Grand Avenue.

Natural Bridges State Beach (all ages)
A few minutes north of Santa Cruz, 2531 West Cliff Dr.; (831) 425-4609. $$ to park.

Named for dramatic sandstone arches, this beautiful beach has tide pools rich with sea life. Guided tide pool tours are available. A short boardwalk from the beach parking lot leads through a eucalyptus forest to the California Monarch Butterfly Preserve. Depending on the time of year—early October through March is best—you'll see hundreds of thousands of butterflies hanging in the trees and moving about in great golden clouds. A 0.75-mile self-guided nature walk begins at the Monarch Trail and heads for Secret Lagoon, where blue herons, mallard ducks, and more freshwater and seagoing birds live.

Santa Cruz Beaches

- **Cowell Beach.** Beach Street, Santa Cruz; (831) 429-3747. The main Santa Cruz beach at the boardwalk and the pier. A popular piece of sand for sunning, swimming, volleyball, and **free** concerts. A special beach-going wheelchair is available from the lifeguard. Restrooms.

- **Santa Cruz Yacht Harbor and Beach.** End of 5th Avenue and East Cliff Drive, Santa Cruz; (831) 475-6161. Kayak and sail, sunbathe, and watch more than 1,200 boats go in and out of the harbor. RV parking, restrooms, restaurants, shops. **Free** water taxi.

- **Twin Lakes State Beach.** Below East Cliff Drive at 7th Avenue, Santa Cruz; (831) 429-2850. Where the windsurfers go. There are fire rings here, outdoor showers, restrooms, and a wild bird sanctuary at Schwan Lagoon and Schwan Lake. You can kayak and canoe on the lake.

- **Seacliff State Beach.** State Park Drive off Highway 1, Aptos; (831) 685-6444. Two miles of shoreline backed by steep sandstone cliffs. A 500-foot wooden pier and the wreck of a concrete ship are roosting spots for birds, and you can fish off the pier. There are a campground and a small visitor center where you can sign up for walking tours to see the fossilized remains of multimillion-year-old sea creatures lodged in the cliffs' sides. On the inland edge of the beach is a paved pathway frequented by joggers, parents with strollers, and skateboarders.

- **Rio Del Mar Beach.** Just south of Capitola at Aptos; (831) 688-3241. A wide stretch of sand with a jetty and lifeguards. Shopping and restaurants are within walking distance.

Seymour Marine Discovery Center at Long Marine Laboratory (all ages)

100 Shaffer Rd., Santa Cruz, near Natural Bridges; (831) 459-3800; www2.ucsc.edu/seymour center. $$; kids 3 and under **free.**

This University of Santa Cruz research facility, open to the public, features an aquarium, an 87-foot blue whale skeleton, and touch tanks where kids can pick up sea animals. A new shark and ray pool gives visitors a chance to see these mysterious creatures up close and feel the "dermal teeth" that give shark skin its sandpaper texture. Three times a day docents take you behind the scenes where scientists do research.

Wilder Ranch State Park (all ages)

1401 Coast Rd., 2 miles north of Santa Cruz; (831) 423-9703 or (831) 426-0505; www.parks .ca.gov. Parking $$.

A 6,000-acre dairy ranch since the 1800s is now a leafy, meadowy park with beaches and wetlands. Picnic in the apple orchard; see historic displays in the Victorian home and take a guided walk on weekends; or hike, horseback ride, or bike on your own on 34 miles of well-marked trails. Bluffs Ride is a wide, easy 4-mile (one-way) trail leading to several beaches.

Davenport (all ages)

About 9 miles north up the coast from Santa Cruz on Highway 1.

The hamlet of Davenport makes a nice half-day trip from Santa Cruz. On the bluff, the Davenport Overlook is a perfect vantage point from which to see California gray whales on their annual trips to and from Mexico. The beach here is less crowded than others and a favorite of windsurfers. On the highway, the New Davenport Cash Store and Restaurant is definitely worth the drive for grilled chicken sandwiches, homemade soup, omelets with homemade chorizo, and big killer brownies in a wood-floored, sunny cafe; it's popular for weekend breakfasts. The gift shop sells guidebooks, masses of jewelry, and a surprising array of African trinkets and crafts.

Nine miles north, at Waddell State Beach, kids love to explore the tide pools and watch the kitesurfers—it's the newest rage—windsurfing with a kite to lift the rider as high as 60 feet off the water.

Henry Cowell Redwoods State Park (all ages)

101 North Big Trees Park Rd., Felton; (831) 438-2396 or (800) 444-7275; www.parks.ca.gov. $.

A rare opportunity to see first-growth redwoods in 1,800 acres of stream canyons, meadows, forests, and chaparral-covered ridges along the meandering San Lorenzo River and Eagle Creek. An observation deck overlooks the Monterey/Santa Cruz coastlines and the mountains. A lovely shaded picnic grove on the river has barbecues and water. Among 20 miles of trails is the short, easy Redwood Grove Nature Trail to the Big Trees Grove. The redwood-dotted campground in the park contains more than 100 tent and RV sites, for vehicles up to 24 feet, with no hookups (831-438-2396).

Nearby is a photo op at the Felton Covered Bridge. Built in 1892, this is the tallest bridge of its kind in the country and one of the few left in the state.

Big Basin Redwoods State Park (all ages)

From Boulder Creek on Highway 9, go 9 miles west on Highway 236 to the park entrance; (831) 338-8861 or (800) 444-7275; www.bigbasin.org, www.parks.ca.gov. Store, snack bar, shop, restrooms. Camping in RV and tent sites, walk-in sites, tent cabins, hike and bike sites. $ fee per vehicle.

California's first state park comprises 18,000 acres of 1,000-year-old redwood groves, fern canyons, waterfalls, and 80 miles of trails: a lush, green world for hiking, camping, picnicking, horseback riding, and mountain biking. The Sea Trail drops 11 miles from high mountain ridges through dense woodlands, past waterfalls and astonishing sea and mountain views all the way down to Waddell State Beach.

Family **Hosteling**

Golden Gate Council Hosteling International: www.norcalhostels.org. For a brochure describing all Northern California hostels, call (415) 863-1444. Hostels are not just for the young and footloose anymore. Many American hostels have private rooms and cabins for families and small groups. The advantages are cost (as low as $10 per person; a few dollars higher in big cities), location (nearby natural and cultural attractions that families want to see and explore), and the chance to meet travelers from all over the world.

You cook your own meals in a fully equipped common kitchen and socialize with other hostelers in a common living room. Clean beds are provided (bring your own linens/sleeping bags), as are laundry facilities and common bathrooms with showers. Some hostels ask you to do brief chores. On the coast of California are several hostels that are perfect for vacationing families. They are popular, so reserve well in advance.

• **Pigeon Point Lighthouse Hostel.** 210 Pigeon Point Rd. at Highway 1, Pescadero; (650) 879-0633. Four family houses, each with a fully equipped kitchen, clustered around one of the tallest lighthouses in the United States. An incredible location on a dazzling stretch of coastline, near state parks, tide pools, beaches, redwood forests, and the famous Año Nuevo State Reserve, where hundreds of elephant seals are a sight to behold.

• **Point Montara Lighthouse Hostel.** 25 miles south of San Francisco on Highway 1, P.O. Box 737, Montara 94037; (650) 728-7177. The 1875 Point Montara Fog Signal and Light Station became a hostel in 1980. Shared and private family rooms; fireplace in the community room; Wi-Fi; laundry; espresso bar; great location near beaches, boat harbors, and Half Moon Bay.

• **Hidden Villa Ranch Hostel.** 45 miles south of San Francisco and 15 miles north of San Jose, 26870 Moody Rd., Los Altos Hills; (408) 949-8648. On a 1,600-acre ranch in the foothills of the Santa Cruz Mountains, the first hostel in California, established in 1937. Rustic, heated cabins, plus a fireplace and piano in the common room. This is a working farm with organic gardens. Nearby are hiking trails and parks.

• **Santa Cruz Hostel.** P.O. Box 1241, Santa Cruz 95060; (831) 423-8304. Newly renovated cottages close to downtown and the beach.

The easiest and most popular trail, the Redwood Nature Trail opposite the headquarters, is a 0.6-mile loop tour of redwoods and Opal Creek. You'll see the Chimney Tree, the Mother of the Forest—329 feet tall—and the Father of the Forest, a really, really big-around redwood.

Roaring Camp and Big Trees Railroad (all ages)
Just south of Felton on Graham Hill Road, near Henry Cowell Redwoods State Park in the Santa Cruz Mountains; (831) 335-4400; www.roaringcamp.com. Ages 3 and up $$$; kids under 3 free.

Tops on kids' favorite places in the Santa Cruz Mountains, this is a re-creation of an 1880s logging town, complete with a covered bridge, a general store, and a wonderful narrow-gauge steam train to ride up through forests of giant redwoods to the summit of Bear Mountain on the steepest railroad grade in North America. A second route runs along the San Lorenzo River down to Santa Cruz beaches. A chuckwagon barbecue serves charcoal-broiled steak and chicken burgers in a forest glade, or you can have your own picnic on the mountain.

New are two ziplines: one for older kids, with tree-to-tree lines at heights nearing 150 feet, and a less scary one, over elevated footbridges and platforms, perfect for introducing little ones to ziplining.

Among annual events, 10,000 eggs are hidden at the Eggstraordinary Egg Hunt, and Civil War battles and camp life are reenacted at the largest encampment in the United States. The Jumpin' Frog Jamboree happens in July, and a Harvest Fair in October, with 1880s crafts, scarecrow contest, pumpkin carving, and free pumpkins. Sunday melodramas are free.

Quail Hollow Ranch (all ages)
800 Quail Hollow Rd., off Graham Hill Road, Ben Lomond; (831) 454-7900.

This meadowy former ranch has a historic house, a pond, a shady picnic area, and 5 or 6 miles of hiking trails. Take an easy, flat footpath, or trek up the 2.8-mile round-trip Sunset Trail to big views of the valley and explore the dwarf redwood forest.

Where to Eat

Crow's Nest. 2218 East Cliff Dr. at the Santa Cruz Harbor; (831) 476-4560; www.crows nest-santacruz.com. A casual, multilevel restaurant overlooking the busy harbor, with a heated, glassed-in deck. The food is not gourmet, but it's good, with plenty of fresh seafood and good choices for children. $–$$

Gayle's Bakery and Rosticceria. 504 Bay Ave., on the corner of Bay and Capitola Avenues, Capitola; (831) 462-1200. Besides pies, cheesecake, and pastries, Gayle's is famous for breakfast and homemade pasta, pizza, and spit-roasted meats. They will pack you a picnic lunch. A new covered patio is warm and bright with a fireplace and mosaic artwork. $–$$

Gilbert's Fire Fish Grill. 25 Municipal Wharf, Santa Cruz; (831) 423-5200. Newly renovated, new menu, new name, long-time family-owned restaurant on the wharf with panoramic bay views. Yummy bread-bowl clam chowder, sandwiches, salads, mesquite-grilled, fresh local fish; house-made dressings and sauces. Kids loves their own menu: burgers, grilled cheese, chicken nuggets, plain buttered noodles. Try the salmon burgers, and don't miss Exotic Bomba, a dessert extravaganza of mango, raspberry, and passion fruit sorbet in a white-chocolate blanket. Wine tasting and gift shop here, too. For quicky meals, stop in next door at Gilbert's serve-yourself outdoor venue, Woodies Cafe. $$–$$$

Kelly's French Bakery. 402 Ingalls St. in the courtyard, just off West Cliff Drive, Santa Cruz; (831) 423-9050. Breakfast, lunch, and early dinner in a casual environment; order at the counter, sit under an umbrella. Luscious pastries; soups, sandwiches, comfort food like chicken potpie. While the kids hang out in the gardens, parents cruise in and out of upscale shops, and indulge in wine and beer tasting here in the Swift Street Courtyard. $

Sea Food Mama's. 820 Bay Ave. at the Crossroads Center, Capitola; (831) 476-5976. The menu is printed every day with a huge variety of what's fresh in seafood. This is a casual, fun place with a jukebox. $–$$

Tony and Alba's Pizza and Italian Food. 817 Soquel Ave., Santa Cruz; (831) 425-8669. A favorite family place for wonderful brick-oven pizza. Also located in Capitola and Scotts Valley. $

Train Place Deli. 1820 41st Ave., Capitola; (831) 475-0150. On hundreds of feet of track, G-gauge toy trains trundle around the dining room and right by your table, while families dig into big, homemade sandwiches, soups, and cookies, and more than a dozen varieties of subs from Italian meatball to chili dog. $–$$

Walnut Avenue Café. 106 Walnut Ave., Santa Cruz; (831) 457-2307. At a table or a booth, at the counter, or outdoors at this old-fashioned coffee shop, breakfast all day: Mighty Mouse pancakes, French toast, tofu or

egg scrambles, traditional and exotic choices; plain and fancy sandwiches for lunch. Portions are huge. Try to get here off-peak hours, as it can be super busy; open until 4 p.m. $–$$

Wharf House. 1400 Wharf Rd. at the end of the Capitola Wharf, Capitola; (831) 476-3534; www.wharfhouse.com. With bay and beach views; breakfast; burgers, sandwiches, clam chowder, and fish-and-chips for lunch; dinner; and weekend jazz brunch. Rooftop deck is open in the summertime. Ask about the family discount. $–$$

Zachary's. 849 Pacific Ave., Santa Cruz; (831) 427-0646. Voted Best Breakfast in Santa Cruz; sourdough pancakes, scones, corn bread, and much more. Breakfast, lunch, brunch. $–$$

Where to Stay

Dream Inn. 175 West Cliff Dr., Santa Cruz; (831) 426-4330; www.jdvhotels.com. Right above Cowell Beach and the wharf, 165 four-star rated, retro-chic, boutique-style rooms with private, oceanfront balconies or patios, all recently renovated. Ocean-view swimming and wading pools; Wi-Fi, flat-screen TVs, and refrigerators. Suites with sofa beds and soaking tubs; some rooms with 2 queens. $$$$

Fern River Resort Motel. Near Roaring Camp, 5250 Hwy. 9, Felton; (408) 335-4412; www.fernriver.com. A nice, small, rustic resort with little red housekeeping cabins, some fireplaces, a private sandy river beach, and 4 acres of lawns, trees, and fern gardens. Fireplaces, kitchenettes; no pets. $–$$$

Sea & Sand Inn. 201 West Cliff Dr.; (831) 427 3400; www.santacruzmotels.com/sea_and_sand. Fresh from a complete renovation, 22 motel rooms with ocean views, within walking distance of the boardwalk and the beach. Spacious family suite and studio have sitting area, minifridge, microwave, dishes, fireplace, 4-person hot tub. **Free**

continental breakfast, Wi-Fi, flat-screen TVs. $$$–$$$$

Seascape Resort. 1 Seascape Resort Dr., off San Andreas, Aptos, 9 miles south of Santa Cruz; (831) 688-6800 or (800) 929-7727; www.seascaperesort.com. Right at the beach, spacious, nautical-theme condos and villas for up to 8 people, with ocean views, fireplaces, fully equipped kitchens, and small private balconies or patios. On-site are 3 ocean-view swimming pools, tennis courts, an excellent 18-hole golf course, a full-service spa, a fitness center, and shopping nearby. The beach stretches for miles in both directions.

Kid's Club in the summer offers supervised activities for children ages 5 to 10—everything from water balloon tosses to nature hikes, tennis, sand castles, pizza parties, and swimming; evenings are fun with videos and cookies and milk. Guests with children ages 5 and under get a **free** safety pack with electrical outlet plugs, night-lights, and tub faucet covers.

The sleek, Italian-contemporary restaurant is pricey and a little formal for families; lunch on the terrace is doable, with outdoor heaters and sea views. The nearby shopping center has cafes and a grocery.

A unique amenity at Seascape is "Fires-to-Go": A bellhop arrives with firewood and snacks for a beach bonfire and drives your family to the private beach, where he or she builds and lights the fire! $$$–$$$$

Tyrolean Inn and Cottages. 9600 Hwy. 9, Ben Lomond; (831) 336-5188. Seven simple cottages within walking distance to town and the river; fireplaces, kitchenettes; no pets. German/American restaurant on-site. $–$$

Villa Vista. 2-2800 East Cliff Dr., 10 minutes from downtown Santa Cruz; (408) 866-2626; www.villavista.com. Two perfectly wonderful condo units; each contains 3 master bedrooms with baths, gourmet kitchen, sea-view patio, home entertainment center, laundry facilities. Great for several couples or a large family. $$$$

For More Information

Santa Cruz Visitors Bureau. 1211 Ocean St., Santa Cruz; (831) 425-1234 or (800) 833-3494; www.santacruzca.org. Stop in at the Kids' Korner for **free** coloring books and sunglasses and at the computer for information on top kids' attractions.

Monterey

A Portuguese navigator sailed into Monterey Bay in the mid-1500s, and the Spanish landed there in 1602, beginning a 200-year occupation. A rich architectural heritage remains today. Gnarled old olive trees and courtyard gardens surround graceful tile-roofed adobes and haciendas built by the early conquistadors—the town looks like old Spain. A "Path of History" wanders between historic buildings and museums.

You're likely to spend much of your time on Monterey's waterfront on the edge of the miraculous Monterey Bay, on Fisherman's Wharf, at Cannery Row, and on the seaside walking trail. Seals, sea lions, and otters provide **free** entertainment offshore.

Most sights and amusements are within walking distance of downtown. Get a self-guided-tour map and ask for the brochure *25 Fun Things To Do with Kids in Monterey County* at the visitors bureau at 380 Alvarado St. (831-649-1770) and hop on and off the "WAVE" shuttle bus.

The annual Whalefest in January on Fisherman's Wharf is a multifaceted event that families love. Attractions include mural painting, whale-watch cruises, **free** entertainment, and special exhibits and tours.

On Tuesday in the late afternoons and early evenings all year, the Old Monterey Market Place downtown features nearly 150 vendors of prepared foods and produce, arts, crafts, and lots of music and **free** fun.

Monterey State Historic Park
"Path of History" (all ages)

A district roughly from Fisherman's Wharf south to Pacific and Madison and east to Camino El Estero; (831) 649-7118; www.parks.ca.gov. Tickets for all 40 Path of History buildings: adults $$; youth and children $; available at all historic buildings open to the public.

In the oldest part of the city, historic buildings and museums are close together in a pleasant, garden-y network of streets. Plan on a leisurely half-day's exploration to do the complete 2-mile walk, with plenty of time for rest stops at little parks along the way.

Children particularly enjoy the Colton Hall Museum at Madison and Pacific, a century-old school on a grassy knoll, with little wooden desks and photos of the pupils from days gone by. Behind the school and around this part of town are small adobes, some of the first homes built in California. Every April, you can take a narrated tour of more than 25 adobes and see courtyard gardens inhabited by docents in period costumes.

The Cooper Store at Munras and Alvarado Streets sells antique toys, postcards, and souvenirs. Walk through the store to another museum and to gardens beneath a huge cypress tree.

Fisherman's Wharf and Wharf #2 (all ages)

Del Monte Avenue and Washington Street, Monterey; (831) 649-1770; www.monterey wharf.com.

Side by side stretching into Monterey Harbor, Wharf #2 is the home of the commercial fishing fleet and several seafood restaurants, while Fisherman's Wharf is a breezy boardwalk, delightfully weather-worn and smelling of salt spray and caramel corn, and crowded with cafes, souvenir shops, fish markets, galleries, and sightseeing and tour companies. From here you can rent kayaks, go whale-watching, and take a bike ride or a walk around the edge of the bay. One of the most fun things to do is to rent an overgrown bicycle, which is powered by two adults in back, with room for two little kids to ride in front.

Across from the entrance to Fisherman's Wharf, Custom House Plaza is the site of festivals and special events, terraced lawns, fountains, and bocce courts.

Monterey Peninsula Recreational Trail (all ages)

The paved path from Cannery Row, past Fisherman's Wharf, to Asilomar State Beach, is part of an 18-mile hiking, biking, and walking trail connecting the greenbelts and parks on the coast. Along the way are historic landmarks, drinking fountains, benches, picnic sites, restrooms, and bike racks. It's fun to dodge brown pelicans and watch sea lions barking to get your attention. Binoculars are great to have for spying otters floating on their backs in the kelp beds offshore, knock-knocking on abalone shells; children are drawn to the friendly looking, inquisitive faces of the hairy little animals. Point Piños Lighthouse and Lovers' Point playground are two stops to make. Pets must be leashed, and skateboards are allowed only in designated areas.

Adventures by the Sea (all ages)

299 Cannery Row and other locations; (831) 372-1807; www.adventuresbythesea.com. $$–$$$$.

Rent a 4-person surrey bike and cruise up and down the waterfront trail. You can also rent surfboards, Segways, regular bikes, and tandem kayaks (kids 5 and up; child-size life jackets provided) to paddle around the quiet parts of the bay to see otters, harbor seals, and kelp forests up close. Ask about tours that include instruction and marine life narration.

Cannery Row (all ages)

A boulevard on the waterfront running from the American Tin Cannery and the Monterey Aquarium for several blocks south; www.canneryrow.com.

A major tourist hub on the shores of Monterey Bay, Cannery Row includes about 100 shops, plus oceanfront restaurants and amusement venues—somewhat of a tourist trap, yet a pleasant one, with lots of ocean vistas and pocket parks, and a small beach. Historic sites relating to the old days of sardine canneries and John Steinbeck's classic novel *Cannery Row* can be found between the businesses. Have some fun at the Spirit of Monterey Wax Museum and Oceans Blacklight Mini-Golf. Rent a 4-wheeled surrey or bikes and baby joggers at Bay Bikes, build teddy bears and pet sea stars, paint pottery, bead a necklace, and take in an IMAX movie. Buy a colorful kite at Windborne Kites and make sand castles at San Carlos Beach Park; dig into shrimp cocktail at Bubba Gump Shrimp Company and a banana split at Ghirardelli Ice Cream and Chocolate Shop.

Peter Hay Golf Course (ages 10 and up)

1700 17 Mile Dr., Pebble Beach; (831) 622-8723. $$$ (17 Mile Drive fee is refunded with purchase of one greens fee); ages 13 to 17 $; ages 12 and under **free.**

This 9-hole, par 3, pitch-and-putt course across the street from the famed Pebble Beach Golf Links is a great place for kids and beginners to learn and practice; wide open fairways with no water hazards. Drinks, golf balls, and snacks are available; restrooms. No jeans or short shorts; collared shirts required.

Maritime Museum of Monterey (all ages)

5 Custom House Plaza, Monterey; (831) 373-2469. $; kids under 12 **free.**

Some 18,000 feet of exhibits focused on the Monterey Peninsula's long seagoing history. Priceless marine artifacts include the 16-foot-tall, 10,000-pound lens that once operated atop the Point Sur Lighthouse. When everyone in the family is ready for a 20-minute rest, take in the historical film here—it's **free**.

Kayaking Monterey Bay (ages 8 and up)

Monterey Bay Kayaks (693 Del Monte Ave., Monterey; 831-373-KELP) or Sea Kayak Monterey Bay (32 Cannery Row and 645 Cannery Row, Monterey; 831-647-0147). They also have bicycle, in-line skate, and boat rentals.

Join the otters and sea lions in their watery living room by paddling around the bay. It's much easier than you might think. A child must be 4½ feet tall and weigh 80 pounds, and can share a double kayak with a parent.

Monterey Bay Aquarium (all ages)

886 Cannery Row, Monterey; (831) 648-4888; www.montereybayaquarium.org. Adults, seniors, and youths $$$$; kids under 13 $$$; 3 and under are free. On weekends and holidays, arrive when the building opens at 10 a.m. (9:30 a.m. in summer); otherwise, you may stand in a long line. Advance tickets are strongly recommended; purchase online or by phone at (866) 963-9645.

In a cross between an old sardine cannery and a contemporary architectural masterpiece, more than 7,000 sea creatures in 200-plus galleries and exhibits reside in giant kelp forests and rocky reefs. It's been called the best aquarium for kids in the United States. You'll see an amazing variety of creatures in the 90-foot-long Monterey Bay Habitat—leopard sharks, brightly colored nudibranchs, anemones, eels, otters, dolphins, sharks, and hundreds more species. The 3-story Kelp Forest is the world's tallest aquarium exhibit. Playful sea otters and bat rays have their own glassed-in homes. An interactive exhibit, Mission to the Deep, features HD video of robots exploring the deep sea, and a hands-on experience where you can use high-tech tools to explore a whale skeleton, map undersea mountains, and discover alien life forms.

When your feet wear out, sit down to watch live videos from an unmanned research submarine prowling Monterey Bay, as deep as 3,000 feet. From the aquarium's decks overlooking the harbor, peer down and watch otters and seals peering up at you.

Inside the building are an elegant restaurant (fresh seafood, pasta, appetizers, full bar service, and complimentary binoculars; reservations, 831-648-4870), an oyster bar, and a self-service cafe (pizza, pasta, Mexican food, clam chowder in a sourdough bowl, sandwiches, and salads), all with fabulous bay views.

Exhibits include Sharks: Myth and Mystery, Ocean's Edge: Coastal Habitats of Monterey Bay, a walk-through wave crash, larger venues for the giant octopuses, and added interactive experiences. Aquarium Adventures programs include overnight camp-ins, behind-the-scenes, and SCUBA, a basic version of scuba diving for kids. During the 3-hour Day Sail, passengers ages 10 and older are marine scientists on Monterey Bay, working alongside naturalists aboard the *Derek M Baylis*, a 65-foot sailboat designed for ocean research.

TopTen Aquarium Zones for Kids

1. Anchovies: Thousands of them swim overhead at the Outer Bay.

2. Touch Pool: Feel a sea cucumber, crabs, and other sea creatures.

3. Bat Ray Exhibit: Touch one of the sea's strangest animals.

4. Wave Crash: At the Shores exhibit, a (wet) surprise!

5. Otter Mealtime: Watch hungry otters chow down at 10:30 a.m. or 1:30 or 3:30 p.m.

6. Feed the Animals: At 11:30 a.m. or 4 p.m. at the Kelp Forest, see a diver feed the fish.

7. Flippers, Flukes, and Fun: Try on seal fins, test your skills, and catch whale food.

8. Bubble Windows: Get a fish's-eye view at the Bay Habitats.

9. Kelp Lab: Touch Kelp Forest creatures and view them under a microscope.

10. Splash Zone: Dive into bright coral reefs; roam rocky shores; and visit eels, sharks, and penguins.

The Outer Bay exhibit contains open ocean species such as a 10-foot-tall, 1.5-ton sunfish, huge stingrays, green sea turtles as big as dining room tables, vast schools of yellowfin tuna, and species of sharks too big for aquariums—until now.

The Splash Zone family galleries have doubled in size; younger kids can stand inside a simulated penguin home, crawl into a coral tunnel and a kelp forest, touch sea creatures in new and larger touch pools, enjoy entertainment, and play in a supervised area. There is even a play area for babies and toddlers. The exhibit Secret Lives of Seashores continues through 2012. Allow at least 3 hours for the aquarium; it can be crowded and sometimes overwhelming for little kids, so take breathers on the outdoor terrace, where salty breezes and the passing scene of watercraft will revive the spirits of even the crabbiest toddler. Before you arrive, check the website for the schedule of activities throughout each day, such as feeding times and live programs—most are only 15 minutes long, making them perfect for brief rest stops.

Asilomar Conference Center (all ages)

800 Asilomar Rd., Pacific Grove; (831) 642-4242; www.visitasilomar.com. $$$–$$$$.

Unknown to most tourists, this secluded, rustic, historic resort hides in a pine and oak forest above beautiful Asilomar State Beach. Conference attendees sometimes fill up the place, but, when space is available, individuals and families rent rooms, cottages, and suites here at reasonable rates that include a bountiful, full breakfast buffet in a bright and pleasant, if noisy, dining room. Breakfasts, hearty lunches, and dinners are available both to guests and visitors, and they are a good deal, with discounts for kids; purchase meal tickets at the reception desk. There are 317 rooms clustered in small lodges that have a common living room and fireplace; blissfully, no TVs or phones, except in public areas. Sleeping 2 to 7 people, some rooms have private patios or balconies, and fireplaces.

Bikes are available, and you can take off right from here for the 17 Mile Drive, the Monterey Bay Aquarium and Fisherman's Wharf, and the 18-mile Monterey Peninsula Recreational Trail.

There is a heated pool, volleyball, a game room with billiards and table tennis, a small general store, and easy accessibility to the wonderful tide pools and the wide, sandy beach, which is unsuitable for swimming or wading. Sixty acres of dunes are traversed by a 1-mile-long boardwalk, and a trail leads to wildflowery cliff tops and stunning sea views. There are also self-guided 2-hour walking audio tours, a fascinating rundown on architecture, history, wildlife, and ecology; the cost for the audio rental is $5, and well worth it.

Dennis the Menace Playground (ages 1 to 10)
On Pearl Street next to the El Estero Ballpark, Monterey; (831) 646-3866.

A unique park designed by Hank Ketcham, the cartoonist who created "Dennis," with fantastic structures such as a steam locomotive, a giant swing ride, a roller slide, and a special play area for the handicapped. A skateboard park is located adjacent to the playground behind the ball field. Kids love powering their own paddleboats on Lake El Estero, and you can rent kayaks and canoes, too (831-374-1484).

Monterey Sports Center (all ages)
301 East Franklin St., Monterey; (831) 646-3700; www.monterey.org/sportscenter. Adults $$; ages 6 to 17 $; ages 5 and under free.

Open for day use at reasonable rates with 2 heated indoor pools, a 112-foot water slide, basketball, volleyball, table tennis, badminton, babysitting from 6 months old, towels and lockers, and a simple cafe. Call or check website for pool hours. This could save your family vacation when it's raining outside.

Elkhorn Slough at Moss Landing (all ages)
Off Highway 1, 25 miles south of Santa Cruz and 20 miles north of Monterey; (831) 633-2133. Walking trails $; visitor center, picnic area, weekend tours free.

A nice day-trip destination to view wetlands wildlife, Elkhorn Slough is home to thousands of sea- and shorebirds and animals. You can walk on 4 miles of easy trails in the mudflats and salt marshes and visit the Moss Landing Marine Laboratory, which is operated by 9 California state universities (831-728-2822). A California record was set here for the most bird species seen in a day. You are likely to see herons, teal, plovers, golden eagles, terns, peregrine falcons, and dozens more wading and flying birds. Guided kayak and pontoon boat tours with natural history narration are the best ways to see wildlife. Try Slough Safari (831-633-5555), Venture Quest (831-427-2267), Kayak Connection (831-724-5692;

www.kayakconnection.com), and Monterey Bay Kayaks (800-649-5357; www.monterey baykayaks.com). Boat tours are scheduled to take advantage of the tides, and the guides know where to find leopard sharks, bat rays, seals, otters, and other creatures.

Here at Moss Landing is a block or so of old store buildings devoted to antiques and "junque" shops, where in July, a big antiques and flea market takes place. Have a seafood lunch at Phil's Fish Market and Eatery or Mexican food at the Whole Enchilada.

The Farm (all ages)

Fifteen miles east of Monterey on Highway 68, off the Spreckels Road exit; (831) 455-2575; www.thefarm-salinasvalley.com. Admission is free, tours $–$$; free for ages 2 and under.

Showcasing the agricultural heartland of California, the Farm is a unique education center, demonstration farm, and produce stand. You can buy fresh, organic produce and take a farm tour at 1 p.m. daily where kids can do a little farm work, learn about tractors and other machines, and taste produce.

The oversize, outdoor art figures of farmers and farm workers offer great photo opportunities. Check the website for harvest and holiday activities, lectures, and cooking demonstrations.

Mirror Maze and Lazer Challenge (all ages)

751 Cannery Row, Monterey; (831) 649-MAZE; www.montereymirrormaze.com. Adults $$$; ages 3 to 6 $$; under 3 are free; lazer challenge is extra.

At a new high-tech attraction on Cannery Row, you navigate a huge walk-through, mirrored labyrinth blazing and blinking with strobe and pulsating lights—wild and crazy fun, yet not for toddlers or for those who tend to be claustrophobic; no strollers allowed. Just when you think you have found your way out, you realize you've gone in a complete circle and are back where you started. In the Lazer Challenge, the object is to navigate the maze quickly without breaking a laser beam, as you jump, crawl and climb your way through an obstacle course of bright green, highly sensitive lasers radiating from the walls—it's addicting, and plenty of families come back again and again. Allow at least a half hour for each activity.

National Steinbeck Center (all ages)

1 Main St., Salinas; (831) 796-3833; www.steinbeck.org. $$; free for children under 5.

Sometime during their schooling, most American youngsters read John Steinbeck's *East of Eden, Of Mice and Men,* and *The Grapes of Wrath.* If your family's trip to the Monterey area coincides with your child's interest in Steinbeck, make the 20-mile drive inland from Monterey. The museum is uniquely child friendly, with interactive displays of the author's books and the time and place in which he lived. You can open a drawer to see his childhood treasures, feel the chill of an "ice packed" boxcar filled with lettuce, experience the smells and the sounds of "Doc" Rickett's science lab on Cannery Row, and learn of migrant life in the Salinas Valley. There are vintage photos, ongoing videos and movies, doors and windows that open into historic vignettes, and Steinbeck's charming camper truck in

The Invasion of the Butterflies

Millions of bright orange and black monarch butterflies escape winter cold and fly thousands of miles, returning to the same groves of eucalyptus, pine, and cypress on the California coast each year between October and March—a phenomenon occurring in a handful of places in the world. The city of Pacific Grove calls itself Butterfly Town USA and holds an annual children's parade to welcome the monarchs.

These are the most accessible places to see the unusual sight of the butterfly migration:

- **Monarch Grove Sanctuary.** Ridge Road off Lighthouse Avenue, Pacific Grove; (831) 373-3304. Self-guided or interpretive tours. **Free.**

- **Butterfly Parade and Bazaar.** October, in downtown Pacific Grove; (831) 646-6540. Elementary school bands and children in butterfly costumes march to welcome the monarch's return to its winter home in Pacific Grove. A charming, beautiful hometown event.

- **Natural Bridges State Beach.** Off West Cliff Drive, Santa Cruz; (831) 423-4609; www.santacruzstateparks.org. Boardwalk and wheelchair-accessible observation area. Self-guided or interpretive tours. In February a Migration Festival is held to welcome the butterflies. Parking $$.

- **Point Lobos State Reserve.** Three miles south of Carmel, on Highway 1; (831) 624-4909; www.pt-lobos.parks.state.ca.us. At the park entrance ask the ranger where to find the butterflies. Admission $$ per car.

- **Butterfly Trees of Pismo Beach.** Pismo State Beach, 2 miles south of Pismo Beach, south of San Luis Obispo; (831) 489-1869. Guided tours offered. **Free.**

which he motored with his dog and wrote *Travels with Charley*. The multimedia "Valley of the World" wing celebrates the agricultural heritage of the Salinas Valley with audio clips, photographs, films, and memorabilia. My granddaughter Melati spent over an hour in the activities room, rearranging hundreds of magnetic words on a huge board and creating a quirky poem. Kids can climb aboard a life-size horse and design their own vegetable crate labels, among other hands-on activities.

The cafe here is light and airy, with a sunny patio and reasonably priced snacks and lunches.

A few blocks away, Steinbeck's boyhood home is a beautifully restored, elaborately decorated Victorian loaded with memorabilia (132 Central Ave.; 831-424-2745). You can have lunch here, although it's a rather stuffy atmosphere for kids.

Wild Things (all ages)

400 River Rd., Salinas; (800) 228-7382, www.wildthingsinc.com. $$; call ahead for tours.

On the east side of Monterey County near Salinas, see more than 100 exotic animals and birds, all lovingly trained for use in films and television. Elephants, giraffes, bears, cheetahs, tropical birds, snakes, alligators, and dozens more creatures, including Josef, the live model for *The Lion King*. The animals are very friendly. Year-round special events and packages include feeding and bathing the pachyderms, nighttime flashlight tours and "Roar and Snore" sleepovers. Come for a tour, or stay overnight in a canvas-walled safari cabin.

Where to Eat

Abalonetti's. 57 Fisherman's Wharf, Monterey; (831) 373-1851. A family-operated restaurant on the wharf for over 40 years, with an outdoor deck and indoor cafe, and a comfortable vantage point for watching the gulls fly. Enjoy the freshest seafood in town, plus pizza and pasta. $–$$

Bubba Gump Shrimp Company. 720 Cannery Row, Monterey; (831) 373-1884. Fresh shrimp in dozens of dishes, fresh fish, steak; informal and fun. Yes, this is Gump as in *Forrest Gump*. $$

First Awakenings. American Tin Cannery, 125 Ocean View Blvd., a block from the aquarium on Cannery Row; (831) 372-1125. Tops for breakfast and lunch: crepes, breakfast burritos, apple pancakes, omelets, grilled sandwiches; outdoor patio with heaters. $–$$

Old Monterey Cafe. 489 Alvarado St., Monterey; (831) 646-1021; www.cafemonterey .com. Voted Best Breakfast in the county. Try the buckwheat pancakes, huge omelets, and great salads and soups for lunch. $–$$

Pasta Mia. 481 Lighthouse Ave., Pacific Grove; (831) 375-7709. Voted Best Italian Restaurant; homemade pasta, veal, grilled fish; country chic decor. $$

Where to Stay

Cypress Gardens Inn. 1150 Munras Ave., Monterey; (831) 373-2761 or (877) 922-1150; www.cypressgardensinn.com. Rooms with tiny balconies or patios, with a king bed or 2 queens, refrigerators. **Free** continental breakfast, large swimming pool, fitness equipment, laundry. Walk to downtown Monterey. Ask about aquarium discounts. $$$–$$$$

Lighthouse Lodge. 1150 Lighthouse Ave., Pacific Grove; (831) 858-1249 or (800) 858-1249. On the seaside at Point Piños; 29 suites with ocean views, fireplaces, Jacuzzi tubs. Full breakfast, afternoon refreshments. Casual, with space to run and play; popular with families. $$–$$$

Lone Oak Lodge. 2221 North Fremont St., Monterey; (831) 372-4924; www.loneoak lodge.com. A "best kept secret" for inexpensive family lodgings. Rooms, suites, kitchenettes, some fireplaces, sauna. $–$$

Monterey Bay Inn. 242 Cannery Row, Monterey; (831) 373-6242 or (800) 424-6242; www.montereybayinn.com. A small, upscale seaside hotel; each room has a king-size bed and oversize double sofa bed, a refrigerator, game table, and a pair of binoculars to watch the sea from your private balcony! Continental breakfast on the sunny garden patio is **free.** Private path to a small beach. $$$

Monterey Bay Lodge. 55 Camino Aguajito, Monterey; (800) 558-1900; www.monterey baylodge.com. Nice, basic motel at Monterey State Beach, within walking distance to downtown and the waterfront, across the street from El Estero and Dennis the Menace parks, with a swimming pool. Rooms with 2 queens, and 2-room suites with bunk beds, kitchenettes, video games, and refrigerators; on-site restaurant. Ask about aquarium and other packages. $$$

Sanctuary Beach Hotel. 3295 Dunes Dr., Monterey; (831) 883-9478, (866) LUXE-411; www.thesanctuarybeachresort.com. Ten minutes north of Monterey, 60 luxurious rooms and suites with outdoor spa tubs, fireplaces, private ocean-view balconies or patios, and gorgeous bathrooms. Two-bedroom suites are perfect for a small family; ask about aquarium packages. One of the 2 swimming pools is designed especially for kids. Complimentary use of golf carts to cruise the property, and a full-service spa. For walking and biking, the 18-mile Monterey Peninsula Recreational Trail starts here. The hotel is adjacent to RJ's Ranch House Steakhouse, an upscale dinner house with cozy booths, Western artwork and relics, 8 fireplaces, and an ocean-view patio. $$$$

Victorian Inn. 487 Foam St., Monterey; (831) 373-8000 or (800) 232-4141; www.victorianinn.com. Near Cannery Row and the aquarium, rooms with 2 doubles, coffeemakers; balconies, patios, or window seats; fireplaces; continental breakfast, afternoon wine and cheese. Concierge rooms have whirlpool tubs, feather beds, Wi-Fi. Two family suites have dining areas, kitchenettes, and living areas with sofa beds and video games. Ask about aquarium packages. $$$–$$$$

Monterey Peninsula Reservations. (888) 655-3424; www.monterey-reservations.com.

For More Information

Monterey County Convention and Visitors Bureau. Camino El Estero at the foot of Franklin Street, between Fremont and Del Monte Avenues, P.O. Box 1770, Monterey 93942; (888) 221-1010; www.montereyinfo.org.

Monterey Peninsula Visitors and Convention Bureau. 380 Alvarado St., Monterey; (831) 648-5360; www.monterey.com.

Carmel

A square-mile village of rustic country cottages and shingled beach houses, Carmel—the queen of quaint—nestles in an idyllic pine forest above a white-sand beach. Wandering the lanes off Ocean Avenue, the main street, you will see peaked-roofed doll's houses side by side with miniature castles and small summer cabins built in the 1920s and 1930s.

Shopping, shopping, shopping happens in hundreds of boutiques on Ocean Avenue and nearby streets, tucked into garden courtyards and in Carmel Plaza. Originally a Bohemian artists' and writers' colony, Carmel has more than 75 art and photography galleries.

There are kid-friendly shops, restaurants that welcome families, inland and coastal parks, beaches, and a fascinating California mission to explore.

Carmel is particularly dog friendly. Dogs are allowed on leashes throughout the town and can run free on Carmel Beach. Some lodgings and even some restaurants make special accommodation for canine family members. In the Carmel Plaza shopping center, look for the Fountain of Woof drinking fountain.

Mission San Carlos Borromeo Del Rio Carmel (all ages) (icons)

Rio Road, on the south side of town near the beach, Carmel; (831) 624-1271. $; kids under 5 free.

The second mission founded by Father Junipero Serra, a glorious Spanish-Moorish cathedral surrounded by lovely gardens. Inside, the church is sienna, burnt umber, and gold, with soaring ceilings and star-shaped stained-glass windows. On a warm summer's day, walk beneath shady colonnades and sit beside a trickling fountain.

A warren of thick-walled rooms, restored from original mission buildings, holds a magnificent museum collection of Native American, religious, and early California artifacts. In September, the Carmel Mission Fiesta is a family affair.

Shopping with Kids in Carmel

- **Carmel Doll Shop.** Court of the Golden Eagle; (831) 624-2607. A fairyland of antique European dolls, teddy bears, and Victorian gewgaws.

- **Fairy Tales.** Ocean Avenue between Lincoln and Monte Verde in the Court of the Golden Bough; (831) 620-1110. Magical fairies, dragons, wizards, merlins, mermaids, gargoyles, garden sculptures, and more.

- **Cottage of Sweets.** Ocean Avenue between Monte Verde and Lincoln; (831) 624-5170; www.cottageofsweets.com. Thirty varieties of licorice. British sweets, homemade fudge, gummies, old-fashioned American "penny candy."

- **Toys in the Attic.** Carmel Plaza; (831) 622-9011. Collectibles, classic toys, Madame Alexander dolls, Steiff animals, Beanies, die-cast cars, tin windup toys, stuffed animals and dolls, and mechanical banks.

- **Total Dog.** 26366 Carmel Rancho Lane, across from the Barnyard; (831) 624-5553. Dog raincoats and boots, dog jewelry, books and toys, figurines, plush doggie beds, and treats.

- **Gibson Gallery of Animation.** San Carlos and 7th Streets; (831) 624-9296. From Disney and other animation studios, a fabulous, changing collection of original animation cels and vintage cels. Provides a fascinating look at how animated movies are made.

- **Thinker Toys.** 7th and San Carlos Streets; (831) 624-0441; www.thinker toys.com. One of the world's greatest toy and game emporiums.

- **The Mischievous Rabbit.** Lincoln between Ocean and 7th; (408) 624-6854. A warren of Peter Rabbit–inspired treasures—hand-painted baby clothing, rabbit videos and books, carrot surprises.

On Rio Road across from the mission (or at Mountain View and Crespi or 11th Street and Junipero), you can access Mission Trail Park, 35 acres of cypress and pine forest and native vegetation, with 5 miles of easy walking trails.

Carmel Beach (all ages)
At the bottom of Ocean Avenue, the main street of Carmel; (831) 624-3543.

Fine, soft, white granite and quartz sand makes this a popular place to watch the sun sink into the ocean. A kite-flying contest takes place here in May. A big annual event is the Sand Castle Contest in fall, when architects and amateurs vie for the biggest, best sand structure.

Carmel River State Beach (all ages)
Highway 1, just south of Carmel; (831) 624-4909.

Adjacent to Monastery Beach and the Carmel River Bird Sanctuary, this beach is frequented by a wide variety of waterfowl and shorebirds, a place to wander the dunes and pick up driftwood and shells or make a 2-mile round-trip run or walk. Swimming is dangerous when the surf is up. You may see scuba divers getting ready to descend into the kelp forests of the Carmel Bay Ecological Reserve offshore. Restrooms, picnic sites.

Point Lobos State Reserve (all ages)
Four miles south of Carmel, on Highway 1; (831) 624-4909.

Named for the sea lions who lie about on offshore rocks, the rocky, forested point surrounded by a protected marine environment includes several miles of trails, pebbled beaches, and one of only two naturally occurring stands of Monterey cypress (the other is at Pebble Beach). Robert Louis Stevenson called it the "most beautiful meeting of land and sea on earth."

From 6 miles of coastline in the park, visitors often see whales, harbor seals, otters, scuba divers, and pelicans, gulls, and cormorants. In the meadows, mule deer tiptoe through purple needlegrass and wild lilac. Point Lobos is completely protected—the land, the marine life on the beach, the tide pools, and underwater. Not a thing may be removed or disturbed, dogs are not allowed, and visitors are required to stay on hiking trails or beaches. Kids particularly like Sea Lion Point, accessed by an easy half-hour walk to Headland Cove, where sea lions bark and you can see the otters. Bird Island Trail offers access to two beautiful sandy beaches, Gibson and China Cove. It will take a half day to enjoy the sights of Point Lobos, and you are advised to come early on weekends. Guided interpretive walks are conducted by park rangers.

Where to Eat

Bruno's Market and Deli. 6th and Junipero, Carmel; (831) 624-3821. Voted Best Grocery Store in the county. Wonderful gourmet sandwiches and salads, ready-made entrees, sushi, barbecued chicken and meats, beautiful produce. $

Caffe Napoli. Ocean between Dolores and Lincoln, Carmel; (831) 625-4033. Pizza, pasta, and bruschetta on checkered tablecloths. $

Carmel Coffee and Cocoa Bar. Carmel Plaza; (831) 622-0660. A charming European coffeehouse with a decadent cocoa menu, fresh cakes and cookies, quiche, sandwiches; breakfast, brunch, lunch, afternoon tea; in a cozy cafe or on the patio. $

Carmel Mission Ranch. 26270 Dolores St., Carmel; (831) 625-9040. Overlooking the Carmel River with views of Carmel Bay and Point Lobos, here cowboys and cowgirls kick back and eat steak, local fresh fish, and California cuisine in casual surroundings. $$–$$$

General Store and Forge in the Forest. Corner of 5th and Junipero, Carmel; (831) 624-2233. At an umbrella table under the oaks, on a heated patio, or inside by the fireplace, fresh fish, burgers, and salads are the best. $$–$$$$

Katy's Place. Mission Street between 5th and 6th, Carmel; (831) 624-0199. French toast with strawberries, 9 kinds of eggs Benedict, and a million omelets. A locals' favorite, serving breakfast and lunch like Grandma used to make. $–$$

Village Corner. Corner of 6th and Dolores, Carmel; (831) 624-3588. Inside and on the sunny patio, sandwiches, salads, and lower prices than at most such places in Carmel. This is a locals' hangout. I often lunched here with my mom, while she commiserated with her neighbors about how Carmel wasn't like it had been before the tour buses came to town. Breakfast, lunch, and dinner. $–$$

Where to Stay

Carmel Mission Ranch. 26270 Dolores St., Carmel; (831) 624-6436 or (800) 538-8221. Plush, pricey rooms here are in charming former ranch buildings and can be great for family groups; some accommodations have several bedrooms, fireplaces, living rooms, and memorabilia from Clint Eastwood's movies (he owns the place). $$$–$$$$

Carmel River Inn. 2660 Oliver Rd., Carmel; (831) 624-1575; www.carmelriverinn.com. On the south end of Carmel at the Carmel River bridge overlooking the river, with a swimming pool and simple rooms and cottages, all with private deck or patio. Some have fireplaces, 2 bedrooms, kitchenettes, and refrigerators. The Trail's Head Cafe here serves breakfast, lunch, and dinner, specializing in fresh local seafood. $$$–$$$$

Carmel Village Inn. Ocean Avenue and Junipero Streets, Carmel; (831) 624-3864; www.carmelvillageinn.com. Lovely landscaped grounds; 34 rooms, some with 2 queen-size beds; microwaves, refrigerators, suites with kitchens and fireplaces; **free** continental breakfast. $$–$$$

Carmel Wayfarer Inn. 4th and Mission Streets, Carmel; (831) 624-2711. Small rooms, some perfect for families, with fireplaces, kitchenettes, queen-size and twin beds. $$$–$$$$

For More Information

Carmel Visitor Center. San Carlos between 5th and 6th, P.O. Box 4444, Carmel 93921; (831) 624-2522; www.carmelcalifornia.com. Located upstairs in the Eastwood Building; you can pick up a walking-tour map and brochures here.

Carmel Valley

A few miles inland from Carmel, the Carmel River runs between two small mountain ranges through horse farms and farmland. The tawny climate is warm and dry when fog blankets the coastline. Near tiny Carmel Valley Village, 11.5 miles from Highway 1, are a few small ranch resorts and not much else except horseback-riding and hiking trails, tennis courts, and swimming pools. Inexpensive lodgings, fewer people, and good weather make the valley a great headquarters for family trips to the Monterey and Carmel areas.

Shopping is one of the primary activities in the town of Carmel, but dragging young kids through quaint shops can quickly turn into a family disaster. One of the easiest and most fun places I've ever seen for shopping with kids is the Barnyard, at the entrance to Carmel Valley.

The Barnyard (all ages)
At the intersection of Highway 1 and Carmel Valley Road, 5 minutes south of Carmel; (408) 624-8886; www.thebarnyard.com.

A rambling complex of shops and restaurants in contemporary barn buildings, this is a shopping place that children like. They can run around outside on terraces among a riot of blooming plants and flowers, or sit on a bench with a book or a game while parents browse. A horticulturist leads a guided tour of the voluminous gardens on Friday. On selected Sunday afternoons in the summertime, live music and wine make this a place to linger. There are several casual restaurants in the Barnyard, including a pizzeria, a Japanese open-hearth grill, an English pub, and a casual sandwich place.

The delicate sounds of hundreds of wind chimes fills the air among the weather vanes, fountains, and fantastical plant "pictures" at Succulent Gardens and Gifts (831-624-0426). My granddaughters love Avalon Beads (831-624-4520), where they spend hours planning their jewelry projects. In the huge inventory are Japanese seed beads, precious and semiprecious stones, and Venetian glass beads. (The website, www.avalonbeads.net, shows other Central Coast locations.)

The Thunderbird Bookshop (831-624-1803), with its large children's section, has been a beloved fixture in Carmel Valley for decades. Sandcastles-by-the-Sea (831-626-8361) features wooden toys, games, kits, costumes, musical instruments, and well-made, sturdy things that parents feel good about. Twiggs (831-622-9802) delights all ages with gnomes, trolls, raccoons, bunnies, twittering birds, and fantastical creatures.

Garland Ranch Regional Park (all ages)
About 8.6 miles east of Highway 1, on Carmel Valley Road, Carmel Valley; (831) 659-4488.

The primary public venue for outdoor recreation in the valley, the park runs along the river and up onto the ridges in oak forests—5,000 acres of wilderness crisscrossed by trails. The most popular paths are the easy Lupine Loop, the Buckeye, and the Waterfall Trail to the mesa. In springtime wildflowers explode in great colorful clouds, water rushes over the falls, and lush grass surrounds the pond on the mesa. Up here views of the entire valley are mesmerizing.

Near the parking lot, picnic sites beside the river are pleasant on hot days. John Steinbeck wrote in *Cannery Row,* "The Carmel [River] crackles among round boulders, wanders lazily under sycamores, spills into pools, drops in against banks where crayfish live . . . frogs blink from its banks and the deep ferns grow beside it. It's everything a river should be."

Earthbound Farm Stand (all ages)

Three miles east of Highway 1, 7250 Carmel Valley Rd.; (831) 625-6219; www.ebfarm.com.

In a beautiful setting between the foothills and a green hillside, a roadside stand laden with organic fresh and dried fruits, herbs and vegetables, flowers, artisanal cheeses, prepared picnic foods, and homemade bakery goods. Stop for a cold drink or a snack, and to shop for gifts. Wander the Kids' Garden, the cut-your-own herb garden, and the aromatherapy labyrinth; call ahead to join **free** harvest walks and chef-led tours in 60 acres of garden, and to participate in garlic braiding, crafts workshops, and more events and classes. This unique farm is now America's largest grower of certified organic produce.

Where to Eat

Baja Cantina. 7166 Carmel Valley Rd., Valley Hills Center, Carmel Valley; (831) 625-2252. On a heated patio overlooking the valley or inside surrounded by funky auto memorabilia of the early 1900s, eat grilled and spit-roasted meats, fresh seafood, salads, and great enchiladas, tacos, and more California-style Mexican food. $$

Bon Appetit. 7 Delfino Place, Carmel Valley Village; (831) 659-3559. Sit outdoors under an umbrella, watch the passing scene of the village, and enjoy bouillabaisse, paella, mesquite-grilled fresh fish, and gourmet pizzas; notable wine list. $$–$$$

Rio Grill. 101 Crossroads Blvd., Carmel, in a shopping center near Highway 1 and Carmel Valley Road; (831) 625-5436. Santa Fe–style decor, butcher-paper-covered tables with crayons for the creative, and tons of awards, such as Best Restaurant in Monterey County, make this a top choice for Southwestern-style food. A wood-burning grill and an oakwood smoker produce savory fresh fish, meat, and poultry specialties. $$–$$$

Running Iron Restaurant and Saloon. 24 East Carmel Valley Rd., Carmel Valley Village; (831) 659-4633. The oldest continuously operating eating place in these parts, opened in the 1940s. Cowboy boots and spurs hang from the ceiling, and steaks and south-of-the-border specialties are on the menu. $$–$$$

Where to Stay

Blue Sky Lodge. Carmel Valley Road at Flight Road, Carmel Valley; (831) 659-2256; www.blueskylodge.com. Large family units, living rooms and fireplaces, heated pool. Pets welcome. Walk to the village. $$–$$$

Riverside RV Park and Saddle Mountain RV Park. A mile off Carmel Valley Road on Schulte Road, Carmel Valley; (831) 624-9329. Tree-shaded RV sites, most with nice views of the valley. Large, attractive swimming-pool terrace, with picnic tables under oak trees. Day use is available for the pool and barbecues. $

Valley Lodge. 8 Ford Rd., Carmel Valley; (800) 641-4646; www.valleylodge.com. Small, quiet, reasonably priced, with pretty patio rooms and suites with 2 queen-size beds; fireplace cottages with 1 or 2 bedrooms, living rooms, kitchens, Shaker furnishings, garden patios or decks. Sixty-foot heated swimming pool, sauna; dogs welcome. $$$–$$$$

For More Information

Carmel Valley Chamber of Commerce. Oak Building, Carmel Valley Road, Carmel Valley; (831) 659-4000; www.carmelchamber .com.

Big Sur

Beginning just south of Carmel along Highway 1, Big Sur is a sparsely developed stretch of coastal wilderness that runs 90 miles south to San Simeon. High cliffs and river valleys are hemmed in by the rugged Santa Lucia Mountains on one side and a largely inaccessible seacoast on the other, with sheer 1,000-foot drops to beaches below. Offshore are natural arches and sea stacks, rocky remnants of ancient shores. The 2-lane highway is crossed by nearly 30 bridges over wild canyons, deep valleys, and creeks that rush down mountains into ferocious ocean surf—a scenic drive but rather unrelentingly curvy for younger children if you drive more than a half hour or so at a time. One of the top-10 highest single-span bridges in the world, the spectacular 714-foot-long Bixby Creek Bridge has linked the world to Big Sur since 1932.

Fortunately, there are many stops to make for walks in forest parks, beach explorations, and lunches and snacks at a few—just a few—cafes. In several river and forest parks, including the Los Padres National Forest, are good campgrounds and walking and hiking trails.

On Highway 1 along the entire Big Sur coastline, deer and other wildlife frequently wander onto the road, especially at night, so it is best to drive slowly and enjoy the views safely! Be aware there are only a handful of gas stations and grocery stores on the Big Sur highway, and prices are astronomical.

Point Sur Light Station (all ages)
Nineteen miles south of Rio Road in Carmel on Highway 1; (831) 625-4419; www.parks.ca .gov. $.

A historic 1889 stone lighthouse, blacksmith and carpentry shops, and an interpretive center are open for guided tours, with reservations. The 2- to 3-hour tour includes a 0.5-mile walk with a 300-foot gradual climb to the lighthouse, located on a dramatic 360-foot-high promontory over the sea. Wildflowers and whales are frequent rewards.

Andrew Molera State Park (all ages)
Twenty-two miles south of Carmel, on Highway 1 (access not suitable for RVs); (831) 667-2315. Day use $.

The Big Sur River flows down from the Santa Lucias through 4,800-acre Molera State Park, falling into the sea at a long sandy beach. One of many hiking trails runs along the river through a eucalyptus grove, where monarch butterflies overwinter, to the river mouth, where you can see a variety of sea- and shorebirds. Besides ancient redwoods, you will encounter the Santa Lucia fir, found only here, and possibly the endangered peregrine falcon and bald eagles.

Reservations are not accepted for the walk-in tent campground in a meadow; the facility has picnic sites, a horseback-riding concession, biking trails, and restrooms. For trail maps and information, write in advance to the US Forest Service, 406 South Mildred, King City 93930 (408-385-5434).

Watch Out for **Poison Oak!**

A common native shrub throughout Northern California and a menace for hikers and mountain bikers, poison oak is rampant along foothill and low-elevation trails, creeks, rivers, and forested areas. Even if you are not allergy-prone, you may get itchy, long-lasting rashes from rubbing against the leaves, particularly in the winter and spring when the leaves are full of moisture and oils. My children seldom got through a summer without at least one or two bouts of poison oak; it seems to be a given at summer camp.

- If your family is unfamiliar with poison oak, ask locals or park rangers to describe it, or better yet, show it to you.

- Look for shrubs with groupings of three separate small leaves, 1–2 inches long, that are bright green in spring and summer, red or reddish yellow in fall and winter.

- Take care not to burn unfamiliar branches and leaves in a campfire, as poison oak smoke can seriously inflame the lungs.

- After hikes and bike rides in areas where poison oak is present, have everyone in the family wash carefully with soap as soon as the outing is over, and do not handle the clothes until they are laundered.

- Tell your children not to touch their faces, and especially their eyes, while hiking, camping, and mountain bike riding.

- Got the dreaded rash? Don't worry; it goes away in a few days. In the meantime, stay out of the sun and avoid overheating the skin.

- Don't scratch! Scratching can spread the rash.

- Use cortisone-based lotions to cover and soothe the rashes.

- If anyone has poison oak rash around their eyes, and the eyes puff up and close, or almost close, promptly take them to a doctor or emergency room; a cortisone shot is the usual remedy.

One of the most unforgettable ways to see Big Sur is on horseback. Molera Trail Rides offers daily 2-hour rides in the park, each featuring a different perspective, such as the beach, redwood groves, mountain ridges, and sunset excursions (831-625-5486 or 800-942-5486).

Pfeiffer Big Sur State Park (all ages)
Twenty-six miles south of Carmel, on Highway 1; (831) 667-2171 or (831) 667-2315. Day use $.

The most popular, easily accessible, and family friendly park in the area, this is a good place to hike, picnic, and fish on the Big Sur River. Short trails around the campground lead to giant redwoods, a waterfall, river boulders, and pools. A 1.8-mile creekside loop brings you to 60-foot Pfeiffer Falls in a fern canyon and to dazzling ridgetop views. Docent-led nature walks to Pfeiffer Beach are given in summer (on your own, access to Pfeiffer Beach is just past the park entrance, marked by a row of mailboxes, on Sycamore Canyon Road).

There are more than 200 developed, tree-shaded campsites on the river, and bath-houses, motel/cabins, picnic areas, a restaurant, Laundromat, and camp stores. Next to the park at Big Sur Station, park rangers hand out trail maps and give advice on trail conditions.

Julia Pfeiffer Burns State Park (all ages)
Thirty-seven miles south of Carmel, on Highway 1; (831) 667-2315. Day use $.

A glowing jewel of forest and coastline on 3,600 acres of undeveloped wilderness. A 0.5-mile, easy trail along McWay Creek leads to glorious coastal views and to a waterfall that plunges over an 80-foot cliff into the ocean. The Partington Creek Trail goes through a canyon and a 100-foot rock tunnel to Partington Cove Beach, where sea otters play in the kelp beds. Beyond the state park, 60 miles south of Carmel, Jade Cove is actually a string of coves, where Monterey jade is found at low tide and following storms.

Where to Eat

Big Sur Bakery and Restaurant. Highway 1 near the post office in Big Sur; (831) 667-0520. In a garden setting with sweeping views of Big Sur Valley, the restaurant serves breakfast, lunch, and dinner, including pizza from a wood-fired oven; hearty, healthy comfort food; and veggie specialties. Super-yummy baked goods. $–$$

Nepenthe. Twenty-nine miles south of Carmel, on Highway 1; (831) 667-2345. For decades a favorite destination for visitors in the Big Sur area, the restaurant features stone patios perched 800 feet above the sea that offer a long and magical view of a spectacular shoreline. Try the ambrosia burger, local artichokes, or the fresh fish, and plan to spend a leisurely lunchtime, or sit by the fire pit at sunset. $$

Ripplewood Resort. Twenty-four miles south of Carmel on Highway 1, Big Sur Valley; (831) 667-2242. Good for breakfast, lunch, and Mexican dinners. $–$$

Rocky Point. Ten miles south of Carmel on Highway 1; (831) 624-2933. Spectacular views of the coast from the dining room and the terrace make breakfast, lunch, and dinner into memorable experiences. Try the enchiladas, the crab salad, or one of the fabulous steaks. $$

Where to Stay

Big Sur Lodge. Twenty-six miles south of Carmel in Pfeiffer Big Sur State Park; (831) 667-2171 or (800) 424-4787; www.bigsur lodge.com. Cozy, simple cottages in a forest; kitchens, fireplaces; lovely views; pool. The casual, family-oriented restaurant serves California cuisine, pasta, local seafood, and stuff kids like; the patio overlooks the Big Sur River—heavenly. $$–$$$

Deetjen's Big Sur Inn. Thirty-one miles south of Carmel, on Highway 1; (831) 667-2377. Quaint, rustic, Norwegian-style inn in a redwood grove; 20 simple cottages; fireplaces or wood-burning stoves; down comforters. Each cottage has 2 or 3 separate guest rooms with shared bath (choose your unit carefully, as some can be noisy). Good American food in 4 charming, rustic, sun- or candlelit rooms; good, hearty breakfasts and dinners. $$–$$$

River Inn. Pheneger Creek, Big Sur; (800) 328-2884. Eighteen queen rooms and family suites with balconies overlooking the river; simple, rustic accommodations. Restaurant and bar, swimming pool, general store; near state parks. $–$$

Riverside Campground and Cabins. Twenty-five miles south of Carmel, P.O. Box 3, Big Sur 93920; (831) 667-2414. Campsites, RV sites, communal bathhouse. $

Treebones Resort. 71895 Hwy. 1, Gorda Springs; (877) 424-4787; www.treebones resort.com. On a cliff with a spectacular sea view, at the end of a narrow, rutted dirt road between Nepenthe and Hearst Castle, are 16 yurts—round, canvas-covered tents with pine floors, queen-size beds with patchwork quilts, heaters, and skylights. Communal bathhouses; yurts 8, 9, 10, and 16 have the best views. Main lodge for meals and a big stone fireplace; includes do-it-yourself waffle breakfasts. Self-serve lunches are extra. $$–$$$

Ventana Big Sur Campground. Thirty miles south of Carmel, on Highway 1; (831) 667-2712; www.ventanawildernesscamp ground.com. A lovely 80-site private campground in a redwood grove, with bathhouses; reserve well ahead. $

For More Information

Big Sur Chamber of Commerce. P.O. Box 87, Big Sur 93920; (831) 667-2100; www.big surcalifornia.org.

The
Big Valley

California's rich agricultural heartland rolls for hundreds of miles between the Sierra Nevada Range and the Coastal Range. Freshened with many lakes and reservoirs, almost a dozen rivers, and 1,000 miles of inland Delta waterways, a string of verdant valleys—the Sacramento, the Santa Clara, and the San Joaquin—is paradise for families who love to fish, water-ski, houseboat, play outdoors, and camp.

The state capital and three good-size towns along the north–south valley route, Highway 99, are gateways to the central and southern Sierras, three national parks, and several national forests. And a tiny inland village, founded by the Spanish and the original Native American residents, is a side trip not to be missed.

Sacramento

The mighty Sacramento River—wide, cool, and green; fringed with overhanging trees; and loaded with fish—nourishes a valley that feeds the world. Astride the river, the state capital, Sacramento, was a simple homesteader's fort that became a boomtown during the gold rush in the mid-1800s and was the western terminus for the Pony Express and the Transcontinental Railroad. The main historic and recreational attractions for families are the California State Capitol, Old Town Sacramento, the State Railroad Museum, and the river itself. Several excellent marinas, with outdoor restaurants and boat tie-ups, are found along the Garden Highway on the northern edge of the city. Thousands of magnificent old trees and glorious Victorian mansions line the downtown streets. Beautiful homes are found from 7th to 16th Streets, and from E to I Streets; don't miss the Heilbron home at 740 O St. and the Stanford home at 800 N St.

Summer days average temperatures in the 90s, with many days topping 100-degree temperatures, yet this is a city of more than a million trees, as well as access to the water, so relief is never far away.

THE BIG VALLEY

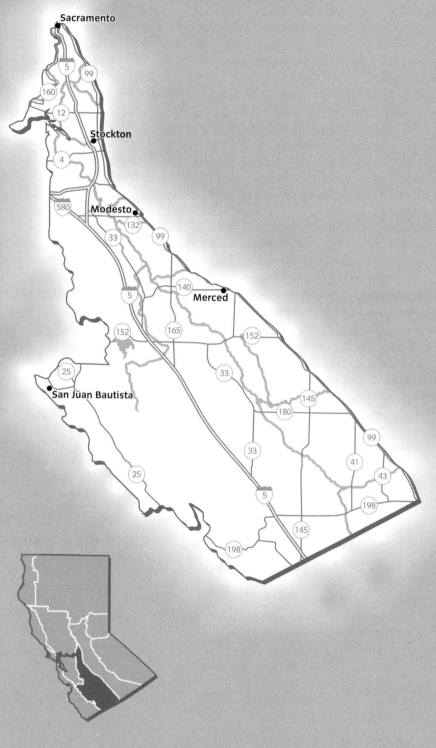

One of the largest of the annual events is the Sacramento Jazz Jubilee on Memorial Day weekend, when jazz fans assemble in droves in Old Sacramento and venues around the city to hear some of the top Dixieland bands in the world, and Latin jazz and Big Band music, too. This is definitely a family affair during the day; look for the kids' stage and the children's parade.

CalExpo in Sacramento is home to the California State Fair and other annual family-oriented events, such as dog shows, outdoor recreation shows, and even a Baby Expo (www.calexpo.com). There is an RV park here, too, Raging Waters, a huge, multifaceted water park that was taken over in 2008 by a national chain. A major freshening-up and several exciting new rides and slides have greatly improved the property. *Good Morning America* called it one of the top 10 water parks in the nation (www .rwsac.com). When you check into your lodgings, ask for the **free** Sacramento Gold Card, entitling you to discounts at restaurants, popular attractions, and shops. For instance, you get two-for-one deals on bike rentals and several museum admissions, the zoo, parks, and more. Check the website for participating hotels (www.discover gold.org/visitors/goldcard).

California State Capitol (all ages)
10th Street and Capitol Mall, Sacramento; (916) 324-0333; www.statecapitolmuseum.com. Free.

The circa-1870, double-domed capitol is surrounded by 40 acres of Capitol Park, a century-old botanical garden that explodes into pink and white clouds of camellias, azaleas, dogwood, and tulips every spring. You can take a **free** guided tour of the gardens or stroll around on your own.

With toddlers and little kids, take a self-guided tour and let them meander up and down the marble hallways while you peek in at the museum displays and re-created historic rooms. You'll see magnificent carved staircases, elaborate crystal chandeliers, marble parquet floors, and historic artwork. You might even be able to sit in on a legislative session. With children about 8 years old and older, take the guided historic tour, where you'll hear stories of California's colorful politicos (call ahead to reserve). On-site are a gift and book shop, and a cafeteria.

Old Sacramento (all ages)
Between I Street, Capitol Mall, the Sacramento River, and Highway 5; (916) 808-7777 or (916) 442-7644; www.oldsacramento.com.

Early in the morning when the mist hangs low on the Sacramento River and footsteps echo on the boardwalks, you can imagine this rollicking port during the California gold rush, when as many as 800 sailing vessels tied up here at the docks. Reeling from months of sailing around the Horn, gold seekers raced down the gangplanks, bargained for provisions and livestock, and then rode away in wagons and on horseback to seek their fortunes in the Sierra foothills. "Forty-niner" days are still alive in the restored wooden false-front saloons, firehouses, dining halls, and emporiums of Old Sacramento, a National Historical Monument.

Browsing 100 boutique shops, more than 20 restaurants, and museums and historic sites will take a full day or two. Annual events in Old Sacramento include the Festival de la Familia, with hundreds of vendors and **free** entertainment, such as Latin, Caribbean, and Native American music. At the Pacific Rim Festival in May, live entertainment includes the thrilling Japanese *taiko* drummers and martial arts demonstrations; kids can make art while parents browse for arts and crafts and try the exotic foods (www.pacificrimstreet fest.com). The Gold Rush Days festival over Labor Day weekend re-creates early days, with horse-drawn carriages, characters in period costumes, exciting Wild West gunfights, gold panning, and living-history events and performances; Old Town streets are authentically dirt-covered.

California State Railroad Museum (all ages)

North side of Old Sacramento; (916) 445-7387 or (916) 445-6645; www.csrmf.org. Adults $$; ages 6 to 17 $; 5 and under are free.

A 100,000-square-foot display of three dozen antique locomotives and railcars in pristine condition, the museum is a dream come true for kids fascinated by rail travel. You can hop aboard a real sleeping car that rocks back and forth and sounds as if it's rolling along. Retired conductors spin tales of the rails. One of the magnificent engines weighs a mere million pounds. Small Wonders: The Magic of Toy Trains includes a century's worth of toy trains, a collection so vast, it's shown in changing, interactive exhibitions. Children can climb around several cars indoors and outdoors and take a 6-mile steam train ride up and down the river. Next to the museum, the Railroad Museum Gift Shop sells myriad toy trains, books, and railroad-related souvenirs. The annual California Railroad Festival is held here in June (916-445-7387). Just down the street from the museum is the Silver Palace, a re-created depot cafe, good for comfort-food lunches, "Steam Whistle Chili," and snacks.

Jedediah Smith Memorial Bicycle Trail/ American River Parkway (all ages)

A paved biking and walking path follows the river for 26 miles, from Old Town to Folsom Lake, in the foothills of Gold Country. Guided walks on the parkway are available through the Effie Yeaw Nature Center (916-489-4918). For a trail map contact the Parks Department (916-875-6961). Summer temperatures on the trail are often 100 degrees or higher, with balmy evenings.

California Museum for History, Women and the Arts (all ages)

1020 O St. near the Capitol, Sacramento; (916) 653-1020; www.californiamuseum.org. Ages 6 to adult $$; ages 5 and under free.

The old California State History Museum has a new name, a new focus, and a new high-tech, interactive environment. It now showcases more than 200 of the state's remarkable women, including today's luminaries, and the rich history of the state in photographs, media presentations, hands-on activities, artifacts, an archive, and much more. Exhibits are vivid and appealing, featuring such stars as Milton Berle, Steve Jobs, Willie Mays, Rita

Things to Do in Sacramento

- **Discovery Museum,** 101 I St.; (916) 264-7057; www.thediscovery.org. In a circa-1850 city hall, you will find a huge gold nugget collection, a planetarium, hands-on science and technology exhibits, and simulated space travel in the Challenger Learning Center. Nature trail and okay-to-touch animals in the Nature Center, history exhibits, and more. $; free for kids 3 and under.

- **Towe Auto Museum,** 2200 Front St.; (916) 442-6802; www.toweauto museum.org. Crazy for cars? Visit this cache of more than 200 antique and classic cars and trucks, including every Ford car from 1903 to 1953. The kids can climb up behind the wheel of a Model T flatbed truck and other wheeled beauties. Adults $$; kids $.

- **Old Sacramento Schoolhouse,** 1200 Front St.; (916) 483-8818; www.scoe .net/oldsacschoolhouse. A replica of an 1884 one-room schoolhouse. Sit at a wooden desk with a slate and chalk; read the list of punishments for bad behavior (Telling Tales out of School, eight lashes); ring the school bell; swing on swings in the schoolyard. Free.

- **Southern Railroad Excursions,** Front Street at the railroad depot; (916) 446-6645; www.csrmf.org. Weekends April through September, vintage steam-powered trains chug along on a 40-minute route beside the Sacramento River. Choose from enclosed coaches or open-air gondolas. The whistle blasts, the steam pours out, and the river breezes blow! Adults $$; ages 6 to 12 $; ages 5 and under are free.

- **Sutter's Fort State Historic Park,** 2701 L St.; (916) 445-4422. The valley's earliest European settlement, founded in 1839. Pioneer and early California artifacts, carpenter and blacksmith shops, bakery, dining room, living quarters—an easy, fun introduction to the early days. Call ahead about Living History Days and Pioneer Demonstration Days, when costumed docents authentically re-create the past and visitors participate. $.

- **Hornblower Historic River Tours,** 1206 Front St.; (888) 467-6256; www.hornblower.com. Hour-long yacht cruises up and down the Old Town riverfront. $$$.

Moreno, Jackie Robinson, Jonas Salk, John Steinbeck, Elizabeth Taylor, and Tiger Woods. Thank Maria Shriver for this inspiring and educational venue.

Scandia Family Fun Center (all ages)

5070 Hillsdale Blvd., Sacramento; (916) 331-5757; www.scandiafamilycenter.com. For unlimited play, adults and those under 54 inches $$$; less for individual attractions; free for toddlers.

You will have a hard time getting the kids to leave here once they see the bumper cars, bumper boats, and the arcade. For less competitive fun, play minigolf on two 18-hole courses or whack baseballs in the batting cages.

Sacramento Zoo/William Land Park (all ages)

3930 West Lane Park Dr., Sacramento; (916) 264-5885. Zoo: ages 13 and up $$; ages 3 to 12 $. Fairytale Town: $.

Remodeled and expanded, with national recognition for the rare cat, primate, and bird collections, and the red panda exhibit.

Across the street from the zoo, Fairytale Town is heaven for the littlest angels, with play structures themed to Mother Goose, puppet shows, and more (www.fairytaletown .org). Also here is Funderland, an amusement park with rides for kids of elementary school age (pay per ride). William Land Park is a large city park with playgrounds, picnic areas, and a duck pond.

Jelly Belly Candy Factory (all ages)

Off Highway 80, take Highway 12/Rio Vista to 1 Jelly Belly Lane, Fairfield; (800) 953-5592; www.jellybelly.com. Free.

The most popular flavors of Jelly Bellies are buttered popcorn, very cherry, licorice, juicy pear, and watermelon. There is a 40-minute tour to watch the jellies being made, and you can see close-ups on TV monitors; best on weekdays when the factory is in operation—come early in the day to avoid crowds. Other fun here is the jelly bean art gallery, free samples, lunch in the Jelly Belly Cafe, espresso drinks at the Java Bar, and ice-cream cones.

Nut Tree Village (all ages)

1661 East Monte Vista Ave., Vacaville; (877) 688-8733; www.nuttreeusa.com. Rides $.

Just off Highway 80, a half hour south of Sacramento, is a new upscale shopping and restaurant complex with an amusement park designed for kids up to about 10 years old. In a park setting, there is a beautiful carousel, a little passenger train, boats in a pond, non-scary rides, hobby horses, Skee-Ball, and more. Among pricey eateries is Fenton's Creamery, an ice-cream parlor that serves meals.

Western Railway Museum (all ages)

Ten miles east of Fairfield on Highway 12, Suisun; (707) 374-2978; www.wrm.org. Adults $$; kids 3 to 12 $; families $$$.

Ride on and explore more than 100 historic cars: trolleys, streetcars, Pullmans, and steam locomotives. Exhibits trace railroad history, and there is a shop selling train-related books, toys, and souvenirs. Have a picnic here under the trees.

Sacramento River Train (all ages)
Boarding in Woodland; (800) 866-1690; www.sacramentorivertrain.com. $$$$.

A steam locomotive pulls open-air and enclosed passenger cars through agricultural lands along the river and the Yolo Wildlife Refuge about 16 miles one-way, and over an 8,000-foot-long wooden trestle to West Sacramento. You will have the chance to sample and purchase local produce at Uncle Ray's Fruit Stand. Special-event trains with music, food, and entertainment include murder mystery and train robbery, Mother's and Father's Day, the Christmas train, and more.

The Great Outdoors Near Sacramento

- **Folsom Lake Recreation Area,** 25 miles east of Sacramento off Highway 50, between Folsom and Auburn; (800) 444-7275. Parking $. Extending 15 miles up the canyon of the North Fork of the American River, an 18,000-acre lake that's great for camping, boating, swimming, hiking, and fishing. You can rent horses and bikes here for exploring more than 80 miles of trails. At the marina, reserve a campsite at one of the tent and RV camps, bike camps, or equestrian camps (916-988-0205). Windsurfing is popular, especially in April and May.

- **Brannan Island State Recreation Area,** Highway 160, 3 miles south of Rio Vista; (916) 777-7701. Parking $. Another windsurfing paradise is Windy Cove, right in the middle of the Delta on the Sacramento River. Windy Cove was developed by local surfing fanatics and is one of the primo spots in the state. Hot summers are great for swimming, camping, and picnicking. Rangers lead canoe tours.

- **Grizzly Island.** Take Highway 12 toward Rio Vista, go south on Grizzly Island Road at the Sunset Shopping Center, and then proceed 9 miles to the wildlife preserve; (707) 425-3828. Entrance fee per car, $. You'll see river otters, turtles, tule elk, egrets, herons, coots, wigeons, grebes, and many more animals and birds in this 12,900-acre wildlife preserve in the Sacramento Delta. A relaxing place to take an outdoor break between Sacramento and the Bay Area, Grizzly Island is best in winter, when thousands of migratory waterfowl stop to feed and rest in the Suisun Marsh surrounding the island (avoid October through mid-January, which is duck-hunting season).

Where to Eat

Crawdads River Cantina. 1375 Garden Hwy., Sacramento; (916) 929-2268; www .crawdadsontheriver.com. Try the Cajun popcorn (shrimp fried in beer batter) and watch the river roll by; children's menu, festive American food. Closed in the winter. $$

Fanny Ann's. 1023 2nd St., Old Sacramento; (916) 441-0505. Five floors of a crazily antiques-crammed restaurant and bar, a fun place to take the kids during the day; an adult crowd gathers at night. Play pinball and foosball while you wait for American comfort food, burgers, salads, and sandwiches. $–$$

Ford's Real Hamburgers. 1948 Sutterville Rd., near William Land Park, Sacramento; (916) 452-6979. Big, wonderful, old-fashioned burgers from kiddie-size to the Pounder. Also grilled chicken, turkey burgers, thick shakes. One order of fries is enough for a small army. $

Joe's Crab Shack. 1210 Front St.; (916) 553-4249. When Crawdads is closed in the winter, try Joe's for boiled shrimp, barbecued Dungeness crab, and music and dancing. $–$$

Leatherby's Family Creamery. 2333 Arden Way, Sacramento; (916) 920-8382. An old-fashioned ice-cream parlor and cafe serving light lunches, dinners, and homemade ice cream. $

Old Spaghetti Factory. 1910 J St., Sacramento (also in Roseville and Rancho Cordova); (915) 443-2862. Sit in the trolley car or at a wooden table under the stained-glass chandeliers in a bright, Old Town environment. The good, traditional Italian food is inexpensive, especially at lunch. $

Rocky Mountain Chocolate Factory. 1039 2nd St.; (916) 448-8801; www.rmcf .com. Hand-dipped ice-cream bars, caramel apples, chocolate-covered strawberries, and fresh, homemade candy. You could be in trouble here. $–$$

Roxy Restaurant. 2381 Fair Oaks Blvd., Sacramento; (916) 489-2000; www.roxyres taurantandbar.com. Paris meets the ranch with "New Ranch Cuisine" and American West grub, cowhide booths, and country and western music. Sourdough pancakes at breakfast; buffalo and beef burgers, steaks, and pasta at lunch; Lucky Dog Ranch Beef and hearty dishes at dinner. Pricey for families; super-fun and worth it for a splurge. $$–$$$

Tower Café. 1518 Broadway, Sacramento; (916) 441-0222. Look for the art deco tower of the landmark Tower movie theater. Sit under the trees for breakfast, lunch, dinner, and brunch at a much-beloved casual restaurant. Open late in the evening. Terrific American and Mexican food, and a good kids' menu. $–$$

Vic's. 3199 Riverside Blvd., near Land Park, Sacramento; (916) 448-0892. For more than 50 years, homemade ice cream in a soda fountain diner with booths; thick shakes, egg creams. Try the turkey-salad special sandwich, a cheese dog, or egg-salad sandwich. $

Where to Stay

Embassy Suites Riverfront Promenade. 100 Capitol Mall; (916) 326-5000; www .embassysuites.com. Walk across the street to Old Sacramento, restaurants, shopping, and museums—you can't beat the location and the value. Right on the river, with a soaring garden atrium and 242 spacious rooms, each with a separate bedroom, living room with sofa bed, wet bar with microwave, refrigerator, and coffeemaker; 2 televisions, guest laundry, indoor pool, sauna, fitness, and complimentary breakfast and afternoon drinks/ snacks. California-Tuscan food and river views at casual Tower Bridge Bistro; salads, snacks, sandwiches, and wood-fired pizza in the Marketplace Café. $$$–$$$$

Radisson Hotel Sacramento. 500 Leisure Lane, Sacramento; (916) 922-2020 or (800) 333-3333; www.radissonsac.com. A 5-minute drive from Old Town, this comfortable oasis has swimming pools, a parcourse, bike rentals, gardens around a small lake, and several restaurants. Each room or suite has a balcony or patio overlooking 18 acres of gardens. $$

For More Information

Sacramento Convention and Visitors Bureau. 1608 I St., Sacramento; (800) 808-7777; www.discovergold.org.

Visitor Information Center. 1004 2nd St., Old Sacramento; (916) 442-7644.

California Division of Tourism. 801 K St., Sacramento; (916) 322-2881 or (800) 862-2543; www.visitcalifornia.com. Information and brochures for travel statewide.

Stockton

The largest of the Delta towns, Stockton is a deepwater port anchoring hundreds of miles of inland waterways. If your family likes to fish and mess about in boats, the Stockton area has it all. Fed by the Sacramento River, the San Joaquin, and five more rivers with origins in the snowpack of the Sierras, the Delta is one of the largest recreation areas in the country. Exploring this enormous labyrinth of sloughs, canals, and meandering rivers can be done on foot on a shady path; on slow, sweet days motoring about on a houseboat; or on water skis behind a speedboat. For the locations of launching ramps and marinas and to find out what's biting, call or stop in at a local sports equipment store.

In this town of literally a million trees, enjoy a lovely historic district and a fairyland amusement park. The 10-block, downtown waterfront has undergone dramatic development, including a Cineplex, an amphitheater and vast lawns for concerts and events, and the new Stockton Ballpark, where home-run "splash landings" into the river are fun to see. Stroll the breezy DeCarli Waterfront Square promenade, enjoy the view, and let the kids loose in the nautical-theme playground and, on a hot day, in the fabulous Weber Point Water Fountain jets that erupt out of the courtyard. The Waterfront Warehouse houses casual cafes and delis.

Head to the "Miracle Mile" on Pacific Avenue between Castle Street and Harding Way to browse antique shops and galleries, see the art deco Stockton Royal Theatre, and try out ethnic restaurants. Have a picnic in leafy Victory Park at Pershing and Argonne, and if you're here on a Wednesday in July or August, stay for the **free** outdoor concerts.

Just north of Stockton, the last undammed river flowing from the Sierras through the Central Valley—the Consumnes—provides unparalleled wildlife viewing. The Nature Conservancy preserve on the river has easy trails through wetlands and forests rich with birdlife.

Magnolia Historic District (all ages)

A rough rectangle between Flora Street and Harding Way, and El Dorado and California Streets. Get street maps from the Visitor's Bureau, 46 West Fremont St., Stockton; (800) 350-1987.

Take a short drive or an hour's stroll around Stockton's lovely old residential district to see homes from as early as 1860—extravagantly decorated Victorians, romantic Spanish Revival mansions, and Craftsman cottages, a rich architectural cache on tree-shaded streets.

Pixie Woods/Louis Park (ages 1 to 10)

Monte Diablo and Occidental Avenue, Stockton; (209) 937-8206; www.stocktongov.com/pixie woods/index.cfm. $.

Kids can ride a stagecoach and ponies in this fairyland–theme park built in the 1950s. Big shade trees and lawns make this a pleasant place for parents to linger while children enjoy

Family Friendly Events in Stockton

- **Stockton Community Labor Day Powwow,** University of the Pacific, 3601 Pacific Ave.; (209) 933-7425; www.powwows.com. Native Americans from around the country gather to celebrate the culture and traditions of their tribes. A vividly colorful and exciting **free** event, with authentic food, dancing, singing, and crafts.

- **Great Italian Street Painting Festival,** www.visitstockton.org. In May, stroll the artfully decorated sidewalks, where kids can get into the act of painting, too. Entertainment and food.

- **Open Air Asian and Farmers' Market,** under the freeway at San Joaquin and El Dorado Streets; (209) 464-5246. On Saturdays, an amazing array of exotic produce, herbs, fish, and sweets of Southeast Asia.

- **Downtown Stockton Farmers' Market,** East Main Street between Hunter Square and San Joaquin Street; (209) 464-5246. Every Friday, a lively street fair with local produce, baked goods, arts and crafts, and entertainment.

- **Outdoor Ice Rink,** (209) 937-8206. November through December at the waterfront park, with a heated rest area and refreshments.

- **Planetarium Shows,** www.stocktonastro.org. Once a month at the newly refurbished Delta College Planetarium, Friday and Saturday night shows at 7:30 p.m. $$; (209) 954-5110. The Friday night shows coincide with **free** "Sky Tours" hosted by the Stockton Astronomical Society, whose members set up telescopes and help visitors observe the night sky.

the playground. Special shows are featured in the Toadstool Theater on Sunday. The park opens for the season in March. Kids to about 10 years old will love riding the little train past Frontier Town, the carousel, and the steam paddlewheeler on the lagoon. Snacks and fast food available.

Wat Dharmararam (all ages)

3732 Carpenter Rd., Stockton; (209) 943-7711; www.visitstockton.org. Free

A unique and fascinating place where Buddhist monks will guide you around to see their Cambodian temple, complete with 2 huge statues of the Buddha and nearly 100 more brightly painted and decorated statues—some are encrusted with jewels. At this sort of Buddhist Disneyland, kids will flock to the 50-foot-long reclining Buddha and to the goddess that floats on a cloud. The Cambodian New Year is celebrated with a festival in mid-April.

Micke Grove Park and Zoo (all ages)

Eight miles north of Stockton off Highway 99; take 8-Mile Road to 11793 North Micke Grove Rd., Lodi; (209) 953-8840; www.mgzoo.com. Vehicle entry $; zoo $; kids 2 and under free.

A great place to spend an afternoon. The zoo houses a nice variety of wild animals, plus tropical birds and an endangered species exhibit. You can picnic under the oaks, try out the playground equipment, go swimming in the public pool, or take a turn on the merry-go-round at the Funderwoods amusement park, which is designed for kids ages 2 to 10. A large museum complex in the park has historic exhibits and nearly 100 tractors displayed outdoors. In the fall, maples and ginkgo trees are aflame in the Japanese Garden, a peaceful place with a waterfall and a stone pagoda.

Children's Museum of Stockton (ages 1 to 10)

Across the street from Waterfront Warehouse, 402 West Weber Ave.; (209) 465-4386. Open Wed through Sun. $; under 3 free.

Hands-on, play-based, educational exhibits and activities, from fire trucks to banks, a grocery store, post office, doctor's office, and other child-size businesses.

Houseboat Rentals in Stockton

For more information and brochures call the **Delta Rental Houseboat Hotline:** (209) 477-1840.

- **King Island Resort,** 11530 8-Mile Rd.; (209) 951-2188.
- **Paradise Point Marina,** 8095 Rio Blanco Rd.; (209) 952-1000.
- **Herman and Helen's Marina,** Venice Island Ferry; (209) 951-4634.

Haggin Museum (all ages)

1201 North Pershing Ave., Stockton; (209) 462-4116; www.hagginmuseum.org. $; children 9 and under **free.**

The history of Stockton represented in a variety of exhibits and the impressive collection of Native American baskets and artifacts distinguish this museum. Art from around the world includes paintings by famous 19th-century artists such as Albert Bierstadt. Look for the 1919 Caterpillar tractor—invented by the founder of Stockton—and a letter by Daniel Boone; a mummy, a great display of antique dolls, and "Willy the Jeep" from World War II.

Houseboating (all ages)

There is nothing like a houseboat for a real Huck Finn experience. From 28-footers to big, luxurious 50-footers, the boats are like floating apartments, furnished with every convenience for up to 12 people. You bring aboard bedding and food and pay for the gas, about 3 to 5 gallons an hour. No experience is necessary, and the boats move at a leisurely pace, about 10 miles an hour. For day trips try a "patio boat," a kind of small floating barge with a roof, seating areas, and not much more. They move a little faster and are fun for camping, picnicking, and fishing expeditions.

Tower Park Marina Resort (all ages)

14900 West Hwy. 12, at the Little Potato Slough drawbridge, Lodi; (209) 943-5656.

This large riverside resort has 400 RV sites, a guest marina, watercraft rentals, boat launching, a general store, picnic sites, and a beach. All tables face the water at the Terminus Tavern restaurant at Tower Park. An annual boat show in May, Deltafest, is held here; in addition to a huge show of boats in the water and ashore, live entertainment, fishing clinics, demonstrations, and food booths are part of the fun.

Consumnes River Preserve (all ages)

Twenty-six miles north of Stockton, take the Twin Cities Road exit off Highway 5; (916) 684-2816. Launch your own boat or take a guided kayak tour; (415) 456-8956.

Great numbers of migrating and resident ducks, geese, swans, and other waterfowl and land birds are found on this 5,400-acre preserve owned by the Nature Conservancy. Stop in at the interpretive center for self-guiding maps to the wetlands, riverside, and oak forest trails; on weekends you can take a guided tour. From spring through July the wildflowers are extraordinary. One-mile Lost Slough Trail has a boardwalk through marshy nesting grounds; Willow Slough Trail is an easy, 3-mile route meandering through beautiful cottonwoods along the river.

Delta River Cruises (all ages)

445 West Weber Ave., Stockton; (916) 399-9342; www.deltarivercruise.com. $$$$.

Take the 1.5-hour cruise on the San Joaquin Delta aboard a 149-passenger catamaran, the *Princess of Whales*, featuring 2 spacious decks and a galley serving snacks and meals.

Houseboating Tips for Families

- **Plan ahead:** Make reservations several months in advance for high-season weekends. Just like motels and campgrounds, houseboats "sell out" quickly.

- **It's not cheap:** A boat sleeping 6 to 10 people in the summer and on holiday weekends will cost $1,000 to $3,000 a week, plus gas, which runs about 3 to 5 gallons per hour, depending on size, speed, weight, and weather.

- **A good night's sleep:** If your group of friends and family fill up the houseboat and you plan to have children sleep on the floor, consider bringing sleeping bags and maybe a tent, for sleeping on the riverside.

- **Getting around:** Don't hesitate to bring with you or rent an outboard skiff to tow behind the houseboat. You'll be glad to have it for zipping to marinas for ice and groceries, for fishing quietly, and for getting away from what may be a noisy, lively life on the houseboat.

- **Anchor early:** Look for a tie-up spot in a protected cove by midafternoon. Boaters like to have their privacy and to be away from wave action generated by passing craft. On weekends, it may take some time to find a good spot.

- **Save money on food:** Shop for groceries before you get to the houseboat marina. Food and drinks are expensive once you get there—the marina stores are more like convenience stores than supermarkets.

- **Upgrades:** Consider making this a truly primo family vacation by going for upgrades such as a water slide, air-conditioning, and an extra bathroom.

Watch fishermen in their boats and on the riverbank, tugboats pushing huge ships, stately waterfront homes, and abundant birdlife. Kids get to steer!

Where to Eat

Angelinas Spaghetti House. 1563 East Fremont, Stockton; (209) 948-6609; www .angelinas.com. Since 1976, homemade spaghetti sauce like no other, and other pasta dishes such as lasagna, tortellini, and fettuccini with various sauces. Also French dip sandwiches, tri-tip, steak, chicken and a pasta buffet, all at reasonable prices. $–$$$

Café Amore Spaghetteria. 40 North Sutter St., Stockton; (209) 462-6811; www .cafeamorestockton.com. Old Tuscan family recipes: lasagna, pizza, seafood, and grilled meats. A small, popular place. $–$$

Garlic Brothers. 6629 Embarcadero Dr., Village West Marina, Stockton; (209) 474-6585; www.garlic-brothers.com. Have refreshments on the deck above 14-Mile Slough, then go for the hearty meat, poultry, and seafood grilled on a wood fire or rotisserie. You can arrive by boat or car. $$

On Lock Sam. 333 South Sutter, Stockton; (209) 466-4561. For more than 100 years, the Wong family has been serving Chinese food to the Stockton community—don't miss this one. $

Waterloo Restaurant. 10447 East Waterloo, Stockton, Highway 99 for 6 miles to Waterloo Road East; (209) 931-4019; www.thewaterloo.com. Serving BBQ-style food for more than 20 years, a very popular place on weekends, when you may have to wait for a table. Barbecued ribs, chicken, fish, steaks and wild game, luscious sandwiches and burgers, homemade clam chowder in a bread bowl, minestrone, and famous pesto. Kids get junior-size portions of yummy ribs or chicken. $–$$$

Where to Stay

Marriott Residence Inn. 3240 West March Lane, Stockton; (209) 472-9800; www.marriott.com. Fairly new and extra nice; studios, 1 and 2 bedrooms; kitchens, fireplaces; pool, guest laundry, continental breakfast. $$

Snug Harbor. (916) 775-1455; www.snugharbor.net. Take the Rio Vista Bridge or the little auto ferries onto Ryer Island, home to Snug Harbor on Steamboat Slough, a quiet inlet where waterfront RV sites; simple, fully equipped cabins; and full marina facilities are popular with vacationing families and fishermen. This is a great headquarters for exploring the delta. $–$$$

For More Information

Stockton Visitors Information. Historic Waterfront Warehouse, 445 West Weber Ave., Stockton; (209) 547-2770; www.visitstockton.org. Call or visit the website to order a brochure.

Delta Rental Houseboat Hotline. For information and brochures call (209) 477-1840.

California Delta Chamber and Visitor's Bureau. Tower Park Marina, 14900 West Hwy. 12, Lodi; (209) 367-9840; www.californiadelta.org.

Modesto

Within a short drive of the Sacramento Delta and the Sierras, Modesto—awarded the title of All-American City—is surrounded by vast fruit orchards and veggie fields: almonds, apricots, peaches, walnuts, and more. Spring is a glorious time in the Modesto area and throughout the Central Valley. Wildflowers—vibrant blue lupine, goldfields, poppies, mustard—cascade in great waves across the grasslands and in the riparian areas. If you are in the area between late February and mid-March, call to ask which almond, peach, and apricot blossom tour routes are in full bloom (209-384-2791).

The town is a good jumping-off point for recreation on the Stanislaus River, where nine US Army Corps of Engineers–maintained areas are located along 59 miles of the river; between Modesto and Knights Ferry are more than 16 drive-in, boat-in, and walk-in campgrounds.

The movie *American Graffiti* was based on director George Lucas's boyhood experiences in Modesto in the '50s and '60s, when cruising was a way of life. For a peek into the past, go to the A&W Root Beer drive-in at 14th and G Streets, where carhops still cruise to your car on roller skates. Classic car shows are held in June. Elvis, Marilyn, and other celebs show up on Friday nights.

McHenry Mansion and Museum (all ages)
15th and I Streets, Modesto; (209) 577-5344; http://mchenrymansion.org. Free.

In the heart of the lovely old home district and built in 1883, a spectacular, fully furnished and decorated Victorian Italianate mansion. A block away on I Street at the McHenry Museum, in a 1912 library are displays from pioneer days through the mid-20th century, from Native American baskets to 1950s advertising posters. Magnificent oaks, elms, redwoods, palms, and magnolias shade the grounds.

West Bear Creek (all ages)
Off Highway 165, 40 minutes south of Modesto; (209) 826-3508.

In the wintertime, until mid-March, a 2-mile auto tour of the West Bear wetlands is a peaceful experience. Half a million waterfowl rest here while migrating along the Pacific Flyway. White-tailed kites and harriers wheel above, while sandhill cranes, pelicans, and a variety of ducks and geese ply the ponds. This is a small segment of the vast San Luis National Wildlife Refuge.

Great Valley Museum of Natural History (all ages)
1100 Stoddard, Modesto Junior College, Modesto; (209) 575-6196. Family admission $.

Exhibits focus on the flora, fauna, and natural history of the Central Valley, with habitat dioramas; stuffed lions, tigers, and bears; Native American displays; and a native plant garden. Younger children like the interactive Discovery Room and the shop, which sells games, puzzles, toys, and educational books.

Caswell Memorial State Park (all ages)
South Austin Road off Highway 99, Ripon; (209) 599-3810; www.parks.ca.gov. $.

Just north of Modesto along the Stanislaus River, this state park has the largest stand of oak riparian woodlands in the Central Valley and a lush understory of native plants and trees—a green and glorious place, winter through late spring (summers are super hot). The campground here is popular because of the swimming beaches and the fishing for bass, catfish, and crappie. Among a network of footpaths, the Riverlands Nature Trail is a 0.75-mile route that accommodates wheelchairs and strollers. Near the 64 campsites are restrooms with showers. On summer weekends, park rangers put on campfire activities, guided walks, and Junior Ranger programs.

Free Tastes & Tours Near Modesto

- **Bloomingcamp Apple Ranch,** 10528 Hwy. 120, 2 miles east of Oakdale; (209) 848-8881. Stock up on dreamy apple pies and tarts, fresh-pressed cider, apples, jams, dried fruits and nuts, and fresh baked goods. This is a good place to make a rest stop, picnic by the duck pond, and enjoy the playground. Open daily from July through Dec 23.

- **Blue Diamond Growers Store,** 4800 Sisk Rd., Salida, 5 miles northwest of Modesto on Highway 99; (209) 545-1602. See a film of a day in the life of an almond grower, watch almonds being processed, and taste the various seasoned nuts.

- **Hershey's Visitor Center,** 120 South Sierra Ave., Oakdale; (209) 848-8126. Stop in for your chocolate infusion—the smell of freshly baked chocolate-chip cookies will do the trick. All the varieties of Hershey's bars and candy specialties are here, plus gift baskets, Hershey souvenirs, and those killer cookies. Closed Sunday.

- **Hilmar Cheese Company,** 9001 North Lander Ave., Hilmar, 18 miles south of Modesto off Highway 99; (800) 577-5772. The largest cheese producer, at one site, in the world. A wide variety of luscious cheeses is available to taste, and the cheese-making process can be viewed Mon through Sat. In the Over the Moon Deli, try homemade fudge, cheese pie, a sandwich, or ice cream. Shop for packaged foods and collectibles, and take a walk under a waterfall to the picnic area.

- **Oakdale Cheese and Specialties,** 10040 Hwy. 120, Oakdale; (209) 848-3139. At this Gouda cheese factory and European bakery operated by a couple from the Netherlands, watch cheese being made through windows and on video, and tour the aging rooms. Besides yummy cheese and bakery items, locally grown fruits, vegetables, and nuts are on sale. Kids like the farm-animal petting zoo and picnics under the trees by the ponds, which are inhabited by over 100 koi fish.

Knights Ferry Recreation Area (all ages)

On the Stanislaus River off Highway 108-12, Sonora Road, Knights Ferry; (209) 881-3517. A "Flow Fone" gives up-to-date information on water conditions (916-322-2327).

Stop in at the US Army Corps of Engineers Information Center for information and maps on where to camp and fish on the Stan. Cast for big rainbow trout in the rapids, riffles, and deep pools between Goodwin Dam and Oakdale. Try for bass and catfish below Orange

Blossom Bridge. Rabid river rafters put in above Knights Ferry for 4 miles of surging white water. Canoes and lighter-weight craft should stick to the river below Knights Ferry.

The 355-foot-long covered bridge is the longest west of the Mississippi, crossing the river near an old gristmill. Closed to vehicles, this is a scenic spot for photos. The park here has pretty picnic areas with barbecues. At the northeast end of the bridge, a hiking trail leads to sandy beaches and to swimming and fishing holes.

Sunshine River Adventures (ages 6 and up)

P.O. Box 1445, Oakdale 95361; (800) 829-7238; www.raftadventure.com. From $$$ per person; discounts for kids.

Guided whitewater rafting trips on the Stanislaus, as well as canoe and raft rentals. An easy introduction to river rafting is the Knights Ferry to Orange Blossom Park Float, a self-guided, 4- to 5-hour trip popular with families (kids must be 6 or over). Bring a small ice chest, tennis shoes, a litter bag, bathing suits, and sunscreen. No pets. Return shuttle is provided. Rates include raft, paddles, life vests, and instructions.

Oakdale Cowboy Museum (all ages)

355 East F St., Oakdale; (209) 847-51632; www.oakdalecowboymuseum.org. $.

Fabulous leather saddles, action photos, branding irons, boots, spurs, and chaps in ranching, farming, and rodeo exhibits that are interactive and educational, and kids get to dress up like cowboys and cowgirls!

Boomers Modesto (all ages)

4215 Bangs Ave., Modesto; (209) 545-5248; www.boomersparks.com. Pricing varies according to full-day, half-day, and day of the week: $$–$$$$.

Go-karts, minigolf, bumper boats, laser tag, climbing wall, batting cages, games arcade, and a climbing-crawling-sliding play area for kids 48 inches and under; plus a snack bar. A madhouse on holiday weekends.

Lake Don Pedro (all ages)

31 Bonds Flat Rd., La Grange; (209) 852-2396; www.donpedrolake.com. See also Moccasin Point Marina on Jacksonville Road (www.foreverresorts.com).

At a low elevation northeast of Modesto, Don Pedro is a sprawling body of water with 160 miles of shoreline and several meandering arms. Summers are hot and dry, perfect for waterskiing, sailing, windsurfing, and using personal watercraft. Fishermen head to the northern, skinny arms of the lake, away from the noise and action, where fishing is good for bass, trout, salmon, crappie, bluegill, and catfish. You can lounge on a sandy beach by the swimming lagoon on the south shore, at Flemming Meadows. Two full-service marinas provide boat rentals, groceries, restaurants, gas stations, showers, and laundry facilities. Many of the 500 campsites have full RV hookups and are lakeside, enabling campers to moor their boats within view of their campsites.

Where to Eat

Barkin' Dog Grill. 940 11th St.; (209) 572-2341; www.barkindoggrill.org. Best organic burgers and hot dogs in town, homemade chili and soups, shakes, floats, and live music, too! $

La Panaderia Mexican Bakery. 1001 Kansas Ave., Modesto; (209) 577-2990. Don't fail to stop in here for the *dulce de leche* cake and exotic empanadas filled with pumpkin, pineapple, or custard, and the treats shaped like little pigs. $

Modesto Stanislaus Firehouse Pub and Grille. 924 15th St., near the McHenry Mansion, Modesto; (209) 575-3473. Home-style soup, sandwiches, burgers, ribs, pub food; 117 beers. $–$$

Olive Garden. 220 Plaza Pkwy., Modesto; (209) 544-8057; www.olivegarden.com. How do you feed a car full of kids for not a lot of money? Platters of Italian food here are so big you can split them. $–$$

Pacifica Grill. 1700 McHenry Ave., McHenry Village, Modesto; (209) 526-9999. A bright, colorful cafe with an inventive south-of-the-border menu: ceviche tostadas; teriyaki chicken, veggie, and fresh fish burritos; and simpler choices for kids. Everything is grilled, nothing fried. Try La Peninsula Caesar with green olives, pine nuts, avocado, and Cotija cheese. $–$$

Where to Stay

Big Bear Park and RV Campground. Twelve miles east of Modesto, on Highway 132; (209) 874-1984. A water-ride and campground combo, with shaded lawns, a half-acre lake with swimming beaches, and fishing and swimming in the Tuolumne River. $

Red Lion Inn Modesto. 1612 Sisk Rd. (Briggsmore exit off Highway 99), Modesto; (209) 521-1612. The inn has 186 rooms on 7 acres; in-room movies and games; room service; and guest laundry. Also a spacious indoor pool, basketball, games arcade, barbecue area, and fitness center. Meals all day and evening at the Palms Atrium Café or Sunset Grille. $$–$$$

For More Information

Modesto Convention and Visitors Bureau. 1150 9th St., Modesto; (888) 640-8467; www.visitmodesto.com. Pick up a self-guided CD for a driving tour.

Merced

Directly west of Yosemite, at the junction of Highways 99 and 140, the small town of Merced is within striking distance of a plethora of things that families like to do. A half-hour east of town are two beautiful, low-elevation recreation lakes, and a world-class museum of vintage aircraft that is well worth a stop.

More than a century old and designated as a Tree City USA, Merced has wide, shady streets with Victorian mansions and miles of off-street bike trails connecting an open-space park system. If you are here on a Thursday night, May through September, plan to enjoy the live music, ethnic foods, craft booths, and children's activities at the farmers' market downtown. Browse the old-fashioned main street for antiques shops and a comic book store. From Merced you can take comfortable, reasonably priced public transportation into Yosemite National Park, departing several times daily (VIA, 800-842-5463; and YARTS, 877-98-YARTS).

The new University of California Merced campus has brought attractions and facilities to the area, including a 750-acre vernal pool habitat preserve and other natural areas threaded with walking and biking trails (209-724-4400; www.ucmerced.edu).

Lake Yosemite (all ages)

Five miles northeast of Merced, on North Lake Road; (209) 385-7426. Day use $$.

Within biking distance of town, a day-use park for picnicking, windsurfing, sailing, and fishing. Rent a rowboat ($$)! You're guaranteed to catch bass all year long. There are restrooms, a snack bar, and shady picnic grounds. Lifeguards are on duty on summer weekends.

Lakes Recreation Area (all ages)

In the Sierra foothills, 25 miles northeast of Merced off Highway 59; (209) 378-2521; www.lakemcclure.com. Camping $.

Two meandering, warm bodies of water, Lake McClure and Lake McSwain form a sprawling recreation area popular with houseboaters, water-skiers, and campers year-round. Activities and public facilities cluster around five marinas, at elevations of 400 to 1,000 feet, in pine and oak woodland settings. Summers are quite dry and very warm; daytime temperatures can reach the low 100s, perfect for swimming and lying on sandy beaches. Six hundred campsites are available at the two lakes, many with shade and RV hookups. The cooler the season, the better the fishing in the lakes for the stocked fish: trout, king salmon, bass, crappie, catfish, and shad.

McClure has over 80 miles of shoreline and is abuzz in the summertime with fishing boats, WaveRunners, houseboats, patio boats, and ski boats, which are available to rent at the marinas. Swimming is primarily near the campgrounds. If you crave a quieter experience, with no waterskiing or houseboating allowed, the smaller Lake McSwain is your best bet. You can fish for trout here and enjoy the nice swimming beach.

Applegate Park and Zoo (ages 1 to 8)

1045 West 25th St. between M and R Streets, Merced; (209) 385-6840. $.

Acres of green beneath shady umbrellas of trees, with a little zoo, playgrounds, a skateboard park, and summertime amusement rides for younger children. Open June through Sept.

Castle Air Museum (all ages)

Six miles north of Merced at Castle Airport; (209) 723-2178; www.castleairmuseum.org. $; 7 and under are free.

One of the country's finest collections of World War II and Korean War aircraft, plus recent planes. It's quite impressive for children to stand beneath the wings of the black, batlike SR-71s, B-29s, B-17s, big transports, helicopters, and more—a dramatic array of 50 or so planes. Indoors are wartime memorabilia, a gift shop, and a coffee shop. The annual West Coast Antique Fly-In happens here in June.

Merced Agriculture Museum (all ages)
4498 East Hwy. 140 in the back of a fruit stand, Merced; (209) 383-1912. Free.

Antique farm equipment, gas engines, horse-drawn buggies, corn huskers and other old gizmos, and a working blacksmith shop.

Merced County Courthouse Museum (all ages)
21st and N Streets, Merced; (209) 723-240; www.mercedmuseum.org. Open Wed to Sun, 1 to 4 p.m. Free.

In a spectacular, 3-story 1875 Italianate edifice that is on the National Register of Historic Places, 150 years of history of the county and the settlers of the Great Central Valley, and Chinese and Native American heritage are showcased in extensive exhibits. Kids are entranced by the antique fire equipment, a flamboyant red-and-gold Taoist temple, Victorian wedding dresses, and much more. The small gift shop specializes in guidebooks and photos of the region, Native Americans, and Yosemite. Surrounding the museum is a lovely park populated with towering magnolias and palms.

McConnell State Recreation Area (all ages)
Off Highway 99 at Delhi, between Turlock and Merced; (209) 394-7755. Parking $.

Swim, fish, picnic, and camp at this delightful park beside the Merced River.

Merced National Wildlife Refuge (all ages)
From Merced, 8 miles south on Highway 59, then 8 miles west on Sandy Mush Road; (209) 772-3508; www.fws.gov. Free.

From September through June huge flocks of lesser sandhill cranes, geese, herons, egrets, pheasants, pintails, teal, sandpipers, and many more stunningly beautiful migrating and overwintering birds and waterfowl flock here to the thousands of acres of grasslands and seasonally flooded wetlands. You can take a slow, 5.2-mile drive-through, stopping at pull-outs and the observation platform; there is an easy 0.6-mile walking trail. Call ahead, as the refuge is closed to visitors during hunting season.

Where to Eat

The Branding Iron. 640 West 16th St., Merced; (209) 722-1822; www.thebranding iron-merced.com. Look for the neon sign of a cowboy, where for more than 50 years, locals have loved this dinner house for prime rib, steaks, fish, and poultry; Rustler's Stew; gazpacho; fresh sourdough rolls; and down-home American food. Hundreds of branding irons declare a Western ranch theme. $$–$$$

Main Street Cinema Cafe. 460 West Main, Merced; (209) 725-1702. In a delightful court-yard, all-American comfort food, sandwiches and soups, homemade pastries, ice cream. Breakfast and lunch. $

Merced Fruit Barn. 426 East Hwy. 140, Merced; (209) 385-2222; www.mercedfruit barn.com. On the way to Yosemite, a huge array of fresh, local produce and dried fruits, and packaged gourmet items. Sit in a casual cafe or at picnic tables outdoors to enjoy fresh juices, salads, and sandwiches. $

Soul Food Café. 1540 Yosemite Park Way, Merced; (209) 726-1510. Barbecue ribs and chicken, sweet potato pie, catfish, frog's legs, peach cobbler, fried okra, and collard greens—one of the only places in California where you can get really good, authentic Southern American cooking. $–$$

Where to Stay

Ramada Inn. 2000 East Childs Ave., Merced; (800) 2-RAMADA; www.ramada.com. Rooms with sitting areas and sofa beds, coffeemakers, microwaves, and refrigerators. Large pool, access to sports club and golf course, and adjacent to a very good restaurant, the Eagle's Nest, which has a good children's menu. $$–$$$

For More Information

Merced Convention and Visitors Bureau and California Welcome Center. 710 West 16th St., Merced; (209) 384-2791 or (800) 446-5353; www.yosemite-gateway .org. In a vintage Southern Pacific Depot, this offers an official California Welcome Center with an extensive array of brochures, maps, and the latest information for traveling in the region and the entire state. You can check your e-mail here, make hotel reservations, and have a picnic. From here, take the Historic Merced Walking Tour to see Victorian-era mansions in a lovely old neighborhood.

San Juan Bautista

A Spanish village since the late 1700s, San Juan Bautista is a perfectly preserved, precious fragment of early California. In an agricultural setting in the Salinas Valley between the tawny Gabilan Mountains on the east and the coastal range of the Santa Lucias on the west, the town encompasses a large state historic park, one of the most beautiful of the California missions, and a few charming streets of antiques shops and Mexican restaurants shaded with pepper, mimosa, and black walnut trees. Everything is within a few short blocks. Among the charming shops in the tiny town, most of which are housed in Spanish, Victorian, and Renaissance Revival buildings, kids love the rocks and flashy minerals at Tops, which specializes in stones from around the world (5 2nd St.; 831-623-4441). At Reyna's World Gallery, all ages enjoy the fascinating Native American clothing, artifacts, and crafts (311 3rd St.; 831-623-2379).

Annual festivals and fairs focus on Native American entertainment and cultural events and on arts, crafts, antiques, and flea markets. In June, Early Days in San Juan Bautista is a celebration of early mission days, with carriage rides, period costumes, music, and dance.

One of the nicest characteristics of the mission complex is the proximity of the museum buildings to the large, grassy plaza. Children who can't bear to look at another artifact can run around outside on the lawn while parents soak up the history.

Mission San Juan Bautista (all ages)

2nd and Mariposa Streets, San Juan Bautista; (831) 623-4528; www.san-juan-bautista.ca.us. $.

Built between 1803 and 1812, this is one of the largest and most impressive of all California mission churches, with 3 aisles and a glorious, 40-foot-high ceiling of grayed beams in traditional viga-lattia construction. Light floods the cathedral, making vibrant the rust- and blue-painted decoration, much of it created by a Boston sailor who jumped ship in Monterey and worked at the mission in exchange for room and board. The animal prints in the floor tiles were created while the tiles dried in the sun. Before and during the Sunday masses, local families mingle and chat near the giant entry doors, and the soft singing voices of the congregation float out the door into the sunshine of the plaza.

Surrounding the cathedral are a series of open rooms housing a museum of early Indian, Spanish Colonial, and Victorian artifacts and one of the best collections of Mission furniture in the world. You will also see a small kitchen from which 1,200 people were fed from iron pots in an open fireplace.

The mission gardens are cool and lovely, with old cacti, aromatic lavender, and climbing roses. Behind the church, under ancient olive trees, more than 4,000 Native Americans and some early pioneers are buried. Look in the mission shop for educational books and small gifts for kids.

San Juan Bautista State Historic Park (all ages)

2nd and 3rd Streets; San Juan Bautista; (831) 623-4881. $.

Full of carriages and wagons today, the Plaza Stable was headquarters for 7 stage lines in the 1860s, when as many as 11 coaches a day arrived, loaded with silver and gold miners, traders, and other travelers. Dusty travelers headed first to the Plaza Hotel to get a beer or something stronger in the bar and to book a room for the night. The owner of the hotel, Angelo Zanetta, built himself a magnificent house on the plaza, and the structure—the Zanetta House—now contains an outstanding collection of early California furnishings and personal items. The red-tile-roofed Castro/Breen House was owned by a family from the Donner Party who struck it rich in the gold rush. Behind the house is a glorious, 150-year-old pepper tree shading beautiful gardens.

Outside in the park, look for a modern-day earthquake monitor, which keeps track of the movement of the San Andreas Fault that runs beneath the town (the mission church was nearly destroyed in the notorious 1906 earthquake that flattened San Francisco).

Living History Day is held in the state park on the first Saturday of each month, from noon to 4 p.m. Here costumed residents demonstrate blacksmithing, mountain man encampments, food preparation, and other activities, while regaling visitors with tales of the old days in San Juan.

If the park surroundings look familiar to you, and you are of a certain age, it may be because in Alfred Hitchcock's 1958 movie classic *Vertigo*, a freaked-out Kim Novak breathlessly described a town that haunted her dreams—it was this town.

Gilroy Gardens Family Theme Park (ages 1 to 12)
3050 Hecker Pass Hwy./Highway 152 West, Gilroy; (408) 840-7100; www.gilroygardens.org.
$$$$; ages 2 and under free.

This is one of the nicest and most beautiful family theme parks, with 19 old-fashioned rides and 27 attractions, and hundreds of acres of gorgeous gardens and thousands of mature trees, from tropical plants in a giant greenhouse to trees grown into animal and other fanciful shapes, called the "circus trees." Among the charms are a 1927 carousel, a rock maze, a butterfly house, a monorail, the Quicksilver Mine Coaster, a swan ride, a miniature car ride, and some carnival games. My grandchildren's favorite rides are on the miniature antique roadsters; they "drive" Chevy Corvettes and Model Ts on a winding route through tunnels, forests, and gardens. There is also the Splash Garden, a water play area with a water-sprayed teeter-totter, spinning water wheels, an 18-foot-tall tree house with platforms of cascading water and a slide, tip-over buckets of water, a squirter station (look out!), and more bubbling fun, fabulous on those very hot summer days in the valley. Dining outlets are reasonably priced and offer barbecue, tacos, pasta, deep-fried artichokes, orange freezes, and more. Although teens will likely be bored, grade-schoolers, parents, and grandparents love this place.

Pinnacles National Monument (all ages)
East entrance is 45 minutes south of San Juan Bautista, off Highway 25, Paicines; (831) 389-4485; www.nps.gov/pinn. $$ day-use fee.

Spires and crags rising dramatically out of the valley are what's left of an ancient volcano; the other half is 195 miles to the southeast, thanks to the San Andreas rift. The 24,000-acre wilderness park attracts rock climbers, hikers, cave explorers, and picnickers. Short, easy paths (some suitable for strollers) make ferny creeks and mountain views easily accessible.

Spring is spectacular, with riots of wildflowers, which bloom here earlier than in most parts of the state. Winters are mild, fresh, and green. Midsummer can be extremely hot and dry, with temperatures in the 100s. Call ahead about ranger-led walks and hikes, and spectacular night hikes. A nice private campground at the entrance to the park has a swimming pool (408-389-4462).

Wings of History Museum (all ages)
Six miles north of Gilroy in San Martin, at 12777 Murphy Ave., across the street from the airport; (831) 683-2290.

On display are planes from 1928 to the 1950s, such as a Sopwith Pup, a Bowlus Albatross, and a Benson Gyrocopter.

Fremont Peak State Park (all ages)
Off Highway 156, 11 miles south of San Juan Bautista on San Juan Canyon Road; (831) 623-4255; www.parks.ca.gov.

A winding country road meanders through canyons and hillsides dotted with oak, pine, and madrone. At the viewful summit on clear days, you can see Monterey Bay, the Gavilan

Range, the Salinas Valley, and the Santa Lucia Mountains. Hiking trails spread out along ridges and in wildflowery grasslands. Park rangers operate a small observatory with a 30-inch telescope, and put on stargazing nights in spring and summer; call ahead. You can camp here, and there are shady picnic grounds. As in most of the Central Valley, outdoor recreation is best from early spring through early summer, and late fall through winter, avoiding the hot dry days of summer.

Casa de Fruta (all ages)

Off Highway 101, 2 miles east of Highway 152/156 junction on Pacheco Pass Highway, Hollister; (408) 842-9316; www.casadefruta.com.

Antique farm machinery, shade trees, and fruit trees create a pleasant, country atmosphere at this farm-theme roadside stop. Since 1908, when they planted a cherry orchard, the Zangers have produced luscious fruit in the Pacheco Valley. Today you can purchase a wide variety of picture-perfect, locally grown produce at their huge fruit stand. You and the kids can also ride a miniature locomotive ($); linger at the playground; have some homemade pie, candy, and ice cream at Casa de Sweets; see goats, ducks, rare white deer, llama, Longhorn steer, and a buffalo; and pan for gemstones and minerals—lots to do and see, and worth at least a couple of hours. Open 24 hours a day, the restaurant serves good American comfort food.

Events are scheduled on some weekends, including a Native American powwow, a Civil War reenactment, crafts fairs, and a pumpkin festival in October. You can stay here, too, in a nice RV park or the Peacock Inn motel.

McAlpine Lake and Park (all ages)

900 Anzar Rd., 5 minutes from town off Highway 129, San Juan Bautista; (831) 623-4263; www.mcalpinelake.com.

Fish for trout, catfish, and bass; as the lake is privately owned, fishing licenses are not required. Kids can take fishing lessons and try their luck in a "Sure Catch" pond. Shady, grassy RV and tent sites, and 4 cabins; general store, laundry, showers.

Where to Eat

Dona Esther Restaurant. 25 Franklin St., San Juan Bautista; (831) 623-2518. Real Mexican food in a warm, friendly atmosphere, with local art and photos decorating the walls. Inexpensive children's menu of simple dishes. Outdoor patio; live entertainment and all-you-can-eat buffet on Sun. $–$$

Felipe's Restaurant and Bar. 313 3rd St., San Juan Bautista; (831) 623-2161. Where the locals go for Mexican and Salvadoran food. Salvadoran dishes are not complete without the zippy pickled cabbage, *curtido.* Try the

specialties of the house: fried plantains and fried ice cream. $

Jardines de San Juan. 115 3rd St., San Juan Bautista; (831) 623-4466; www.jardines restaurant.com. A Mexican restaurant with a big, popular, Mission-style garden patio. Guitarists strum; breezes ruffle the fig and maple trees; lunches and dinners are served at umbrella tables or indoors in cool, art-filled dining rooms. On the children's menu are mildly flavored burritos, quesadillas, and plain rice and beans with tortillas. Parents go for the fresh red snapper Veracruz and for *pollos borrachos*—chicken cooked in sherry, an old Puebla recipe. $$

JJ's Homemade Burgers. 100 The Alameda, San Juan Bautista; (831) 623-1748. Shakes, fries, salads, sandwiches, and famous burgers with such additions as chiles, mushrooms, blue cheese, and guacamole. Outdoors or in the soda fountain–like cafe. $

Margot's Ice Cream Parlor. 211 3rd St., San Juan Bautista; (831) 623-9262. Icy delights, plus sandwiches and salads, espresso, and chocolates. $

Mission Cafe. 300 3rd St., San Juan Bautista; (831) 623-2635. Voted by the town as the best place for breakfast, and it's true! Lunch, too. The owner, Quirina Luna-Costillas, is a member of the Mutsun tribe, who lived here before the mission was built—and several hundred tribal members still do. $

Where to Stay

Mission Farm RV Park. 400 San Juan–Hollister Rd. on the southeast corner of town, San Juan Bautista; (831) 623-4456. Old barns and a small store; tree-shaded sites surrounded by a walnut orchard. Sites for tents and RVs. $

San Juan Inn. 410 Alameda St., San Juan Bautista; (831) 623-4380. Small motel with simple rooms, some with refrigerators and microwaves; swimming pool; gardens. $–$$

For More Information

San Juan Bautista Visitors Information. 33 Washington St., San Juan Bautista; (831) 623-2454; www.san-juan-bautista.ca.us. Stop here for a historic walking tour map and check out the calendar of events online.

Gold Country

The foothills of the California Gold Country stretch more than 300 miles along the western slopes of the Sierra Nevadas, all the way to the southern gate of Yosemite National Park. Fed by snowy peaks, six major rivers carve dramatic, steep-sided canyons and rush down the valleys into the heart of the state.

Along the Yuba, American, Mokelumne, Stanislaus, Tuolumne, and Merced River corridors, dozens of boomtowns exploded in population when gold was discovered in the mid-1800s, only to be abandoned by the miners and adventure seekers when the lodes were exhausted a decade later.

Still looking much as they did more than a hundred years ago, small "forty-niner" gold rush towns on the "Golden Chain"—Highway 49—from Nevada City in the north to Jamestown in the south are both living museums and thriving towns of today. These communities that sprang up overnight for the miners and gold panners are carefully preserved, with wooden false-front stores and saloons, board sidewalks and gas lamps, and balconied Victorian hotels.

There is so much to see and do in Gold Country, and the area so vast, that your family may want to plan several trips, combining outdoor fun—such as rafting, fishing, and hiking—with sightseeing at historical sites.

Nevada City & Grass Valley

The sights of Nevada City and its adjacent sister city of Grass Valley, plus historic gold mines and outdoor pleasures on the banks of the Yuba and American Rivers, add up to busy vacation days in this area. Just a few miles to the east, 1.2 million acres of wilderness afford endless hiking, camping, fishing, and cross-country skiing opportunities.

The most completely original gold rush town in the state, Nevada City has more than 100 Victorian mansions and Western saloons and hotels clustered cozily together on a radiating wheel of tree-lined streets on small hills. At an elevation of about 2,840 feet, the

GOLD COUNTRY

Nevada City

Grass Valley

20

99

70

113

Auburn

65

80

50

49

16

Sutter Creek

Jackson

99

88

12

San Andreas

26

Angels Camp

Columbia

4

Jamestown

49

120

132

99

140

41

168

99

180

180

63

245

whole place turns red and gold in fall, when thousands of maples, aspens, and oaks turn blazing bright.

There is much to discover today within the 8-block area surrounding Broad, the main street. As soon as you cross the bridge into town, take the first right to the visitor center for a walking-tour map. Step into the National Hotel at 211 Broad St. to take a look at the oldest continuously operating hotel west of the Rockies and see the elaborate long bar, shipped around the Horn more than a century ago. Near Broad, Boulder, and Sacramento Streets, take a short, easy walk along Deer Creek, stopping at six stations that describe gold prospecting in the early days. Running through town, the creek once yielded a pound of gold a day.

Inhabited during the gold rush by thousands of English and Irish miners who worked five major gold mines in the area, Grass Valley is honeycombed with underground tunnels and shafts. On Mill and Main Streets remain dozens of buildings built in the mid-1800s,

Gold Country **Shops That Kids Like**

- **Confectionary Mine,** 236 Broad St., Nevada City; (530) 265-3448. Handmade ice-cream bars, drumsticks, chocolates, coffee drinks, smoothies, shakes and sundaes, and toys.

- **Earth, Science and Nature Store,** 310 Broad St., Nevada City; (530) 265-0448. Educational kits and toys for kids, including books, clothing, and entertainments you can feel good about purchasing.

- **Foothill Mercantile,** 121 Mill St., Grass Valley; (530) 273-8304. Board games and puzzles, dolls and stuffed animals, action figures, Christmas villages and other seasonal decorative stuff, and candy, plus all sorts of gifts and decorative items for the home.

- **Golden Eagle,** 308 Broad St., Nevada City; (530) 265-6478. Fancy collectible dolls, swords, daggers, decorative clocks, fairies, angels, animal and dolphin items, and myriad gifts and decorative things for the home. A dangerous store for toddlers.

- **Mountain Pastimes Fun and Games,** 320 Spring St., Nevada City; (530) 265-6692. The shop is always full of people trying out the gizmos and the toys and games for all ages.

- **Tanglewood Forest Gallery,** 313 Broad St., Nevada City; (530) 478-1223; www.tanglewoodforest.com. A fantasy gallery featuring the work of local doll artist, Marci Wolfe. An enchanted world of fairies, elves, gnomes, pixies, sages, and wizards in a magic forest setting.

when this was the richest mining town in the state. Antiques shops are clustered on Main Street and its side streets. At 212 West Main, the Holbrooke Hotel has been, since 1862, the grand old lady of Grass Valley. A glance in the hotel register turns up such famous guests as Presidents Cleveland and Garfield. Families take Sunday dinner and brunch in the dining room. A block off Main, take a stroll on Neal and Church Streets to see rows of magnificent Victorian mansions and churches.

Firehouse No. 1 Historical Society Museum (all ages)
214 Main St., Nevada City, next door to the visitor center; (530) 265-5468; www.nevada countyhistory.org. **Free.**

In a much-photographed building, circa 1860, with a bell tower and gingerbread trim, 2 floors of gold rush and Native American artifacts, from Donner Party relics to a Victorian dollhouse and Maidu Indian artifacts.

Grass Valley Museum (all ages)
Mount St. Mary's Convent, 410 South Church St., Grass Valley; (530) 273-5509. Weekdays only. **Free.**

A restored 1865 school and orphanage exhibiting gold rush artifacts and domestic items. The fascinating cemetery on the grounds dates to 1852.

North Star Mining Museum (all ages)
On the south end of Mill Street, Grass Valley; (530) 273-4255. **Free.**

A delightful, shady spot for a picnic on the lawn beside an old powerhouse on Wolf Creek. Among the many pieces of antique equipment here are a working stamp mill and the largest Pelton wheel in the world, a waterwheel that produced power from the creek for the North Star Mine. A large collection of photos traces mining history, and there are hands-on demos for kids.

Nevada County Traction Company (NCTC) (ages 1 to 12)
Behind the Northern Queen Inn, 400 Railroad Ave., on the south end of Nevada City; (530) 265-0896; www.northernqueeninn.com. Adults $$; children $.

Take a 1.5-hour ride in a forested area on a restored narrow-gauge train, while the conductor-owner, Al Flores, talks about local history. Part of the trip entails a short walk to see Maidu grinding holes and a fascinating Chinese cemetery; in October a pumpkin farm is part of the fun. The railroad is located on the grounds of the Northern Queen Inn, one of the best family motels in the area (see "Where to Stay").

Malakoff Diggins State Historic Park (all ages)
Twenty-seven miles northeast of Nevada City, on Highway 49; (530) 265-2740. Day use $.

The largest hydraulic mine site in the world, a rather shocking and strangely beautiful remnant of gold mining in the 1800s, when giant water jets called monitors destroyed entire mountains. A mile of hillside here was washed away, the soil and rocks clogging rivers and

Book Towns

Grass Valley and Nevada City are famous for their bookstores, with more than 20 booksellers between them; the local radio station even has a "Book Town" program. The annual Gold Rush Book Fair at the fairgrounds attracts crowds of readers, prominent speakers, and booksellers from around the state. Here are a few stores that children will enjoy.

- **Wisdom Cafe and Gallery,** 426 Broad St., Nevada City; (530) 265-4204. A good place to plan your bookstore tour, with cappuccino and hot chocolate, smoothies, healthy lunches, and dinners indoors or on the patio; use the **free** Wi-Fi, too. Browse the shelves here for local hiking and travel guidebooks.

- **Toad Hall Books,** 108 North Pine St., Nevada City; (530) 265-2216. A life-size Tin Man greets kids at this children's used bookstore. Also here is Brigadoon Books, specializing in used and rare Californiana and Western Americana, and books on Scotland.

- **The Bookseller,** 107 Mill St., Grass Valley; (530) 272-2131. A general bookstore, plus an entire floor for the Children's Cellar.

- **Ames Bookstore,** 309 Neal St., Grass Valley; (530) 273-9261. In 5 buildings, more than 300,000 used books.

- **Main Street Antiques and Books,** 214½ Main St., Nevada City; (530) 265-3108. A tiny establishment packed with Americana, from cowboy comics to *The Boy Scout Handbook*, ephemera and antique toys, wonderful wind-ups.

- **Booktown Books,** 107 Bank St., Grass Valley across from Caroline's Coffee; (530) 272-4655. In a pleasant, airy environment, 16 sellers of general used, rare, and out-of-print books, among them specialists in horses, comic art, philosophy, and history.

streams until the practice was outlawed late in the century. Weird and colorful pinnacles, domes, spirals, and a milky lake remain, fringed with pines.

There are reconstructed buildings and hiking trails in the park, swimming at Blair Lake, and a campground. Swimming and fishing holes on the South Yuba River and a 21-mile river corridor park are accessible near the Diggins. On weekends and holidays, rangers lead **free** gold-panning tours.

Empire Mine State Park (all ages)

Just south of Grass Valley off Highway 49, take the Empire Street exit; (530) 273-8522; www
.empiremine.org. $.

This is one of my favorite Gold Country parks, where big trees and lawns are a cool respite
from hot summer days. At this beautiful mining estate, the largest, deepest, and richest
hard-rock gold mine in California operated for over 100 years, producing $100 million in
gold from 360 miles of underground channels, some 11,000 feet deep. On a 1-hour ranger
tour, see an extensive complex of buildings and equipment, including part of the main
shaft. A visitor center recounts history in photos, exhibits, and films.

Sweeping lawns beneath 100-foot sugar pines surround the mine owner's home,
Bourne Cottage, an outstanding example of a Willis Polk–designed English country manor
with lovely gardens and a fountain pool. Also here are hiking and cycling trails and picnic
areas. Come for the Miners' Picnic in June and enjoy the food, contests, gold panning,
and entertainment. On weekends from May through October, docents in 1905 period costumes entertain visitors at the Cottage.

Bridgeport Covered Bridge (all ages)

Pleasant Valley Road, southwest of Grass Valley near Penn Valley; (530) 432-2546.

On the Yuba River, this is one of only a dozen covered bridges still standing in the state.
At 256 feet, it may be the longest single-span covered bridge in the world, with sugar pine
shingles and massive, old-growth Douglas fir beams that are reminders of when buggies
and mule teams clattered across the wooden floorboards. Here in the South Yuba River
State Park (www.parks.ca.gov) are nice picnic spots, wading and swimming pools, and
good kayaking. An easy footpath runs just over a mile, one-way, upstream. During much of
the year, docents and rangers teach gold panning and conduct interpretive tours.

Rock Creek Nature Trail (all ages)

Eight miles east of Nevada City off of Highway 20; (530) 265-4531

Winding along mossy, gurgling Rock Creek, a marked, flat, shady 0.8-mile walking trail in
the Tahoe National Forest, through madrones, firs and dogwoods. Markers explaining the
flora, fauna, and history of the area. Picnic sites and restrooms.

Pioneer Park (all ages)

Nimrod Street on the outskirts of Nevada City; (530) 265-2521.

Spend the afternoon under the trees here at the playground, picnicking; playing sand volleyball, horseshoes, and tennis; or swimming in the public pool (June through August). (In
Grass Valley on Minnie Street, Condon Park has similar facilities, plus disc golf and walking
trails; 530-274-4390.)

Teddy Bear Castle Museum (all ages)

203 South Pine, Nevada City; (530) 265-5804; www.teddybearcastle.com. $; ages 12 and
under free.

Thousands of teddies, in elaborate costumes and in furry plainness, inhabit decorated scenes in a charming, circa-1860 Victorian house. Open by appointment on weekends. Organized by the museum, the International Teddy Bear Convention is held in town in April.

Lake Spaulding (all ages)

Located 30 miles from Nevada City, on Highway 20; (530) 527-0354.

A glacier-carved bowl of granite, at 5,000 feet, the lake is surrounded by huge boulders and a forest. This is a great day-trip destination, with good fishing for trout, small lakeside beaches, and powerboating and sailing. A small, developed campground for tents and RVs is here, too.

Three Easy Wilderness Hikes
Near Nevada City

- **Independence Trail.** Eight miles north of Nevada City on Highway 49, just before the arched Yuba River Bridge (watch carefully for the sign); (530) 477-4788. My favorite Gold Country trail, because it's easy for all ages and abilities, and you get into eye-popping scenery within a minute, on 7 miles of packed dirt paths and a boardwalk that is wheelchair and stroller accessible. The trail meanders through forests and at times is dramatically suspended over the Yuba River Canyon. Along the way there are picnic platforms as well as ramps leading to fishing holes.

- **Sierra Discovery Trail.** From Highway 20 take Bowman Lake Road 0.6 mile to the parking lot; (530) 386-5164. A delightful loop along the Bear River, this easy 1-mile trail is popular, for good reason. The partly paved, partly gravel, partly boardwalk path is accessible to wheelchairs and strollers as it winds through a pine and cedar forest. Meadows are awash with wildflowers, and a small waterfall rushes year-round. Watch for water ouzels at the waterfall—they are the only American songbirds that dive into the water.

- **Bullards Bar Trail.** North from Nevada City on Highway 49 to Marysville Road, turn left and follow signs to Dark Day Picnic Area; turn right for 0.5 mile; then take left fork to trailhead; (530) 288-3231. Along the edge of Bullards Bar Reservoir, this is a flat, scenic trail. Stop and take a swim, catch a fish, ride mountain bikes, and enjoy a picnic under a giant ponderosa pine.

Scotts Flat Lake (all ages)

Twenty minutes from Grass Valley off Highway 20; (530) 265-5302; www.scottsflatlake.net.

A nice day trip for swimming, fishing, hiking, or waterskiing, or for lakeside camping in the national forest. Two campgrounds have developed tent and RV sites, sandy beaches, a store, paddleboat rentals, a cafe, and picnic areas. Afternoons are perfect for windsurfing, and there is a network of forest trails around the lake.

49er Family Fun Park (ages 5 and up)

314 Railroad Ave., Grass Valley; (530) 272-4949. $–$$.

Rocket around in single or double go-karts. Putt around a gold rush–themed, 18-hole minigolf course. Swing away in a batting cage, or play some of 60 arcade games.

Auburn State Recreation Area (all ages)

Access off Highway 49 at Auburn or from Auburn-Foresthill Road; (530) 885-4527 or (530) 367-2224; www.parks.ca.gov. Day use $.

Along 40 miles of the North and Middle Forks of the American River, the state maintains trails, 4 campgrounds, and other development for wonderful hiking, swimming, boating, fishing, biking, horseback riding, motorcycle riding, and whitewater rafting. Boat-in campgrounds at Lake Clementine are popular with fishing and waterskiing families, with good swimming beaches at the campgrounds. For information about the designated Offroad Vehicle Area, call (530) 885-5821.

Nevada County Narrow Gauge Railroad and Transportation Museum (all ages)
From Highway 49 just south of Nevada City, take the Gold Flat Road exit to 5 Kidder Court, Nevada City; (530) 470-0902; www.ncngrrmuseum.org. Free.

A display of narrow-gauge railroad cars and massive engines built between the late 1800s and early 1900s—antique stock cars, boxcars, coaches, cabooses, and more. Open weekends in winter and daily in summer.

Where to Eat

Awful Annie's. 160 Sacramento St., Auburn; (530) 888-9857; www.awfulannies .com. On the shaded porch or in the cozy dining room, enjoy sumptuous scrambles, breakfast burritos, and 5 kinds of waffles for breakfast; homemade soup, grilled sandwiches, and salads for lunch; and a variety of steak, seafood, and poultry dishes for dinner. Come early—or you may be standing in line. $–$$

Charlie's Angels Café. 145 South Auburn St., Grass Valley; (530) 274-1839. A busy locals' place, famous for chicken-fried steak, biscuits and gravy, big breakfasts, and burgers. Kids love the aquarium, the green eggs and ham, and Mickey Mouse pancakes. $–$$

Dedrick's Cheese. 405 Commercial St., Nevada City; (530) 265-6564; www.dedricks cheese.com. Fab picnic fare, from 250 types of cheese to an olive bar, locally baked

356 716

breads and pastries, Italian-style cured meats, cookies, and chocolates. $

Ikeda's. 13500 Lincoln Way (take Foresthill exit off Highway 80), Auburn; (530) 885-4243; www.ikedas.com. On the way to and from the Gold Country, this has been a stop off the highway for homemade pies, fresh produce, smoothies, and burgers for more than 30 years. Also in Davis (26295 Mace Blvd.; 530-750-3379). $

Marshall's Pasties. 203 Mill St., Grass Valley; (530) 272-2844. Introduced by English miners, Cornish pasties are delicious, flaky, hand-size turnover pies in which savory fillings are baked, such as potato and vegetables, ham and cheese, and fruit combinations. In forty-niner days, each miner carried a 3-tiered tin lunch pail every day. The bottom was filled with tea, the pasty was placed in the middle section, and a bun was on top. The miner lit a candle under his pail at the beginning of his shift and, by the time he ate, his meal was warm. Some of the best pasties in town are baked at Marshall's: broccoli and cheese, apple-figgy, sausage, and many more. (Another good place to get pasties in Grass Valley is **Mrs. Dubblebee's** at 251 South Auburn St.; 916-272-7700.) $

Posh Nosh. 318 Broad St., Nevada City; (530) 265-6064. On a tree-shaded patio, sandwiches, pasta, salads, and homemade desserts. $–$$

Tofanelli's. 302 West Main, Grass Valley; (530) 272-1468. On the garden patio or in the bustling dining room, enjoy a hearty American menu with huge plates of food, breakfast burritos, and raspberry chicken. Breakfast, lunch, dinner, and Sunday brunch. $–$$

Where to Stay

Grass Valley Courtyard Suites. 210 North Auburn St., Grass Valley; (530) 272-7696; www.gvcourtyardsuites.com. A block from Main Street, a lovely, unique property with a small heated pool and a laundry room. The suites have equipped kitchens, gas fireplaces, decks or balconies, dining rooms, sofa beds, and rollaways; some have 2 queen-size beds. Continental breakfast is included, and dogs are welcome. $$$–$$$$

Northern Queen Inn. 400 Railroad Ave., off Highway 49, Nevada City; (530) 265-5824; www.northernqueeninn.com. This is the best, and most popular, place for families to stay in the area. Motel rooms are simple and spacious; chalets on the creek have loft bedrooms and kitchens. Covered swimming pool; a very good, family-oriented restaurant with a deck over a waterfall; and narrow gauge train tours on the property. $$$ Mandy $79.00 $79.00 $1710.00 +5 -10

Sierra Motel. 816 West Main St., Grass Valley; (530) 273-8133; www.sierramountaininn.com/about.htm. Circa-1930 small motor-court-style motel is a good value and conveniently located. Recently renovated with marble baths, some rooms have 2 beds, and there are 2-room suites and a small cottage; some kitchenettes; full breakfast included. $$$ 1 Qn, Full $139.00 Joe

For More Information

Nevada City Chamber of Commerce. 132 Main St., Nevada City; (530) 265-2692 or (800) 655-6569; www.nevadacitychamber.com. In the stone and brick Yuba Canal Building, built in 1850 on the banks of Deer Creek.

Grass Valley/Nevada County Chamber of Commerce. 248 Mill St., Grass Valley; (530) 273-4667; www.grassvalleychamber.com. Located in the home and museum of Lola Montez, a notorious dance hall entertainer of the 1800s. Pick up excellent maps here for hiking and mountain and road biking.

California Welcome Center. 13411 Lincoln Way, Auburn; (530) 887-2111; www.visitplacer.com.

$115 2 queens. 2 queens. $197, 2 Bed King $900 2 queens 50 Ft. Danielle

Sutter Creek

My favorite Gold Country town, Sutter Creek is surrounded by rolling pasturelands, vineyards, and orchards—a postcard-perfect settlement with white frame houses and picket fences, giving it a New England look. Clapboard houses with porches and balconies, coupled with steepled churches, look down from the hillsides over Main Street, which is riddled with antiques shops and quaint boutiques. Among the blizzard of shops, children like My Dolly's Department Store for dolls, teddies, Beanies, and Sanrio; and Lizzie Ann's Books and Gifts for children's books and collectibles. In the Gold Miner Candy Shoppe, barrels of "penny candy" (no longer costing a penny) line the aisles. A nice hotel here caters to families, and plenty of exploring can be done on country roads near town. Two miles north of here, Amador City is also an antiques center. The Saturday morning farmers' market is the place to meet locals.

Chatter Box Cafe (all ages)
29 Main St., Sutter Creek; (209) 267-5935. $.

My favorite cafe in my favorite town, a walk back into the 1940s. It's an old-fashioned soda fountain, nostalgic with World War II posters, Big Band record covers, and a long counter where town regulars meet for burgers with homemade buns, grilled cheese sandwiches, world-class onion rings, and pies, floats, sodas, and thick shakes.

Daffodil Hill (all ages)
Thirteen miles east of Sutter Creek on Shake Ridge Road off Sutter Creek–Volcano Road; (209) 296-7048. Free.

One of the loveliest and most rewarding of California back roads promises a golden surprise between mid-March and the end of April, when wildflowers and 300,000 daffodils, crocuses, hyacinths, lilacs, and tulips are a riot of bloom in a farmer's field. Since the late 1800s, the McLaughlin family has planted bulbs on "Daffodil Hill" on their homestead, and they welcome visitors during the blooming season. Against a backdrop of pine trees, an old barn, wagon wheels, antique mining and farming tools, peacocks, chickens, and a flock of sheep make this is a photogenic place. Picnic sites here, too. Call ahead to check bloom status. Another flower-filled site to visit is the **Amador Flower Farm** (22001 Shenandoah School Road near Plymouth, 209-245-6660; www.amadorflowerfarm.com), where you can stroll through 12 acres of tulips, daffodils, hundreds of types of daylilies, and other perennials.

Little Amador Railroad (ages 1 to 7)
10760 Pig Turd Alley, Amador City; (209) 267-5129. Open weekends Mar to Dec, weather permitting. Free.

Next to the old green firehouse on Main Street, take the footbridge across a creek to watch a tiny G-scale train that bumbles along about a mile of garden-landscaped track, meandering through dwarf evergreens, over trestles, and past replicas of local gold mines, lumber mills, and farms. Ask to see the train room.

Sutter Gold Mine (ages 4 and up)

On Highway 49 between Sutter Creek and Amador City; (866) 762-2837; www.suttergold
.com. Adults $$$; children 4 to 13 $$; under 4 free. Minimum age for underground tours
is 4 years.

If your family really gets interested in gold mining and its history, this is the nicest, best-
organized place to try gold panning and learn about the process. You ride in a cool "Boss
Buggy" shuttle truck, go underground into a mine in your hard hats, and observe gold
extraction and equipment.

Volcano and the St. George Hotel (all ages)

Near Daffodil Hill, in Volcano; (209) 296-4458; www.stgeorgehotel.com. $–$$.

In a circa-1850 building, have lunch and dinner in a charming, rather eccentrically decorated dining room where the menu depends on the chef's whim of the day. In the little
burg of Volcano, a clutch of historic buildings remain. Sit on the hotel veranda and imagine
the village of 1,000 people when it was the center of a rich mining area that produced
over $90 million in gold.

The General Store has been in continuous use since 1852. Behind an impressive
arched stone facade is the community theater, and nearby, the Sing Kee Store and the jail.
Look for "Old Abe," a bronze cannon cast in 1862 and smuggled into Volcano in a hearse
during the Civil War. (Although the hotel's rooms are not appropriate for families, they do
offer a simple garden cottage sleeping 4, with a four-poster queen bed and a daybed with
trundle.)

Indian Grinding Rock State Historic Park (all ages)

Pine Grove–Volcano Road, Pine Grove; (209) 296-7488. $ per car.

More than 1,000 grinding holes used by Miwoks are gouged out of a vast limestone surface, and you will see many petroglyphs and replicas of bark dwellings. The museum displays beautiful baskets and artifacts. Once a month Miwok elders spend time at the park,
telling stories and recounting tribal history to park visitors. Nature trails and a small, first-
come, first-serve campground with RV sites, restrooms, and showers are here, too.

Where to Eat

Bellotti's. 53 Main St., Sutter Creek; (209)
267-5211; www.bellottis.com. Bountiful family-style Italian dinners in the oldest continuously running hotel and saloon in California,
established in 1858. $

Caffe Via d'Oro. 36 Main St., Sutter Creek;
(209) 267-0535; www.caffeviadoro.com. A
surprising Mediterranean influence emerges
in unique pizzas and calzones, homemade
pastas, polenta, and seasonal specials at a

cafe owned by a former Chez Panisse part-
ner. Parents like the exceptional wine list;
kids are quite comfortable. $–$$

Susan's Place Wine Bar and Eatery. 15
Eureka St., in the courtyard, Sutter Creek;
(209) 267-0945; www.susansplace.com.
Under the arbor on the patio, cheese boards,
salads, soups, and sandwiches. Lunch and
dinner. $–$$

Sutter Creek Ice Cream Emporium. 51 Main St., Sutter Creek; (209) 267-0543. Have a root beer float, some fudge, or a snack in this charming soda fountain out of the late 1800s, with creaky wooden floors and ragtime piano music. Lunch menu, too. $

Where to Stay

Aparicio's Sutter Creek Hotel. 271 Hanford St., Sutter Creek; (209) 267-9177. Spacious rooms with 2 queen beds or 2 doubles, plus 2-room suites. Contemporary Victorian-style architecture. $–$$

Far Horizons 49er Village. 18265 Hwy. 49, Plymouth; (800) 339-6981; www.49ervillage .com. Over 300 paved, tree-shaded RV sites with full hookups; Laundromat, showers. Volleyball and other outdoor games, pool tables; cafe serving basic meals, ice cream, and snacks; adult-only and family swimming pools. Small air-conditioned cabins for rent. $–$$

Historian Inn. 271 Hanford St./Highway 49, Sutter Creek; (209) 267-9177. Right in town; double queen-bed rooms and suites make this a good choice for families. $$

For More Information

Sutter Creek Visitor Center. 11-A Randolph St., P.O. Box 600, Sutter Creek 95685; (209) 267-1344 or (800) 400-0305; www.sutter creek.org.

Amador County Chamber of Commerce. At junction of Highways 49 and 88, 125 Peak St., Jackson; (209) 223-0350 or (800) 649-4988; www.touramador.com.

Jackson

As you approach from above on Highway 49, Jackson looks like a toy town. Picturesque streets are lined with churches and balconied houses from the mid-1800s. In my opinion, the Amador County Museum here is the premier museum of everyday life in the early days of the Gold Country. A scattering of recreational lakes is located within a short drive. Nearly 80 shops and restaurants in historic buildings line the main street.

Every year, families congregate in Calaveras County for a number of events: Snyder's Pow Wow, a May weekend of arts, crafts, gems, minerals, food, and fun on a working cattle ranch (209-772-1265); a Civil War Reenactment in September (209-728-1251); and a Lumberjack Day in October, featuring a parade, logging competitions, music, and food (209-293-4324).

Amador County Museum (all ages)

Above Main Street, 225 Church St., Jackson; (209) 223-6386. Free.

In a neighborhood of churches and homes from the mid-1800s, one of the oldest houses in town shelters a huge collection of artifacts and antiques. On the hottest summer day, it's cool and quiet in the house. Hundreds of photos re-create the gold rush, and you'll find a fine collection of Indian baskets, women's and men's fashions, furniture, and many domestic items from throughout the era. Part of the thousands who worked the mines and built Western railroads, the Chinese are featured in displays of clothing, musical instruments, and tools. A working scale model shows the Kennedy Mine, whose 5,000-foot

Winter Fun near Jackson

Bear River Lake Resort, 42 miles east of Jackson, on Highway 8; (209) 295-4868; www.bearrivercampground.com. At 5,840 feet in the Eldorado National Forest are groomed and ungroomed trails for cross-country skiers around the lake. Several snow-play hills are perfect for sleds, saucers, and inner tubes, with rentals available. A 50-mile snowmobile road loops around the lake. A general store, a snack bar, and a small resort and campground are open all year.

shaft was one of the world's deepest. Bring a picnic and take a rest under the trees while the kids run around on the grass.

Kennedy Gold Mine (all ages)
One mile north of Jackson off Highway 49; (209) 223-9542; www.kennedygoldmine.com. Adults $$; ages 6 to 12 $; under 6 free.

One of the best places to learn about mining history through a film, equipment, and guided tours of the mine buildings. On the north end of Jackson, in a city park, are two of the original four giant wooden Kennedy Mine tailing wheels—58 feet in diameter—that were built in 1912 to remove more than 500 tons of mine tailings a day.

National Hotel (all ages)
2 Water St., Jackson; (209) 223-0500.

Take a look at the lobby and public rooms of the most notorious of gold rush hostelries. With brass chandeliers and red velvet walls, it's still infused with a spirit of cowboy-style elegance. Across the street, the 1862 IOOF Hall once housed Wells Fargo offices, where more than $100 million in gold dust and bullion were weighed.

Mokelumne Hill (all ages)
Ten minutes south of Jackson, at the bottom of a canyon of the Mokelumne River.

The once lawless town of "Mok Hill" is a quiet ghost of its former rowdy self, now a village of winding streets shaded by magnificent old locust and oak trees. Have a cold drink on the veranda of the Hotel Leger at 8304 Main, or stay for a sumptuous Italian meal served family-style—rosemary garlic chicken, calamari, polenta, and pasta at reasonable prices (209-286-1401). Across the street, take a peek into the Adams and Company Genuine Old West Saloon and Museum.

Calaveras County Museum and Archives (all ages)
30 North Main, San Andreas; (209) 754-6513. Free.

A unique collection of Native American and mining artifacts, interesting old documents and papers, re-created miners' cabins and stores, and a Miwok teepee. The jail out back is where Black Bart, the famous stagecoach robber and poet, languished for a time.

Roaring Camp Mining Company (all ages)

Highway 88, P.O. Box 278, Pine Grove 95665; (209) 296-4100.

An old gold camp on the Mokelumne River, featuring prospectors' cabins, modern bathhouses, a wildlife museum, a trading post, and a snack bar; and you can bring your own picnic. They drive you in for a 5-hour tour, with fishing, gold panning, and swimming, and you can also stay here in a simple cabin or pitch a tent, and enjoy a Saturday night steak cookout.

Angels Camp (all ages)
At Highways 49 and 4; (800) 225-3764.

The site of the Calaveras Country Fair and Jumping Frog Jubilee every May. Commemorating Mark Twain's famous story "The Celebrated Jumping Frog of Calaveras County," the popular frog competition is open to all—thousands of people and about 500 frogs show up. You can even rent a frog and try your own version of the wild gyrations necessary to make the frogs win the jumping contests (www.frogtown.org).

The setting for Brett Harte's famous story "The Luck of Roaring Camp," the town of Angels Camp is a complex of historic buildings, shops, hotels, and museums, enough to fill an afternoon. In a grassy, midtown park is equipment from five mines that pulled in more than $20 million in gold between 1886 and 1920. The Angels Camp Museum at 753 Main (209-736-2963) displays pioneer and gold rush antiques and artifacts, carriages, mining and farm equipment, and a steam locomotive. New in the museum is a comprehensive exhibit about Mark Twain's stay in the area.

Near Angels Camp, the town square of the tiny burg of Copperopolis makes a nice stop for a meal, gallery and shop browsing, and picnicking in the park. Check the website to find out about the frequent annual and special events held there, from **free** concerts to festivals, car shows, chili cook-offs, and lots of Christmas holiday happenings (www .copperopolistownsquare.com).

Where to Eat

Angels Creek Cafe. 1246 South Main St., Angels Camp; (209) 736-2941. Stop in for local gossip and advice on the area at this popular breakfast spot. Dig into Sue's big omelets and platters of eggs and home fries with homemade biscuits. $

Cafe Max. 140 Main St., Jackson; (209) 223-0174. Open early for Swiss pastries fresh out of the 1865 brick oven, and all day for sandwiches, salads, and desserts. $–$$

Piaggi's. 1262 South Main St., Angels Camp; (209) 736-4862. Fresh pasta, cioppino, steaks, burgers. $–$$

Upstairs Restaurant. 164 Main St., Jackson; (209) 223-3342. Upstairs is a "ferny," art-filled environment for a sophisticated California cuisine menu; downstairs, the Streetside Bistro is perfect for sandwiches and pizza lunches. Both are casual enough for kids. $–$$

Lakes, Fishing & **Water Sports**

- **New Melones Lake,** 7 miles south of Angels Camp, Highway 49; (209) 536-9094 or (877) 468-7326; www.houseboating.org. More than 100 miles of tree-lined shore dotted with campgrounds and marinas, headquarters for fishing, sailing, waterskiing, and houseboating. At the Museum and Visitor Center see exhibits of regional history and wildlife, and get maps, brochures, and advice. Ask about ranger-led hikes and interpretive programs. Stop at Glory Hole Sports (2892 Hwy. 49; www.gloryholesports.com) for fishing tackle, water toys, camping equipment, groceries, and gas.

- **Pardee Lake,** 12 miles from Mokelumne Hill, off Highway 26; (209) 772-1472. Popular for trout, kokanee fishing, and sailing. Swimming, water-skiing, and Jet Skis are not allowed in the lake. Also there are a nice playground, a campground, and a swimming pool.

- **Lake Amador,** 9 miles from Jackson, off Highway 88; (209) 274-4739. Some 425 surface acres of warm water for fishing, sailing, and boating, plus an acre swimming pond with sandy beaches, as well as a coffee shop and play-grounds. At an elevation of 500 feet in the Sierra foothills, it can be very hot and dry in midsummer and early fall. Developed campground and RV sites.

- **Lake Camanche,** 15 miles southwest of Jackson, off Highway 88; (209) 772-1472. A big stretch of water, 33 miles around, created by a dam on the Mokelumne. You'll find it all here: large campgrounds, marinas, and cottage resorts; everything from riding stables, a dance pavilion, tennis courts, bike rentals, and water slides to Jet Skis.

- **Lake Tulloch,** 7 miles southeast of the center of Copperopolis; (209) 785-8200; www.laketullochresort.net. Every water sport imaginable: boating, fishing, skiing, wakeboarding, wakesurfing, wakeskating, windsurfing, kaya-king, Jet Skiing or playing around on the waverunners. Boats and equipment can be rented at the resort and at the campground.

Where to Stay

Angels Inn Motel. 600 North Main St., Angels Camp; (209) 736-4242. Nice motel rooms; and big family units with kitchens, dishwashers, refrigerators, microwaves, books, king-size beds, 2 sofa beds, large liv-ing rooms, and 2 TVs. Small pool, laundry. $–$$

Jackson Lodge. 850 North Hwy. 49 at Highway 88, Jackson; (866) 333-0486; www.thejacksonlodge.com. Adjacent to a pretty wooded area; 28 rooms, some double-doubles. Eight cabins have living rooms with sofa beds and equipped kitchens, and fenced patios (good for toddlers and pets). The

40-foot-long pool has been recently remodeled; complimentary continental breakfast. $–$$

Saddle Creek Resort. 1001 Saddle Creek Dr. off Highway 4 near Angels Camp; (800) 611-7722; www.saddlecreek.com. An upscale golf resort near Gold Country lakes and towns, with 17 lovely 2-bedroom, 2-bath bungalows on a top-notch golf course, with kitchens, large living rooms, patios. Fitness center, game room with large-screen TV,

junior Olympic-size swimming pool, wading pool, tennis courts, bocce ball, hiking trails, horseback riding. $$$–$$$$

For More Information

Amador County Chamber of Commerce. 571 South Hwy. 49, Jackson; (209) 223-0350 or (800) 649-4988; www.touramador.com.

Calaveras County Visitors Center. 1192 South Main St., Angels Camp; (209) 736-0049 or (800) 225-3764; www.gocalaveras.com.

Columbia

The most perfectly re-created Mother Lode settlement in the United States, Columbia is a state historic park where the 1850s are relived by costumed performers, by horse-drawn vehicles, and by sights and sounds of the past that make you feel as if you've fallen back in time. When gold was discovered here, the population exploded within a month from less than 100 to 6,000 people, and 150 saloons, gambling halls, and stores opened up. Many of the Western false-front and 2-story brick buildings with iron shutters remain, housing the shops, restaurants, and museums of today.

The town is absolutely captivating to children, who love the costumed storekeepers and wagon drivers, the innkeepers and blacksmiths, the street musicians and itinerant actors. Musicians and performers are encountered on the street corners and in the restaurants and theater. Horse-drawn stages clip-clop up and down the main street, which is free of auto traffic, while artisans demonstrate horseshoeing, woodcarving, and other vintage crafts. You can pan for gold in the creeks near town, take a horseback ride, and have a sarsaparilla at an old-fashioned ice-cream parlor.

The town is crowded with visitors and hot during summer vacation, although pines and maples do shade the boardwalks. The mild months of spring and fall are the best times to visit. A lively schedule of festivals and special events is conducted all year in Columbia, from the Fireman's Muster in May to a "Glorious Fourth" celebration in July and the Fiddle and Banjo Contest in October.

William Cavalier Museum (all ages)
Main and State Streets, Columbia; (209) 532-0150. Free.

The Columbia experience is enriched by "talking buttons" outside several storefronts. Push the museum buttons to hear about the museum displays in the windows. Tread the creaky floorboards within to see photos of people who lived here during the gold rush, as well as to eye huge chunks of ore, quartz, and semiprecious stones. At the height of

River **Rafting**

Wilderness rafting on one of the big rivers of the Sierra Nevada can be the highlight of a childhood and a never-to-be-forgotten family memory. Be sure to connect with an experienced company that caters to families, choose your river and your time of year carefully, and start with a day trip. The water is high and rough in early spring, and it's cold; in the summertime, the water is warmer and the rapids calmer. The South Fork of the American River, the Lower Klamath, and the Merced River are the most popular choices for families with younger children and first-time rafters. The waters are warm, the rapids are exciting but not too scary, and there are plenty of quiet swimming holes.

- **Outdoor Adventure River Specialists (O.A.R.S.),** P.O. Box 67, Angels Camp 95222; (800) 346-6277; www.oars.com. Over 30 years in the business of guiding families on the river, with special parent-child trips and games and toys for kids ages 4 to 13, plus activities for teens. Their Sierra Nevada Family Adventure Camp takes in rafting on the American, kayaking on an alpine lake, exploring Marshall Gold Discovery State Park, and more activities.

- **Zephyr Whitewater Expeditions,** P.O. Box 510, Columbia 95310; (800) 431-3636; www.zrafting.com. Long-established rafting company on the American, Tuolumne, Merced, and Kings Rivers. You can camp at the company's private campground near Yosemite; bring a nanny to take care of younger kids in camp while you hit the river, or switch off—one parent stays in camp while the other goes rafting, and vice versa. Free wet suits and paddle jackets; family rates.

Columbia's fame as the Gem of the Southern Mines, $1.5 billion in gold was weighed on the Wells Fargo Express scales.

Columbia Grammar School (all ages)

On the north end of Main Street, Columbia. Free.

In use from 1860 to 1937, the school has an endearing collection of antique desks, inkwells, books, and slates that children used.

Columbia Stage (all ages)

Catch the stage on Main Street at the Wells Fargo Express, Columbia; (209) 588-0808. $–$$.

One of the greatest treats for younger children is a ride through town and into the woods and hills nearby.

Jack Douglass Saloon (all ages)
Main Street, Columbia; (209) 533-4176. $.

Push open the swinging doors and step right into this classic Western bar (children welcome) for a sarsaparilla and watch the street scene through the open shutters. Established in 1857, the saloon serves sandwiches, hot dogs, chili, tacos, salads, and big platters of nachos. From May to September, come in for the live music every weekend afternoon.

Coyote Creek at Natural Bridges (all ages)
Parrott's Ferry Road, near Columbia.

A short, easy walk on a streamside nature trail. You may see people swimming here and rafting through a colorful limestone cave—not as scary as it looks.

Columbia State Historic Park (all ages)
11255 Jackson St., Columbia; (209) 588-9128; www.parks.ca.gov. Free.

Experience the gold rush era firsthand in this living historic town complete with costumed shopkeepers, stagecoaches, saloons, and more. Watch candles and soap being made, taste homemade chocolates, or dress up for a photograph (fees for some of these offerings). Free 1-hour guided walking tours depart from the main museum at 11 a.m. on Saturday and Sunday year-round, and daily during the summer. The second Saturday of each month is Gold Rush Day, with many special exhibits and hands-on activities.

Shops on **Main Street**

- **Columbia Candy Kitchen.** Four generations of the Nelson family make fresh taffy, brittles, fudge, and penny candy. Watch it being made in the big copper kettles and on the marble-topped tables.

- **Cosmos Daguerrean.** Dress up the family in the forty-niner costumes provided and have your tintypes taken.

- **Village Pharmacy.** Rows of bottles of strange remedies, plus dentist's office exhibits with hand drills and anything-but-painless tools for the teeth.

- **Bearcloud Gallery.** American Indian art and curios.

- **Columbia Candle and Soap Works.** In an old feed store, watch soaps and candles being freshly milled in clove, chocolate, lavender, and more scents, and buy a candle kit to take home.

- **Pioneer Emporium.** A dry-goods store selling household sundries and gifts; old-time brass, tin, and textile wares; and items of Native American culture.

Where to Eat

Brown's Coffee House and Sweets Saloon. Main Street, Columbia; (209) 532-1850. Fresh-baked cookies and ice cream, coffee, and espresso drinks; lunches. $

Columbia House Restaurant. 22738 Main St., Columbia; (209) 532-5134. Hearty American fare for breakfast and lunch. $–$$

Goldstreet Bakery Cafe. 22690 South Gold St., Columbia; (209) 533-2654. Just outside the state park; open early for breakfast and lunch. Owner Anne-Marie Holmes uses organic ingredients and local produce in healthy menu items like homemade soups, salads, and vegetarian dishes; inch-thick French toast; and fruit pastries. Breads are baked here, and juices are fresh squeezed. Sit outside under the trees. $

Lickskillet Cafe. 11256 State St., Columbia; (209) 536-9599. American home-style cooking: rosemary roasted chicken with mashed potatoes and roasted garlic gravy, rib-eye steak, Cajun meat loaf, curried chicken— bring your appetites. In a historic cottage behind the museum, dine inside or on the porch; lunch and dinner served. $$

Where to Stay

Columbia Gem Motel. One mile from Columbia, 22131 Parrotts Ferry Rd.; (209) 532-4508; www.columbiagem.com. Simple cottages and motel rooms in a pine grove; well-behaved pets okay. $–$$

Columbia Inn Motel. Adjacent to Columbia State Historic Park, 22646 Broadway St., Columbia; (209) 533-0446; www.columbiainn motel.net. Two-bedroom units, plus suites sleeping 4; simple accommodations. Pool, restaurant, and picnic area. $–$$

Marble Quarry RV Park. 11551 Yankee Hill Rd., Columbia; (209) 532-9539; www .marblequarry.com. Wooded setting, pool, playground; new cabins. Walk to the state park. $–$$

Trails End RV Park. 21770 Parrotts Ferry Rd., Columbia; (209) 533-2395. One of several RV parks near Columbia, offering shady sites, a store, and nightly campfire gatherings. $

For More Information

Columbia State Historic Park. Fourteen miles south of Angels Camp, off Highway 49, Columbia; (209) 532-0150; www.parks.ca.gov and www.columbiacalifornia.com.

Jamestown

Boomed and busted several times in the past 150 years, Jamestown retains an anything-can-happen Wild West atmosphere, from the days when it was just a cluster of tents on a dusty road. When the gold began to rush, saloons and dance halls were erected, then hotels and homes. Antiques and curio shops line Main Street today, and almost as many saloons and restaurants. This is one town where children enjoy the shops as much as their parents do. Most of the restaurants in town are casual and reasonably priced for family groups.

You can pan for gold near Jamestown, stay in a vintage hotel, and take a ride on a steam train. If Jamestown looks familiar to you, it may be because the movie *Butch Cassidy and the Sundance Kid* was filmed here. As in most of the Gold Country, summer temperatures are in the 90s and higher. If you have any doubt about whether there is still gold in them thar hills, a 60-pound slab of pure gold was discovered in the Jamestown Mine in 1993.

Visitors and residents get into the spirit of the Mother Lode by dressing in period costume for annual theme events such as Old West reenactments. You can purchase or rent beautiful Victorian and Western apparel at Dragoons (18231 Main St.; 209-984-1848). David and Deborah Wright will outfit you in cowboy boots and hats, fancy dresses and feathered

Underground Adventures

If your family has never toured underground caverns, you'll be fascinated by how beautiful they are. On a hot summer day in Gold Country, it's totally cool to see fantastic crystalline formations; gigantic, multicolored mineral towers; and stalagmites and stalactites. Caverns are not particularly claustrophobic—believe me, I would know. Family members do need to be able to walk easily up and down stairs. No children carried in backpacks; front packs and slings are okay. Toddlers might be scared if/when the lights are turned off for a moment, which is sometimes done to show how dark the dark can be; ask about this possibility before you buy a ticket.

- **California Caverns,** 8 miles east of Highway 49 off Mountain Ranch Road, San Andreas; (866) 762-2837; www.caverntours.com. Open to the public since 1850. Eighty-minute tours wind through narrow passageways and limestone chambers 200 feet high. Adults $$$; ages 3 to 13 $$; under 3 free.

- **Mercer Caverns,** 1 mile north of Murphys, at 1667 Sheep Ranch Rd.; (209) 728-2101; www.mercercaverns.com. One-hour tour featuring magnificent mineral formations. $$.

- **Moaning Cavern,** Parrots Ferry Road, 2 miles south of Vallecito; (866) 762-2837; www.caverntours.com. A 45-minute tour, featuring a 100-foot spiral staircase. For the adventurous this cavern offers a 3-hour, 180-foot descent by rope in the main chamber, with equipment supplied. Adults $$$; ages 3 to 13 $$; under 3 free.

- **Black Chasm,** between Volcano and Pinegrove, off the Volcano-Pinegrove Road; (866) 762-2837; www.caverntours.com. Descend steep and narrow stairways into a dreamlike world of wavering, dripping draperies of flowstone; glowing subterranean lakes; crystal formations; stalactites; and stalagmites. It is a steady, damp 60 degrees year-round. Children must be able to walk on their own or be small enough to fit into a front carrier; no strollers. Adults $$; ages 3 to 13 $, children under 3 free.

hats, beaded purses, and fringed buckskin jackets and vests. The days of the desperadoes are re-created every September at the Jamestown Shoot 'Em Up, when bewhiskered cowboys and wild-eyed outlaws swagger up and down the sidewalks, their six-guns smokin'.

Railtown 1897 State Historic Park (all ages)

5th Avenue and Reservoir Road, Jamestown; (209) 984-3953; www.railtown1897.org. Admission is free. Rides and tours: adults $$; children $; ages 5 and under are free.

Plan a half-day visit at this 20-acre exhibit of vintage steam locomotives and passenger cars, a roundhouse, and a railroad shop. Take a 1-hour train ride through the foothills or the 2-hour Twilight Limited, a sort of sunset cruise with refreshments, entertainment, and a barbecue dinner at the end. Trains operate weekends, April through October, and there are special theme excursions on holidays. This is a great place for a picnic at tables or on the lawns under the aspens and maples, within sight and sound of the exciting action on the track—whistles, bells, steam, and smoke.

Costumed conductors and workers are railroad and train lovers, and they are loaded with great stories and information. You can take a guided or self-guided tour of the roundhouse to see 100-ton locomotives and a blacksmith at his fiery task. Around the site are numerous photogenic artifacts from the many movies that were shot here, including *Dodge City, High Noon, Back to the Future III,* and *Wild Wild West.* In the train station shop is a huge collection of railroad- and train-related books and lots of fun things for kids, from games and toys to books and kits.

Gold Prospecting Adventures (all ages)

18170 Main St., Jamestown; (209) 984-4653 or (800) 596-0009; www.goldprospecting.com. Panning on the sidewalk $; trips $$$$.

When you see people panning for gold in a wooden trough on the main street, you're here. They will give you information about panning and prospecting day trips and about rafting trips on nearby creeks and rivers. One gold-bearing creek is less than 5 minutes away. They run a special 1-day excursion to a re-created mining camp on Wood's Creek. You will get more gold on this trip than on others because of the use of a sluice box, and you can camp there, too.

The Mossy Bog (ages 5 and up)

18145-8 Main St., Jamestown; (209) 527-1845.

If your child loves fairies, gnomes, and elves, he or she will find this a magical place. Whimsical home and garden accessories and gifts are densely packed into this tiny shop, from frogs hiding under mushroom umbrellas to flying angels and colorful bird feeders. Toddlers with busy fingers might get into trouble here as many of the collectibles are within their reach.

Where to Eat

Here's the Scoop. 18242 Main St., Jamestown; (209) 984-4583. Incredible banana splits, shakes, and ice-cream concoctions, plus homemade desserts, sandwiches, salads, and espresso drinks. $

Historic National Hotel. 18183 Main St., Jamestown; (209) 984-3446; www.national hotel.com. In a shady garden courtyard, lunch, brunch, and dinners are among the best in town; the wine list is a *Wine Spectator* award winner. Kids may be uncomfortable in the elegant dining room, yet they will like sitting outdoors and digging into an Italian burger, potato skins with bacon and cheese, and cheese tortellini. Adults are partial to such sophisticated dishes as escargot, halibut with apricot glaze, steak sandwiches, and trout. A historic landmark built in 1895, the hotel is a beauty. $$

Michelangelo's. 18228 Main St., Jamestown; (209) 984-4830. In an ultramodern, Euro-cafe atmosphere, Michelangelo's is the best in town for pizza, nouvelle Italian food, and pasta. The circa-1910 building served as the post office for decades. $–$$

The Smoke Cafe. 18191 Main St., Jamestown; (209) 984-3733. Tex-Mex specialties, Southwest decor. Lunch and dinner. Built in 1927, the building is a good example of pueblo revival architecture popular in the 1920s. $–$$

The Willow Steakhouse. 18273 Main St., Jamestown; (209) 984-3998. In a roadhouse built in 1862, dig into platters of steak of every description, from filet mignon to pepper steak to London broil, plus hot and cold sandwiches. Ask about the ghosts. $–$$

For More Information

Tuolumne County Visitors Bureau. 542 Stockton St., Sonora; (800) 446-1333; www .tcvb.com. Among Gold Country souvenirs you can purchase from the website are gold nuggets, the book *California Desperadoes,* a Roy Rogers and Dale Evans T-shirt, and maps and guides to the area.

Jamestown Visitor's Information Center. 18239 Main St., Jamestown; (209) 984-4616.

High Sierra South

idwam in the 400-mile wave of California's great Sierra Nevada Range, Yosemite National Park is a jewel box of granite monoliths sparkling with some of the highest waterfalls on the continent. Within the 1,070-square-mile park are snowy alpine peaks, subalpine forests, and meadowlands, all crisscrossed with hundreds of miles of hiking trails.

Add to this groves of giant sequoias—the largest living things on earth—and two mighty rivers, the Merced and the Tuolumne, plus historical museums, theaters, campgrounds, and lodges, and it's no wonder that more than three million tourists visit annually. Families return year after year to tent in sunny campgrounds along the Merced, to hike silent trails in the High Country, and to marvel again at El Capitan and Half Dome in Yosemite Valley. In fact, it's the most revisited national park in the country, as well as the oldest.

North of Yosemite, in a spectacular meadow at 7,200 feet, Bear Valley is surrounded by a panorama of snowcapped mountains. In summer families go mountain biking and hiking, play tennis, swim and float on the Stanislaus River, and camp and fish at eight nearby lakes. In winter a casual, reasonably priced ski resort brings families back to the valley.

A busy gateway to the south gate of Yosemite, the town of Oakhurst is a mecca for antiques lovers and for families on their way to Bass Lake and the Sierra National Forest. The small town offers family friendly motels and restaurants, plus a few surprises. Within a few minutes' drive are a wonderful steam train, a magnificent sequoia grove, and a unique luxury resort that caters to families.

Bear Valley

Poised 7,200 feet high in Stanislaus National Forest, Bear Valley means good times on mountain lakes and quiet forest trails, along with laid-back Nordic and downhill skiing. Your family can spend several days here hiking the trails in Calaveras Big Trees State Park

HIGH SIERRA SOUTH

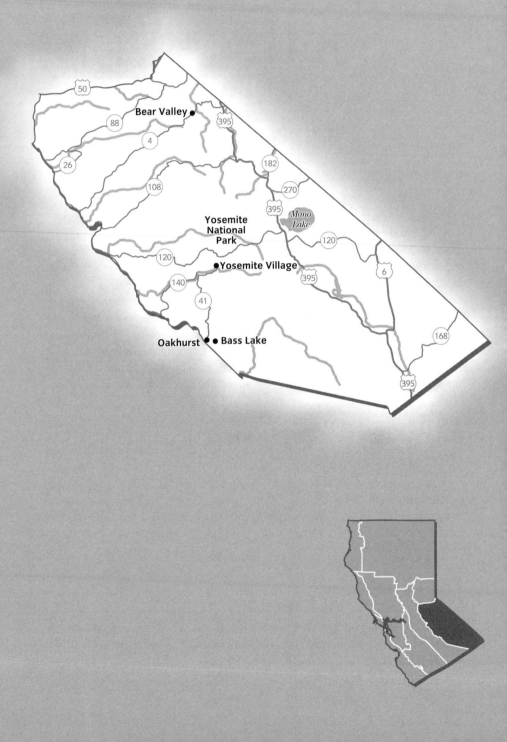

and camping and fishing on the Stanislaus River. Alpine lakes are sprinkled about nearby Ebbetts Pass and the Carson-Iceberg Wilderness area. Mountain biking and, on the river, canoeing and kayaking are popular summer sports. The midsummer Bear Valley Music Festival is a popular annual event that brings hundreds of visitors to hear big-name classical, opera, and jazz performances outdoors in spectacular mountain meadow settings (800-458-1618).

Winter fun consists of skiing on one of the most extensive networks of cross-country trails in the nation, skiing downhill on Mount Reba, and skating on a frozen pond. Saturday nights around the ice rink are out of a storybook, with music, lights, and a bonfire.

With 450 inches of snow annually at Bear Valley, the white stuff can pile up. My children and I spent a weekend here learning to ski, and we literally climbed into and over 3 feet of snow to our cabin—which was fun . . . sort of. The next time I'll call ahead to be sure a path is cleared before we arrive. What I liked best about skiing with the kids here is that everything at the ski resort and within the village is close together, and the atmosphere definitely is family-oriented and reasonably priced.

Above Bear Valley on Highway 4, 8,730-foot-high Ebbetts Pass is the road to glory in spring, when heavy snowmelt rushes off in a million waterfalls and wildflowers run riot over the meadows and beneath aromatic forests of Jeffrey pine, incense cedar, white fir, oaks, and the massive sequoias. In 2005, a 58-mile stretch of Highways 4 and 89, from the east end of Arnold to Markleeville, was declared the Ebbetts Pass National Scenic Byway (www.byways.org).

Snow Play

Around the valley and along Highway 4 above Bear Valley are several snow-play areas and cross-country ski trailheads, including US Forest Service roads used by both skiers and snowmobilers. Besides the developed areas (listed below), watch for roadside play hills from Dorrington to Bear Valley.

- **Cottage Springs,** 8 miles east of Arnold, on Highway 4; (209) 795-1209. Tube hill and rentals; sledding hill for kids to age 10. There is also downhill skiing for beginners—a good, inexpensive place for younger kids to take lessons.

- **Bear Valley Sledding Hill,** Highway 4 in Bear Valley; (209) 753-2834. For kids 4 to 10, $$ including sled rental.

- **Lake Alpine Snow Park,** 2 miles west of Bear Valley, off Highway 4; (209) 795-1381. Sledding hill with rentals; restrooms. You must buy a parking permit at the ranger station on Highway 4, near the Mount Reba Ski Area turnoff.

Just past the state park on Highway 4, on the way to Bear Valley, stop at Dorrington, a tiny former stagecoach stop, where you can take a peek in the vintage saloon and have a Northern Italian dinner at the hotel. Ask for directions to the largest sugar pine in the world—32 feet around, 220 feet tall. Board's Crossing Road near Dorrington leads to several campgrounds on the Stanislaus River.

Bear Valley Village
Forty-five miles east of Angels Camp, on Highway 4; (209) 753-2327.

Two carved wooden grizzlies greet you at the entrance to the village, a small complex anchored by Bear Valley Lodge and the Village Center, where you'll find a general store, a coffee shop, a few galleries, and places to buy sports clothing and equipment (shop for groceries and essentials on the way up here in Arnold, 20 miles south, where prices are more reasonable). Surrounded by condos and houses that are rented by the day or the week, the village is the headquarters for the ski area and for renting summer sports equipment and boats. Most roads are not plowed in winter, giving the valley a picturesque, alpine look. Highway 4 stays open year-round to about 3 miles above Bear Valley Village.

Bear Valley Lodge
P.O. Box 5038, Bear Valley 95223; (209) 753-2327; www.bearvalleylodge.com. $$–$$$$.

Simple, spacious rooms in a 5-story lodge, plus a pool, tennis courts, restaurants, and an inviting atrium lounge with a huge fireplace made of king-size boulders; European-style breakfast buffet. Among the accommodations are rooms with 2 twins and a double; rooms with 2 doubles; and nice suites with a queen and a sofa bed. In winter you can cross-country ski and access the lifts from the lodge. If you decide to stay more than a day or two, condominiums and cabin rentals in the village are the way to go (800-794-3866).

Calaveras Big Trees State Park (all ages)
Four miles east of Arnold, on Highway 4; (209) 795-2334 or (800) 444-7275 (camping reservations); www.bigtrees.org. Open all year. Day use $.

In spring white-flecked branches of blooming mountain dogwood hover over your vehicle as you drive into the park on South Grove Road. Like red Christmas candles, snow plants burst up in flaming spikes through the last remnants of snow.

The really big trees, the sequoias, are here. One giant stands 320 feet high, and another measures 27 feet around. The biggest trees—1,300 of them—are found in the South Grove, 1 mile from the parking lot up the Big Trees Creek Trail. Short nature trails are accessible near the visitor center, and a network of trails leads to high ridgetops above the valley.

Winding through the park, the Stanislaus River has sandy, pebbly beaches for swimming and wading. Developed campsites are set up for RVs to 27 feet, and environmental campsites are available for backpackers; reserve campsites at (800) 444-7275. Ask about summer interpretive programs, family adventures, and guided hikes.

The park is a popular cross-country ski area. A 1-mile loop near the main parking area and an outer 3-mile loop are groomed; snowmobiles are not allowed. At 4,800 elevation, snow is not always present, so it's best to call ahead for snow conditions.

Family Day at the park in August includes storytellers, face painting, games, hikes, hands-on arts and nature crafts, fly-fishing demonstrations, Smokey the Bear, Miwok demonstrations, "cocked hat" bowling, as well as food and drink, from 10 a.m. to 4 p.m.

Bear Valley Mountain Resort (all ages)

Highway 4 at Highway 207, P.O. Box 5038, Bear Valley 95223; (209) 753-2301; www.bear valley.com. All-day lift tickets: ages 13 and up $$$$; seniors and ages 7 to 12 $$$; kids 6 and under **free.**

At this family-oriented ski mountain, the emphasis is on beginner and intermediate skiing. Special programs are set up for little kids ages 4 to 8 (Skiing Bears), for 9- to 12-year-olds (Bear Scouts), and for teens and adults. There is all-day "Bear Care," too. The Grizzly Snowboard Den is a boarder-only rental and lesson center; snowboarders have a snazzy terrain park. Among features of the recent multimillion-dollar expansion are a new 300-foot Panda Carpet lift for beginner lessons, a huge dining deck overlooking the gigantic Mokelumne Canyon, and a children's equipment rental center.

First-timers are VIPs, with **free** guided ski tours of the mountain on weekends. Lift ticket and rental prices are considerably cheaper here than at Lake Tahoe ski resorts. You can ski to Bear Valley Village on Lunch Run or Home Run, or get to and from the village on the **free** shuttle.

The cross-country ski area has the largest track system in the central Sierras, 65 miles of groomed trails with warming huts and endless acres of unmarked meadows (209-753-2834; www.bearvalleyxc.com).

Ice skating is popular on a frozen lake. On weekend nights, lights, music, and a bonfire make skating fun to try and to watch. You can take lessons, too.

Bear Valley Adventure Company

Highway 4 and Bear Valley Road, Bear Valley; (209) 753-2834; www.bearvalleyxc.com. Open all year. Rental and lesson prices vary.

In the summer families can rent kayaks, canoes, and mountain bikes here, and get fishing, camping, tennis, and rock climbing equipment and bait, as well as outdoor apparel. You can rent a fishing pole for $5 and pick up snacks at the minimart. This is a good place to get maps and advice about recreation in the area and get a copy of the *Bear Valley Mountain Bike Trail Guide*. Ask about the Morning Meadow Bike Tour, which meanders through a scenic private meadow and the east bike trail to Lake Alpine (call ahead for reservations; kids must be able to ride a two-wheeler without assistance). Here you can also arrange for half-day kayaking lessons on Lake Alpine and for "Moonlight Paddles." In winter rent cross-country skiing, sledding, ice-skating, and snowshoeing equipment. All year, check the website for updates on accessibility of biking, hiking, and ski trails.

Sierra Nevada Adventure Company (all ages)

2293 Hwy. 4 across from Meadowmont Center, Arnold (also in Sonora and Murphys); (209) 795-9310; www.snacattack.com.

Outdoor gear and clothing, rental equipment for hiking, paddling, skiing, snowboarding, climbing, backpacking, camping, and more, for every season; kayaks and canoes; snowshoes and skis; USGS maps. Bring in your dog for a dog pack and a dog life vest.

Lake Alpine (all ages)

Two miles northeast of Bear Valley, off Highway 4; (209) 795-1381; www.lakealpine.com.

The closest lake to the village, Lake Alpine is popular for kayaking, canoeing, and sailing and is regularly stocked with rainbow trout. Hiking and equestrian trails lead to the Carson-Iceberg Wilderness and into the Mokelumne Wilderness. Situated around the lake are 4 campgrounds, a backpackers' camping area, 2 swimming beaches, a restaurant, and a general store; facilities are generally open from Memorial Day to Labor Day. At Lake Alpine Lodge you can rent a variety of boats, canoes, kayaks, and windsurfing boards. In the summertime this is a popular, crowded, sometimes noisy, yet idyllic, mountain lake.

A snow-play area lies just south of the parking lot. Snowmobilers and cross-country skiers head from here into the backcountry on the road to Mosquito Lake.

Utica, Union, and Spicer Meadow Reservoirs (all ages)

Four miles west of Bear Valley, off Highway 4; (209) 795-1381.

At 6,200 feet in elevation, usually open from June to October, this area is quieter and less developed than the popular Lake Alpine and great for launching your own small boat and fishing for trout, bass, and catfish. No waterskiing, no Jet Skis—ah, heaven. A lyrical day trip can be had by renting lightweight kayaks and a car rack and spending the day paddling and picnicking and messing around on one of the reservoir lakes. Surrounded by dark forest and sun-warmed boulders, with plenty of shallow spots for wading, these glittering gems are easily accessible.

A 60-unit campground is available at Spicer, with day-use facilities that include picnic tables, barbecue grills, and restrooms. Boating here is restricted to a speed limit of 10 miles per hour.

Bear Valley Music Festival (all ages)

(209) 753-2574 or (800) 458-1618; www.bearvalleymusic.org.

For more than 40 years, the annual midsummer music festival has attracted crowds of visitors to hear classical, opera, country, pops, and jazz performances and Hollywood-style shows, outdoors in spectacular mountain meadow settings and under a 1,250-seat tent. A full symphony orchestra, international soloists, and top-name entertainers are on the schedule. Kids flock to the **free** children's concert and Teddy Bear picnic. During the festival, the annual Bear Valley Star Party takes place at the new moon. Telescopes are provided, and during the day there are lectures on astronomy and the universe, and photo displays (www.bearvalleystarparty.com). If you are not staying at Bear Valley, you can arrange to join bus transport, leaving from San Andreas, Angels Camp, Murphys, and Arnold. Food and drinks are available at the tent, and you can put together your own tailgate picnic in the parking areas and on the roadsides—patrons come early with their tables and chairs and gourmet dinners.

Where to Eat

Creekside Dining Room. Bear Valley Lodge; (209) 753-2325. California cuisine and American comfort food are on the menu for dinner in the lodge dining room; light meals are also available in the Grizzly Lounge. $–$$

Headwaters Coffee House. In the Village Center, Bear Valley; (209) 753-2708. Yummy baked goods, ice cream; breakfast and lunch; pizza, microbrews, and espresso drinks. Check your e-mail here. $

Lake Alpine Lodge. Two miles from Bear Valley off Highway 4; (209) 753-6358. By the stone fireplace or outdoors on the deck, enjoy chicken and mushroom fettuccine Alfredo, prime rib, and steak for dinner, and charbroiled sandwiches, soups, and salads for lunch. Hearty appetizers are served in the lounge. Children get the usual spaghetti and chicken nuggets on their menu, plus tri-tip steak and pasta primavera. $–$$

Where to Stay

Bear Valley Condominium and Cabin Rentals. Alpine Condo Management; (209) 753-2503. Bear Valley Condo Management; (209) 753-6201. Bear Valley Real Estate; (209) 753-2334. $$$–$$$$

Lake Alpine Lodge. Two miles from Bear Valley, off Highway 4; (209) 753-6358; www .lakealpinelodge.com. A family-oriented resort on the lake offering housekeeping and tent cabins, a general store, a restaurant, boat and bike rentals, laundry facilities, and showers. $–$$$$

Tamarack Pines Inn. 18326 Hwy. 4, 2.5 miles west of Bear Valley; (209) 753-2080 or (209) 753-2895. In a quiet, family friendly, historic inn, recently redone, simple rooms have queens, and multibed suites have microwaves, refrigerators, and coffeemakers. Guests gather in the common kitchen and living room with stone fireplace, video library, books, Internet, and a play nook with games, toys, and books. Complimentary sleds and snowshoes are provided for the on-site sledding hills and the cross-country/snowshoe trail that circles the property. Just down the hill, Cottage Springs X-Terrain Park offers tubing hills; all the winter activities of Bear Valley are nearby. A complimentary big breakfast is included. $–$$$

For More Information

Calaveras Visitors Bureau. 5005 Fairgrounds Rd., Mariposa; (800) 225-3764; www .visitcalaveras.org.

Calaveras Ranger District. 5519 Hwy. 4, Hathaway Pines; (209) 795-1381.

Yosemite National Park

Spring in Yosemite means wildflowers and waterfalls. The shining water curtains of Bridalveil, Nevada, Vernal, and Yosemite Falls are all visible from the valley floor. Within the spectacular view corridor of Yosemite Valley are Half Dome, El Capitan, Cathedral Spires, Royal Arches, and myriad granite columns, domes, and pinnacles created by millions of years of glacial activity. Like the Grand Canyon, Yosemite Valley is one of those places that you and your children must see at least once in your lifetimes.

Campgrounds, lodges, and most of the public facilities—including grocery stores, theaters, and restaurants—are located in the eastern end of the valley. Sightseeing in the valley is best done on foot, on 12 miles of bike trails, and on **free** shuttle buses. Little kids can come along on a bike ride—at Yosemite Lodge or Curry Village, rent a bike with a trailer that fits one child (or two small toddlers or babies); helmets are **free.** You can also rent strollers and jogging strollers.

You can get away from people and midsummer heat by heading for the Tuolumne High Country, to campgrounds, lakes, and cool, wildflower-bedecked Tuolumne Meadows at 8,600 feet.

From spring through fall, the park service offers guided horseback rides in Yosemite Valley, Tuolumne Meadows, and Wawona; longer rides and wilderness pack trips are available, and you can rent horses or bring your own (209-372-4386). Rafting and tubing on the Merced River in Yosemite Valley are popular during the hot summer months, and that stretch of river is calm enough for first-timers and children. Rent a raft or bring your own nonmotorized flotation device; kids must weigh at least 50 pounds (209-372-4386). The two main beaches for cooling off and inner tubing are Cathedral and Sentinel.

In what some claim is the world's premier rock climbing area, climbing lessons for all abilities are conducted in the valley and at Tuolumne Meadows, with equipment provided (209-372-8344).

Everyone Comes to **Yosemite**

One million people visit Yosemite in July and August, 80 percent of them remaining in the valley, which is just 1 percent of the park, where most of the public facilities and the best-known postcard views are found.

To avoid crowded campgrounds, high-season traffic, and people glut, opt to come in spring or fall. If summer is your only choice, come on weekdays and stick to the two quieter but no less attractive areas of the park, Wawona and Tuolumne. The southern section of the park, Wawona, is loaded with historic architecture, shady camping spots along a tributary of the Merced, and some of the tallest and oldest trees in the world.

When the snow flies in Yosemite, the number of visitors drops dramatically, and activities center on Crane Flat, Badger Pass Ski Area, and Yosemite Valley. Rangers lead snowshoe walks and ski tours from several locations. With icicle-clad Half Dome looking on, skating is fun to try or to watch at the outdoor rink in Curry Village.

If you are nervous about driving on snowy roads, take a 2-hour, narrated winter sightseeing tour of Yosemite Valley in a comfortable motor coach with large windows.

Plan your trip in advance by reading about the events, activities, and seminars offered throughout the year—download seasonal issues of *Yosemite Today* from the National Park Service at www.nps.gov/yose/planyourvisit/guide.htm. This is the **free** tabloid that is handed to you at the park entrance gates. You can also download the *Yosemite Guide,* which provides more general information, and check out "Plan Your Visit" on the website for detailed information not shown in the publications. The park is open year-round, 365 days a year, 24 hours a day. Reservations are not required to enter the park; private vehicles are always welcome. The park entrance fee is $20 per vehicle and all occupants.

Summertime midday temperatures in the park, particularly in the valley, may top 90 degrees, and the sun is intense at this elevation, between 3,000 and 4,500 feet. Plan young children's strenuous activities for times other than between late morning and midafternoon. Have them carry a daypack loaded with water, sunglasses, a hat, sunscreen, and insect repellent.

Visitor Center (all ages)
Yosemite Village, shuttle stop 5; (209) 372-0299.

In a recently renovated and rearranged facility, get information and advice from park service rangers; make reservations for guided walks, hikes, classes, live theater, musical programs, and exhibits. Watch slide shows and films; browse dioramas and exhibits on geology, Native Americans, and early history; browse the excellent bookstore for guidebooks, posters, videos, maps, and great books for children. You will find a handy courtesy phone with which to make lodging reservations. If you plan to take an extensive hike or backpack trip, stop at the Wilderness Center next to the post office to get wilderness permits, maps, and information (209-372-0740, www.nps.gov/yose/wilderness).

Ansel Adams Gallery and Photo Walks (all ages)
Yosemite Village, shuttle stops 5 and 9; (209) 372-4413; www.anseladams.com.

The works of the world-famous photographer of Yosemite, Ansel Adams, are on display and for sale here, along with fine-art prints, photos, calendars, posters, handcrafted home accessories, Indian-motif silver jewelry, great books for kids, and a terrific collection of fiction and nonfiction books, all in a serene, elegant atmosphere. Ask about the **free** photography walks that start here daily. (Check at Yosemite Lodge about the Sunrise Camera Walks held there.)

Top Ten Yosemite **Sights for Families**

- **Lower Yosemite Fall.** Walk a short path to the base of the third-highest waterfall in the world, dropping 2,425 feet in two mighty cataracts. The lower fall is the tallest waterfall in North America, crashing to the ground in an avalanche of vibrating sound and a refreshing, misty spray. An extensive area at the base of the falls has received a much-needed restoration of habitat, new footpaths, nature trails, benches, and alcoves, resulting in a much-improved, tranquil environment. New interpretive exhibits showcase natural history and Native American culture.

- **Mist Trail.** From Happy Isles it's 0.7 mile on a paved trail to Vernal Fall bridge for astonishing views of the fall. With more time, continue on a 0.5-mile steep trail to the top of the fall. A spectacular route, it may be strenuous and slippery for kids under 7 or 8. Rewards are close-up views of the fall dropping over a 317-foot cliff and knockout vistas of peaks, domes, and water cascades.

- **Mirror Lake.** Take the popular, scenic, 0.5-mile walk on a paved path to a small, glassy lake for fabulous views of Half Dome. The wildflowery trail around the lake takes an hour or so.

- **Bridalveil Fall.** Near the Highway 140/Highway 41 junction, a short, paved trail leads to the base of the fall, a miraculous, wispy sheet of water floating 620 feet to the valley floor. The fall flows year-round and is often decorated

Happy Isles Nature Center (ages 5 to 12)
Shuttle stop 16; (209) 372-0287.

Films, puppet shows, exhibits, and wildlife programs designed for kids. Here and at Tuolumne Meadows, a Junior Ranger Program is conducted for 8- to 12-year-olds. To earn a Junior Ranger patch, the children listen to interpretive talks on ecology, Native Americans, and wildlife and go on ranger-guided treks.

At the Happy Isles bookstore, consider checking out an Explorer Pack, a daypack filled with a guidebook and activity suggestions. Each pack has a theme, such as Featuring Feathers, a bird identification kit, and Rocking in Yosemite, for rock and mineral discoveries. For children ages 3 to 6, purchase the *Little Cub Handbook* here or online at www.yosemitestore.com. A fun teaching tool, the book is about matching animals with their homes, taking a hike, learning about bears, and more. When they have attended a ranger program and completed the book, kids receive a Little Cub button.

by rainbows. In the springtime, turn around for a view of Ribbon Fall, the highest single fall in the park, at 1,612 feet. The creek here is fun to play in on a hot day.

- **Glacier Point Road.** Bring cameras for the 32-mile drive past dazzling alpine scenery topped by stupendous views from Glacier Point, 3,200 feet above the valley, with peaks, domes, and massive cliffs in a dizzying array.

- **Happy Isles Nature Center.** Excellent source for kids' activities, exhibits, and tours.

- **Indian Village of Ahwahnee.** Wander the paths of a replica Miwok/Paiute village.

- **Pioneer Yosemite History Center.** On the banks of the Merced, a fascinating compound of 19th-century buildings with costumed docents, tours, wagon rides, and events.

- **Badger Pass.** Winter headquarters for snowboarding, downhill and cross-country skiing, snowshoeing, and tubing.

- **Mariposa Grove.** A magical world inhabited by the world's largest living things; walking trails and a tram ride to see the tallest trees in the world.

You can leave children at Happy Isles for **free** 1-hour walks and talks on nature, birds, and forest lore. This area of the park is full of streams perfect for wading and scattered with mossy boulders. The open forest calls for a game of hide-and-seek. Happy Isles is the start of several trails, including the Mist Trail.

Art Activity Center (ages 10 and up)
Yosemite Village, shuttle stop 2; (209) 372-1442. Free.

Outdoor art classes are conducted in watercolor, sketching, and mixed media. Children over 10 with long attention spans and genuine interest in art may participate; those under 12 must be accompanied by a parent or guardian. You will find here a small, well-stocked shop selling artists' materials and equipment, including top-quality watercolor paints and oils, brushes, paper, pens and pencils, and children's art kits. The store is open spring through fall.

A Very **Beary Place**

Bears live in Yosemite, and they love campers' food. A few precautions are essential or you may be awakened in the middle of the night by a furry creature eating your hamburgers and marshmallows.

- Put every bit of food into the bear lockers provided, never in your car.
- Or, hoist your food by rope 10 feet or more up into a tree, and hang pots and pans from your food bag as an alarm.
- If bears arrive, make as much noise as possible and throw rocks.
- Before you set up in a campground or High Country hike-in site, ask a ranger about bears in the area.
- Take your children to the talk entitled "Thinking Like a Bear," held once a week at Happy Isles Nature Center.

Indian Village and Yosemite Museum (all ages)
Next to the Visitor Center; (209) 372-0282. Free.

Yosemite's native Miwok and Paiute hunter-gatherers from 1850 to the present are featured in photos; see priceless baskets, feather capes, and other artifacts. Local artisans demonstrate basket weaving, beadwork, and traditional games. Upstairs in the research library, which is open to all, wonderful 19th- and 20th-century photos and books are worth a look.

Behind the museum in a pine and oak forest, a self-guided trail introduces the daily life, history, and language of the Southern Miwoks in a reconstructed Miwok-Paiute village of 1872. Basketry, food preparation, and arts of the Ahwahneechee people are on display in the model village, and ranger talks and walks are offered frequently.

The Ahwahnee
Shuttle stop 3; (801) 559-4884; www.yosemitepark.com. Room rates $$$$; packages are available.

A stunning masterpiece of art deco and California Craftsman architecture, the Ahwahnee opened in 1927 and has been one of the icons of Yosemite Valley ever since, a must-see tourist attraction and a fabulous place to stay. Native American baskets and artifacts, historic photos and artworks, and Persian and American Indian rugs create a museum-like atmosphere. Notice the photos of cowboys and Indians in the Great Room.

Hung with baronial chandeliers, the 130-foot-long dining room is world famous for its beauty and views through sky-high windows. A pianist plays for dinner, and on the menu are top-notch California cuisine and American comfort food. The dining room is elaborately decorated and glowing with candles and merriment every Christmas season, when the medieval-style Bracebridge Dinners are held.

The gift shop is loaded with pricey Yosemite-theme gifts and guidebooks, calendars, and postcards. You can purchase polo shirts, sweaters, purses, and Native American–inspired items such as kachina dolls, rawhide drums, handcrafted silver jewelry, pottery, and rugs. "Native Critters" are fanciful figures decorated with fur, feather, and leather, with price tags in the hundreds.

There is a pool, and you can walk or bike from here, or take the shuttle, to all valley sites.

Each with a glorious view through big windows, guest rooms have been redecorated in mountain lodge style, with comfy sofas and chairs, original art, and nice, if small, bathrooms. Some are parlor rooms with separate sitting rooms. Recent upgrades included new mattresses, carpeting, down bedding, and luxurious fabrics. Also recently outfitted are the cottages; in a forest glade, they are spacious, with fireplaces. Ask about midweek and off-season rates, and special event and ski packages. Among thoughtful amenities are honor libraries, newspapers at your door, refrigerators, and bathrobes.

The lobby bar has been redone in rich fabrics and warm colors, with booths in a cozy alcove, and historic photographs and art. Light meals are served in the bar and on the outdoor terrace.

High season and special events are booked months in advance; I like late fall, winter, and early spring, when we often have the public rooms to ourselves.

Experience "love" on the Ahwahnee's tennis courts tucked into a meadow beneath Royal Arches, within view of Yosemite Falls. Hotel guests seem to be occupied with sightseeing and other activities, so the courts are often empty. The meadows behind the hotel are among the few overlooked areas in the valley, as is the riverbank behind the Awahnee cottages—just amble back there and picnic under a tree, alone.

Children's Corner in the LeConte Memorial Lodge (ages 3 to 12)
Yosemite Valley at shuttle stop 12; (209) 372-4542; www.sierraclub.org/education/leconte. **Free.**

In the charming, rustic Sierra Club museum in midvalley, a corner is set aside for kids to spend quiet time coloring, leafing through nature books, and playing with hand puppets, while their parents browse the library and displays. **Free** evening talks, slide shows, and programs are held on such topics as geology, history, Native Americans, flora, fauna, and the like. The lodge is open Wed through Sun, May through Sept.

Valley Campgrounds
National Park Reservation Service, (877) 444-6777 or (800) 427-7623; www.recreation.gov. To check campsite availability, visit www.yosemitesites.com.

Although they are crowded in the high season, and sometimes noisy with road traffic and RV generators, North, Upper, and Lower Pines Campgrounds are convenient to walking and biking throughout the valley and to most public facilities and trailheads. Many valley campers prefer North Pines, as it is a little more isolated than the others and is shaded

Family Programs in Yosemite

Check the **free** tabloid *Yosemite Today* for more information.

- **Explore Yosemite Family Program.** Curry Village; (209) 372-4386. Offered two or three mornings a week in the summertime, a 3-hour program introduces families to the natural and cultural world of Yosemite; topics are wildlife, geology, Ahwahneechee culture, and ecology; a couple of miles of easy walking are involved. Cost is $12 for the first child, $10 for each additional child, and two parents per child are **free** (at least one parent must accompany each family's kids).

- **Family Adventures in Yosemite Valley.** (209) 379-2321; www.yosemite .org. Just for families, a 2-day expedition throughout the valley is sponsored by the Yosemite Association. Parents and kids scramble through rocks and caves, search for remnants of Indian villages, climb a dome, learn legends, wade in a lake, and more. From 3 to 6 miles of easy hiking are involved; cost is about $200.

- **Evening Programs.** Nightly talks and slide shows present the natural and cultural history of Yosemite. Learn about the secret life of bats, see Yosemite in the early 1900s through the eyes of a buffalo soldier, and view photography slide shows. Held at Curry Village, Yosemite Lodge, Lower Pines Campground, and Le Conte Memorial Lodge, the hour-long programs are **free** and require no preregistration.

- **Old-Fashioned Campfires.** June through September, families gather around blazing campfires in a gorgeous setting beneath tall pines and

by tall pines; sites near the river are the first to go, so make your reservations well in advance. For quieter, cooler places to camp, away from the valley, consider Bridalveil, Wawona, or Tuolumne Campgrounds. You can bring an RV up to 40 feet to some, not all, campgrounds.

Curry Village

Shuttle stops 13A, 13B, 14; on the eastern end of the valley; (801) 559-5000 or (209) 375-8232. Lodging $–$$$.

Sprinkled for 0.5 mile under cedars, oaks, and pines at the foot of Glacier Point, this spot is the coolest in the valley in the summertime, the coldest in the winter. Established in 1899, this is the camp that thousands of people remember from their childhoods. Expect lots of people, a lively atmosphere, and plenty to do within walking distance, perfect for families. Open spring to fall, and weekends and holidays in the winter.

silvery granite cliffs. The program includes family friendly interactive activities, songs, and stories; ranger talks about Yosemite history, ecology, and geology; and a marshmallow roast at the end. Campfires are limited to 65 people; purchase tickets at Yosemite Lodge or Curry Village; $20 per family. Outside the valley, **free** campfire programs are offered in some campgrounds.

- **Ranger Walks and Talks.** See *Yosemite Today* for days and times. Stroll with a park ranger as he or she talks about geology, Yosemite history, wildflowers, or fauna in the park. The **free** talks are offered throughout the park, departing from campgrounds, popular attractions, and lodgings; reservations are not required. Walk along the Tuolumne River, learn about fire ecology, identify poisonous and edible plants, take a twilight trek to see nocturnal creatures, and find out about rivers and waterfalls.

- **Children's Storytime,** (209) 372-4413; www.anseladams.com. On Saturday at 4 p.m. on the front porch of the Ansel Adams Gallery, a staff member reads from the great collection of children's books in the store.

- **Wee Wild Ones,** (209) 372-4386. For ages 6 and under, **free** 45-minute programs of stories, games, and fun surprises based on wildlife and geology. In summer they're in the outdoor amphitheaters at Yosemite Lodge and Curry Village; in other seasons, go to the Great Room of the Ahwahnee. A parent must accompany a child; preregistration is not required.

You have your choice of nice, motel-like rooms with sleeping lofts, cabins with or without bath, and canvas tent cabins with wood floors, propane heaters, electricity but no outlets, screened windows, and a central bathhouse. A recent extensive redecoration of all accommodations here included new bedding, mattresses, carpeting, furnishings, and other upgrades.

Curry Village is headquarters for outdoor recreation in the valley, including the Yosemite Mountaineering School and bicycle and river raft rentals in the summer. The Mountain Shop sells pricey outdoor, camping, and mountaineering equipment—everything from backpacks, sleeping bags, parkas, footwear, ponchos, and tents to guidebooks, maps, freeze-dried food, cooking utensils, and water filtration systems.

There are several food outlets, a gift shop and general store, a large swimming pool with lifeguards, and a post office. Almost daily, interpretive programs and entertainment are presented in the Curry Village Amphitheater. And the historic Lounge is a wonderful

Biking the Valley

You can rent six-speed bikes and baby trailers at Yosemite Lodge in all seasons (shuttle stop 8), and Curry Village rents bikes April through October (shuttle stop 21). Helmets are **free,** and bikers under 18 years of age must wear a helmet. No mountain bikes are available, although you are welcome to bring your own. Stop in the Visitor Center or the main desk at your lodgings for Yosemite Valley bike trail maps. Strollers, pets, and all bicycles, including mountain bikes, are prohibited on unpaved pedestrian and hiking trails.

An easy 2-mile route starts from Curry Village and goes past the stables and on to Mirror Lake. On the way back, stop at the stables and visit the friendly horses and mules. For a 5-mile round-trip, ride from Yosemite Lodge across the meadow and over the bridge toward the chapel, continuing past Le Conte Memorial and on to Curry Village for an ice cream. Follow the signs to Yosemite Village for an easy loop around the valley.

place to sit by the fire or on the porch, reading or making new friends; take a look at the vintage photos and artifacts around the room.

The outdoor skating rink here is a cozy place to be, with a warming hut, skate rentals, and hot drinks. You can rent one-speed bikes, a great way to get around the valley on 8 miles of bike paths in addition to the roads.

Glacier Point

Required sightseeing. Early morning or late afternoon is the best time for the 32-mile road trip to Glacier Point, to avoid gridlock and to see the dazzling array of granite monoliths when the light is most dramatic (early morning is when hang gliders sail off Half Dome).

From Glacier Point, a rock outcropping hanging out over the edge of the valley, you get a breathtaking bird's-eye view from 3,200 feet. Looking down into the chasm of the valley, your children will spot the river snaking far below and antlike cars crawling on the main roads. With the help of the plaques provided, it's fun to search for the landmarks. The Ahwahnee is easy to locate, at the foot of Royal Arches; Happy Isles is right below your feet; and Half Dome, with half its roundness chopped off as if by a tomahawk, seems to fill up half the sky to the east. Look for climbers making their ascent to the 7,000-foot summit of El Capitan, a startling vertical mass four times as large as the Rock of Gibraltar. The faint booming sound you hear in springtime is Nevada Fall, 2 miles away.

A relaxing way to get to Glacier Point is on a narrated bus tour that runs three times a day from the valley ($$$$; 209-372-1240). You can also take the bus one-way up and walk all the way down to the valley, a 4.8-mile, 3.5-hour hike for the superfit family.

Tuolumne Meadows

Overnight backpacking requires a wilderness permit, which is free and not necessary for day hikes. Trailheads have quotas that are occasionally "sold out" in the high season, so request permits online at www.nps.gov/yose/wilderness or by mail: Wilderness Office, P.O. Box 577, Yosemite 95389; (209) 372-0740. A hiker's bus from the valley will drop you off near Tioga Road trailheads.

An enormous open space at 8,600 feet, bordered by the snow-fed Tuolumne River and surrounded by peaks and glacier-polished domes. The boiling waters of two forks of the river come together here, then drop into the Grand Canyon of the Tuolumne. A hub for backpacking trails, the 2.5-mile-long meadow is the largest in the Sierras at the subalpine level. It may sparkle with frost or be awash in purple nightshade, golden monkey flowers, and riots of magenta lady's slipper orchids. A variety of ranger-guided walks begin here. The "Night Prowl," an after-dark caravan around the meadow, turns up great gray owls, spotted bats, and other nocturnal denizens of the High Sierras.

For good fishing and swimming, take the 1.5-mile one-way trek to Dog Lake, a little steep at first, but easy enough for kids age 6 and up.

At the Tuolumne Meadows Visitor Center, get information on where to picnic and take day hikes, and sign up here for guided walks and presentations (209-372-1240). Exhibits explain geology, alpine and subalpine ecology, bears and other wildlife, wildflowers, and human history.

The Olmsted Point turnout on the Tioga Road has been transformed to the tune of $1.5 million. A new short trail leads from the road to an overlook vista point, at 8,400 feet in elevation, with breathtaking views of Half Dome, Cloud's Rest, Mount Starr King, and the spectacular Clark Range country.

Wawona

Southern section of the national park, 36 miles south of Yosemite Valley on Highway 41.

Families with small children love Wawona for the quiet, riverside campground; for the fun of the Mariposa Grove tram ride; and for the Pioneer Yosemite History Center, where costumed docents reenact 19th-century life. Beaches and swimming spots are easily accessible on the South Fork of the Merced River as it runs through Wawona.

Even toddlers can manage part of the 3-mile, flat loop trail around Wawona Meadow, and they like watching the herds of grazing deer (do not feed or touch them).

From Wawona take the Chilnaulna Fall Road 1.5 miles to a parking lot, then follow the trail to the lower cascade of Chilnaulna Fall, about 0.5 mile, uphill. For more spectacular falls crashing over massive boulders, hike another 4 miles on the trail.

Opened in 1917, the Wawona Golf Course is a 3,035-foot-long 9-holer on easy, rolling terrain bordered by towering cedars and pines; you can walk or take a cart, and clubs are available to rent. Horseback riding is offered at Wawona, and it is a perfect area for snowshoeing and Nordic skiing.

The best places to fish on the south fork of the Merced River in Wawona are upstream from the Wawona Campground, downstream from the "swinging bridge," and in Big Creek—cross the golf course and walk about 0.5 mile to Big Creek.

Wawona Hotel

Near the south gate of the park on Highway 41; (801) 559-4884. $$–$$$; kids under 12 are free. Ski packages are available.

The oldest resort hotel in the state was built in 1870s, and she is in fabulous shape. Rooms in several beautiful, vintage buildings and cottages vary in size, and all have been redone in sumptuous fabrics, with armoires, new furnishings, and nice bathrooms with amenities. Some families return every summer to stay in their favorite rooms; some of the best choices are number 137 (3 beds); Little White cottage (3 adjoining rooms and private porch); and upstairs in the main building, connected rooms with shared baths. A small pool, sweeping lawns, a 9-hole golf course, wonderful walking trails, tennis, horseback riding, and swimming and fishing on the Merced River are nearby. Or you can just sink into a rocker on the covered porch. You don't need a car; just jump on one of the **free** shuttles to the valley and the Mariposa Grove, operating year-round.

The Victorian dining room, open for all meals, serves a cross between California cuisine and comfort food, with seasonal specials; don't miss the pine-nut pie and the summer barbecues (restaurant reservations, 209-375-1425). Every December the hotel is decorated in elaborate Victorian style with natural materials and vivid ribbons and fripperies. The lobby Christmas tree is lit at a special occasion calling for hot chocolate, cider, and cookies, while resident musician Tom Bopp leads guests in caroling.

Pioneer Yosemite History Center (all ages)

One-half mile from the Wawona Hotel.

A compound of circa-1880 buildings, offering antique horse-drawn vehicles, a covered bridge, a real live blacksmith, and stagecoach rides. Costumed docents reenact the period between 1890 and 1915, as blacksmiths, artisans, soldiers, and pioneer families. The walking tour is easy for all ages and abilities year-round, except during extreme snow conditions. For just a few dollars, you can ride a horse-drawn wagon in the summertime. About 200 yards upstream from the covered bridge are small swimming and wading pools in a river tributary, the warmest waters in the park. You can leave your vehicle on the side of the road and wade across to big, flat boulders warmed by the sun—one of my favorite places to picnic. A small grocery store and deli are located here.

Gas Up

Gas is available in El Portal outside the Arch Rock entrance; at Crane Flat, 15 miles inside the Big Oak Flat entrance; at Wawona; and during the summer only at Tuolumne Meadows. No gas is available in Yosemite Valley.

Mariposa Grove

A 5-minute drive east of the Pioneer Yosemite History Center, or take the free shuttle from the Wawona Store; (209) 375-1621. Tram tour tickets: adults $$$, children $$.

The largest of three sequoia groves in Yosemite. It's the home of the 209-foot, 300-ton Grizzly Giant, the Columbia (290 feet), and dozens more 2,000- to 3,000-year-old sequoias, the world's largest living things. One branch of the Grizzly Giant is more than 6 feet in diameter, and the cinnamon brown bark is 24 inches thick.

The narrated, open-air tram tour stops frequently for passengers to hop on and off to wander nature trails on the way to a vista point at 6,810 feet, overlooking the vast Wawona forest basin. Instead of taking the tram back to the parking lot, wander the 2.5-mile, easy downhill route on footpaths beneath the fragrant branches. In the cool stillness you'll hear only bustling chipmunks and the prattle of Steller's jays; trillium and wild iris spring from carpets of moss and fern.

Badger Pass Ski Area

Off Glacier Point Road; (209) 372-8430. Lift tickets for adults $$$$, ages 12 and under $$$; inexpensive equipment rental, lessons, and tours. Ask about family ski packages at Yosemite Lodge and Wawona Hotel.

Five lifts take skiers to the 8,000-foot summit to 10 runs. The emphasis is on beginners and intermediates at the downhill, snowboard, and cross-country ski schools, with 85 percent of the slopes designed for them. This is the oldest ski school in the state and still one of the best and most reasonably priced. Except on holiday weekends, you won't wait in lift lines; the dining decks and all facilities are just steps away from the lifts. Take it easy, and take the comfortable shuttle buses from your accommodations up the (sometimes icy) hill to Badger.

Kids ages 4 to 6 like the Badger Pups program. Little kids get group lessons, equipment rental, and Turtle rope tow tickets; certified babysitters provide care and games while parents are on the slopes, too.

Within the park are 350 miles of accessible trails and roads, more than 90 miles of marked trails, and 25 miles of machine-groomed trails and skating lanes; no trail fees. You can rent "pulk" sleds, designed for pulling little kids behind you on the trail (209-372-8444). Cross-country track and skating lanes are groomed from Badger Pass to Glacier Point (a 21-mile round-trip), and a 1.8-mile track runs to scenic Old Badger Summit.

Winter Fun (all ages)

Most valley walking trails are open and relatively dry during the winter. Usually just a dusting of snow remains on the ground, so with boots you can get around on foot just fine. After a few days of dry weather, the Yosemite Falls trail is a great winter hike. Fit hikers carry their snowshoes up the John Muir Trail to Little Yosemite Valley and trek around, enjoying the incredible views. The low elevation of Wawona, about 4,000 feet, means that walking trails in that area of the park are usually quite accessible.

If you have never tried snowshoeing, it is easier than you think, with the new high-tech, streamlined, lightweight equipment. Daily, ranger-led, interpretive snowshoe walks

Snow **Play**

- **Crane Flat** on Highway 120, developed snow-play hill and rentals ($); free to play.

- **Curry Village** toboggan hill, saucer rentals ($); free to play.

- **Goat Meadow** hill, 0.5 mile outside the South Gate/Highway 41 entrance to the park; free to play.

- **Badger Pass** has a 100-yard-long snow-tubing hill with a generous run-out and stopping berm at the bottom. Two-hour tubing sessions are scheduled at 11:30 a.m. and 2 p.m. daily ($$$ per person, including equipment). You are not permitted to use your own tubes or sliding devices, and a parent must accompany children ages 10 and younger.

($) at Badger Pass and at the Mariposa and Tuolumne Groves move at the pace of the slowest person. Tours take about 2 hours, and you can just show up. Wear warm clothes that can be peeled off and any kind of waterproof boots for this moderately strenuous trek. While snowshoes are provided, the sizes available are not recommended for children under 10 years of age.

The end of the season is heralded by a big ski carnival at Badger Pass in April, the Yosemite Springfest, with races for all ages, a barbecue, a costume contest, and snow sculptures. At the Pioneer History Center, costumed docents recount early Yosemite winters, and there is caroling by candlelight and hot cider and cocoa in the old barn (209-742-6231).

Hite's Cove Trail (ages 5 and up)
Thirteen miles east of Yosemite next to Savage's Trading Post, 9486 Hwy. 140 East, El Portal; (209) 379-2301.

In March along the highway, vivid orange California poppies and other flowers wash the hills, and thousands of redbud trees burst brilliant, magenta-colored blossoms. Here is the trailhead to one of the best wildflower trails in the West. Massed with blooms in the spring, the narrow, curving footpath winds high above the South Fork of the Merced River. On just a short walk and for several miles down the trail, you will see dozens of species of flowers: magenta-colored owl's clover; vivid purple and pink Chinese pagodas; shooting stars; bright red Indian pinks; and many more. Grab a cold soda at the Trading Post and browse the shop and art and gift gallery, full of pottery, rugs, baskets, and jewelry from Native American tribes throughout the western states; there is a nice collection of history, art, and children's books, too. Also here are a dozen or so houses and suites available to rent; simple, fresh, affordable accommodations (888-742-4371).

Where to Eat

Curry Village. Shuttle stops 13A, 13B, 14; at the east end of the valley; (209) 372-8333. The Dining Pavilion is a big, airy cafeteria with a nice mountain atmosphere, serving good old American food buffet style at moderate prices; terrific chuckwagon barbecue in the summertime. At the Hamburger Deck, breakfast, lunch, and dinner to eat outdoors or take out, burgers, grilled sandwiches, salads, snacks; share the big orders of fries. At the Pizza Patio, good, fresh pizza and ice cream, for outdoors at an umbrella table with a meadow and forest view, or to take out. Sports fans huddle around the big-screen TV. There is a taco stand, and the Coffee Corner is the place for fast takeout of espresso drinks, pastries, muffins, and Danish; yogurt, juices, hand-dipped ice cream, and prepackaged sandwiches and snacks. $–$$

Degnan's Deli, Cafe, and Pizza Loft. Yosemite Village, shuttle stop 10; (209) 372-8454. In the deli, custom-made and premade deli sandwiches, salads, snacks, espresso drinks, and other beverages to take out. The cafe serves gourmet sandwiches, homemade soups and pastries, soft-serve ice cream, burgers, and light meals. A central fireplace and valley views make the upstairs pizza and pasta place a cozy spot. $

Food Court at Yosemite Lodge. Shuttle stop 8; (209) 372-1274. The cafeteria of old is now an attractive food court with a tree-shaded patio and umbrella tables; you can charge purchases to your lodgings. Freshly made choices include prepacked lunches, custom deli sandwiches, vegetarian and meat-based entrees, ethnic dishes, and specialty sauces at the pasta station. Seafood, fruit and veggie salads, a grill station for hamburgers, garden burgers, and chicken and fish sandwiches; and a hot and cold breakfast station. At the bakery-dessert station are muffins, bagels, Danish, cakes, pies, and espresso drinks. $

Mountain Room at Yosemite Lodge. Shuttle stop 8; (209) 372-1274. Blond wood paneling, low lights, and the killer view of Yosemite Falls make the Mountain Room a grand, if casual, dinner house. Mountain climbing is featured in photos, art, and a mural. Grilled and roasted meats are featured. This is one of the few places in the valley where outdoor dining is available. No reservations are accepted, and the wait can be considerable—come early. Children are welcome in the Mountain Room Lounge, where a round fireplace is inviting. The casual lounge serves alcoholic beverages, light meals, sandwiches, salads, and snacks. Four TVs are tuned to sporting events, family-oriented sitcoms, and news. While parents enjoy views of Yosemite Falls, kids can get a s'mores kit and a child-safe roasting stick to make their favorite treat in the fireplace. $–$$

Tuolumne Meadows Lodge and Grill. Highway 120 East, Tuolumne Meadows; (209) 372-4471. A restaurant in a tent in the High Country of the park, serving American comfort food for breakfast and dinner. Box lunches are available, as well as beer and wine. Dig into Meadow Scramble in the morning, prime rib or veggie specialties for dinner. Next to the post office at the Grill, sit at the counter or take away sandwiches, snacks, hot breakfasts, lunches, and light dinners. In midsummer when the Tuolumne food outlets are overflowing with hungry campers, drive out of the park, east about 2 miles on Highway 120 to the Tioga Pass Resort, where you can get three meals a day of hearty American food and divine homemade pie. $–$$

Village Grill. Yosemite Village, shuttle stop 10. Pretty good fast food from a walk-up window: hamburgers, fries, onion rings, chicken strips, and the like. Eat at a table outdoors or take it away. $

White Wolf Lodge. Highway 120 between Tuolumne Meadows and Yosemite Valley;

(209) 372-1316. This great old clapboard dining hall with a fireplace serves hearty American breakfasts and dinners. You can buy sandwiches at the adjacent store. $–$$

Where to Stay

Cedar Lodge. 9966 Hwy. 140, El Portal; (888) 742-4371; www.yosemitemotels.com. Near the Arch Rock entrance to the national park, on the Merced River, nearly three dozen whimsically carved wooden bears delight children on the motel grounds. Ask for the **free** *Kids' Guide* that includes fun Yosemite facts and games, including a hunt for the wooden bears, and enjoy the plethora of teddies in the gift shop. Two hundred motel rooms of several types and sizes, including a master suite that sleeps 14 and family suites with kitchenettes; small indoor and outdoor swimming pools; a small beach on the river. $$–$$$

High Country Campgrounds at Yosemite. (801) 559-4884. Rustic tent cabins with woodstoves are at Tuolumne Meadows Lodge and the Tuolumne Meadows Campground. Tuolumne Meadows is the largest campground in the park, with 325 sites; the most desirable are on the east side near the river. Campfire programs and special children's get-togethers with songs and stories are held most nights. Nearby are a grocery store, stables, and a restaurant serving substantial American fare. Tent cabins with woodstoves are in a picturesque setting near the river. White Wolf Campground is summertime-only headquarters for backcountry trails, with rustic tent cabins, a first-come,

first-served campground, store, stables, and a lovely old clapboard dining hall. $–$$

Housekeeping Camp. Shuttle stop 12; (801) 559-4884. If you like to camp but do not enjoy sleeping in a tent or on the ground, this could be for you. There are 266 tent cabins sleeping up to 6 that have concrete walls and floors and canvas roofs; each has a fire ring. A canvas curtain separates the sleeping and cooking/dining areas. With electricity but no phones or plumbing, the cabins are close together, with minimal privacy. Facilities include central restroom and shower facilities (soap and towels are provided), a laundry, and a small grocery store. Bring your own linens or sleeping bags, cooking equipment, dishes, and food. $

The Redwoods. Chilnaulna Falls Road off Highway 41, Wawona, in the national park; (209) 375-6666; www.redwoodsinyosemite .com. Choose from more than 100 privately owned cabins and houses to rent in a wooded setting near the river. Homes are varied sizes, all fully furnished and equipped. Make reservations months ahead for holidays; call early in the year for the December holidays. $$$–$$$$

Yosemite Lodge at the Falls. Midvalley; (801) 559-5000. Nearly 500 rooms, from traditional rooms with balconies or patios to rustic cabins with or without baths. An extensive recent remodeling includes all new fabrics, bedding, mattresses, drapes, and carpeting, and, for the first time, the addition of TVs, irons, hair dryers, and other amenities. Internet access is now available in the

Pets

Kennel facilities, (209) 372-1248. Pets are allowed in the national park if they are leashed at all times and never left unattended. No pets are allowed on trails, in the backcountry, or in lodgings.

Mountain Room Lounge, the outdoor amphi-theater, and in the lobby; Internet kiosks are located in the lobby. The compound includes a cafeteria and restaurants, a post office, gift shops, a swimming pool, an outdoor theater, and a tour desk (539-375-1240). **Free** nightly programs. $$–$$$

Yosemite National Park. (801) 559-4884; www.yosemitepark.com. Campgrounds, cab-ins, hotels, lodges. For sites requiring reser-vations call three months to a year in advance to ensure your space. For campgrounds operating on a first-come, first-serve basis, be sure to arrive early in the morning to avoid disappointment.

Yosemite View Lodge. 11159 Hwy. 140, El Portal; (800) 321-5261; www.yosemite-motels.com. Near the Arch Rock entrance to the national park, a large, recently reno-vated motel with balconies or patios over-looking the roaring Merced River. Rooms and family suites are spacious and attractive with rustic mountain lodge–style furnish-ings; some have equipped kitchenettes with microwaves, refrigerators, toasters, and 2-burner stoves, plus flat-screen TVs, fireplaces, sofa beds, and deep double whirl-pool tubs. Nicely decorated standard rooms are set up with 2 double-size beds. There are small outdoor pools and a larger indoor pool, a pizza place, and a small restaurant by the river serving breakfasts and dinners, with a cocktail lounge, a convenience store, and gift shop. From here you can take a bus in and out of the valley ($$); bus fee includes park entrance. $$$$

Yosemite West. Seven miles from Badger Pass, 30 minutes from Yosemite Valley; (209) 296-7364; www.yosemitewest.com. A wide variety of year-round vacation homes and condominiums in the Wawona area within the park. The website shows details and photos of everything from studios to luxury lodge homes sleeping 10 people. Many of the homes and condos have sundecks

with mountain or forest views; fireplaces or woodstoves; TV, DVD; hot tubs or spas; and all have fully equipped kitchens. Many of the homes have been recently renovated; some have private riverside patios. The office will supply you with sleds and saucers, games, videos, snowshoes, play equipment, and even extra kitchen appliances. $$–$$$$

For More Information

Yosemite National Park. P.O. Box 577, Yosemite 95389; general information, (209) 372-0200 or (800) 436-PARK; road and weather information, (209) 372-0200, ext.1. Admission to the national park: $$$ per car. Weather changes rapidly in the Sierras; snow can fall as early as September, and storms can occur any month of the year. Before you leave home, call to check on weather, road, and trail conditions, and ask about the avail-ability of campsites if you plan to camp with-out reservations.

Sierra National Forest Ranger District. (559) 297-0706.

Yosemite Websites:

- **www.yosemitepark.com.** Book lodging and campgrounds on this site and get infor-mation on shopping, dining, and activities from Delaware North Companies Parks & Resorts at Yosemite, Inc. (DNC), the com-pany that operates concessions, tours, and lodging in Yosemite.

- **www.recreation.gov.** Camping reservations.

- **www.yosemite.org.** Yosemite Associa-tion, visitor information, bookstore, classes and seminars, weather, and live-camera views.

- **www.nps.gov/yose.** Official National Parks Association site.

- **www.yosemite.com.** Travelers' informa-tion, lodging, road conditions, and weather.

Transportation Tips:

Y.A.R.T.S. (877) 98-YARTS; www.yosemite .com/yarts. From Merced, Mariposa, and Mammoth, big motorcoaches have reclining seats, large windows, bike racks, and restrooms. The Highway 120 East route from Mammoth may use multipassenger vans; riders with children requiring car seats or with bicycles should call ahead on this route. YARTS connects with Amtrak and Greyhound in Merced. Fares $$ and $$$, including park admission; kids are discounted; with each adult passenger, a child 16 or younger rides **free.**

Amtrak. (800) USA-RAIL; www.amtrak.com. Ask about off-season discounts and special family fares for departures from throughout the state to the park; you arrive in Merced or Fresno, with **free** connections to the park by bus.

Sightseeing Tours and Activities:

• **Delaware North Companies Parks & Resorts at Yosemite, Inc. (DNC) Tour Desk.** Yosemite Lodge, Curry Village; (209) 372-4386; www.yosemitepark.com. All year-round, daytime and evening talks and slide shows, classes, guided walks and hikes, fireside gatherings and old-fashioned campfires, and theater presentations, all showcasing the natural and cultural history of Yosemite. Learn about the secret life of bats, see through the eyes of a buffalo soldier in the 1900s, meet John Muir, take a wilderness survival class, learn to use a digital camera. Some are **free** and require no preregistration, others are fee-based with advance sign-up. Ask at the Visitors Center and Yosemite Lodge, see *Yosemite Today* for schedules, and get information online.

• **National Park Service Tour Desk.** Visitor Center, Yosemite Village; (209) 372-0200; www.nps.gov/yose. Ranger-led tours, hikes, films, and talks.

Oakhurst & Bass Lake

Between Yosemite and Kings Canyon National Park, the Lake Country of the Central Sierras remains relatively undiscovered by vacationers. Some 700 miles of trout streams, along with numerous lakes, reservoirs, and campgrounds, make this an area your family will want to explore.

Fourteen miles from the southern Yosemite gate, Oakhurst is an antiques center and a busy stopover point for travelers on the way to the national park and the national forests. Just up the road at an elevation of 3,400 feet lies the popular recreation area of Bass Lake, with rustic resorts and campgrounds; marinas for sailing, fishing, and waterskiing boats; and endless hiking trails in the surrounding Sierra National Forest.

My favorite time of the year in the Central Sierras is after Labor Day. Traffic is light, and the weather has cooled from the high 90s of midsummer to the 70s. Nights are delightfully crisp, and color is beginning to show in the maples, dogwoods, and oaks.

The Talking Bear landmark in the center of Oakhurst, at Highway 41 and Road 426, is a great photo op. Around town, notice the elaborate chain-saw sculptures of bears, pine trees, eagles, and other flora and fauna. This does seem to be the chain-saw art capital of the Sierras.

Fresno Flats Historical Park (all ages)

One mile from Oakhurst, on Road 427; (559) 683-6570; www.fresnoflatsmuseum.org. **Free.**

A re-created Western town from the region's early timber and ranching era. Old buildings have been moved here from all over the county—jails, schools, barns, wagons, buggies, and a furnished home. You can ramble around on your own anytime, or check in at the museum and gift shop to ask about guided tours. There are outdoor concerts on weekends, a playground, picnic tables, barbecues, and horseshoe pits, making this a busy hometown park.

Yosemite Mountain Sugar Pine Railroad (all ages)

Between Oakhurst and Yosemite, on Highway 41; (559) 683-7273; www.ymsprr.com. Most train rides ages 3 to 12 $$; kids under 3 **free.**

A major destination for families with younger children. You might want to plan a couple of hours here riding the train, picnicking, and enjoying the beautiful forest. An 84-ton vintage locomotive—the largest ever built for a narrow-gauge track—pulls open cars 4 miles through forestlands into Lewis Creek Canyon. It's exciting to climb aboard at the tiny station while steam rolls out from under the huge engine and black smoke belches into the sky. A conductor spins tales of when the railroad hauled timber out of the Sierras.

Watch out for masked horsemen, who are known to stop trains searching for passengers' loot. There is a gift and sandwich shop, and the Thornberry Museum in a 140-year-old cabin. For a fun preview of the train whistles, bells, brakes, and other exciting noises, and to see a few photos of the trains, go to www.ymsprr.com/sightsnsounds.html. From June through September a "Moonlight Special" evening train excursion ends with a steak barbecue and live music around a campfire ($$$$).

Next door at the Narrow Gauge Inn, the Victorian era and the Old West come together in the restaurant and Bull Moose saloon—cozy in cool weather when logs burn in the big stone fireplaces (209-683-7720).

Oakhurst River Parkway (all ages)

Oakhurst Community Park; (559) 683-4636.

An easy, 3-mile walking trail just off the main street of Oakhurst meanders past Fresno Flats Historical Park, the Fresno River, China Creek, and Oak Creek—the water flows in late winter, spring, and early summer. Stroll along the water and watch ducks, beavers, red-winged blackbirds, and other wild creatures; have a picnic or a barbecue in the small, grassy park.

Sierra Mono Museum (all ages)

Malum Ridge Road/Road 274 and Mammoth Pool Road/Road 225, North Fork; (209) 877-2115; www.sierramonomuseum.org. $.

On display are Native American artifacts, basketry, and beadwork, as well as a grizzly bear, a mountain lion, elk, moose, antelope, wolves, and other wildlife. In August the Sierra Mono Indian Fair Days and Pow Wow are held here, featuring traditional dances, crafts, and games. Call ahead before driving up here, as sometimes the museum is closed.

Hit the **Trail**

- **Oakhurst River Parkway,** Oakhurst Community Park, Civic Circle, Oakhurst; (209) 683-7766. An oak-shaded 3-mile loop trail along the Fresno River and Oak Creek.

- **Lewis Creek National Recreation Trail,** 5 miles south of the southern Yosemite Gate, off Highway 41; (209) 683-4665. From the highway parking area, walk 0.25 mile south on the trail to Corlieu Falls, then 1.8 miles north to Red Rock Falls, through dogwood, azalea, and pines along Lewis Fork Creek. The creek is stocked with trout and is popular with anglers.

- **Shadow of the Giants Trail,** 10 miles north of Oakhurst on Highway 41, take Sky Ranch Road for 6 miles. A National Recreation Trail, an easy 1-mile walk with interpretive signs along the banks of Nelder Creek, leading to a miraculous grove of over 100 specimen sequoias and one of the largest trees in the world, the Bull Buck. Insiders know that this trail is less traveled and more beautiful than the Sequoia grove trails in Yosemite. The biggest and best trees are at the far end of the loop, so get there!

- **Way of the Mono Trail,** along Road 222 at Bass Lake; trailhead between the Forks Resort and the California Land Management Office. A nice, easy 0.5-mile walk to learn some American Indian history and see some great views of the lake.

- **Goat Mountain Trail,** trailheads at Spring Cove Campground and Fork Campground at Bass Lake; (209) 683-4665. Four strenuous miles one-way to the summit and the fire lookout, with nonstop views of the lake and the forested valleys along the way. Cut the distance and the degree of difficulty of this beautiful trail in half by starting at one campground, leaving a car at the other, and turning back where the two trails meet on the way up.

The Mono, Miwok, and Chuckchansi tribes call the southern Sierras their home, and many of them are artisans whose works are displayed and sold in shops and at fairs throughout the region. On Thursday, elders gather to weave, bead, and talk, and in the fall they crack acorns; ask about guided tours.

The Forks Resort (all ages)

39150 Rd. 222, Bass Lake; (559) 642-3737; www.theforksresort.com. $$–$$$$.

Families return here year after year for their summer vacations in cabins on the southwest corner of the lake. Conveniently grouped together are a general store selling groceries and fishing and camping gear; a marina renting patio and fishing boats; and a casual, 1950s-style cafe serving three meals a day. The cabins are actually spacious houses in the trees, most with lake views. They are completely outfitted with everything you might need for a day or a week—just arrive with your clothes.

Bass Lake (all ages)

Fourteen miles from Oakhurst off Highway 41, on Road 222; (559) 683-4665.

The warm waters of this popular lake reach 78 degrees in summer. Situated in the Sierra National Forest at 3,400 feet, the lake is good spring and fall fishing for trout, bass, catfish, and bluegill, and in summer for partaking in water sports and camping. You can rent Windsurfers and boats for canoeing, sailing, rowing, and waterskiing. At three main resort areas—Pines Village, Forks Resort, and Miller's Landing—are shops, groceries, gas, and rentals of all kinds.

At Pines Village you can take waterskiing lessons and hire a boat driver, or cruise the lake at your leisure in a party barge (800-585-9283; www.basslakeboatrentals.com). In the winter you can rent snowmobiles here, too. Besides watercraft rentals, Miller's Landing rents a few nice cabins (559-642-3633; www.millerslanding.com).

Where to Eat

Castillo's. 49271 Golden Oak Loop, Oakhurst; (559) 683-8000. Terrific tacos and homemade Mexican food. It's a cantina, too; try the blackberry margaritas. $

Ducey's on the Lake. Pines Village, Bass Lake; (559) 642-3131. Overlooking the lake, the dining room looks like a cross between a yacht and a hunting lodge, with great old photos on the walls. Ask for a comfy booth. The dinner menu includes steaks, lamb, and prime rib of pork; plus crab cakes, lobster, and more fresh seafood. On the sunny deck at lunchtime, have grilled chicken, salads, burgers, fresh fish, or pasta. Traditional American breakfasts, eggs Benedict, French toast, and omelets. Friday evenings from late May through late August, enjoy live jazz outdoors and fireworks. $$

The Pines Resort. Pines Village, Bass Lake; (559) 642-3121. Good barbecue and American food; indoor/outdoor casual dining. $$

Sierra Meadows Ranch Golf Course. 6516 Opah Dr., just west of Oakhurst off Highway 41, Oakhurst; (559) 642-1343; www.sierrameadows.com. A pleasant place to be on a sunny Sunday for the breakfast buffet, from 9 a.m. to 2 p.m. Call ahead to get a table on the deck, overlooking the golf course. Prices are reasonable for a big brunch. $$

Tenaya Lodge. 1122 Hwy. 41, Fish Camp; (800) 635-5807; www.tenayalodge.com. The Sierra Restaurant offers an upscale casual atmosphere, fresh fish, local produce, Italian cuisine, a fireplace, and mountain views. The Parkside Restaurant is a casual coffee shop serving sandwiches, salads, and deli takeout. Breakfast, lunch, and dinner are offered at both restaurants. $$

Three Sisters. 40291 Junction Dr., Oakhurst; (559) 642-2253; www.threesisterscafe.com. In a bright, colorful, casual atmosphere, exotic and fabulous food. For breakfast the San Francisco–style Joe's Special, chicken quesadillas, banana-nut French toast, eggs Benedict with crab, exotic omelets, and traditional breakfast fare. On the extensive lunch menu may be asparagus, shrimp, and Brie crepes; seafood cioppino; Thai chicken salad; and sandwiches. Gourmet dinners include Oysters Rocksisters, chicken cacciatore, veal stew, spicy Asian entrees—the list goes on. Definitely make reservations. $$$–$$$$

Where to Stay

Bass Lake Recreational Resort. 39744 Rd. 274, near Pines Village, Bass Lake; (800) 700-7795; www.basslake-rvresort.com. A membership club affording privileges around the country. Cabins, RV sites, RV rentals; lodge clubhouse with fireplace, playground, rec room, cafe, swimming pool. Near restaurants, movies, and stores. $–$$

The Pines Resort. Right on Bass Lake, P.O. Box 109, Bass Lake 93604; (800) 350-7463; www.basslake.com. Rustic condos and chalets at the lake and luxury suites; restaurant; tennis, swimming pool, sauna, hot tub; boat rentals. $$–$$$

Tenaya Lodge. 1122 Hwy. 41, Fish Camp; (800) 322-2547; www.tenayalodge.com. A destination resort overlooking forested mountains and valleys, 5 minutes from the southern gate of Yosemite National Park. The 2-story atrium lobby and the restaurants have a casual yet luxurious feel and are decorated with Indian artifacts and Western-style furnishings. Some of the spacious rooms have 2 double beds and a sitting area with sofa bed. Recreational facilities include a full-service spa and fitness center, saunas, indoor and outdoor pools, a playground, and a snow-play area. Tours from the hotel get you into the park and to the Badger Pass ski area.

Kids can pick up an activity pack at the front desk. Camp Tenaya day camp is popular with 5- to 12-year-olds who like volleyball, table tennis, swimming, games, movies, music, crafts, and nature hikes. There are evening programs, too, and babysitting can be arranged.

You can hike right from the lodge through pine forests and along streamsides. Bikes are available at the hotel, and you can walk to a stable for guided horseback rides. Cross-country ski out the door and rent equipment here, too. Barbecue evenings start with a horse-drawn wagon ride to the cookout, with campfire singing and marshmallow roasting with cowpokes. $$$–$$$$

US Forest Service (USFS) Campground Information and Reservations. The forest service operates many campgrounds, seasonally, near Yosemite in the Inyo, Sierra, Stanislaus, and Toiyabe National Forests. Many are on a first-come, first-served basis; in some campgrounds, at least half the sites may be reserved (877-444-6777; www.recreation.gov, www.fs.fed.us). The USFS Summerdale Campground at Fish Camp has a nice, streamside location. Off Highway 41 near Fish Camp, the tiny, tents-only Summit Campground is 6 miles down a gravel road near good fishing on Big Creek.

Yosemite Gateway Inn. 40530 Hwy. 41, Oakhurst; (559) 683-2378 or (800) 545-5462. Motel and family units in a parklike setting, with oak trees, some kitchens, indoor and outdoor pools, restaurant, barbecue area, playground, laundry, and mountain views. Some 2-bedroom family units. $$–$$$

For More Information

Yosemite Sierra Visitors Bureau. 41969 Hwy. 41, Oakhurst; (559) 683-4636; www.yosemitethisyear.com.

Bass Lake Chamber of Commerce. P.O. Box 126, Bass Lake 93604; (559) 642-3676; www.basslakechamber.com.

South Bay & East Bay Towns

The cities and the countryside surrounding San Francisco are easily accessible and packed with opportunities for family adventures—from ridgetop hikes in the East Bay hills to science museums, ethnic festivals, and a wild water park.

Hop a fast underground train to Berkeley for a day on a university campus, or shop in the outlet stores, and later take a hike in a ridgetop forest. Ride the ferry to Oakland for a seafood dinner in Jack London Square and to an art museum that kids like. Spend the day in San Jose at high-tech play-and-learn centers; you will need another whole day to play at California's Great America theme park, and yet another to explore a mystery house and a cool museum of mummies and Egyptian tombs.

Highway 280 is the fastest route south to San Jose. Take Highway 80 across the Bay Bridge to Oakland and Berkeley, or a ferry or BART across the bay.

Berkeley

Just a skip and a jump across the bay from San Francisco, Berkeley is the home of one of the largest and most beautiful university campuses in the western United States, the University of California at Berkeley. Attractions here for visiting families are museums, educational buildings, walking paths, and shady glades on the campus itself; ethnic restaurants on the surrounding streets; and recreation in Tilden Regional Park in the verdant hills above the city. You might also enjoy the reasonably priced accommodations and the factory outlet stores.

At the base of a range of forest-covered hills overlooking San Francisco Bay, the small city is laid out on either side of University Avenue, which stretches from a lively marina to the campus. Telegraph Avenue is ground zero for the university students who prowl the coffeehouses and the grungy shops and sidewalk vendors who sell everything from punk music to hip-hop gear, funky art, jewelry, and tattoos. At Telegraph and Durant, Bear Basics offers tons of Cal logo apparel. Crossing University and extending

SOUTH BAY & EAST BAY TOWNS

into Oakland, on College Avenue is a parade of boutiques, restaurants, and markets. North Shattuck Avenue and 4th Street are pleasant boulevards for strolling, shopping, and noshing (www.northshattuck.org, www.4thstreetshop.com).

4th Street **Shops & Cafes**

To reach the restaurant and factory outlet area on 4th and surrounding streets, take the University Avenue exit off Highway 80, then the first left turn; then turn left again onto 4th Street.

- **Bette's Oceanview Diner,** 1807 4th St.; (510) 644-3230. This all-American, circa-1940 cafe with booths and a counter opens at 6:30 a.m. and goes full blast all day long, through dinner; take out and eat in. The epitome of comfort food. $.

- **Royal Robbins,** 841 Gilman Street off 4th; (510) 527-1961. Top-quality outdoor-recreation equipment and clothing, at a discount. My husband has Royal Robbins shorts that he's worn every summer for 20 years. Really!

- **Earthsake,** 1772 4th St.; (510) 559-8440. Interesting eco stuff, including toys, games, and books.

- **REI,** 1338 San Pablo Ave., near 4th Street; (510) 527-4140. Top-of-the-line camping and outdoor-recreation equipment, clothing, bikes, a climbing wall, boots, running gear, guidebooks, and ski stuff.

- **This Little Piggy,** 1840 4th St.; (510) 981-1411. For babies and kids to age 12, super-cute cotton clothes, books and toys, even bath and body items.

- **Goodnight Room,** 1848 4th St.; (510) 548-2108. Cottagy furniture for toddlers to teens.

- **Jest Jewels,** 1791 4th St.; (510) 526-7766. Tiaras, fanciful costume jewelry, nutty sunglasses, and more fun stuff.

- **East Bay Vivarium,** 1827 5th St.; (510) 841-1400; www.eastbayvivarium.com. Snakes, reptiles, spiders, scorpions, turtles, frogs, newts, and more creepy crawlies at one of the largest reptile specialty stores in the country.

- **Sketch,** 809A 4th St.; (510) 665-5650; www.sketchicecream.com. Homemade artisanal ice creams made from organic milk and local fruits, and such enticing flavors as double ginger, baby coconut, organic chocolate, burnt caramel, blood orange, olallieberry—the seasonal list goes on. Try the hot chocolate with ice cream in it. $

Highlights of the **UC Campus**

- **Sather Tower,** central campus, visible from Sather Gate on Bancroft; (510) 642-5215. A campus landmark built in 1914 as a replica of St. Mark's campanile in Venice. Take a heart-stopping ride to the top for 360-degree views of the Bay Area. $.

- **Lawrence Hall of Science,** Centennial Drive near Grizzly Peak Boulevard; (510) 642-5132; www.lawrencehallofscience.org. Get interactive with lasers, computers, medicine, dinosaurs, and outer space; pretend to be a doctor, an archaeologist, and an astronaut. Planetarium shows and physics and biology labs are here, too. The littlest kids like "OK-to-touch" frogs, tarantulas, rabbits, and other animals. Kids love the earthquake simulator and the boulders for climbing, while parents love the bay views. Adults and students $$; ages 3 to 4 $. Children 3 and under **free.**

- **UC Botanical Garden,** 200 Centennial Dr.; (510) 643-2755; www.botanical garden.berkeley.edu. Wander redwood-lined trails past old roses and a Chinese medicinal herb garden, a Japanese lily pond, and more plant displays; take a walk or a bike ride; bring a picnic. Adults $$; seniors and children ages 3 to 18 $; under 3 **free. Free** admission the first Thursday of the month.

- **Valley Life Sciences Building/Museum of Paleontology,** (510) 642-1821. A huge collection of fossils are laid out in the hallways, and a triceratops skull awaits in the library. A 2-story-high Tyrannosaurus rex presides in the atrium, while a pterosaur flies overhead. Cool! **Free.**

- **Phoebe Hearst Museum of Anthropology,** Kroeber Hall on Bancroft at College Avenue; (510) 643-7648. California Native Americans are featured, plus ancient artifacts from all over the world. Adults and students $; ages 12 and under **free;** everyone **free** on Thurs.

- **International House,** 2299 Piedmont Ave.; (510) 642-9460; www.ihouse.berkeley.edu. A chance to have a meal in the company of students from all over the world. Good, basic international cuisine is served from a buffet in a unique Spanish/Moorish–style restaurant, indoors or on the garden patio. $.

University of California (all ages)

101 University Hall, at Oxford Street and University Avenue, Berkeley; (510) 642-5215; www .berkeley.edu. Free tours.

Budding scientists in your family will find a plethora of fascinating museums, as well as the world-famous Lawrence Hall of Science, on the campus. Student-led campus tours are offered daily, and you can get maps for a self-guided tour at the visitor center. Maps are also posted at the campus entrance, or you can get one by mail by sending a self-addressed, stamped envelope to 2200 University Information Center, 2200 University Ave., Berkeley, CA 94720. Call ahead for tour reservations.

I went to school here and now find the campus a little more crowded with buildings and students, yet it's still a great place to spend an afternoon, wandering the garden pathways and having a picnic beneath one of the century-old redwoods or oak trees. The oldest of the UC campuses, established in 1868, this one has a fascinating variety of architectural styles. Delicatessens and casual cafes are clustered on the streets near each campus entrance.

Berkeley Marina (all ages)

West end of University Avenue, west of Highway 80; (510) 981-6903.

Extending 3,000 feet out into the bay, the Berkeley Pier is a good place to stroll, take photos of the skyline, and watch freighter traffic. Many people fish for perch and flounder, and you may see sharks and stingrays being caught. The dependably breezy waterfront park is the site of the annual Berkeley Kite Festival in July, when amateur and professional kite flyers compete. There is a 1.7-mile loop of paved walking trail and room to roam.

Staffed by volunteers, the Adventure Playground is open weekends for low-risk fun on fanciful forts, boats, and towers; a zipline; and supervised activities with hammer, saw, and paint (for ages 7 and up, and younger kids with parents). There is a nature center open weekends, restrooms, a grassy field, and a sea-view restaurant, too.

Tilden Regional Park (all ages)

In the hills above Berkeley, accessed from Spruce Street, from Centennial Drive, and from Grizzly Peak; (888) EBPARKS; www.ebparks.org.

A vast, green open space for hikers, bikers, and picnickers. Little kids like Little Farm, where they can pet and feed animals and birds, as well as ride ponies and a 1911 carousel. Lifeguards are on duty for swimming at the sandy beach, spring through fall, at Lake Anza. Take a ride on a miniature steam train through the redwoods and a tunnel. An easy 1-mile walk through woods and meadows circles Jewel Lake, leading to a marshy pond where frogs and ducks hold court.

Where to Eat

Caffe Trieste. 2500 San Pablo Ave., Berkeley; (510) 548-5198; www.caffetriesteberkeley .com. Listen to the Italian opera on the website to get a taste for this annex of the historic cafe in San Francisco's North Beach. Pastries, bagels, panini, sandwiches, and some of the world's best coffee drinks. A place to linger over the Sunday paper. (Be aware, it's next door to Good Vibrations, an adult accessories/erotica store.) $–$$

Fatapple's Restaurant and Bakery. 1346 Martin Luther King Jr. Way, Berkeley; (510) 526-2260. Wildly popular with families, for burgers, chili, potpies, pork barbecue sandwiches; in-house bakery makes great pies, cakes, and cookies. All at reasonable prices; takeout, too. $–$$

Homemade Café. Sacramento Street at Dwight Way, Berkeley; (510) 845-1940. Super-popular for breakfast all day and lunch; you may wait on weekends. Omelets, whole-wheat pecan waffles, blueberry pancakes, cinnamon swirl French toast, Italian eggs, espresso drinks. To the great home fries, add guacamole, cheese, pesto, salsa, and more toppings. $$–$$$

Long Life Vegi House. University Avenue at Shattuck Avenue, Berkeley; (510) 845-6072. Rub elbows with the locals who like good, inexpensive Chinese, vegetarian, and seafood specialties. Try the moo shu veggies. $

Mondo Gelato. 2106 Shattuck Ave., Berkeley; (510) 883-1568; www.mondogelato.com.

More than 50 flavors of gelato in a Nuevo-Italo gelateria. Choose from exotics like Nutella, Ferrero Rocher, honeymelon, pear, and pistachio, or traditional flavors such as strawberry, milk and dark chocolate, and lemon. $

Pizza Rustica Cafe and Tapas Bar. 5422 College Ave., Berkeley; (510) 654-1601. Some say this is the best pizza in town. $

Where to Stay

Doubletree Hotel & Executive Meeting Center Berkeley Marina. 200 Marina Blvd. on the waterfront, Berkeley; (510) 548-7920 or (800) 243-0625. A big hotel conveniently located to the entire Bay Area; AAA three-star rating. Each room has a balcony or patio. Two indoor pools, fitness center, guest laundry; **free** shuttle to BART, Amtrak, UC campus, and Berkeley shopping; restaurant; pets OK. $$$–$$$$

For More Information

Berkeley Convention and Visitors Bureau. 2015 Center St., ½ block west of the downtown Berkeley BART station, Berkeley; (510) 549-7040 or (800) 847-4823; recorded information on events and more: (510) 549-8710; www.visitberkeley.com.

Oakland

The main family attractions in the port city of Oakland are Jack London Square, Lake Merritt, a spectacular space and science center, and museums. Don't miss the multiethnic foods, exotic produce, snack foods, and live entertainment at Old Oakland Farmers' Market, year-round on Friday (across the street from Chinatown, 9th Street between Broadway and Clay; 510-745-7100). You can get to Oakland from San Francisco on BART and by ferry.

Lake Merritt and Children's Fairyland (ages 1 to 8)
Grand Avenue and Bellevue Street, Oakland; (510) 425-2259; www.fairyland.org. $$; kids 1 and under **free.**

For younger children, a three-dimensional nursery-rhyme playground, a merry-go-round, a puppet theater, train rides, and farm animals. A 3-mile paved path runs around the lake, and you can rent paddleboats, rowboats, and canoes ($$–$$$). Glide on the lake in an authentic gondola built by hand in Venice, complete with serenading gondolier ($$$$; 510-663-6603). On the lakeshore, the Camron-Stanford House is a beautifully restored museum of the Victorian period. You can take a guided tour on Wednesday and Sunday afternoons (1418 Lakeside Dr.; 510-444-1876; www.cshouse.org). Cost $$; seniors and children 12 to 18 $; kids 11 and under are **free.** **Free** to all on the first Sunday of every month.

Jack London Square

Broadway at Embarcadero, Oakland; (510) 814-6000; www.jacklondonsquare.com.

Named for the notorious and prolific adventure story author Jack London, who was a roustabout in Oakland early in the 20th century, the waterfront is a hodgepodge of old and new seafood restaurants and cafes, souvenir shops, a few historic sites, toy stores, bargain bookstores, and Cost Plus. The Sunday farmers' market is great fun, and so is the monthly antiques fair and the weekend artisan fairs. There is a waterfront walking path, a movieplex, and inexpensive hotels within easy reach of the Oakland airport. Ferries ply the bay between here and downtown San Francisco, Pier 39, Fisherman's Wharf, and Angel Island. On Friday afternoons the ferry becomes a pleasure cruiser, complete with music. The Jack London Water Taxi, a kind of covered barge, will take you on a cruise in the Oakland Estuary from the square to Alameda, dropping off at dockside restaurants (510-839-7572). Amtrak trains arrive and depart from here, too (www.amtrak.com).

The California Canoe and Kayak company is based here, too, where you can rent boats to paddle the estuary ($$$–$$$$; www.calkayak.com). And stop in at Timeout for Fun and Games, a small, friendly store chock-full of toys and games (510-444-4FUN). At Whales and Things, kids get lost in the aisles of fun and educational things related to wildlife, art, science, and ethnicity, from whale dolls to stickers, books, videos, toys, games, and cards (510-763-0585). Look for Tin Plate Junction on 4th Street, an emporium of toy and miniature trains (510-444-4780). A gigantic Barnes & Noble is open late and has a cafe with tables in a shady grove of trees. You can join a free, city-sponsored, guided Jack London History Walk (510-627-1670) or guide yourselves, following the bronze "wolf tracks" to trace the history of the square. At the Museum of Children's Art are art displays, open studios for kids to come in and create masterpieces, and a store selling art-related stuff for kids (560 2nd St., http://mocha.org).

USS *Potomac* (all ages)

540 Water St. at Jack London Square, Oakland; (510) 627-1215; www.usspotomac.org. Adults $$; ages 6 to 12 $; under 6 are free.

FDR's "Floating White House" is a sweet reminder of a beloved president who escaped humid Washington summers and the pressures of World War II and the Depression by cruising on this yacht, which has been beautifully restored. While browsing the artifacts of that tumultuous era, you can imagine FDR playing poker with his buddies and poring over his stamp collection. Elvis was another famous owner.

USS *Hornet* Museum (all ages)

Pier 3, Alameda Point, Alameda; (510) 521-8448; www.uss-hornet.org. Adults $$$; ages 5 to 17 $$; 4 and under are free.

A restored aircraft carrier with sea, air, and space exhibits focused on World War II and Apollo moon landings. On view are fighter jets, propeller and jet helicopters, and more. Most of the docents are Navy vets, many were naval aviators, and some served on the ship in World War II or in Vietnam. On the third Saturday of every month, Living Ship Day re-creates life at sea, with planes being moved by giant elevators to the flight deck, PA announcements echoing throughout the hangar bays, and guest speakers sharing their sea stories.

Chabot Space and Science Center (ages 4 and up)

10000 Skyline Blvd., Oakland; (510) 336-7300; www.chabotspace.org. $$, with separate admission to theater and planetarium.

Plan most of a day for the huge educational center with one of the largest public telescopes in the United States, the most advanced planetarium in the world, and an IMAX theater showing fabulous films of outer space, the ocean floor, volcanoes, and more. Explore planetary landscapes, meteorites, the sun, and the solar system; build a telescope; see a lunar lander. The amazing telescopes are free for viewing on weekend nights, and on nights of meteor showers, lunar eclipses, and other astronomical events. Be an astronaut or an engineer on a simulated space mission at the Challenger Learning Center. Take a break on 6 acres of nature trails and at the Celestial Cafe, an indoor/outdoor cafe serving simple, hearty American food, and slurpees! Call ahead for special events. Back home, kids can interact with the center online at the Virtual Science Center.

Lake Chabot (all ages)

In the hills above San Leandro (see website for directions); (888) EBPARKS; www.ebparks.org/parks/lake_chabot. $ parking.

A tree-lined lake for nonmotorized boating and fishing for bass and trout. You can rent rowboats, canoes, pedal boats, kayaks, Duffy boats, and boats with electric trolling motors. Walking and biking on the 15-mile lakeshore trail, plus paved walking paths; dogs are okay. There are also a small cafe, bait and tackle shop, picnic sites, and playgrounds.

Rockridge (all ages)

From the beginning of College Avenue at Broadway, up College to the Oakland/Berkeley border.

Spend an afternoon strolling, noshing, and shopping in a charming, leafy neighborhood that seems lost in the early 20th century. Shop the fresh produce, fruit, cheese, and bakery vendors at the pleasant, open-air Market Hall; peruse the spectacular tile murals at the BART station; buy outdoor- and nature-oriented books and gifts at Sierra Club Books. Grab burgers at Rocky's, Chicago-style pizza at Zachary's, satay at Sabuy Sabuy Thai, toys and games at Rockridge Kids, and a treat at Buttercup Bakery.

Oakland Museum (all ages)

1000 Oak St. at 10th Street, Oakland; (888) 625-6873; www.museumca.org. $$; kids 6 and under free.

Not just another boring museum, this one is a playful construction of three tiers topped by a 4-acre roof garden of outdoor sculpture and a koi pond. The open layout makes this a child-friendly, comfortable place to see contemporary and vintage California art. Stop at the video stations to watch Native American demos and interviews with artists. A cafe serves sandwiches, salads, and yummy desserts.

Oakland Aviation Museum (all ages)

8252 Earhart Rd., Building 621, at the Oakland International Airport; (510) 638-7100; www .westernaerospacemuseum.org. Adults $$; ages 5 and under are free.

Among the fabulous aircraft in a lofty hangar are a giant flying boat used in the movie *Raiders of the Lost Ark,* a Lockheed Electra similar to the one flown by Amelia Earhart, an A-6 fighter, bombers, and a couple of dozen others. Artifacts, memorabilia, and photos trace the history of aviation.

Redwood Regional Park (all ages)

7687 Redwood Rd., Oakland; (510) 562-7275; www.ebparks.org.

In a hidden forest not far from downtown, trails wind through lush redwood, oak, and bay laurel woods. From the French Trail, connect to the easy East Bay Skyline National Trail for high views. See several park entrance locations on the website. Adjacent to this park is Roberts Redwood Park, where picnic sites, a baseball diamond, a playground, and grassy fields attract families on every sunny day.

Oakland Zoo (all ages)

In Knowland Park, 9777 Golf Links Rd., Oakland; (510) 632-9525; www.oaklandzoo.org. Ages 2 and up $$; under age 2 are free; parking $.

Well over 400 creatures in natural settings, from camels, lions, and elephants to meerkats, giraffes, chimps, exotic birds, tigers, and many more. Check the website for film times and special events. Within the main zoo, the Children's Zoo is beloved by little kids who hang out on the play structures and investigate bugs, snakes, frogs, turtles, otters, and spiders. Also here are inexpensive rides, including a mini train, the Sky Ride chairlift, and a merry-go-round.

Where to Eat

Flippers Gourmet Burgers. 2060 Mountain Blvd., Montclair Village; (510) 339-2082. A favorite of kids who like the burgers (both meat and veggie), sandwiches, salads, the booths, and the fish tank. Flippers is one of dozens of restaurants within a quaint, 4-block village of shops and eateries. After lunch, on the same block, drop in at Le Bonbon for chocolates, or the Montclair Malt Shop for sundaes. $

House of Chicken 'n Waffles. Jack London Square, 444 Embarcadero at Broadway,

Oakland; (510) 836-4446. In a very popular, retro-diner-style restaurant, grab a booth or counter stools for down-home soul food: fried chicken, fluffy waffles, candied yams, corn bread, greens, grits, biscuits, and homemade pies and cakes, accompanied by '60s and Motown recorded music, gospel on Sunday mornings. Open to midnight on weeknights; to 4 a.m. on weekends. $–$$

Il Pescatore. 57 Jack London Sq., Oakland; (510) 465-2188. Overlooking the Oakland Estuary, a pleasant place for fresh seafood and Italian-American food. $–$$

Ratto's. Corner of 9th and Washington Streets, Oakland; (510) 832-6503. Founded in 1897, a turn-of-the-20th-century-style grocery store filled with wooden bins, barrels, and jars offering products in bulk and prepared foods. Browse the fantastical assortment of gourmet deli items, homemade pastas and soups, imported foodstuffs, cheeses, oils, and spices; then order sandwiches to eat at outdoor tables or take away. $

Red Tractor Cafe. 5634 College Ave., across from Market Hall in the Rockridge district; (510) 595-3500. Down-home comfort food, from macaroni and cheese to sumptuous meat loaf and garlic mashed potatoes, barbecued chicken, and chicken-fried steak and gravy. Kids get crayons and Big Bird plates. Lunch, dinner, weekend brunch. $

Where to Stay

Executive Inn and Suites. 1755 Embarcadero, Oakland; (510) 536-6633 or (800) 346-6331; www.executiveinnoakland.com. A sheltered swimming pool with a view of the Oakland Estuary; private balconies; complimentary, expanded continental breakfast; a fitness room; guest laundry; and **free** Internet access make this tops for families. All 226 rooms and suites were recently redecorated. Add to that the **free** shuttle to Oakland International Airport, Jack London Square, Alameda, the San Francisco ferry, BART, and Amtrak. A typical 500-square-foot suite has a sitting area, refrigerator, microwave, and 2 queen-size beds. Smaller, more basic rooms also have 2 queens. $$–$$$$.

Waterfront Plaza Hotel Oakland. 10 Washington St., Oakland; (800) 729-3638; www.jdvhotels.com. One of the fabulous Joie de Vivre boutique hotels. At Jack London Square, 143 newly decorated, nautical-theme rooms and suites, some with 2 queen-size beds, balconies, fireplaces, Nintendo, and bay views, with breakfast buffet. Fitness center, valet parking, pool/sauna, Wi-Fi, private boat dock, restaurant. $$$–$$$$

For More Information

Oakland Convention and Visitors Bureau. 474 14th St., Oakland; (510) 839-9000; www.oaklandcvb.com.

San Jose

Families visiting in the Bay Area may have heard of California's Great America theme park, but many are unaware that several other fantastic family-oriented attractions are located in the South Bay. Your big and little cyber-nerds can spend their time in three dazzling technology museums: the Tech, the Intel, and the Children's Museum. In the main downtown park, Plaza de Cesar Chavez, adjacent to the Tech, the Museum of Art, and the Fairmont Hotel, kids splash and play in the 4-foot-tall water spouts, and tuckered tourists rest on the lawns and benches. In the trendy arts and dining hub, SoFA (South 1st Street), it's fun to explore sidewalk cafes, galleries, and bookstores. A refurbished "Old Town" district downtown, San Pedro Square is a dining mecca with delightful shade trees, landscaping, and sidewalk cafes. Kids run up and down, and parents push strollers on 3 miles of landscaped paths in Guadalupe River Park; look for the carousel and a visitor center in the south end of the park at Arena Green.

Near downtown, between Jackson and Taylor, and 1st and 7th Streets, Japantown is lined with historic buildings, Japanese groceries, restaurants, and shops; come to see exotic produce at the Sunday Farmers' Market (www.japantownsanjose.org). Adding to San Jose's value as a family destination are a water park, the urban oasis of Kelley Park, an eerie mystery mansion, and one of the premier Egyptian museums in the world.

Annual events that families like best are the Japanese Obon Festival in July, the Cinco de Mayo parade and festival in May, and Hoi Tet—the Vietnamese New Year celebration—in February. The wildly colorful International Folklórico Festival is held in May at the Mexican Heritage Plaza, a lively headquarters for Hispanic music, art, and performing-arts events all year (www .mhcviva.org). In December an incredible "Christmas in the Park" at Plaza de Cesar Chavez features 400 decorated trees and an animated village and nutcracker display; a block away, an outdoor ice-skating rink is set up from late November through mid-January.

Children's Discovery Museum of San Jose (ages 3 to 12)
180 Woz Way, San Jose; (408) 298-5437; www.cdm.org. $$.

In a bright purple building, the largest hands-on science facility in the West is loaded with educational and fun activities for children through grade-school age: drive a fire truck; make tortillas; climb on a movable jungle gym; invent thingamajigs; crawl through tunnels; play on computers; conduct an orchestra; walk through an ambulance; get your face painted.

Light spills in through 2-story glass walls onto indoor city streetscapes complete with traffic lights. Get here early (the facility opens at 10 a.m.) to avoid crowds and noise, pick up a map to the 150 exhibits, and let the kids go. The museum shop sells great toys, games, and puzzles. Get snacks and light meals in the Kids' Cafe, or have a picnic and tumble on the grass in adjacent Discovery Meadow.

The Tech Museum of Innovation (ages 5 and up)
201 South Market St., San Jose; (408) 294-TECH; www.thetech.org. $$; kids under 3 are admitted free.

Silicon Valley is the birthplace of the personal computer and world headquarters for technology-oriented businesses. It's no wonder that their dazzling mango-colored edifice of learning and tech fun is state of the art. More than 100 exhibits are mostly interactive, including experimenting with the virtual bobsled simulator, piloting a real robot on the ocean floor, floating in a jet pack like the astronauts, designing a roller coaster, making your own movie, and much more—an IMAX theater, a Robot Zoo, computer games, demos of high-tech inventions, and a cafe. For the techie in your family, this could be an all-day affair.

Intel Museum (ages 7 and up)

Take the Montague Expressway exit off Highway 101 to 2200 Mission College Blvd., Santa Clara; (408) 765-0503; www.intel.com/museum. Free.

Learn about the life and times of the microprocessor chip through hands-on exhibits and demos that make tech science comprehensible to all of us. You can also find out about clean rooms, transistors, and memory technology, and try out the hands-on computer-based learning lab. The gift shop is great fun, with techie souvenirs, clothing, and semiconductor jewelry.

San Jose–Area Parks

- **Guadalupe River Park and Gardens,** west of Highway 87, with attractions around Spring Street and Taylor, the Alameda and Delmas, and Woz Way—see map on website; (408) 277-5904; www.grpg.org. A 3-mile-long park along the Guadalupe River. More than 3,700 varieties of roses; playground of net structures; shaded picnic area; carousel ($); toddlers' play lot, a refreshment kiosk, and restrooms. Visitor center is on the north side of Santa Clara Street at the river, in the pocket park of Arena Green across from the San Jose Arena. A good place to start the river walk is at the Children's Discovery Museum on Woz Way.

- **Kelley Park,** 1300 Senter Rd.; (408) 277-3000. Happy Hollow Zoo, a miniature train ride, the **free** Historical Museum, an outdoor complex of Victorian buildings, a trolley barn and firehouse with old engines, all laid out on beautiful Coyote Creek. Younger children love the merry-go-round and the petting zoo. Parking $$; zoo and rides $$; under 2 **free.**

- **Lake Cunningham Regional Park,** Capitol Expressway and Tully Road; (408) 277-4319. Adjacent to Raging Waters, picnic areas, windsurfing, bike paths, marina with pedal boat rentals, and fishing. Parking $; boat rentals $$$.

- **Los Gatos Creek Trail,** above Los Gatos at Lexington Reservoir; (415) 691-1200. For biking, walking, and skating, 9 miles of trail along a riparian corridor.

- **Castle Rock State Park,** 15000 Skyline Blvd., Los Gatos; (408) 867-2952. More than 3,000 acres of semiwilderness with big views, waterfalls, forests, meadows, hiking and horse trails, picnic areas. Parking $$.

Winchester Mystery House (ages 6 and up)
525 South Winchester Blvd., San Jose; (408) 247-2000; www.winchestermysteryhouse.com. Ages 13 and up $$$; ages 6 to 12 $$; under 6 are **free.**

In a Victorian mansion with 160 rooms, doors open into blank walls, stairways lead nowhere, and ghosts and spirits are afoot in a strange and spooky atmosphere. Also here is a large collection of antique Tiffany glass windows. The house tour (a mile long) is guided, yet you can wander the vast, glorious gardens on your own. Come at Halloween for entertainment and flashlight tours.

Rosicrucian Egyptian Museum (all ages)
1342 Naglee Ave., San Jose; (408) 238-9900. $$; kids 5 and under **free.**

Do you love your mummy? A large collection of fascinating stuff: Sphinxes, temples, chariots, statues from ancient Thebes, gods of the Nile, a pharaoh's tomb, and delightfully scary, shrouded mummies are a few of the artifacts and reproductions here, the largest Egyptian museum in the West. Kids love it. Little ones can run around in the gardens.

Raging Waters (ages 5 and up)
2333 South White Rd., San Jose; (408) 238-9900; www.rwsplash.com. Open mid-May to mid-September. Kids 48 inches and above $$$$; under 48 inches $$$; late afternoon discounts; kids 2 and under **free.**

A 23-acre water park with more than 30 exciting slides, a huge wave pool, the Pirate's Cove water fort, and the Dragon's Den. The little ones have their own wading pools and minislides; big kids take off in the Barracuda Bluster! Adjacent to the water park, Lake Cunningham Regional Park offers picnic areas, windsurfing, bike paths, fishing, and a marina with pedal boat, canoe, and sailboat rentals.

California's Great America (all ages)
Great America Parkway, Santa Clara; (408) 988-1776; www.cagreatamerica.com. $$$$; ages 2 and under **free.**

Plan one long day here to enjoy more than 50 rides, coasters, and live entertainment. This is the only theme park in the state with a water park—Boomerang Bay has 30 water slides, lagoons, rushing rivers, and surfable waves (in the Tazmanian Tornado, you slide through a completely dark, 300-foot cavern and rocket out into a funnel that tosses your raft around). Toddlers like Kookaburra Cay, a quiet, shallow pool with waterfalls. The big thrills are the roller coasters—the Vortex, a rare stand-up coaster; SURVIVOR The Ride, the world's first reality roller coaster, based on the hit TV series, which rocks and spins riders past fiery torches and tribal masks; and Invertigo, the first inverted face-to-face coaster in North America, propelling riders through a 180-degree turn with double inverted sidewinders and a 72-foot-high vertical loop before rocketing to the top of the second 138-foot lift and back! FireFall sends 40 passengers to 60 feet, then subjects them to high-speed inversions and in-your-face fire and water special effects. For smaller kids and less brave adults, there are many easy, fun rides, too, like Rugrats Runaway Reptar, Psycho Mouse, and the pint-size Taxi Jam coaster. The fancy double-decker carousel is the tallest in the

Highlights of **Stanford University**

In Palo Alto, bordered by El Camino Real, Stanford Avenue, Junipero Serra Boulevard, and Sand Hill Road. Visitor center at 551 Serra Mall, Memorial Auditorium Lobby; (650) 723-2560; www.stanford.edu. Bring your bikes to cruise the rambling, tree-shaded campus, which is studded with lovely Spanish colonial landmark buildings. Take the elevator to the top of 285-foot-tall Hoover Tower for the view, and to get your bearings. You can picnic in the Oval, hike in the foothills, walk and bike scenic paths, and enjoy the gardens and the dining options. I find that eateries on college campuses are among the least expensive and most fun and satisfying places for families to dine; check the website for locations and descriptions of several food outlets on campus.

- **Cantor Arts Center.** Lomita Drive and Museum Way; (650) 723-4177; www .museum.stanford.edu. Treasures from Renaissance paintings to African masks, and the largest collection of Rodin bronze sculptures outside Paris. You can look at them while having snacks or lunch on the patio of the Cool Café. On the museum's website, choose from several guided tours, to the Papua New Guinea sculpture garden and to the extensive outdoor collection of 20th-century sculpture in the quad and south campus areas—a way for parents to drink in some culture while kids get fresh air and an easy walk.

- **Stone River.** Across from the Cantor, 128 tons of sandstone blocks compose world-famous artist Andy Goldsworthy's impressive snaking sculpture. He used salvaged pieces from buildings that toppled in the 1906 and 1989 earthquakes.

- **Linear Accelerator Center.** 2575 Sand Hill Rd., Menlo Park; (650) 926-2204; www.slac.stanford.edu. Call ahead to book the free 2-hour tour of the accelerator, the Gallery (offering an incredible photo op of the 2-mile tunnel), the Collider, and more. The Klystron Gallery is the longest building in the world, housing 2 miles of cutting-edge scientific machines and devices. If you have children (ages about 11 and up) who are mad scientists and interested in subatomic collisions, synchroton radiation, antimatter, quarks, and leptons, they will love this place.

western states and may be the tallest in the world. One admission price gets you on all the rides and into live and filmed extravaganzas. See IMAX movies, spectacular ice-skating shows, rock bands, Dora the Explorer Sing-Along Adventure, Hip-Hop Explosion, a magic show, Backyard Circus, and more live entertainment.

New in the park is Planet Snoopy with rides for little ones, and hugs from Snoopy, Charlie Brown, and their friends. Also new is *Snoopy Rocks,* a 35-minute ice-skating show.

Santana Row (all ages)

400 South Winchester Blvd., San Jose; (408) 551-4643; www.santanarow.com.

A unique, European-style arcade of upscale shops and cafes makes this a nice stop for a couple of hours. Between the sidewalks, a wide, tree-shaded park is filled with fountains and water features, gardens, and 16 chess tables with pieces provided. Sit in an outdoor cafe, browse the Sunday farmers' market, or catch an outdoor movie or live music in the summertime. As for the glittering boutiques and shops, either endanger your credit cards or limit yourselves to window-shopping.

Where to Eat

Maggiano's Little Italy. 3055 Olin Ave. in Santana Row, San Jose; (408) 423-8973; www .maggianos.com. Luscious traditional Italian food in an upscale, comfortable environment, from meatball sandwiches to chicken Parmesan, gnocchi, ravioli, pizza, many pastas, and much more. Don't miss the Family Dinner menu that offers large portions to share. $–$$$

Old Spaghetti Factory House. 51 North San Pedro Ave., San Jose; (408) 288-7488. Good, traditional Italian food; fun, casual surroundings. $–$$

Original Joe's. 301 South 1st St., San Jose; (408) 292-7030; www.originaljoes.com. Owned by the Rocca family since the early 1970s. American comfort food in large portions for lunch and dinner: steaks, burgers, chicken, pasta. For breakfast, the famous menu item is Joe's Special, a hearty spinach-beef-onions-eggs concoction. $–$$

Peggy Sue's. 185 Park Ave. across from the Tech, and at 29 North San Pedro St. in San Pedro Square, San Jose; (408) 294-0252. In classic '50s-style diners, thick shakes, juicy burgers, soup, salad, sandwiches; breakfast, too. $

Peninsula Fountain & Grill. 566 Emerson St., a block south of University, Palo Alto;

(650) 323-3131. A classic soda fountain and '50s diner serving meat loaf, chicken potpie, burgers, pies, pancakes, milk shakes, banana splits; breakfast, lunch, and dinner. $

Sam's Bar-B-Que. 1110 South Bascom Ave., San Jose; (408) 297-9151; www.sams bbq.com. Beloved by the locals and serving barbecued brisket, ribs, chicken, and burgers. A model train entertains the youngsters. $

Where to Stay

Holiday Inn San Jose. 1740 North 1st St., San Jose; (877) 863-4780, (408) 793-3300; www.holidayinn.com. A 512-room, newly renovated hotel near main San Jose attractions, with an airport shuttle, a pool and garden courtyard, a fitness center that was updated in 2008; a parcourse, an on-site jogging path, some refrigerators, and a coffee shop and pool cafe. Kids 12 and under eat **free** from the childrens' menu when accompanied by a family member dining from the regular menu; limit 4 kids per family. $$–$$$$

Residence Inn San Jose South. 6111 San Ignacio Ave., San Jose; (408) 226-7676; www .marriott.com. Apartment-like 1- and 2-bedroom suites and studios with kitchenettes, living areas with sofa beds; swimming pool, video games, exercise room, sports court, laundry; near restaurants, groceries, and freeway. **Free** full breakfast, afternoon snacks, evening cookies, and juices and coffee all day; **free** parking. $$–$$$$

Wild Palms Hotel. 910 East Fremont Ave., Sunnyvale; (800) 538-1600; www.jdvhotels .com. New owner, new Mediterranean look with courtyards, murals, and mosaics. Complete renovation of 208 compact "bungalow-style" rooms (some with 2 doubles) done up in fresh colors, with refrigerators, coffeemakers, Wi-Fi. Suites have a king bed and a living room with sofa bed, 2 TVs, armchairs, and oversize desks. Complimentary breakfast, heated pool, poolside office cabanas, fitness room. Great value in pricey Silicon Valley. $$–$$$

For More Information

San Jose Convention and Visitors Bureau. 408 Almaden Blvd., San Jose; (408) 295-9600 or (888) SAN-JOSE (recorded events: 408-295-2265); www.sanjose.org. Ask about travel packages that include lodgings and admission to local attractions and events.

Santa Clara Convention and Visitors Bureau. 1850 Warburton Ave., Santa Clara; (408) 244-9660; www.santaclara.org.

Valley Transportation Authority (VTA). (408) 321-2300; www.vta.org. Light-rail service in San Jose, Santa Clara, and throughout Silicon Valley, and historic trolleys downtown.

Bay Area Rapid Transit (BART). (510) 441-2278; www.bart.gov. High-speed trains between major cities in the Bay Area, including Santa Clara.

San Francisco

Families who may not have been to San Francisco for a few years will find it more magical than ever before and worth planning for extra vacation days. The entire bayside from the Golden Gate Bridge to beyond AT&T baseball park has been transformed into one of the most spectacular and multifaceted city waterfronts in the world. Footpaths and natural areas have been restored at Crissy Field, a new indoor/outdoor marketplace is open at the Ferry Building, and one of the country's most fetching baseball parks sits right on the bay.

Old favorite attractions are the cable cars, Alcatraz, Golden Gate Park, and Chinatown. More than 200 parks and playgrounds are places to let off steam and have a picnic. Kids love playing on Marina Green and buying souvenirs at Fisherman's Wharf, while parents like the romantic Victorian neighborhoods, the museums, and the choice of over 3,500 restaurants—more per capita than any other American city. A visit to San Francisco is not complete without a ferry ride around the bay and a walk across the Golden Gate Bridge!

South of Market Street at Yerba Buena Gardens is a massive complex designed for children and families: a rooftop play and learning garden; the Zeum, a tech-based visual, performing, and media arts center for older kids; an ice-skating rink; a bowling center; a historic carousel in a glass house; and looming above all this, Metreon is a 3-story block-buster of a family entertainment emporium.

Only locals know of the more than 300 hidden stairways that wind up and down the hills, through forest glades and lush gardens. With a little investigation your family will discover the stairways and other hidden treasures, such as mysterious Chinese temples smoky with incense, a museum of antique nickelodeon games, and a students' cafe with knockout views and yummy, inexpensive food.

Walking is the best way to explore Italian North Beach, the multiethnic Mission District, Japantown, and Chinatown, as well as the neighborhoods inhabited by the "Painted Ladies," as the city's thousands of early 20th-century mansions are called.

Local mariners share the bay with visitors on sightseeing sails, whale-watching cruises, and deep-sea fishing expeditions. Whale-boaters row, kayakers paddle, and flotillas of

SAN FRANCISCO

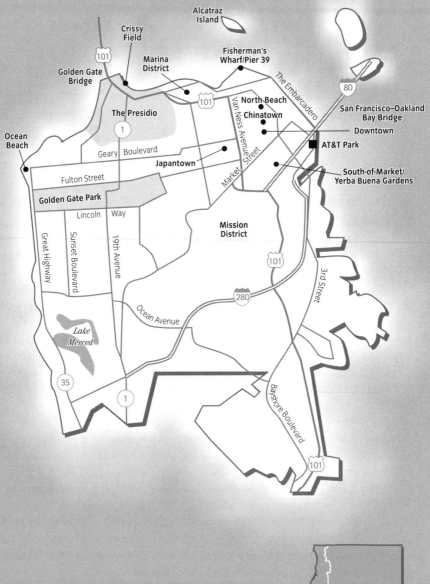

Alcatraz
Island

Crissy
Field

Fisherman's
Wharf/Pier 39

101

Marina
District

Golden Gate
Bridge

101

North Beach

San Francisco–Oakland
Bay Bridge

Chinatown

80

The Presidio

1

Downtown

Ocean
Beach

Van Ness Avenue

Geary   Boulevard

AT&T Park

Japantown

Market Street

South-of-Market/
Yerba Buena Gardens

Fulton Street

Golden Gate Park

Lincoln   Way

Mission
District

Great Highway

Sunset Boulevard

19th Avenue

3rd Street

Ocean Avenue

280

101

Lake
Merced

35

1

Bayshore Boulevard

101

windsurfers flit like butterflies. A new landing and **free** public boat dock have opened at Pier 1½ on the Embarcadero, for use by sea kayakers and recreational boaters; plans are under way for Bay Quackers water taxi service between here and Hyde Street Harbor at Fisherman's Wharf.

Parking is scarce and expensive, and streets are congested throughout the city, so preplanning and lots of walking is advised, with the occasional use of a taxi to get from one district to another. Bay Area Rapid Transit (BART), the clean, safe, and on-time subway and commuter rail system, connects the city with the East and South Bays and the San Francisco International Airport. "Muni," the streetcar and bus system, is neither clean, safe, nor on time; the refurbished vintage streetcars running along the Embarcadero are the exceptions. Bicycles are more popular than ever; parking garages and ferries all have bike parking.

Bring light jackets for the city's mild but changeable marine climate. Summer mornings and evenings can be chilly due to foggy fingers blowing in through the Golden Gate, the city's natural air conditioner. Fall and spring are the best seasons to visit, when days are sparkling clear and warm, and the summer crowds are gone.

Marina District

Marina Green (all ages)

Along Marina Boulevard between Scott and Webster.

A vast greensward on the edge of the bay and a yacht harbor, this is a popular place for jogging, walking, and kite flying. You can get picnic goodies at the Safeway across the street. On weekends and on most breezy days, watch spectacular kites fly, with the spectacular Golden Gate Bridge as a backdrop—from multitiered, champion acrobatic kites to the handmade versions. The **free** Family Day Kite Festival in September showcases all forms of kiting, from kite flying to kite boarding, kite boating, and kite making, while exhibitors present wind and renewable energy and eco-friendly products (415-383-0500; www .fdkf.org). The St. Francis Yacht Club's Big Boat Series usually falls on the same weekend.

The Exploratorium (ages 3 to 16)

3601 Lyon St. in the Palace of Fine Arts; (415) 397-5673; www.exploratorium.edu. Ages 5 and up $$$; ages 4 and under are free; Tactile Dome $$$.

Called the best science museum in the world, the Exploratorium is housed in the Palace of Fine Arts, a fanciful Greco-Romanesque remnant from the Panama-Pacific Exposition of 1915. Here kids and adults are encouraged to play with and explore more than 700 interactive exhibits. It's fun to bend lights, step into a giant kaleidoscope, fly without leaving the ground, touch a tornado, make bubbles 3 feet across, and create on computers. The Playsquare has climbing structures and role-playing venues for toddlers, as well as a place for infants to play with mirrors and experimental toys. Reservations are necessary for the Tactile Dome, a labyrinthine, pitch-black, crawl-through experience of a lifetime! (Call

415-561-0362; not recommended for children under 7.) Special exhibitions have featured animation, digital technology, TV editing, space, weather, music, the physics of toys, the brain, the environment, and dozens more subjects. Call or check the website for the many special events throughout the year.

When you're all reeling from cerebral stimulation, grab a snack in the indoor cafe or a hot dog at the outside food cart, take a walk around the lake, and relax on the lawns. On weekends you'll see wedding parties in full regalia, having their photos taken in the elegant pink rotunda of the Palace of Fine Arts.

Not far from the Palace are 20 brand-new outdoor interactive science exhibits and artworks at Fort Mason. Among the fun and educational installations is the Bridge Thermometer, where the Golden Gate Bridge is transformed into an instrument that lets visitors measure changing temperature patterns; the Tasting the Tides site, and the Wind Arrows wind observatory.

Fort Mason (all ages)
On the east end of the Marina yacht harbor at Bay and Franklin Streets; (415) 441-3400; www.fortmason.org.

A sea-breezy complex of former military buildings on the waterfront, where cultural events are held on weekends. There are small museums and frequent weekend festivals; parking is **free** for up to 12 hours, depending on the parking spot location. The Children's Art Center in Building C offers drop-in and extended art workshops such as clay, printing, and painting for children 27 months to 10 years (415-771-0292; www.childrensartcenter.org).

Check the website for performances by the Young Performers Theatre and other family-oriented troupes. Every year the San Francisco Blues Festival (415-826-6837) is held on the lawns above Fort Mason. There are easy-to-find public restrooms in each of the Fort Mason buildings.

Cooks and Company here is a terrific take-out counter for sandwiches, soups, and scrumptious desserts; picnic tables are just outside, or walk to adjacent Marina Green.

Crissy Field (all ages)
Old Mason Street off Marina Boulevard, at the east end of the Marina; (415) 561-7690; www .crissyfield.org. Free.

Restored to its original duney state, this is a nice place to walk, take photos of the Golden Gate Bridge, sit on a narrow beach, fly a kite, bird-watch in the wetlands, in-line skate or stroll on a 1.3-mile trail, and enjoy watching boating and windsurfing activity offshore. Stop in at the Gulf of the Farallones Marine Sanctuary visitor center to see photos and exhibits of sea creatures, including great white sharks, and touch marine animals in a simulated tide pool. The Warming Hut Cafe and Bookstore is a cozy spot where you can stop for drinks, light meals, and snacks (415-561-3040). Let's Be Frank hot dog cart is often on hand here, too, selling dogs made from special Hearst Ranch beef; try the spicy Devil Dogs, hot Italian sausages with hot pickles and hot peppers. You can walk from here to Fort Point, and on the Golden Gate Promenade, all the way around the Embarcadero to AT&T Park and beyond.

Golden Gate Promenade/Embarcadero (all ages)
Along the north and east waterfronts, from Fort Point under the Golden Gate Bridge to
AT&T Park at China Basin, about 5 miles.

A wide sidewalk perfect for in-line skates, baby strollers, and your feet. Cruise along
through Crissy Field, past the small-craft harbor and the Marina to Aquatic Park, Ghirardelli
Square and the Cannery, past Fisherman's Wharf to Pier 39. Continue along the commercial piers to the Ferry Building and Justin Herman Plaza, beyond the Oakland Bay Bridge

Where to Go in San Francisco

The most popular family attractions are located in these districts of the city.

Marina District (Bordered by San Francisco Bay, Van Ness and Pacific Ave-
nues, and the Presidio.)
- Marina Green
- The Exploratorium
- Fort Mason
- The Presidio
- Fort Point
- Crissy Field

Waterfront (From the Marina east along the Embarcadero.)
- Hyde Street Pier and Maritime
  National Historical Park
- Fisherman's Wharf
- Maritime Museum
- Ferry Plaza
- Pier 39
- Alcatraz
- Bay Ferries

North Beach (The old Italian district, bordered roughly by Broadway, Mason,
Kearny, Lombard, and Telegraph Hill.)
- Washington Square
- Coit Tower
- Italian restaurants
- North Beach Museum

Golden Gate Park/Ocean Beach
- Japanese Tea Garden
- Land's End
- Conservatory of Flowers
- Japan Center
- J-Pop Center
- Academy of Sciences
- Beach Chalet
- San Francisco Zoo
- deYoung Museum

South-of-Market/South Beach
- Yerba Buena Gardens
- MOMA
- Mission District
- Zeum/Rooftop
- Metreon
- AT&T Park

Chinatown
- Chinese Historical Society Museum
- Chinese restaurants and shops

and the outdoor cafes of South Beach, to AT&T Park, enjoying the fishing piers, benches, historic markers, restaurants, and rest stops along the way. Take the F Line trolley back from Market Street to Fisherman's Wharf.

City Tours for Families

- **City Guides Tours.** Main Library, 100 Larkin St. at Grove, Civic Center; (415) 557-4266; www.sfcityguides.org. Free guided and narrated walking tours including Chinatown, Victorian landmarks, Japantown, earthquake and fire history, ghosts, Golden Gate Bridge, gold rush history, Mission District murals, Telegraph Hill, and more.

- **Fire Engine Tour.** Beach Street at Columbus Avenue; (415) 333-7077; www.fireenginetours.com. Outfitted in firefighters' jackets, climb aboard a beautiful 1955 red fire engine for a 75-minute city tour and ride across the Golden Gate Bridge into Sausalito. The lively guides keep up a steady narration of sights and history and lead the group in rousing songs. My grandkids absolutely loved it. $$$–$$$$.

- **Wok Wiz Tours.** (415) 981-8989 or (650) 355-9657; www.wokwiz.com. The ultimate expert on Chinatown, high-energy Shirley Fong-Torres conducts fabulous, fun tours. Choose from I Can't Believe I Ate My Way Through Chinatown; Ciao Chow!, a 2-hour walk highlighting Italian and Asian history; general Chinatown tours; and more. $$$$.

- **Do-It-Yourself Walking Tours.** (415) 346-2000; www.sfhistory.org. Stop in the visitors bureau (see "For More Information" at the end of this chapter) or at the Museum of the City of San Francisco at Pier 45 for maps of great walking routes around the city. A popular trek is the Barbary Coast Trail, a 3.8-mile walk marked with bronze medallions and arrows set in the sidewalk.

- **Mr. Toad's Tours.** From Fisherman's Wharf; (877) 4MR-TOAD; www.mrtoadstours.com. An 80-minute "Hop Around the City" tour, a 2.5-hour "Postcard San Francisco" tour, or a 75-minute "San Francisco by Night" tour, in 10-passenger, propane-powered vintage touring cars.

- **Bay City Bike.** From Fisherman's Wharf; (415) 346-2453; www.baycitybike.com. Rent kids' bikes, trailers, baby seats, and half-wheelers, or take the 9-mile, easy guided ride across the Golden Gate Bridge to Sausalito, with a ferry ride back. Including helmet, sightseeing stops, ferry ticket, and snacks, the cost is about $40.

The Presidio of San Francisco (all ages)

Near the Golden Gate, bordered by Baker Beach, the bay, Lyon Street, and West Pacific Avenue; (415) 561-5300. Maps and information at the Presidio Museum, corner of Lincoln Boulevard and Funston Avenue; (415) 561-4323; www.nps.gov/prsf. Free admission. Free PresidiGo shuttle.

These 1,480 acres of wooded highlands, beaches, and vintage buildings were used by the military for more than 200 years, from the Spanish and Mexican armies to the US Army, from Civil War times to the 1990s. Now part of the National Park System, this magnificent park is threaded by quiet roads and paths for walking and bike riding. You can easily spend a day here, starting with a ranger-led tour or a self-guided expedition of the museums and architectural relics, from 17th-century bronze Spanish cannons to Civil War barracks, pre-earthquake Victorians, adobe walls built by the Spanish conquistadors, and picturesque rows of Queen Anne–style officers' homes. Call for tour reservations: (415) 556-0865. Easy 2-hour walks focus on history, architecture, nature, or historical personalities.

In the San Francisco Film Centre here, the Dish Cafe is a good place for a casual breakfast, lunch, and picnic items. Organic everything, from coffee to fresh juices, homemade soups, pastries, minipizzas, and sandwiches (415-561-2336; closed weekends).

Secluded trails wind through cypress, pine, and eucalyptus forests. Picnic tables are found in sunny meadows, hidden in lush rhododendron groves, or perched on breezy headlands with sea views. A meandering creek and a spring-fed pond are habitats for hundreds of birds. Along the southern border of the Presidio is an excellent playground and playing fields at Julius Kahn Park. At the Letterman Digital Arts Center campus, lawns, benches, and a pond are great for bridge viewing and resting. Near the Arguello entrance, the easy Ecology Trail meanders through a grove of redwoods past meadows dotted with wildflowers. Start from the patio atop Inspiration Point and amble down to the visitor center, stopping off at El Polin Spring to picnic and play in a secluded greensward. While at the center, pick up the *Kids on Trails* brochure, detailing walks for ages 5 to 9 (www.presidio.gov/kids/trails).

On the west side of the Presidio, Baker Beach is unsafe for swimming but great for sunning and shore fishing, and there are World War II bunkers to explore. Smaller, more sheltered beaches and a waterfront promenade are found at Crissy Field beside the bay—also part of the Presidio.

Walt Disney Family Museum (all ages)

104 Montgomery St., San Francisco; (415) 345 6800; www.waltdisney.org. $$$ adults, $$ ages 6 to 17.

Ten colorful galleries focus on the life of Walt Disney himself, from his early years to Hollywood in the 1920s and his technological innovations. Walt lovers will enjoy seeing Oscar statuettes, early drawings of Mickey, animation cels of *Bambi* and *Pinocchio*, plus interactive displays and 200 video monitors, a theater, and temporary exhibits. On-site, Our Cafe features a Wolfgang Puck menu of kid-friendly foods. The museum is housed in a charming barracks built in the 1890s, with a stunning, glass-walled contemporary annex.

Fort Point National Historic Site (all ages)

Under the Golden Gate Bridge adjacent to the Presidio, take Long Avenue to Marine Drive; (415) 556-1693. Open Fri through Sun. Free.

A Civil War–era fort where costumed docents show you around a gunpowder storehouse, barracks, jail cells, and a museum of military artifacts. Little boys really go for the swords, guns, and cannons. Take photos here of the bridge with waves crashing and sailboarders in the bay. You can fish along the seawall. A beach at the foot of the cliffs on the west side of Fort Point is sometimes enjoyed by nude sun worshippers.

Waterfront

Wax Museum (all ages)

145 Jefferson St.; (415) 202-0400 or (800) 439-4305; www.waxmuseum.com. Adults and children ages 12 and up $$$; ages 4 to 11 $$; children under 4 free.

It's downright spooky to see Princess Diana, George Burns, and King Tut in the (waxed) flesh. From their posts in 100,000 square feet of elaborate, movielike settings, nearly 300 celebrities and historic figures look you right in the eye: Caruso, Castro, Chaplin, Cinderella, even Bruce Willis. This is a fun but pricey experience, a genuine Fisherman's Wharf tourist trap. If you decide to go for it, come at opening time, 9 a.m. weekends, 10 a.m. weekdays, to avoid the crowds. The Rainforest Cafe has a beautiful, huge aquarium, live birds, and a 3-story indoor waterfall.

Hyde Street Pier and
Maritime National Historical Park (all ages)

Hyde and Jefferson Streets at Pier 45, Fisherman's Wharf; (415) 556-3002; www.maritime .org. Admission to the museum building is free. Admission to Hyde Street Pier: adults $$; ages 12 to 17 $; under 12 are free with an adult. A family ticket admits 2 adults and up to 4 children under 18, $$$.

The only floating national park, anchorage for the world's largest collection of historic ships. Dozens of antique vessels are open to explore and clamber on, from tiny fishing boats to steam tugs, a houseboat, an 1895 lumber schooner— with 100-foot beams in its hold—and an ornate 1886 square-rigger. Vintage autos line the decks of the *Eureka*, an 1890 ferry. Knot tying, sail raising, and sea-shanty singing take place on weekends. Annual events include the Haunted Halloween Ship, storytelling, engine room tours, birding tours on the pier, navigation, and more. Every Saturday rangers give free presentations, especially for kids: scrimshaw, signal flags, stories, ship models, and knot tying.

Fisherman's Wharf

On the waterfront, from Aquatic Park to about Powell Street; www.fishermanswharf.org.

The bawdy, brawny Barbary Coast of a century ago is now a warren of seafood restaurants, shopping complexes, commercial fishing wharves, museums, tourist traps, and one of the great waterfront promenades in the world.

National Maritime Museum (all ages)

900 Beach St., at the foot of Polk, Fisherman's Wharf; (415) 561-7100; www.maritime.org. **free.**

A glorious and historic art deco building resembling a cruise ship, awash with ship models, figureheads, maritime paintings, photos, and artifacts. Watch ships in the bay through the telescope on the "bridge," and translate Morse code in the World War II–era radio room. The USS *Pampanito,* a World War II submarine, is docked at Pier 45 (a short walk east). Self-guided submarine tour: adults $$; ages 6 to 12 $; ages 5 and under are **free.**

The Cannery

2801 Leavenworth, at the foot of Columbus overlooking the bay; (415) 771-3112; www.the cannery.com.

The largest peach cannery in the world at the turn of the 20th century, this 3-story brick complex now holds dozens of smart shops and restaurants, with an olive-tree-shaded patio for dining and **free** entertainment. The cable car turnaround is ½ block away.

Musée Mécanique (ages 3 to 12)

Pier 45 at Taylor Street; (415) 346-2000; www.museemecanique.org. **Free.**

In a high, airy pier building, next to the docked USS *Pampanito* submarine, a museum of coin-operated arcade games and curiosities. With handfuls of quarters, have fun making them go: Fortune-tellers, dioramas, stereoscopes, strength testers, dancing puppets, road racers, and player pianos are among the 180 vintage machines. The bad news: A few modern arcade games have been added at the back of the building. The good news: Displays of the Museum of the City of San Francisco are here, and you can walk right out onto the breezy dock of the bay.

Ferry Building Marketplace (all ages)

At the foot of Market Street on the Embarcadero; (415) 291-3276; www.ferrybuildingmarket place.com.

Come with an appetite to one of the world's best farmers' markets, the Saturday market at Ferry Plaza, outdoors on the edge of the bay. Gorgeous produce; prepared foods like rotisserie chicken, salads, cheeses, and breads; and **free** tastes are presented by as many as 100 vendors, mostly small regional farmers and ranchers, many of them certified as organic.

Indoors and open every day are the permanent vendors, all top-of-the-line, selling everything from olive oils and deli foods to wines, books, oysters, candy, fish, chocolate, 36 kinds of gelato at Ciao Bella, and more.

Pier 39

On a pier jutting out into the bay from the Embarcadero, Pier 39 is a shopping, restaurant, and entertainment center with over 100 shops, a big games arcade, a mirror maze, a Venetian carousel, the Frequent Flyer bungee trampoline, and breezy bay views (www.pier39.com). Outdoor live entertainment is free, while prices are high for everything else, although you will find souvenirs in the $5 range. Shops focus on such catchy goods as puppets, movie memorabilia, magic, sports, toys, dolls, San Francisco and wildlife souvenirs, and more. The atmosphere is clean and commercial in a Disneyesque way. Sea-view cafes and snacks carts serve fresh seafood, American comfort food, and ethnic specialties.

- **Aquarium of the Bay.** (888) 732-3483; www.aquariumofthebay.com. On moving walkways, travel through 150-foot tunnels surrounded by 700,000 gallons of San Francisco Bay seawater, with exhibits of more than 20,000 marine animals, from bat rays to schooling fish, deep-sea predators, angel sharks, and giant octopus. Touch leopard sharks and other tide pool animals in the "touch pools." Adults $$$; ages 3 to 11 $$; 2 adults and 2 children $$$$.

- **K-Dock.** Herds of 600 or so cavorting sea lions put on a daily show, barking, cavorting, and showing off on the docks at the end of the pier. The males can be 7 feet long and weigh 1,000 pounds.

- **Riptide Arcade.** More than 100 video games in the Cyber Station games arcade. Kiddie rides and some video games are just for ages 3 to 12.

- **Turbo-Ride.** A wild big-screen trip in hydraulic seats to see jolting, tilting, rocking multimedia extravaganzas such as *3-D Dino Island; Deep Sea, the Ride* in 2-D; and *Comet Impact.* Adults and children ages 5 to 12 $$.

- **Eagle Cafe.** (415) 433-3689. Start the day with eggs, country fries, and big buttermilk pancakes taken family-style at long wooden tables.

- **Wipeout Bar and Grill.** (415) 986-5966; www.wipeoutbarandgrill.com. Kids love to watch people and entertainment from outdoor benches and the fire pit at the "beach" at this surf-themed restaurant; sandwiches, burgers, burritos, pastas, pizza, and tacos for lunch and dinner. Surfing and sporting events are featured on TVs and a big projection screen. Order from the Wipeout-To-Go menu at the orange 1966 Volkswagen van window. $$

- **San Francisco Carousel.** The glorious new 2-story carousel was custom-crafted in Italy, a glittering merry-go-round filled with 32 artful marine creatures from sea dragons to sea lions, dolphins, pandas, and of course, horses, and decorated with vivid depictions of San Francisco landmarks. Little ones like the stationary chariots, while adventurous riders go for the spinning tubs.

Alcatraz Cruises (all ages)

Pier 33, Fisherman's Wharf; (415) 981-7625; www.alcatrazcruises.com. Ages 12 and up $$$$; ages 5 to 11 $$$; ages 4 and under free; ask about family tickets.

An island in the middle of the bay is the site of the notorious federal penitentiary that once housed Al Capone and Machine Gun Kelly. The Alcatraz experience takes about 3 hours and includes a ferry ride, a walk in the sea-breezy outdoors, and a choice of several different narrated or self-guided tours of empty cell blocks and other historic buildings, all with stunning views of the Bay Area. Among recent upgrades are better audio tours, a larger museum store, and a nicer theater with a new video. Be prepared to walk steep, hilly paths from the dock to the prison at the top of the island; for those unable to make it, an electric tram trundles up and down hourly (no wheelchairs available). Tours often sell out in summer; make reservations in advance. If seeing the prison up close is not your idea of fun, consider Blue and Gold Fleet's "Escape from the Rock Cruise", a 1.5-hour bay cruise that goes under the Golden Gate Bridge and circles Alcatraz, with live narration about the island and its history.

North Beach

Between Telegraph Hill and Russian Hill near the waterfront.

In the heart of Italian North Beach beneath the towers of the Romanesque masterpiece Church of Saints Peter and Paul, Washington Square is an outdoor meeting hall and social center, where Chinese practice tai chi, Italian grandpas sit on park benches, and artists set up their easels. Surrounding streets are crowded with family-style Italian restaurants, pizza joints, bakeries, and more than a dozen espresso cafes. Picturesque against the murals of Cafe Roma and Cafe Viva, people from all over the world sip cappuccinos. At Caffé Verdi and Cafe Puccini, you'll hear opera, and at Cafe Italia the click of pinball and pool. The tiny Bohemian Cigar Store, famous for focaccia sandwiches, is a good place to pick up picnic goodies (415-362-0536). Just up the street, the fragrance in Molinari's Delicatessen is of dozens of kinds of Italian cheeses and salamis (415-421-2337).

A main tourist attraction in North Beach is Coit Tower on top of Telegraph Hill, overlooking the entire north Bay Area (415-362-0808). The 210-foot-tall art deco tower is decorated with 1930s murals of early California. Take the bus up to the tower, then return to North Beach by way of the woody Filbert Street steps past mansions, pre-earthquake cottages, and gardens. Sit quietly on a bench, and you may see raccoons or a small red fox.

Tucked away on the mezzanine of a bank, the tiny North Beach Museum exhibits fascinating old photos and a few artifacts that make the early days of the city come alive (1435 Stockton, 415-391-6210; free admission; closed weekends).

San Francisco **Soda Fountains**

- **Bill's Place,** 2315 Clement St.; (415) 221-5262. Zillions of celebrity-named burgers, thick malteds, fabulous fries, and rubbing elbows with the locals at vinyl-topped stools at the counter.

- **Daily Scoop,** 1401 18th St. on Potrero Hill; (415) 824-3975. Bring coins for the jukebox at this '50s-style parlor. Perch on heart-shaped wire chairs and lap up the Double Rainbow ice-cream sundaes, malts, and shakes. Good coffee, too.

- **Ghirardelli Soda Fountain and Chocolate Shop,** 44 Stockton St. in Ghirardelli Square; (415) 397-3030. An old-fashioned soda fountain and sweets shop specializing in spectacular sundaes and cones, shakes, and floats. Lots of fancy-wrapped gift baskets and candies.

- **Joe's Ice Cream,** 5351 Geary Blvd.; (415) 751-1950. Take stools at the counter or grab a table to sample an amazing variety of ice creams made in front of your eyes in this five-decades-old, diner-style shop in the Richmond District. Exotic Asian-style flavors like green tea, ginger, and adzuki bean, and all-American flavors like rum raisin, butter brickle, toasted almond, and more. Sandwiches, too.

- **Mitchell's Ice Cream,** 688 San Jose Ave. at 29th Street; (415) 648-2300. The line in the summertime will be out the door at this locals' favorite since the '50s. Wild and crazy flavors like avocado, cantaloupe, and several tropical fruits; yummy traditional chocolate, mint, and praline; and seasonal flavors like pumpkin. No inside seating.

- **St. Francis Fountain,** 2801 24th St. in the Mission; (415) 826-4200. Since 1918, some of the city's best sodas and root beer floats, egg creams, homemade ice cream, grilled cheese sandwiches, BLTs, egg salad, burgers, and more. Like when Grandma was a kid, neon signs, a rotary phone, penny candy, and retro decor.

Golden Gate Park/Ocean Beach

In the 1,017-acre garden that is one of the world's greatest metropolitan parks, you can row on a lake, ride a horse, play tennis, take long walks, browse in museums, or just laze on the lawns. My kids, grown up now, still love having tea and cookies in the Japanese teahouse when the cherry trees bloom in early spring. The Japanese Tea Garden is a fairy tale of a place, with a moon bridge, a brightly painted pagoda, a brooding bronze statue of Buddha, and lily ponds swimming with koi fish. Glorious maples blaze in autumn, and clouds of rhododendrons and azaleas burst into flower in spring.

On a huge network of walking and biking trails, you will pass people playing bocce and tennis, tossing horseshoes, fly casting, and playing checkers and chess in the checkers pavilion. For pot stickers to pizza, make a quick side trip to a clutch of restaurants at 9th Avenue and Irving Street.

On Sunday afternoons the main park road is closed to vehicles, and impromptu in-line skating and skateboarding happen; I mean, they really happen—fantastic **free** entertainment. As in any large urban park, it's advisable to stay together, leave before dark, and avoid isolated areas. Guided walking tours are offered **free** on weekends; call ahead for times and location (415-263-0991). Maps of the park are available at McLaren Lodge, at Stanyan and Fell, weekdays. On weekends, when parking is hard to find, hop on and off the **free** shuttle bus that runs between McLaren Lodge and Ocean Beach, stopping throughout the park at major attractions along the way. You can park at the nearby UCSF parking garage (at Parnassos and 5th Avenue) and shuttle into the park from there.

deYoung Museum (all ages)

JFK and Tea Garden Drives, Golden Gate Park; (415) 863-3330; www.deyoungmuseum.org. $$–$$$.

A colossal, contemporary-design, copper-clad, world-class museum surrounded by the park, with large, open galleries, plenty of places to take breaks, and dramatic, primitive art displays that kids like. Ascend to the top of the tower for 360-degree views of the city, then head for the African and Oceania galleries to see scary masks, fantastical ceremonial costumes and headdresses, towering Maori carvings, and other dramatic pieces that appeal to children. Wander in the other huge galleries of Mesoamerica, Central and South America; and those showing American art of the last two centuries—perhaps less interesting to little kids. Tall glass windows viewing interior courtyards and the park, and the light-filled interior piazza are restful to young eyes.

Check out the Education Gallery (415-750-3658) on the first floor to learn about and interact with art. Offered from 10:30 a.m. to noon on Saturday are **free** tours for ages 3½ to 12, followed by workshops; kids under age 8 must be accompanied by an adult. On Friday nights are special events for all ages involving live music and dancing, artists' demonstrations, and art-making workshops, with food and drink.

Look in the gift shop for toys, games, and art projects. Have snacks or lunch in the excellent cafe, and sit indoors, on the covered patio, or outdoors adjacent to the sculpture garden and lawns. The museum is close to the new Academy of Sciences, the Japanese Tea Garden, and the Conservatory of Flowers—plan to spend the day.

California Academy of Sciences (all ages)

55 Concourse Dr., across from the deYoung Museum in Golden Gate Park; (415) 379-8000; www.calacademy.org. Adults $$$$; ages 7 to 17 $$$; 6 and under **free.**

After four years and $500 million in design and construction, a spectacular, brand-new facility combines an aquarium, planetarium, natural history museum, and research facilities under a unique living roof. Save at least a half day to see a huge, all-digital planetarium; get a bird's-eye view of a Costa Rican rain forest; and see the world's deepest display of living corals. More than 38,000 live animals are on view in the aquarium and natural history exhibits, from 100,000-gallon tanks teeming with sharks, octopus, and jellyfish to gorillas, zebras, and lions in naturalistic settings to alligators in a swamp to creepy creatures in a 3-story rain forest—and more, much more. Toddlers interact with exhibits and play in the Early Childhood Center. On the observation terrace you get a view of the

Best **Playgrounds**

- **Children's Playground Golden Gate Park.** 320 Bowling Green Dr. between JFK and MLK Jr. Drives; (415) 831-2700; www.parks.sfgov.org. The first children's playground in a US public park, opened in 1888; the beautiful carousel has been twirling there since 1912. A recent transformation created a glorious, expanded play space, now known as Koret Children's Quarter, to include a hillside slide, climbing wave walls, sea caves, animal sculptures, a tree house village, the Sharon Art Studio, a water spray area, the playground, and restrooms.

- **KidPower Park.** 65 Hoff St. between 16th and 17th Streets. A small, vividly colorful park with preschool and school-age playgrounds, a fountain, benches, and palm trees, backed by a flamboyant, 3-story-tall tile mural; adjacent to a community garden.

- **Angelo J. Rossi Playground.** Edward at Arguello Boulevard. Newly renovated in 2007, now with colorful rubber mats, sand, grass, restrooms, picnic tables, tennis, an indoor pool, and separate areas for toddlers and for school-age kids (no dogs).

- **North Beach Playground.** Lombard and Mason Streets; (415) 274-0201. Olympic-size pool with special hours for kids, a big playground, and an excellent children's library. Restrooms.

- **Julius Kahn Playground.** West Pacific Avenue—enter off Arguello or Presidio; (415) 292-2004. Surrounded by trees, cool space-age structures in separate, sand-surfaced play areas for toddlers and for school-age kids. Tennis and basketball courts, soccer and baseball fields; picnic tables, restrooms.

- **Mountain Lake Park.** From Park Presidio to 8th Avenue at Lake Street, at the southern end of the Presidio. Separated playgrounds for little ones and school-age kids; tennis, picnic tables, lovely walking trails around the lake and into the Presidio. Ducks, birds, and seagulls in residence.

park and the 2.5-acre, revolutionary "living roof." A store, cafe, and courtyard are places to take breaks.

Conservatory of Flowers (all ages)

JFK Drive, Golden Gate Park; (415) 666-7001; www.conservatoryofflowers.org. $; under 4 **free.**

Shipped around Cape Horn from England in the 1870s, this monumental glass greenhouse encloses a steamy, dreamy jungle of trees, exotic plants, and flowers in a sort of Victorian biosphere. Leaves as big as Hummers, lily ponds, Tarzan vines, gorgeous orchids, and blooming flowers are among the sights. The butterfly enclosure captivated my grandkids, who played for more than an hour with the bright creatures, which perched on their hands and shoulders. Outside are flower beds and vast lawns for running and picnicking. Except on weekends, you can usually park on the street nearby.

Beach Chalet (all ages)

1000 Great Hwy.; (415) 386-8439; www.beachchalet.com. $$.

In a terra-cotta-tiled 1925 masterpiece of Willis Polk architecture overlooking Ocean Beach, this is a charming museum of Depression-era murals, mosaics and wood carvings, a model of Golden Gate Park, and historic exhibits. The bistro/brewpub upstairs is a great place for Sunday brunch or lunch; it's rather noisy, so squirmy kids attract little notice. The menu is robust, featuring sausage sandwiches, beer-battered prawns, macho onion rings, grilled fish, and Cajun/Creole specialties, with some plain choices that kids like. Try the Sandcastle chocolate truffle cake. The Park Chalet Garden Restaurant out back is a casual cafe in a light-filled atrium with park views, a stone fireplace, and indoor/outdoor seating. On the menu are seafood, flatbread pizzas, barbecue, burgers, banana splits, and microbrews; lunch, dinner, and brunch. The museum is **free** and makes a convenient restroom stop at the beach. Daily lunch and dinner.

Land's End Trail (all ages)

Take Geary Boulevard west to the Cliff House Restaurant, where the trail begins; (415) 556-0560.

An easy, 2.5-mile walk, with views of the Golden Gate, the Marin Headlands, and the shore, plus seabirds and marine mammals for company. There are benches along the way.

San Francisco Zoo (all ages)

Sloat Boulevard at 45th Avenue; (415) 753-7083; www.sfzoo.org. Ages 12 and older $$; ages 3 to 11 $; under 2 are **free.**

The zoo shelters many rare and endangered animals, such as black rhinos, snow leopards, condors, elephants, gorillas, and tigers. The feeding of the African lions and the highly endangered Sumatran and Siberian tigers takes place at 2 p.m., a big hit with all ages. A walk through the magical aviary of Rainbow Landing is an intimate encounter with some of the most colorful birds in the world—rainbow lorikeets. Kids can feed them nectar from their hands, then take home a photograph of themselves with these beautiful Australian birds. A sweet home for the North American river otters has climbing logs, pools, and waterfalls. From overhead observation decks in the expansive African Savanna area, watch rare antelopes, zebra, giraffes, and other inhabitants of the grasslands. Little ones like the circa-1920 carousel and the Children's Zoo, where they can feed, pet, and play with barnyard animals.

Japantown (all ages)
Bordered by O'Farrell, Pine, Fillmore, and Octavia; www.sfjapantown.org.

Anchored by a 5-tiered pagoda tower, the Japan Center, and the Sundance Kabuki movie theater, sleek, exciting "J-Town" comprises more than 50 Japanese restaurants, shopping malls, entertainment venues, and a few hotels—this is the largest Japanese neighborhood in the country. Kids love Kinokuniya Stationery (1581 Webster, in the Kinokuniya Building; 415-567-8901), a store jammed with cute and cool, mostly inexpensive collectibles; art, school, and office supplies; and mini everything—Hello Kitty, Neruto, Dragon Ball Z, origami paper, stickers, and more. In the same building, the huge Kinokuniya Bookstore specializes in books, magazines, and manga comics from Japan (415-567-7625). The Sundance Kabuki Cinemas is a main attraction, with 21 screens and a restaurant serving exotic California cuisine, plus a few kid-friendly favorites like pizza and mac and cheese (1881 Post at Fillmore; 415-929-4650; www.sundancecinemas.com). The J-Pop Center screens Japanese films and anime, alongside a bookstore, cafe, and several hip fashion boutiques.

Among annual gatherings in Japantown are the two-weekend Cherry Blossom Festival in April; the huge Asian Heritage Street Celebration in May, featuring Asian DJs, pop culture, j-cars, martial arts, food, karaoke, and much more; the two-day Nihonmachi Street Fair in August; and Kodomo no Hi (Children's Day) in May, when entertainment, food, games, and hands-on fun are all about kids.

Downtown/South-of-Market

MOMA, the San Francisco Museum of Modern Art (ages 4 and up)
151 3rd St.; (415) 357-4000; www.sfmoma.org. $$$ for adults; $$ for students with ID; and free for children 12 and under who are accompanied by an adult. Tickets are half price on Thursday, 6 to 9 p.m. Free admission on the first Thursday or each month.

Like a striped spacecraft about to lift off, this dazzling brick-and-glass temple to the arts was designed by world-famous Swiss architect Mario Botta. Step inside to see the gigantic, upslanting skylight pouring light into the atrium. A whirl of gallery floors flow one into another, showing the works of Matisse, Kline, Warhol, and countless other contemporary masters. A glitzy cafe and an upscale shop with truly fabulous children's educational and artistic toys and games complete the MOMA experience. When popular exhibitions are in residence, avoid standing in line by coming a few minutes before the museum opens at 11 a.m. (10 a.m. during the summer). On Family Sundays, introduce your child to modern art at hands-on workshops in a light-filled workroom, with docent-led gallery activities, live music, and performers, often related to the current special exhibition.

Metreon Entertainment Center (all ages)

101 4th St., at Yerba Buena Gardens; (415) 369-6000; www.metreon.com.

A 4-story dazzler of an entertainment complex housing a 3-D IMAX theater and 14 more movie screens, several restaurants, shops, and a world of high-tech places to play and buy. The place is pricey, commercial, bustling, and fun, and can be rather overwhelming for toddlers. Browse among the latest games and gadgets in Sony Style and in the hands-on Playstation store. Pick up anime collectibles at Kamikazi POP. From Another World specializes in movies, comics, and pop culture collectibles; action figures; model kits; and the like. TILT is a collection of interactive experiences such as Dance Dance Revolution and tons of video games. A wide variety of restaurants includes sushi at Sanraku, Mexican food at Luna Azul, pasta and pizza at Firewood Café, Asian food at Long Life Noodle, and sweets at Just Desserts.

Apple Store San Francisco (all ages)

1 Stockton St.; (415) 392-0202; www.apple.com/retail/sanfrancisco.

In an architecturally spectacular glass-clad store, check your e-mail in the Internet cafe on the Macs or on your own laptop. Register for **free** "getting started" classes on digital photography, digital moviemaking and music, and iPod and iTunes workshops. You can ask the Mac Geniuses at the Genius Bar any tech question. Kids ages 8 to 12 love the **free** 3-hour, summertime Apple Camp sessions on iPhoto, iMovie, and GarageBand (register in advance). This is a busy store—early in the day or evenings are best (open until 9 p.m.; 7 p.m. on Sun).

Contemporary Jewish Museum (all ages)

736 Mission St., across from Yerba Buena Gardens; (415) 655-7800; www.thecjm.org. $$ adults; ages 18 and under **free.**

The museum, in a new home as of June 2008, is housed in a vivid blue steel edifice that tilts up from an 1907 Willis Polk–designed former power station. Exhibitions feature a wide variety of perspectives on Jewish culture, history, art, and ideas, such as "From *The New Yorker* to *Shrek:* The Art of William Steig," a showing of drawings from the cartoonist and beloved author of children's literature. Art, music, film, literature, and debate are among the programs. Bring your children to hands-on, drop-in programs and to seasonal family days; call for information. **Free** with admission are ArtPacks filled with age-appropriate activities. The Cafe on the Square in the museum is a good place to grab a snack or lunch: cafe food and Jewish favorites, indoors or on the patio.

Yerba Buena Gardens

This art and culture area and urban park South-of-Market, **Yerba Buena Gardens** is bordered by 3rd, Folsom, 4th, and Howard Streets. A greensward surrounded by contemporary architecture, museums, and theaters, Esplanade Park is a place to sit at an outdoor cafe, lounge on the lawns, and enjoy the larger-than-life sculpture flanked by a 60-foot-wide torrent of water that creates a misty grotto for trees and a butterfly garden (415-820-3550; www.yerba buenagardens.com).

- **The Rooftop** (ages 2 to 8); (415) 522-9860. **Free.** An outdoor amphitheater where performances are held for young audiences; lawn bowl, robot sculptures, and fabulous playground with rubberized surfaces, too.

- **Yerba Buena Bowling Center** (ages 6 and up); (415) 777-3727. $$–$$$. Twelve lanes of high-tech bowling with "bumpers" that pop up on either side of your lane, the better to corral the ball. Upstairs, Mo's makes its famous smoky grilled burgers, thick shakes, sandwiches, and salads, with views of the surrounding cityscape.

- **Yerba Buena Ice Skating Center** (ages 2 and up); (415) 777-3727; www .skatebowl.com. Adults $$; ages 12 and under $. Surrounded by windows with stunning views of the city, this 100-foot-long, NHL-regulation-size rink flashes with plenty of action—ice dancers, hockey players, and figure skaters of all ages and abilities. It's **free** to watch. You can rent skates and get in on public sessions every afternoon. The Kristi Yamaguchi Holiday Ice Rink is open outdoors at Embarcadero Center from mid-November through December, with rentals available. Just before Thanksgiving a **free** ice show and lighting ceremony takes place (www .embarcaderocenter.com).

- **Zeum** (ages 8 to 18); (415) 777-2800; www.zeum.org. Ages 4 and up $$. Leonardo da Vinci meets R2-D2 at this pumpkin- and mauve-colored visual, performing, and media arts center. Peer docents help kids get involved in multimedia production, animation, web page design, and all kinds of tech-based art and drama. Your children can simply observe and enjoy the exhibitions and performances or jump right into interactive play and learning, from virtual reality games to high-tech puppeteering, making a video, making music, sculpting, or participating in backstage theater production. The average visit is about 3 hours.

Cable Cars (all ages)
Call (415) 673-6864 for information. $.

National Historic Landmarks, the famous cable cars of San Francisco are fun, rain or shine. You get fresh air, great photo ops, and roller-coaster rides up and down the steep hills. To avoid standing in line, very early in the day during the week is the best time to hop on and off the Powell–Hyde, Powell–Mason, and California Street lines, each ending at a "turn-around." From the Powell–Hyde turnaround on Market Street, walk 2 blocks up to Union Square for an exciting ride on one of the St. Francis Hotel's 32-story glass elevators, an eye- and ear-popping, 1,000-feet-per-minute flight with dizzying views at the top.

AT&T Park (all ages)
Between King, 2nd, and 3rd Streets, and China Basin; (415) 972-2400 or (800) 544-2687; www.sfgiants.com.

No other stadium in the world has these views—the San Francisco Bay, the Bay Bridge, and the city skyline—and some home-run balls end up with the fishes. Kids love the Coca-Cola Fan Lot, an interactive play area with slides, a mini ballpark, autograph rubbings, and the world's largest baseball glove and Coke bottle. Along the waterfront from right to center field are portholes where you can watch games at no charge. As few parking spots are available on this South-of-Market site, ferries drop people off right at the park. CalTrain arrives from South Bay cities a block away, and BART is nearby. In the city's tradition of the best food on the planet, the food vendors in the stadium sell everything from cappuccinos to gourmet burritos, cheesecake to chili. Take the Insiders' Tour to see the dugout, clubhouse, field, batting cages, the press box, and more (415-972-1800; tickets are $$ adults, $ ages 12 and under; ask about the doubleheader tour including a bay cruise). Nearby are the Giants Dugout store, Amici's East Coast Pizzeria, and ice cream treats at the Marble Slab Creamery.

Asian Art Museum (all ages)
200 Larkin St., at Civic Center; (415) 581-3500; www.asianart.org. $$; ages 11 and under are free.

A stunningly redesigned historic building, this is one of the largest museums in the Western world devoted to Asian art. Kids are drawn to the huge East Indian stone sculptures, intricately carved Chinese jades, Cambodian buddhas, Japanese kimonos, arms and armor, puppets, and daggers from Indonesia. AsiaAlive is a free interactive program for all ages, with art demonstrations, videos, and hands-on activities. A Family Festival takes place in May, and you can come for free art workshops and storytelling on some weekends. Within the museum, Cafe Asia is a serene indoor/outdoor environment for enjoying Asian-style snacks: bento boxes, rice bowls, noodles, sushi, salads, and sweets.

Wells Fargo History Museum (all ages)
420 Montgomery St., between California and Sacramento; (415) 396-2619; www.wellsfargohistory.com. Open weekdays. Free.

Connecting the bank's history to the California gold rush and early San Francisco, on exhibit are an original 1868 Concord stagecoach, and gold coins and nuggets from the Mother Lode. Kids can operate a telegraph station, handle historic artifacts, ride a replica stagecoach, and take an audio tour to hear stories and sounds of the gold rush.

Museum of the African Diaspora (all ages)

685 Mission St. at 3rd Street; (415) 358-7200; www.moadsf.org. $$.

For kids of all races, in the lower 3 floors of the luxurious St. Regis Hotel, art, history, and culture of African people around the globe are showcased in changing exhibits, films, a culinary center, and ongoing events, with programs for children and teenagers, lectures, concerts, a film series, and much more. Children are fascinated by the 3-story-high mosaic portrait of an African girl composed of some 2,100 photos, and other vivid installations.

Randall Museum (ages 2 to 10)

199 Museum Way, above the Castro District; (415) 554-9600, www.randallmuseum.org. Closed Monday. Free.

Just for kids, interactive, hands-on exhibits of science, natural history, and the arts; a wood shop; art and ceramics studios; a theater; a greenhouse; live animals; and a toddler zone. Lectures and special events, too. The grounds comprise a great play space with a fab view, lawns, a short hiking trail, and big granite animal sculptures to climb on. Drop-in Saturday classes, like jewelry making, woodworking, and photography, are **free.**

Chinatown

Stand at the ornate Chinese Gate at Bush and Grant, and look down Grant at the blizzard of neon signs, pagoda roofs, and dragon-bedecked lampposts, all in the colors of China—blood red, gold, and bright green. Flying from the rooftops of the more elaborate buildings are banners and flags heralding the family and benevolent associations that unite Chinese people with a common heritage. At one of these, the Chinese Six Companies building at 843 Stockton, the steps between the green dogs are a good place for a family photo. Chinatown comprises about 24 square blocks, including most of Grant Avenue and the streets and alleys off Grant.

No visit to San Francisco is complete without a few hours in Chinatown, one of the oldest and most vibrant Asian neighborhoods in the United States. This is the place to give the kids a few dollars and let them cruise around the many gift emporiums, which are loaded with inexpensive trinkets and toys. The larger souvenir stores and Asian antiques emporiums are on Grant, while the small shops are found in the 41 narrow alleys crisscrossing the main street. As you prowl the alleys, watch out for laundry dripping from balconies overhead.

On Washington Street look through the open doorways of the fragrant shops and watch herbalists concoct potions and medicines by scooping fungi, roots, spices, and herbs into paper packets.

A meal in a Chinatown restaurant is a must, from an elegant dining room to a hole-in-the-wall noodle shop or a dim sum emporium. Most of us are familiar with Cantonese-style food—chow mein, sweet-and-sour dishes, fried rice—and you can get that all over Chinatown, but it's fun to try "hot pots" and noodle dishes from northern China or hot-and-spicy Szechuan-style cuisine. In dim sum teahouses, steamed dumplings and stuffed buns and turnovers are rolled by on carts.

Reflecting the large Asian and Pacific Islander population, a "New Chinatown" has emerged in the Richmond district along Clement Street from Arguello Boulevard to 25th Avenue. Here you can shop for the same roasted ducks, ginseng, mangoes, and star fruit as in Chinatown, and browse for old records, flowers, and books. The many family-owned restaurants are multicultural, from Chinese and Japanese to Thai, Persian, French, and Burmese cuisine. You may hear some of the 25 different languages while hanging out with teens at Java Source Coffee Shop or stopping in at Green Apple Books and Vinh Khang Herbs and Ginsengs. Sweet Delite sells popular coconut- and taro-flavored tea shakes with tapioca balls at the bottom, which customers slurp up with a fat straw.

Chinatown Kite Shop (all ages)
717 Grant St.; (415) 391-8217.

At one of the world's great kite shops, there are Asian fighting kites; multilevel, dual-control stunt kites; dragon kites; windsocks; and even plain diamond-shaped paper kites you put together yourself. The nicest ones are made of fabric, and they make dramatic decorative pieces for the home, especially in a child's room. The best place in town to fly kites is on the Marina Green, where you have plenty of room to roam and the chance to see some fabulous, big kites in the air on weekends.

Great Wall Ginseng and Herbs
821 Pacific Ave.; (415) 397-2040.

This is the archetype of the colorful, fragrant, crowded Chinatown shops where herbalists concoct potions and medicines by scooping fungi, roots, spices, and herbs into paper packets—quite an exotic environment. They don't mind if you watch and ask questions.

Golden Gate Fortune Cookies Company
56 Ross Alley; (415) 781-3956.

Workers sit at machines from the 1920s, twisting fortunes into hot cookies as they come off the press. You are welcome to step in and sample the goodies.

Ten Ren Tea Company
949 Grant Ave.; (415) 362-0656.

Wide open to the street, welcoming you for **free** samples of steaming green, jasmine, or black teas. More than 50 varieties of special teas, priced up to $60 a pound, are scooped from big canisters. When tea samples are poured for you, tap your fingers or knuckles on the table to show thanks.

Chinese Culture Center (all ages)

Holiday Inn, 750 Kearny St.; (415) 986-1822; www.c-c-c.org. Free.

In the lobby of the hotel is a small, impressive museum of antique Chinese pottery and musical instruments, beautiful ancient statuary, and the gold-adorned costume of an empress. An annual holiday bazaar is held in December, when reasonably priced Chinese ceramics, toys, gifts, and home accessories are on sale.

Biking the City

San Francisco is a big biking city, with extensive, marked bike lanes everywhere, and bike racks on buses and in parking garages, valet bike parking, and more resources. The San Francisco Bicycle Coalition website (www .sfbike.org.) is full of ideas and maps of bike routes and hill grades so that you can easily navigate the city while avoiding steep hills Also on the site is an online tool giving turn-by-turn biking directions to your desired destinations.

A particularly bike-friendly, flat, beautiful area is Golden Gate Park, which is off-limits to cars on Sunday on John F. Kennedy Drive, a 7.5-mile stretch.

The unforgettable ride across the Golden Gate Bridge is 1.5 miles with stunning views; a workout on windy days. Monday to Friday the east sidewalk is open to cyclists and walkers; weekends, the west walkway is for riders only. From Vista Point on the north end of the bridge, you can cruise down Alexander Avenue into Sausalito.

The Golden Gate Bridge also links to the waterfront Bay Trail to Crissy Field and the Marina District, a 4-mile, flat path just for bikes.

• **Bay City Bike Rentals & Tours,** 2661 Taylor St., (visit website for more locations); (415) 346-BIKE (2453); www.baycitybike.com.

• **Bike & Roll San Francisco,** five locations (see website); (800) RENT-A-BIKE; www.bikeandroll.com.

• **Blazing Saddles Bike Rentals & Tours,** 2715 Hyde St. (five locations throughout the city—see website); (415) 202-8888; www.blazingsaddles .com.

• **Golden Gate Park Bike & Skate,** 3038 Fulton St.; (415) 668-1117; www .goldengateparkbikeandskate.com.

Chinese Historical Society of America (all ages)
965 Clay St.; (415) 391-1188; www.chsa.org. $; **free** for 5 and under; **free** to all on the first Thursday of each month.

In the wonderful Julia Morgan–designed, former YMCA building are displays of clothing, slippers of 19th-century Chinese pioneers, a colorful 1888 Buddhist altar, antique swords, photos, parade dragons, opium pipes, a fishing sampan, and other artifacts tracing the history of Chinese immigration in America from the early 1880s to today. The gift shop here is a good place for inexpensive souvenir shopping.

Chinese New Year (all ages)
January and February; (415) 391-2000.

The most spectacular of annual festivals in the city, starting with the New Year Flower Fair in late January, on Grant and Pacific Streets: plants, flowers, produce, traditional dance, music, art, and cultural displays. A mid-February weekend is the big deal, with a China-town Community Fair—kite and lantern making, arts demos, folk dance, puppet shows—and the big nighttime New Year Parade. With kids and grandkids in tow, my family prowls the parade route for a prime spot where the smaller children can see, and we wait breathlessly to hear the first blast of the firecrackers. Up the street come the glowing lanterns, crashing cymbals, marching bands, booming drum troupes, and famous dragons—roaring, fire-breathing, twisting, leaping, and sparkling red, gold, and green, accompanied by costumed attendants holding long strings of popping firecrackers.

More San Francisco

Mission Dolores (all ages)
Dolores Street at 16th, in the Mission District; (415) 621-8203. $.

The beating heart of the city's Hispanic community, the mission is the oldest and one of the most beautiful structures in the city; it was founded in 1776, 5 days before the signing of the Declaration of Independence. Within the thick adobe walls a miraculous painted ceiling glows in early Native American designs. Next door, the larger church was built in 1918. In a tiny cemetery lie thousands of the Mexican, Spanish, Indian, and Irish builders of America's favorite city by the bay.

Coyote Point Museum (ages 3 to 12)
Five miles south of the airport, take Poplar Avenue exit; 1651 Coyote Point Dr., San Mateo; (650) 342-7755; www.coyoteptmuseum.org. $–$$.

In the walk-through aviary you can ramble around a pond, waterfall, and gardens to get up close to native birds. Designed especially for kids are science and wildlife exhibits, aquariums, films, games, and live animal venues. River otters are fed daily at 12:15 p.m.; foxes at 11:30 a.m.

The museum is within the Coyote Point Recreation Area, which includes Magic Mountain playground, where a 3-story castle, 2 dragons, and more play structures await the children. There is a marina here, a waterfront walking/biking path, narrow beaches, restrooms, and picnic sites.

San Francisco International Airport (all ages)

Thirteen miles south of San Francisco near the junction of Highways 101 and 380; (650) 821-6700; www.flysfo.com.

On the departures/ticketing level of terminal 1, three beautiful aquariums are mesmerizing. In boarding area F, terminal 3, you can rent DVD players and movies for use at the airport, during a flight, or for your entire vacation. Near gate 87A, boarding area F, terminal 3, is the Kids' Spot for interactive exploration with exhibits from the Exploratorium, plus a crawling apparatus, a plasma wall, and other fun stuff. In terminals 1 and 3, special nursery rooms are set up for babies and toddlers who need a change.

About 40 exhibitions at a time are on view throughout the airport, focusing on culture, art, history, and science. You might see Halloween costumes, Indonesian puppets, or American flags. Check the schedule and locations at www.sfoarts.org. In the international terminal is the Aviation Museum, showing vintage planes and exhibits of space travel (650-821-9909).

Don't settle for junk food. Restaurants at SFO are among the most sophisticated and varied of any airport in the world, from Il Fornaio Caffe del Mondo to Max's Eatz, Just Desserts, Jalapeno Taqueria, and Harbor Village Kitchen, a quick-serve version of one of the city's top Chinese restaurants. Kids City and Shift N' Gears are a couple of kids' favorite shops among dozens of upscale retailers in the airport.

Where to Eat

Boudin at the Wharf. Jefferson and Taylor Streets at Pier 43½; (415) 928-1849; www.boudinbakery.com. The aroma will lure you into the bakery, gift shop, 2 restaurants, and museum on the wharf. Through a huge window and from a glass-walled catwalk suspended over the action, watch as 10,000 loaves of that famous sourdough bread are made daily. Sit upstairs in the bistro or on the patio by the fireplace to enjoy chowder in bread bowls, fresh seafood, sourdough pizza, and more only-in-San-Francisco food. A small fee is asked for the full bakery tour. $–$$

The Canvas Café. 1200 9th Ave. at Lincoln, near the Hall of Flowers in Golden Gate Park; (415) 504-0060; www.thecanvasgallery.com. Casual industrial chic in a cavernous room; great breakfasts, sandwiches (including PB&Js), salads, comfort food entrees; Mediterranean appetizers; cream sodas, hot chocolate, coffee drinks. **Free** parking; open late in the evening with live music. $$–$$$

Cliff House. 1090 Point Lobos Ave.; (415) 386-3330; www.cliffhouse.com. A monumental renovation has turned a worn tourist attraction into a gorgeous, if pricey, art deco–style destination at Ocean Beach. Overlooking the crashing waves of the Pacific are a bistro, a take-out counter, and the upscale, 2-story-view Sutro's restaurant; the bistro is best for families. Remember the old Camera Obscura? It's still here on the oceanfront terrace, which is open to the public. $$–$$$$

David's Deli. 474 Geary, near Union Square; (415) 771-0431. Kids like to sit at the counter for gigantic deli sandwiches, hot pastrami to die for, New York–style cheesecake, and huge slices of pie. $

Kate's Kitchen. 471 Haight St.; (415) 626-3984. Let out your belts, belly up to the blue-and-white-checked tablecloths, and tuck into big chunks of French toast, biscuits and sausage gravy, piles of bacon and cheddar cornmeal pancakes, and gigantic scrambled egg concoctions. Tops on the lunch menu are meat loaf sandwiches, homemade chicken soup, and incredible pie. Now, walk the 15 blocks to Golden Gate Park. Breakfast and lunch daily. $

La Taqueria. 2889 Mission St.; (415) 285-7117. Whimsical murals create a festive backdrop for fresh-fruit sodas, smoky *carne asada*, *carnitas* (slow-cooked pork), grilled chicken, and steak tacos and burritos. The neon sign says, THE BEST TACOS IN THE WHOLE WORLD. It could be true. You can sit on a bench inside or outside to eat, or take away. $

Lichee Garden. 1416 Powell St.; (415) 397-2290. Squeeze around a table in the bright, crowded dining room for great dim sum, crispy fried chicken, and lots of veggie dishes—good service, good food for lunch and dinner. $–$$

Mel's Drive-In. 2165 Lombard St., 3355 Geary Blvd., 1050 Van Ness Ave., and 801 Mission St.; (415) 921-3039; www.melsdrive-in.com. No longer a real drive-in, Mel's is *American Graffiti* revisited. Jukeboxes are stationed at every booth; burgers come in a car-shaped box; shakes are cold and thick; and crayons, balloons, homemade apple pie, and banana splits are abundant. Open just about all hours of the day and night. $–$$

R and G Lounge. 631 Kearny St.; (415) 982-7877. Don't bother to open the huge menu, just ask what fresh seafood specialties are being prepared today. Dishes are primarily seafood—wonderful whole steamed fish, crispy fried catfish, salt-and-pepper-roasted Dungeness crab, and savory clay-pot casseroles. The dining room is plain and brightly lit; group tables are upstairs, which is nicer. Lunch and dinner. $–$$

San Francisco Soup Company. 50 Post St. in the Crocker Galleria, and at several locations around the city and the Bay Area; (415) 397-SOUP; www.sfsoupco.com. In a fresh, clean, very casual cafe, step up to the counter to choose made-from-scratch soups, from traditional favorites like vegetable, potato leek, and chicken noodle to gumbo, mushroom barley, and exotic ethnic varieties. In the cafe and on the website is nutritional information for each soup. Also salads, sandwiches, and cookies; hot cereal and pastries for breakfast. $

Sears Fine Foods. 439 Powell St., at Union Square; (415) 986-1160. For years and years, breakfasts of sourdough French toast and tiny Swedish pancakes for tiny tots, plus all-American favorites for breakfast and lunch. $

Swan Oyster Depot. 1517 Polk St.; (415) 673-1101. Since 1912 just a counter with 20 stools and the best clam chowder, cracked crab, and other fresh seafood in town. Breakfast and lunch. $

Where to Stay

Argonaut Hotel. 495 Jefferson St., at Fisherman's Wharf; (866) 415-0704; www.argonauthotel.com. A boutique hotel on the waterfront. Kids can step up to the steamer trunk front desk and choose a welcoming gift from the treasure chest. Families like the rooms set up for four; fresh nautical decor and bay views; flat-screen TVs, DVD/CD players, Nintendo, and Internet access; and fitness center. Dogs are welcome. Some rooms have original brick walls, a separate parlor and bedroom, spa tubs, and brass telescopes; "tall" rooms have extra-long beds. With Starbucks next door, and Hyde

Street Pier, the National Historical Maritime Park, and the cable car turnaround across the street, you can't beat this location. $$$

Hotel del Sol. 3100 Webster St.; (877) 433-5765; www.jdvhotels.com/del_sol. Looking just like a California beach town motor lodge from the 1950s, the 2-story Del Sol is Day-Glo yellow, bright orange, royal blue, and flaming red inside and out, with fabulous striped canvas drapes to pull across the carports. With low rates, a small swimming pool, **free** parking, a sauna, even hammocks, and an unbeatably convenient location near the Marina and Union Street shopping, this is a rare find in this city. Smallish rooms and spacious suites. $$$–$$$$

Hotel Metropolis. 25 Mason St.; (800) 553-1900; www.hotelmetropolis.com. In a mid-downtown landmark a block from the cable car, this hotel has sleek, contemporary rooms with 2 doubles, and 1- and 2-bedroom suites. The 3-room Urban Explorers Kids Suite sports pint-size furniture, bunk beds, an eMac computer, chalkboard wall, toys, and rubber ducky decor in the bathroom. With the connecting 2-queen room and living room with sofa bed, it sleeps up to 6 adults and 3 children. Refrigerator, wet bar, fitness room, library, and Wi-Fi, too. Pet-friendly. On-site Farmer Brown Restaurant specializes in Southern soul food made from locally produced ingredients: mac and cheese, fried chicken, gumbo, pulled pork. Dinner nightly, Sun brunch. $$$–$$$$

Hyatt at Fisherman's Wharf. 555 North Point St.; (800) 233-1234; www.fishermans wharf.hyatt.com. Across the street from the Mason/Powell Cable Car line, the Hyatt has 331 contemporary-urban, newly renovated rooms, some with 2 doubles, armchairs, and desks. Wi-Fi throughout the hotel; **free** transport to the Financial District; new 24-hour fitness center; large outdoor heated pool. Knuckles Sports Bar/Restaurant has big-screen TVs, cafe food, endless popcorn, pool

tables, and shuffleboard in a bright, casual environment. $$$–$$$$

Motel Row. On Lombard Street, between Baker Street and Van Ness. Several inexpensive and medium-priced motels are located on Lombard Street within walking distance of the waterfront, restaurants, and public transportation. Reasonable choices are the **Buena Vista Motor Inn** (800-835-4980), the **Lombard Motor Inn** (800-835-3639), and the **Cow Hollow Motor Inn,** which has big family suites with kitchens (415-921-5800). All have **free** parking and connecting rooms. $$–$$$

Ocean Park Motel. 2690 46th Ave.; (415) 566-7020; www.oceanparkmotel.citysearch .com. In an art deco gem, family-oriented rooms with kitchens, some with separate bedrooms and up to 3 queen-size beds, private entrances, **free** parking. Playground, hot tub, nice gardens; dogs okay. Two blocks to Ocean Beach and bike/walking path, 1 block to the zoo; public transportation at the front door. $$$

San Francisco International Hostel. Bay and Franklin, above Fort Mason; (415) 771-7277; www.norcalhostels.org. For families on a strict budget or for those looking for a unique experience, 2- and 3-bunk private rooms (bring sleeping bags) and a communal kitchen; brief chores are required. The location above Fort Mason is unbeatable. $ per person; also family rates. For a brochure describing all Northern California hostels, call (415) 863-1444 (fax: 415-863-3865).

For More Information

San Francisco Convention and Visitors Bureau. 900 Market St., corner of Powell and Market Streets, Lower Level, Hallidie Plaza; (415) 391-2000; www.onlyinsanfrancisco .com. Ask about lodging, restaurant, and transportation deals and packages. The new Fisherman's Wharf Pass offers a savings of 33 percent on a choice of 6 options, from hop-on, hop-off CitySightseeing on a double-decker bus, a Gray Line Trolley tour, and a bay cruise to Ripley's Believe It or Not!, Pier 39's Turbo Ride and the carousel, the wax museum, and more (www.wharfpass.com). Get the latest news and information at www .facebook.com/onlyinsf.

California Welcome Center. Pier 39, Marina Plaza, 2nd Level, Building P; (415) 956-3493; www.visitcwc.com. Get traveler's information, brochures, and maps for the entire state. Check your e-mail, make hotel reservations, and ask for advice.

San Francisco Hotel Reservations. (415) 974-4499 or (888) 782-9673; www.onlyinsan francisco.com. More than 200 hotels and inns are described by location, type, price range, services, neighborhood, comfort level, and quality ratings, with availability up to a year in advance. and photos.

Bay Area Rapid Transit (BART). (650) 992-2278 or (510) 465-BART; www.bart.gov. Subway and rail connecting San Francisco with Colma, Daly City, and the East and South Bay, including Oakland Airport and SFO. Ticket prices start at $1.10; ages 4 and under ride **free.** Call for schedules, discounts, stations.

Streetcars. (415) 956-0472; www.streetcar .org. One of the nicest ways to ride about the city is on the colorful, historic streetcars.

Beginning at Embarcadero Station, 5 streetcar lines take you along Market Street to various stops west and southwest in the city, including Ocean Beach. The F-line extension runs from AT&T Park to the Ferry Building and around the Embarcadero to Fisherman's Wharf every 10 minutes, stopping frequently.

CityPass. Purchase at visitor center and at the major attractions on the pass. (888) 330-5008; www.citypass.com. Prices: adults $43; ages 5 to 17 $28; younger kids are **free** at most of the venues. If you plan to visit these attractions, you will save at least 50 percent at SFMOMA, Blue and Gold Bay Cruise, Exploratorium, Palace of the Legion of Honor, California Academy of Sciences, Muni transportation, and cable cars.

Bay Trail Maps. (510) 464-7900; www.bay trail.org. Explore the entire San Francisco Bay shoreline with the help of a set of 6 maps that traces 230 miles of trails for walking, biking, and wildlife watching; each route is described in detail. The set costs $15.

Ferries. One of the least expensive and most fun ways to get around the bay is by ferry, from Vallejo, Marin County, and the East Bay to Pier 41 or to the Ferry Building on the Embarcadero. Schedules for seven ferry operators can be found at www.baylinkferry .com.

Golden Gate North:
Marin County

S treaming out of the city like the tide under the Golden Gate Bridge, day-trippers escape into Marin County. Within an hour's drive are Pacific beaches, shady roads for bike rides, and footpaths beneath ancient redwood giants.

The profile of 2,600-foot Mount Tamalpais, the "Sleeping Maiden," lures mountain bikers and hikers into the canyons, forests, and meadows of Mount Tamalpais State Park. Scenic 2-lane Panoramic Highway runs steeply over the mountain and down to Stinson Beach.

For freeway-free getaways take a ferry from San Francisco's Embarcadero to Tiburon or Sausalito for a day in the sun when the city is socked in with fog. With shops, restaurants, and waterfront promenades, the two Mediterranean-style villages overlook San Francisco Bay and the quiet inlet of Richardson Bay.

Miraculous double peninsulas that point jaggedly into the Pacific, Point Reyes National Seashore is one of the greatest coastal wilderness preserves in the world. The tiny towns of Inverness and Point Reyes Station are headquarters for provisions, meals, and lodgings near the national seashore. If your family craves oysters, head for Tomales Bay.

Inverness/Point Reyes

Inverness (all ages)
Highway 1 on the west shore of Tomales Bay; (415) 663-9232; www.pointreyes.org.

A vacation village since the late 1880s, Inverness, population 1,000, is a day-tripper's rest stop and a community of country cottages in the dark forest of Inverness Ridge, overlooking Tomales Bay. Keep your eyes open for cafes, a small marina, and eye-popping scenery.

From February through early summer, the meadows and marine terraces are blanketed with California poppies, dark blue lupine, pale baby blue-eyes, Indian paintbrush, and some wildflowers existing only here. The summit of Mount Wittenberg, at 1,407 feet, is reachable in an afternoon's climb.

GOLDEN GATE NORTH: MARIN COUNTY

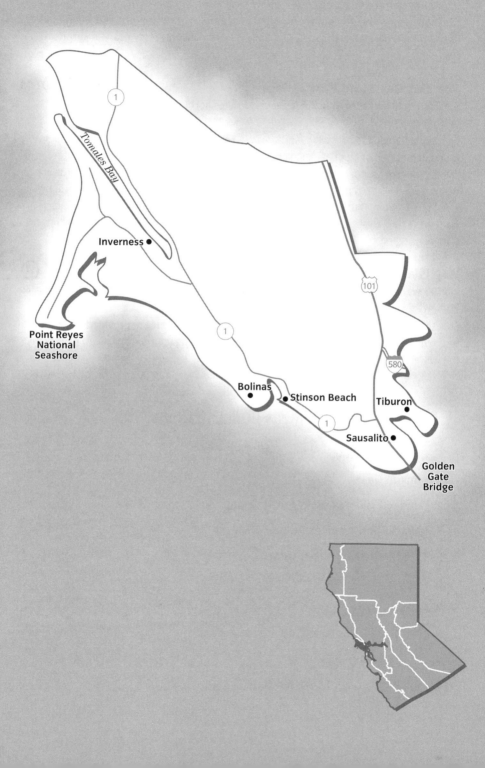

Inverness •

Point Reyes
National
Seashore

Bolinas •

Stinson Beach •

Tiburon •

Sausalito •

Golden
Gate
Bridge

Tomales Bay

1

101

580

1

1

A string of beaches and protected bays, hilltop and meadow trails, and an astonishing variety and abundance of birds and wildlife make the area a magnificent resource for families who love the outdoors. Often cool and foggy in summer, the weather is dependably clear and warm in spring and fall, and midwinter days can be surprisingly mild.

Tomales Bay State Park (all ages)

Adjacent to Point Reyes National Seashore, 8 miles north of Inverness on Pierce Point Road, Inverness; (415) 669-1140; www.parks.ca.gov. Parking $$.

Thirteen miles long, a mile wide, and shallow, Tomales Bay is a quiet finger of water surrounded by acres of mudflats and salt- and freshwater marshes. Commercial oyster farms line the eastern shore. More than 100 species of resident and migrating waterbirds are the reason you'll see anorak-clad, binocular-braced bird-watchers at pullouts on Highway 1 along the shore. Four beaches, hiking trails, and picnic areas. Heart's Desire Beach is a wind-protected, easily accessible beach, great for swimming, sailboarding, kayaking, and clam digging; picnic tables and 6 miles of easy-to-moderate trails.

Hog Island Oyster Company

20215 Hwy. 1, in the Old Marshall General Store, between Point Reyes Station and Tomales; (415) 663-9218; www.hogislandoysters.com.

Shucking knives, waterfront picnic tables, and barbecue kettles are provided—and the best oysters in the world! This is not a restaurant, so bring your own picnic to have with the oysters.

TopTen fun ideas in Marin County

1. Bay Area Discovery Museum

2. Stinson Beach

3. Sunday brunch at Sam's in Tiburon

4. Kayaking on Tomales Bay

5. Tide pooling in Drakes Estero

6. Angel Island State Park

7. Ferry to San Francisco and back

8. Hiking the Palomarin Trail

9. Marine Mammal Center

10. Walking across the Golden Gate Bridge

Tomales Point Hike   (ages 6 and up)

About 2.5 miles past Inverness, turn right onto Pierce Point Road, following signs to McClure's Beach, and continue 9 miles to white ranch buildings and the parking lot; (415) 663-1092.

A breathtaking route on the bluffs above the Pacific, on windswept moors that remind some visitors of Scotland. Wildflowers float in the meadows, whales spout December through February, and a herd of 500 tule elk live in the grassy fields of Pierce Ranch, a historic and photogenic dairy ranch. Stroll around the buildings to discover interpretive signs. The entire loop is 6 miles round-trip.

Point Reyes National Seashore   (all ages)

Bear Valley Road, Highway 1 and Sir Francis Drake Boulevard, Point Reyes; (415) 464-5100; www.nps.gov/pore. Free; camping $.

When the English explorer Sir Francis Drake sailed his *Golden Hind* into the great curve of Drake's Bay in 1579, he knew this was a bit of earth like no other. Part of the national seashore, the bay remains largely as it was 400 years ago—fringed with sandy beaches and tide pools alive with anemones and crabs, sometimes even rays and leopard sharks. North from the point—Point Reyes, where the lighthouse stands—are miles of beaches accessible from Sir Francis Drake Boulevard. Exposed to the full force of storms and pounding surf, these beaches are unsafe for swimming or surfing. The headlands, tide pools, sea stacks, lagoons, wave-carved caves, and rocky promontories are alive with birds—endangered brown pelicans, cormorants, surf scooters, sandpipers, grebes, terns—and sea life such as giant anemones, sea palms, urchins, fish, and even the occasional great white shark offshore of Tomales Point.

At the visitor center are exhibits, guidebooks, trail maps, and daily postings of whale sightings. Rangers are on hand to orient you to the diverse ecosystem and the many destinations within the huge park.

Short, easy walks near the visitor center include Kule Loklo Trail to Miwok Village, where an ancient Indian site has been re-created. On the Earthquake Trail are photos of the effects of the 1906 earthquake and signs explaining earth movement; the entire peninsula was once located some 250 miles to the south!

During the summer, a visitor center operates at Drakes Beach off Sir Francis Drake Boulevard, where you can see exhibits on maritime exploration and marine environments, and a minke whale skeleton (415-669-1250). Here also are restrooms, an outdoor shower, picnic tables, barbecue grills, and a casual cafe.

The weather can be foggy and windy on any day of the year, so warm jackets are advisable; check weather at (415) 663-1092.

Bear Valley Trail   (all ages)

Point Reyes National Seashore; (415) 663-1092.

The American Hiking Society names Point Reyes as one of the top 10 most family friendly hiking areas in the country. It's the most popular of dozens of hiking, biking, and horseback riding trails in the national seashore. Winding through forest tunnels, along creeks, and through meadows, this easy, 8-mile round-trip hike ends on a bluff 50 feet above the sea. Bikes are okay for all but the last 0.75 mile, where a bike rack is located; restrooms are halfway.

Limantour Beach and Limantour Estero Reserve (all ages)
Within Point Reyes National Seashore, at the end of Limantour Road; (415) 663-1092.

Just a few steps from the parking lot, this long stretch of windswept sand is good for surf fishing and sunbathing. Look for the Muddy Hollow Trail for a short bird-watching walk. Bird watching is popular in the 500-acre Drakes Estero, a large intertidal lagoon with a giant tide pool.

Point Reyes Lighthouse (all ages)
Within Point Reyes National Seashore, at the end of Sir Francis Drake Boulevard; (415) 669-1534. Free.

Until the lighthouse was built in 1875, many shipwrecks occurred off the Point Reyes Headlands. The lighthouse is reachable by 308 steps leading downhill from a high bluff, and it can be a windy, windy spot. During whale-watching season, December through March, this is a prime viewing venue; a shuttle bus operates between the lighthouse and the beach. Some 20,000 California gray whales travel the Pacific coastline south to breed in Mexico, returning a few months later with their babies to the Arctic.

Point Reyes Station (all ages)
Highway 1 and Sir Francis Drake Boulevard.

Many century-old buildings remain on the short main street of this picturesque railroad town founded in the 1800s. The train depot is now the post office; the Fire Engine House, a community center. Dairy ranches and commercial oyster companies fuel the rural economy.

Toby's Feed Barn
11250 Hwy. 1, Point Reyes Station; (415) 663-1223.

Hay, feed, souvenirs, T-shirts, and cool stuff crafted by local artists. On Saturday from June through October, a farmers' market takes place here, where vendors sell local produce and flowers, wool, poultry, meats, olive oil, preserves, and more.

Into the Blue (all ages)
In the Livery Stable, corner of 3rd and B Streets, Point Reyes Station; (415) 663-1147.

On the way to the beach, kites, games, and wind toys galore.

Tomales Bay Foods
4th and B Streets, Point Reyes Station; (415) 663-9335.

In a former hay barn, an airy emporium of luscious take-out foods, hot and cold, plus organic produce, homemade ice cream, flowers, and more from local farms, ranches, and

Kayaking Marin

If you haven't been in a kayak since years ago when they were heavy and awkward, you have no idea how easy and safe they are these days. When they say, "for all ages," it's really true. Kayaking companies will teach you the basics, outfit you, and suggest short or long paddling routes. Besides single "open deck" and sea kayaks, these proprietors rent junior-size kayaks, doubles, and triples. Even first-timers can learn in a few minutes with the **free** instruction offered by the kayak companies; kids will feel secure riding with a parent or older sibling. Call ahead to reserve the boats.

- **Blue Waters Kayaking,** next to Barnaby's By the Bay, 12938 Sir Francis Drake Blvd., Inverness, and in the town of Marshall; (415) 669-2600; www .bwkayak.com.

- **Point Reyes Outdoors,** 11401 Hwy. 1, Point Reyes Station; (415) 663-8192; www.pointreyesoutdoors.com. Rent kayaks and/or take a kayaking class or guided tour of Drakes Estero and Tomales Bay. Also hiking tours of Point Reyes.

- **Open Water Rowing,** 85 Liberty Ship Way, Sausalito; (415) 332-1091; www .owrc.com.

- **Sea Trek Ocean Kayaking Center,** Schoonmaker Point, Liberty Ship Way, Sausalito; (415) 488-1000; www.seatrekkayak.com.

wineries. Watch artisanal cheeses being made; wine, seafood and cooking demonstrations on weekends.

Five Brooks Ranch (all ages)

Three and a half miles south of Olema on Highway 1, look for the Five Brooks Trailhead sign; P.O. Box 99, Olema 94950; (415) 663-1570; www.fivebrooks.com. Guided trail rides $$$$; pony rides $$$.

Guided horseback rides in glorious Point Reyes for buckaroos and buckarettes, from a 1-hour slow trail ride to longer treks up the Inverness Ridge and incredible beach rides. The littlest riders like the hand-led pony ride around Five Brooks Pond.

Where to Eat

Barnaby's By the Bay. At the Golden Hinde Inn, 1 mile north of Inverness; (415) 669-1114. A glassed-in dining room and decks overlooking a marina on Tomales Bay; the only waterside restaurant in the area. Clam chowder, deep-fried calamari with cornmeal crust, fresh fish, and barbecued oysters, chicken, and ribs from the apple-wood smoker. $–$$

Bovine Bakery. 11315 Hwy. 1, Point Reyes; (415) 663-9420. Lines of customers are sometimes out the door for gooey morning buns, pastries, muffins, scones, and organic coffees (no espresso); pizza, soup, and sandwiches. Yummy bear claws and fruit scones, chocolate croissants. Most people sit outside on the curb, drinking in the sunshine, the passing scene, and the really good coffee. $

Drakes Beach Cafe. At the visitor center at Drakes Beach off Sir Francis Drake Boulevard, Point Reyes National Seashore; (415) 669-1297. A tiny, cozy cafe at the water's edge, with outdoor tables and a telescope for whale-watching. Hearty, simple American food, barbecued oysters, and corn on the cob. Cowgirl Creamery cheeses. Lunch daily, dinner Fri and Sat. $–$$

Olema Farm House Restaurant. 10005 Hwy. 1, Olema; (415) 663-1264. Once an 1845 stagecoach stop, this farmhouse is decked out with beautiful old bottles, Elvis memorabilia, and antiques. The heated garden patio is the place to be. Fish-and-chips, clam chowder, meat loaf, prime rib, roast chicken, oyster stew, Philly cheesesteak; lunch and dinner, with breakfast on weekends. $–$$$

Station House Cafe. Main Street, Point Reyes Station; (415) 663-1515. In a historic red building, the cafe is good food for breakfast, lunch, and dinner, in the casual dining room or on the garden patio, with live weekend music. Homemade breads, free-range poultry and meats, the harvest from an on-site organic garden, and local products go into an updated comfort-food menu, from pot roast and duck breast with cherry sauce to fresh seafood; don't miss the pecan pie. $$–$$$

Tomales Bakery. 27000 Hwy. 1, Tomales; (415) 878-2429. European-style breads and pastries, pies, amazing calzones, focaccia with exotic toppings, croissants, all made with local ingredients. $

Where to Stay

Golden Hinde Inn. 12938 Sir Francis Drake Blvd., Inverness; (415) 669-1389; www.goldenhindeinn.com. A fresh-looking, white-painted, unassuming motel right at the marina on Tomales Bay, with a small swimming pool and fishing pier. Two-room suites have queen beds and sofa beds, microwaves, refrigerators, and fireplaces. Suite #5 has a king bed, a sofa bed, kitchen, and dining area. Some rooms have kitchenettes, 2 doubles or queen and sofa bed, and fireplaces. $$–$$$

Nick's Cove and Cottages. 23240 Hwy. 1, Marshall; (866) 63-NICKS; www.nickscove .com. On Tomales Bay, just the sweetest lineup of comfy cottages you'll ever see, and a private dock. Each cottage is divinely different, romantic, and spacious—and pricey. The waterfront restaurant here is wildly popular and famous for fresh seafood and local ingredients. $$$$

Olema Ranch Campground. 10155 Hwy. 1, Olema; (415) 663-8001 or (800) 655-2267; www.olemaranch.com. Shade trees and grassy meadows with 150 tent and 80 RV sites and cabins, showers, and laundry. They've thought of everything: mountain bike rentals, kayak tours, volleyball, a US post office, ice-cream socials, storytelling around a bonfire, and buffet breakfast Sunday morning. Dogs okay. $

Point Reyes Hostel. From Bear Valley Road, go about 6 miles on Limantour Road; P.O. Box 247, Point Reyes Station 94956; (415) 663-8811. A ranch house and bunkhouse, with spacious kitchen, outdoor barbecue, and common rooms with wood-burning stoves. A family room is available by reservation. $

Point Reyes Seashore Lodge. 10021 Hwy. 1, Olema; (415) 663-9000; www.point reyesseashore.com. One of the few B&Bs appropriate for families, a luxurious country estate in an idyllic garden setting with sweeping lawns, large trees, and a creek. The best rooms for families have tiny, private patios; some have fireplaces and double Jacuzzis. The complimentary breakfast is generous. The super-comfy Casa Olema cottage has a kitchen, a living room, a spa, and a loft bedroom, and sleeps up to 6. The Creekside Cottage sleeps 4, and some other rooms have queen/twin combinations or 2 doubles. A large library of guidebooks and restaurant menus is a big help. The staff will arrange bike, kayak, and horse rentals for you. $$–$$$$

For More Information

West Marin Chamber of Commerce. P.O. Box 1045, Point Reyes Station 94956; (415) 663-9232; www.pointreyes.org.

Point Reyes Lodging. P.O. Box 878, Point Reyes 94956; (415) 663-1872 or (800) 539-1872; www.ptreyes.com. Check online for information, availability, and links to a long list of cottages, suites, and inns in the area.

Sausalito/Tiburon

Tumbling down steep, forested hillsides to the edge of San Francisco Bay as if it were on the Mediterranean, the small tourist town of Sausalito makes a great day-trip destination. Running along the edge of Richardson Bay, the main street, Bridgeway, is chockablock with galleries and upscale shops, seafood restaurants, and yacht harbors, all sharing postcard views of San Francisco.

Near the ferry terminal in midtown is a large fountain and a small city park with palm trees and huge stone elephants with streetlights on their heads, leftovers from San Francisco's 1915 Exposition. From here, ferries come and go to San Francisco and Tiburon.. A little farther north on Bridgeway, you can wander around the houseboat docks—look for the floating Taj Mahal—and stop in at the Arques School of Wooden Boatbuilding, between noon and 1 p.m. Tuesday through Saturday, to watch the intricate woodworking, casting, and bronzing activities (call first, 415-331-7134). Back toward town, at the end of Liberty Ship Way near the marina, Schoonmaker Beach is palm-shaded patch of sand. Boat owners and kayakers like Le Garage here for bistro-style cuisine on the deck.

A community of 400-plus houseboats, permanently located at the north end of Bridgeway, is a phenomenon in itself and fun to see. In this part of town you can take kayaking and windsurfing lessons on Richardson Bay.

On the opposite side of Richardson Bay from Sausalito, Tiburon is another hamlet of vintage mansions, with outdoor restaurants overlooking the San Francisco skyline and Raccoon Strait. You can get here via ferry from Pier 41 in San Francisco (www.blueand goldfleet.com), as well as by car. On opening day of yachting season in April, decorated pleasure craft sail and motor back and forth while families engage in springlike behavior on the grassy shoreline. June through August, "Friday Nights on Main" are all about food, fun, families, music, and gallery events.

Shopping in Tiburon & Sausalito

Shops, boutiques, and art galleries are plentiful in these two bayside towns, and the majority of them are not of particular interest to children. However, here are a few fun shops the kids might enjoy.

- **Tails of Tiburon,** 34 Main, Tiburon; (415) 789-1301. A fluffy Papillon, Bandit is the "pawpriotor" of this emporium of dog and cat clothing and accessories, toys, and healthy treats. In Sausalito, **Top Paws** is a similar fancy pet boutique (1001 Bridgeway; 415-331-7297).

- **The Harbor Shop,** 100 Bay St., Sausalito; (415) 331-6008. Right at the marina, this shop is the place to outfit yourselves with nautical clothing, hats, and accessories, and buy toys for kids and gifts for yachties. Shop for model boats and planes, a "boat-in-a-bottle," and games. Best sellers are baseball caps, straw hats, and waterproof hats. A tiny coffee corner overlooks the marina.

- **The Attic,** 96 Main St., Tiburon; (415) 435-0351. Open afternoons only. Crowded with vintage video games, comic books, baseball cards, stamps, coins, old postcards, and other finds for avid collectors.

- **The Candy Store,** 7 Main St., Tiburon; (415) 435-0424. Homemade fudge and chocolates, ice cream, and stuffed animals.

- **Games People Play,** 695 Bridgeway Ave.. Sausalito; (415) 332-4151. Not just for kids, this shop has games for the car, for the beach, for the hotel room, and for the brain. Kites, dolls, Groucho Marx glasses, balloons, and lots of little stuff.

- **Sausalito Ferry Company,** 688 Bridgeway, Sausalito; (415) 332-9590; www .sausalitoferry.com. Tchotchkes, gizmos, gadgets, and novelty toys, from plastic fish to whirling lamps, glowsticks, pinkie-size baby dolls, weird T-shirts, lunchboxes, tin rockets, crazy cards, and way, way more.

- **RJ Sax Apparel,** 30 Main St., Tiburon; (800) 709-4449. Aloha shirts, decorated flip-flops, wild and crazy umbrellas and parasols, and gifts for your nuttiest friends.

Bay Model (all ages)

2100 Bridgeway Ave., Sausalito; (415) 332-3870. Free.

From the ferry dock a pleasant 20-minute walk or bike ride north brings you to the 1.5-acre, hydraulic, working scale model of San Francisco Bay and the adjacent Sacramento

River Delta. The natural and cultural histories of the bay are traced in exhibits of wetlands, wildlife, shipwrecks, antique equipment, videos, and video games—kids love it. Check the website for a variety of guided tours and events throughout the year.

Marin Headlands (all ages)

Take the Alexander Avenue exit off Highway 1, the first exit north of the Golden Gate Bridge; (415) 331-1540; www.nps.gov/goga.

Part of the Golden Gate National Recreation Area, wild open spaces with miraculous views. Hiking trails above the Golden Gate are breezy and bracing, and kids like to climb around in the remnants of World War II fortifications. Stop at the visitor center at Field and Bunker Streets for maps to myriad hiking, biking, and equestrian trails and beaches. Besides the Marine Mammal Center (listed below), the main attractions are Rodeo Beach, Rodeo Lagoon, Muir Beach, and the Point Bonita Lighthouse. The lighthouse is perched on a bit of rock at the entrance to the Golden Gate, with incredible views and a (slightly) swaying footbridge over crashing waves; walk down and back on your own and get the history from the ranger in the tiny visitor center, or opt for the guided walk, which takes (it seems) forever. Precipitous cliff-top trails near here are not for little kids. The best time to explore Muir Beach is at low tide, when hundreds of sea stars and vividly colored sea anemones are revealed (always keep an eye on the water, and remind the kids not to turn their backs on the sea).

Muir Woods National Monument (all ages)

From Highway 101 take the Highway 1 exit at Mill Valley; (415) 388-2595; www.visitmuir woods.com. $$ ages 16 and up.

A precious pocket of redwoods, some over 1,000 years old and 260 feet high, live in an isolated canyon just 12 miles north of the Golden Gate Bridge. Trails wander through an idyllic mixed forest of Douglas fir, big-leaf maple, oak, laurel, red alder, and buckeye—glorious in the fall. The easiest trail loops from the visitor center to Cathedral Grove, about a 1-mile, 1-hour walk if you stop to read the nature signs and enjoy Redwood Creek; wide, paved, and wheelchair and stroller accessible. Hillside and Fern Creek trails are longer trails. Midweek is best, as weekends and summertime are busy with visitors from around the world. No bikes, picnics, or pets.

Marine Mammal Center (all ages)

Marin Headlands, Sausalito; (415) 289-SEAL; www.marinemammalcenter.org. Free; donations accepted.

A must-see for families fascinated by the largest denizens of the sea, the center serves as a hospital for orphaned, sick, and injured seals, sea lions, dolphins, otters, and whales. Many of the patients are endangered or threatened species, and you can watch them being fed, treated, and comforted. The twin goals of the center are to ready the animals to return to their watery habitat and to create public understanding of and appreciation for our fellow creatures. During the winter, there are few animals on view. Spring is pupping season, a busy time; between February and June, orphaned or abandoned elephant seal and harbor seal pups are in residence, while during summer and fall, California sea lions are usually on-site. Call ahead or check online to find out what to expect. You can explore on your own, take a docent tour, and/or an audio tour. The gift shop has a nice array of kids' books and guidebooks and some exhibits.

Bay Area Discovery Museum (ages 1 to 10)
Fort Baker, 557 McReynolds Rd., Sausalito, at the south end of Sausalito near the Golden Gate Bridge; (415) 487-4398; www.baykidsmuseum.org. $$; free for kids under 1

An extensive renovation and expansion brings more fun and education to kids. In a complex of historic buildings by the bay near the north end of the Golden Gate Bridge, the museum comprises a Media Clubhouse with games, art, music, animation, video projects, and more on the latest multimedia equipment; a science lab; a maze of illusions with optical tricks; and a fishing boat to climb aboard. Crawl through an underwater tunnel; make ceramics, crafts, and art projects; touch sea animals; develop photos; drop in on a workshop; or ride a carousel. The recently enlarged Tot Spot offers indoor/outdoor, hands-on fun for toddlers, including a walk-under waterfall. Lookout Cove is an outdoor exploration area with a rocky shore, sea cave, and tidal pools. Little architects build and design high-rise construction.

Multicultural shows are put on in the theater, from acrobats to plays and musical presentations. The museum store sells science projects and imaginative toys and books, and the cafe serves reasonably priced sandwiches, soups, and salads. You can take a short walk by the bay and have a picnic on the lawn; don't forget jackets, as it can be windy and cool. The museum is of interest to kids through about fourth-grade age: Children must be accompanied by an adult.

Richardson Bay Audubon Center
and Wildlife Sanctuary (all ages)
At the north end of the Tiburon Bike Path, 376 Greenwood Beach Rd., Tiburon; (415) 388-2524; www.tiburonaudubon.org. Free.

In this lovely wetlands preserve, thousands of waterfowl, birds, and harbor seals show up in the wintertime. There is a self-guided nature trail and a bookstore adjacent to Lyford House, a lemon-yellow landmark Victorian open to the public.

Tiburon Museum (all ages)
1920 Paradise Dr., Tiburon; (415) 435-1853; www.landmarks-society.org. Open Apr through Oct on weekends, 1 to 4 p.m. Free.

On breezy Shoreline Park with fab views of the San Francisco skyline, the Golden Gate Bridge, and Angel Island, a restored building houses the Railroad & Ferry Depot Museum. On the ground floor, a detailed operating HO-scale model shows Tiburon as a railroad town circa-1900, with landscape elements, buildings, trains, ferries, and boats. Upstairs, filled with period pieces and artifacts, is the Depot House Museum is where the station-master's family lived.

Nature Conservancy Ring Mountain Preserve (all ages)
3152 Paradise Dr., Tiburon; (415) 435-6465. **Free.**

In the hills on the north end of Tiburon, a 377-acre ridge top offers 3 miles of walking trails and wonderful views of the Bay Area. It's less than 1 mile to the summit on an easy trail edged with knee-high native grasses dotted with wildflowers in the spring.

Angel Island State Park (all ages)
Accessible via a short ferry ride from Tiburon and from Pier 41 in San Francisco; entrance is included in ferry price (415) 435-3522 or (415) 897-0715; www.angelisland.com. Tram tours: adults $$$; ages 6 to 12 $$; 5 and under **free.**

There are miles of hiking trails and mountain biking roads on this breezy island, plus gull's-eye views of three bridges and the skylines of the Bay Area. Among the historic sites are an ancient Miwok hunting ground, a cattle ranch, and a US prisoner-of-war camp. The easy way to learn some history and get some fresh air is to take the narrated tour in an open-air tram.

Mountain bikes and Segways are available to rent, and you can take sea kayaking tours conducted around the island with historical and ecological interpretation. Have an espresso and a light lunch on the deck of the cafe, or bring a picnic and sit on the lawn to watch sailboats and freighters gliding by. Environmental campsites (800-444-7275). No dogs, skateboards, or in-line skates are allowed.

China Camp State Park (all ages)
North San Pedro Road on the east side of Tiburon; (415) 456-0766.

Along San Pablo Bay, here is a hidden jewel of Bay Area parks, where the protected beach is often warm when fog chills the rest of Marin. Windsurfing is a big deal from May through October. Walk-in campsites are in lovely meadows about 1 mile from parking. Trails along the ridge have views of the north Bay Area, and there is a small museum and remnants of a late-1800s Chinese immigrants' shrimp fishing village. Leashed dogs are allowed.

Tiburon Peninsula Historical Trail (all ages)
Just off Highway 101, from Blackie's Pasture on Tiburon Boulevard to Tiburon; (415) 435-5490.

A beautiful, 3-mile, paved path for biking, in-line skating, and strolling along Richardson's Bay, with lawns for picnicking and kite-flying and benches for resting.

Sausalito Bikeway (all ages)
From Bridgeway and Wateree Street in Sausalito to Tennessee Avenue and Shoreline Highway in Mill Valley; 415-332-0505.

A 3.8-mile flat, paved path between Sausalito and Mill Valley makes a nice bike ride or walk. You will pass the edge of Richardson Bay and Bothin Marsh Open Space Preserve, where shorebirds reside; a heliport, the famous Sausalito houseboats, and an old shipyard.

Sausalito Tours (all ages)

Captain Case Powerboat and Waterbike Rental offers Boston whalers, tours on the bay, sunset cruises, water taxis, and high-tech water bikes to play around with on calm Richardson Bay (85 Liberty Ship Way, 415-331-0444).

It's easier than it looks! Sign on with Segway Tours of Sausalito for a 3-hour, narrated cruise along the waterfront and on the bike path, with a short stop at the Bay Model. About $70 per person, including instruction.

Sign up for guided kayak tours, classes and sunset and full-moon paddles at Sea Trek at Schoonmaker Point (415-488-1000; www.seatrek.com). They rent paddleboards, too, and conduct kayak expeditions at various sites in the Bay Area.

Where to Eat

Fish. 350 Harbor Dr., Sausalito; (415) 331-3474; www.331fish.com. On a patio at the waterfront, sit at picnic tables for fish-and-chips, chowder, sustainably produced seafood, pasta, fish tacos, PB&J, and root beer floats. Very fun, very casual. $–$$

Fish and Chips of Sausalito. 817 Bridgeway, Sausalito; (415) 332-2622. Bad news: It's deep-fried. Good news: It's crunchy and good. Not only fish, but calamari, shrimp, and crab. Also here, locally made Lamppert's ice cream and a hamburger place. Take your lunch and sit in the waterfront park a couple of blocks away. $

Kitti's Place. 3001 Bridgeway Ave., Sausalito; (415) 331-0390; www.kittisplace .com. In a small strip mall, a casual, homey atmosphere and Pan-Asian comfort food extraordinaire, from the very popular home-made soups to salads and entrees. Great sandwiches, Chinese chicken salad, pad thai, savory lettuce wraps, some unexpected Mexican and Indian food, curried turkey burgers, coconut ice cream. Sit at an outside table in the sunshine-with your leashed dog (and leashed kids)! Breakfast, lunch, and early dinner. $–$$

Lappert's Premium Hawaiian Ice Cream. 689 and 817 Bridgeway Ave., Sausalito; (415) 332-8175; www.lapperts.com. Super-premium, rich, creamy, homemade ice cream in luscious tropical flavors like guava, macadamia nut, mango, Kona mocha chip, Kauai Pie, and caramel coconut. Extra yummy, with 16–18 percent butterfat, compared with the average of about 10 percent in most ice cream. Gourmet coffee, too, from Kona and Kauai beans. $

Sam's Anchor Cafe. 27 Main St., Tiburon; (415) 435-4527. One of the all-time best places in the Bay Area to sit on a sunny deck, contemplate the San Francisco skyline, and watch sailboats float by. Tuck into clam chowder, cracked crab, and fresh fish while the kids check out the seagulls and the boats. Bored older children can window-shop on Main Street while you figure out how you can move to Tiburon. $–$$$

Seven Seas. 682 Bridgeway Ave., Sausalito; (415) 332-1304. The best in town for breakfast, indoors or on the patio. Lunch and dinner, too. $–$$

Sweden House Bakery. 25 Main St., Tiburon; (415) 435-9767. On a bayside deck with the locals, you can get pastries, Swedish pancakes topped with fresh berries, and egg dishes; breakfast and lunch. $–$$

Taste of Rome. 1000 Bridgeway Ave., Sausalito; (415) 332-7660, www.caffetrieste.com. Italian pastries, muffins, bagels, sandwiches, salads, wood-fired pizza, and focaccia; breakfast, lunch, and dinner; great espresso drinks. $–$$

Where to Stay

Corte Madera Inn. 56 Madera Blvd., Corte Madera, 5 minutes north of Tiburon on Highway 101; (800) 777-9670; www.bestwestern .com. One of the best choices in the North Bay for families, an attractive, comfortable motel arranged around gardens and lawns, with swimming and wading pools, a laundry, playground, putting green, and an excellent coffee shop. Continental breakfast is **free,** and so is the shuttle to the San Francisco ferry. Walk across the street to a large shopping center and around the corner to a world-class bookstore. Can't beat it! $$$

The Lodge at Tiburon. 1651 Tiburon Blvd., Tiburon; (415) 435-3133; www.thelodgeat tiburon.com. Upscale, pricey, nicely done up in contemporary-style Craftsman decor; located within a short walk from the ferry. Rooms have king or 2 queen beds, work desk, and small fridge, while Residential Suites have king beds, living room with sofa bed, equipped kitchen, armchair and ottoman, work desk, and plush amenities. **Free** Wi-Fi throughout the property; small swimming pool with private cabanas; sunny, rooftop terrace with food service. $$$–$$$$

For More Information

Sausalito Visitors Center. Kiosk next to the ferry landing and also at the Ice House, 780 Bridgeway at Bay; (415) 332-0505 or (415) 331-1093; www.sausalito.org. At the Ice House, the local historical society sells books and maps, maintains a small history museum, and offers guided walks.

Tiburon Peninsula Chamber of Commerce. 96 Main St., Tiburon; (415) 435-5633; www.tiburonchamber.org.

Stinson Beach/Bolinas

A unique tropical undercurrent keeps the waters off Stinson Beach surprisingly warm year-round. Below the western slopes of Mount Tamalpais in a protected "banana belt," the white-sand beach and the village enjoy a mild climate and are favorite destinations for San Franciscans escaping the fog.

A clutch of small cafes and shops, the village of Stinson Beach is ringed with eucalyptus and Monterey pines, where thousands of monarch butterflies spend the winter. Bolinas is even smaller and scruffier and is surrounded by spectacular wildlife preserves, beaches, and hiking trails.

A rustic village inhabited by rogue artists and craftspeople, Bolinas has some charming 19th-century buildings, particularly near the old downtown along Wharf Road. Part of Smiley's Bar dates from 1852 and St. Mary Magdalene Catholic Church from 1878. The Bolinas Lagoon is 1,200 acres of salt marsh, mudflats, and calm sea waters harboring great blue herons and egrets, migrating geese, and ducks—as many as 35,000 birds have been spotted in a single day.

A mile of shallow tide pools are exposed at low tide on the Bolinas Bay shoreline. In the vast intertidal area live gooseneck barnacles, ochre and pink sea stars, purple and giant red anemones, chitons, and more exotic sea life. This is a marine reserve, and not a thing may be removed. At the north end of the reef, Agate Beach is a small county park. Keep an eye peeled for the swift incoming tide.

Stinson Beach Park (all ages)

Highway 1 and Panoramic Highway, Stinson Beach; (415) 868-0942.

A 3-mile-long sandy beach beloved by surfers and swimmers (many Marin beaches are not safe for swimming due to undertows and currents; this one is an exception); great white sharks are occasionally sighted. Picnic tables, barbecues, restrooms, a snack bar, and, during summer, lifeguards. Dogs on leashes are allowed in one area. Rent surfboards, kayaks, and bikes at Stinson Beach Surf and Kayak, 3605 Hwy. 1; (415) 868-2739.

Audubon Canyon Ranch (all ages)

Between Bolinas and Stinson Beach, 4900 Hwy. 1, Stinson Beach; (415) 868-9244; www .egret.org. Open to the public from mid-March through mid-July on weekends and holidays. Free.

A wildlife research center in a beautiful valley where, in the tops of redwoods and pines standing in deep, wooded canyons, herons and egrets make their nests. A short trail leads to fixed telescopes for nest-watching, and you can walk on two 3-mile-long loop trails and a short nature trail. Watch for newts, frogs, fox, deer, and quail. Adjacent to a circa-1870 house are exhibits, a bookshop, and picnic tables.

Slide Ranch (ages 4 to 12)

2025 Shoreline Hwy., Muir Beach; (415) 381-6155; www.slideranch.org. $$$.

A few miles south of Stinson Beach, on a hillside overlooking the sea, lies a ranch built in the early 1900s that is now an environmental education center where your children can milk a goat, harvest veggies, bake bread, and learn how to care for animals and nature. Special days are scheduled for ocean exploration and for children under 5. Call ahead for a reservation.

Point Reyes Bird Observatory (all ages)

Four miles northwest from Bolinas, on Mesa Road; (415) 868-1221. Free.

A lovely, short, self-guided nature trail and a small museum. You are welcome to observe the activities here, which include banding rufous-sided towhees, song sparrows, and other birds. This is the Palomarin Trailhead, leading to four freshwater lakes that are waterfowl habitats and to Double Point Bay, where harbor seals breed and tide pools are inviting to look into (don't touch). Three miles from the trailhead, watch for Bass Lake, a secret swimming spot. There are portable potties near the trailhead.

Where to Eat

Bolinas Coast Café. 46 Wharf Rd., Bolinas; (415) 868-2298; www.bolinascafe.com. Amid a display of vintage surfboards, feast on Drake's Bay oysters, local seafood, and local organic produce, poultry and meats. Fabulous whole wheat sourdough bread, beautiful burgers, yummy Gardener's Pie for vegheads, fish-and-chips, berry pies, eggs Benedict, and more. Lunch, dinner, and Sunday brunch. Sit on the patio on a sunny day. $–$$

Parkside Cafe. 43 Arenal, Stinson Beach; (415) 868-1272. Italian food, burgers, and pizza; breakfast, lunch, and dinner. $–$$

Stinson Beach Grill. 3465 Shoreline Hwy., Stinson Beach; (415) 868-2002. Breakfast, lunch, or dinner, indoors or on the heated deck; fresh seafood, barbecued oysters, pasta, and Southwest cuisine. $–$$

Where to Stay

Golden Gate Hostel. Building 941, Fort Barry, in the Marin Headlands; (415) 331-2777. On the National Register of Historic Places, a spacious, homey place, with 3 kitchens, common rooms, a recreation room, a fireplace, and a piano. Family rooms with bunks. Walk right out the door onto a hiking trail. $

Ocean Court. 18 Arenal, Stinson Beach; (415) 868-0212. Large, simple motel units with kitchens, near the beach. $–$$

Seadrift Company. 2 Dipsea Rd., P.O. Box 177, Stinson Beach 94970; (415) 868-1791; www.seadriftrealty.com. Vacation home rentals. $–$$$

Steep Ravine Cabins. 801 Panoramic Hwy., 1 mile south of Stinson Beach; (800) 444-7275. Simple, rustic cabins from the 1930s, each sleeping up to 5 people, with wood-burning stoves, bunks, water, no electricity. These are rented through the state park. $$

For More Information

Marin County Visitors Bureau. 1 Mitchell Blvd., San Rafael; (415) 925-2060 or (866) 925-2060; www.visitmarin.org.

North Coast

To a child, California's northern coastline means flying kites on the beach, camping among the redwoods, and watching a whale spouting offshore. Parents love the fishing villages and Victorian loggers' towns, the art galleries, and cozy seaside cafes.

The main coastal route, Highway 1, twists and turns atop marine terraces and cliff tops, some as high as 900 feet above the shore. Views of mountains and sea are legendary, but young backseat passengers will demand frequent stops. Several forays to the North Coast will create sweeter vacation memories than trying to see all the sights in just a few days.

Set up your headquarters in Mendocino, Fort Bragg, or Bodega Bay, and make day-trip expeditions to nearby beaches and forest parks. Take time to investigate the historic towns. In Mendocino, for instance, the entire town is a Historical Preservation District of early Cape Cod and Victorian homes and steepled clapboard churches. Point Arena is prime whale-watching country. A chain of beaches stretches north from Bodega Bay, a small fishing village where seals, sailboats, and windsurfers share a harbor.

Fort Bragg

A lumbering and commercial fishing town since 1857, Fort Bragg today carefully preserves a cache of vintage wood-frame houses. Families find that restaurants and accommodations are more reasonably priced here than in Mendocino, 8 miles to the south. There are several coastal and forest state parks nearby, a picturesque fishing port at the mouth of the Noyo River, and the departure depot for the famous Skunk Train.

The annual Whale Festival in March is a two-weekend event with chowder, beer, and wine tasting; a doll show and classic car show; a run; banquet dinners; and a big arts and crafts fair with musical entertainment.

NORTH COAST

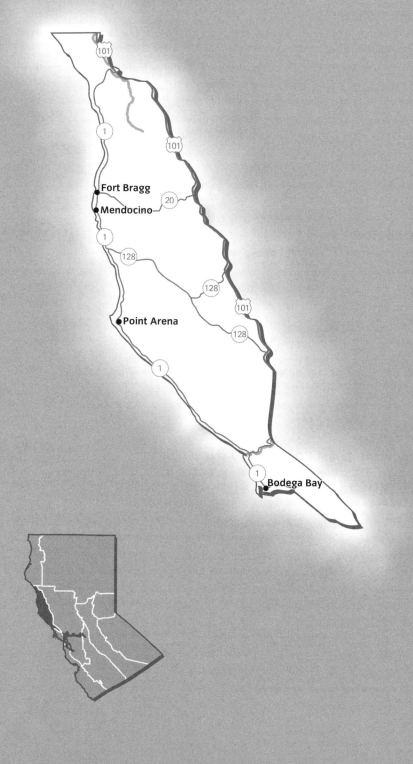

Skunk Train (all ages)

Laurel Street Depot at Main Street, Fort Bragg; (707) 964-6371 or (800) 866-1690; www .skunktrain.com. Adults $$$$; ages 5 to 11 $$$; free for children under 5.

Hauling logs to sawmills in the 1880s, the Skunk Train—actually several historic diesel and steam trains—now takes tourists on half- or full-day trips to Willits and back. The route runs along Pudding Creek through redwood forests, crossing 30 bridges and trestles. In the Fort Bragg train depot are two dozen retail shops and places to eat, scattered among railroad and logging artifacts. Snacks and lunch are available to buy along the way, or you can bring a picnic. Special events, such as barbecue-dinner rides and "Tour de Skunk," a skunk ride one way and bike ride the other, are held annually. The logging trains were nicknamed for their original gas engines, which prompted folks to say "you can smell 'em before you can see 'em."

MacKerricher State Park (all ages)

Three miles north of Fort Bragg off Highway 1; (707) 937-5804.

This 1,598-acre park has 8 miles of beach and dunes, with a popular beach play area and tide pools at Pudding Creek, at the southern end of the park. Two freshwater lakes are stocked with trout. Horseback-riding, mountain-biking, and hiking trails are found through-out bluffs, headlands, dunes, forests, and wetlands. The headlands at Laguna Point are a prime spot for whale-watching, and a permanent population of harbor seals reside here. The boardwalk affords wheelchair and stroller access from the southwest corner of the parking lot. There are 140 developed campsites and RV sites for up to 35-foot vehicles, plus fire rings and toilets. Stretching the entire 8-mile length of the park, the paved Haul Road, a former logging road, is a fabulous jogging, biking, and walking route with ocean views, crossing beautiful sand dunes.

Mendocino Coast Botanical Gardens (all ages)

18220 Hwy. 1, 1.5 miles south of Fort Bragg; (707) 964-4352; www.gardenbythesea.org. Adults $$; kids ages 6 to 17 $; free for kids under 6. Monthly birding tours are free. Leashed dogs are okay.

Wander 2 miles of path in lush gardens through acres of plantings, forest, and fern can-yons. Something is blooming every season, and in the spring the color is lyrical. Rhodo-dendrons and roses, heathers, succulents, camellias, and literally thousands of other plants crowd the gardens. From the bluff overlooking crashing waves, you can see gray whales during their winter migrating season. A picnic site perches on a scenic overlook. More than 100 bird species visit the gardens. Smack in the middle of the gardens, the Country Garden Restaurant and Grill serves lunch, dinner, and brunch at umbrella tables overlooking glorious bloom-ing flowers and trees. Try the grilled fresh fish, grilled eggplant salad, mushroom crepe torte, or the apple-wood rotisseried game hen.

Noyo Harbor (all ages)

Located 1.8 miles south of Fort Bragg, at the mouth of the Noyo River.

Headquarters for a large fleet of fishing trollers and canneries. Barking and posing, sea lions lounge on the wooden piers, waiting for the return of the boats at day's end. You can rent a fishing rod here and fish off the piers or the rocks. One of a handful of seafood restaurants on the harbor, Silver's at The Wharf is a casual, family friendly place to enjoy some fresh fish and watch the sun sink slowly behind gangs of wheeling gulls (707-964-4283). Come on the Fourth of July for the giant salmon barbecue.

You can watch migrating whales from Todd's Point, just south of Noyo Bridge on Ocean View Drive. For small children and for people who get seasick easily, Noyo Harbor is the best place from which to take a whale-watching cruise, as whales are usually sighted within 15 or 20 minutes.

For the Shell of It

344 North Main St., Fort Bragg; (707) 961-0461.

Shell jewelry, seashells, posters, rocks, minerals, folk art—and everything about shells.

Guest House Museum (all ages)

343 North Main St., Fort Bragg; (707) 961-2823. Free.

A beautiful 3-story, shingled Queen Anne home, built in 1892 entirely of redwood and filled with photos and artifacts of local history and antique logging equipment. Explore the lovely garden and be sure to take photos of yourselves by the redwood tree stump next to the museum. It's the largest redwood tree believed to have grown in the county, an incredible 21 feet in diameter. Cut in 1943, the tree rings indicate that the tree lived to be 1,753 years old.

Point Cabrillo Lighthouse (all ages)

Six miles south of Fort Bragg; (707) 937-6122; www.pointcabrillo.org. Free

On a spectacular headland above the sea, a photogenic, restored, century-old lighthouse and outbuildings, museum, and tide pool aquarium. The lighthouse is open year-round on weekends; the preserve is open for wandering every day.

Mendocino Chocolate Company

542 North Main St., Fort Bragg; (707) 964-8800, www.mendocino-chocolate.com.

Here you'll find handmade truffles and chocolates and edible seashells. Or try these specialties: a dark Rambo of a truffle, Mendocino Macho; Mendocino Breakers, dark-dipped caramels rolled in almonds; and old-fashioned Convent Fudge. Free samples; shipping worldwide.

Karen's Favorite Beaches Near Fort Bragg

- **Glass Beach,** at the foot of Elm Street; (707) 961-6300. The sand is sprinkled with pebbles of glass and china that have been tumbled and smoothed in the sea.
- **Pudding Creek,** north of town, past the first bridge. Beach play area and tide pools.
- **Ten Mile River Beach,** 8 miles north of Fort Bragg. Acres and acres of salt marsh and wetlands at the mouth of the Noyo River, inhabited by nesting birds and ducks; a 4.5-mile duney stretch of sand extends south from the river.

Where to Eat

Cafe One. 753 North Main St., Fort Bragg; (707) 964-3309. Healthy, organic, vegetarian food, plus seafood and poultry. Breakfast and lunch, with dinner on weekends. $–$$

Cowlick's Ice Cream Café. 250B North Main St., Fort Bragg; (707) 962-9271. Open late and fun for after the movies. A hometown creamery making world-class ice cream, hot fudge sundaes, banana splits, shakes, and cones; also hot dogs and snacks. $

Egghead Restaurant. 326 North Main St., Fort Bragg; (707) 964-5005. Sit in a comfy booth in a Wizard of Oz environment, complete with yellow brick road, and enjoy big, big omelets, burgers, salads, and sandwiches; breakfast and lunch. $–$$

Mendocino Cookie Company. In the Company Store at 301 North Main St., Fort Bragg; (707) 964-0282. Fresh double-chocolate-chip cookies, homemade muffins, scones, pastries, ice-cream cones, shakes, and smoothies; Wi-Fi. $

North Coast Brewing Company. 444 North Main St., Fort Bragg; (707) 964-BREW. In a casual brewpub indoors or on a (sometimes) sunny patio, enjoy a hearty menu of local fresh fish, Cajun black beans and rice, ribs, Mendocino Mud Cake, burgers, nachos, and Route 66 chili. Voted Mendocino County Restaurant of the Year. Tons of fun. $$

Piaci Pub and Pizzeria. 120 West Redwood Ave., Fort Bragg; (707) 961-1133; www.piacipizza.com. Crispy, thin-crust pizza with traditional and inventive toppings; calzones; and panini. $–$$

Where to Stay

Hi Seas Beach Motel. 1201 North Main St., Fort Bragg; (707) 964-5929. Simple rooms, all with ocean view, adjacent to Haul Road walking/biking route. $–$$

Pomo RV Park and Campground. 17999 Tregoning Lane, 1 mile south of Highway 20, Fort Bragg; (707) 964-3373. Secluded, spacious sites in a parklike setting. $

Surf Motel and Gardens. 1220 South Main St., Fort Bragg; (800) 339-5361; www.surfmotelfortbragg.com. Located next to a shopping center, the motel has rooms with

2 queen beds, microwaves, and fridges, and 2-room suites with kitchens, sleeping 6. The grounds are lush with native plants. Breakfast and Wi-Fi are **free.** $–$$$

For More Information

Fort Bragg/Mendocino Coast Chamber of Commerce. 332 North Main St., Fort Bragg; (707) 961-6300 or (800) 726-2780; www.mendocinocoast.com.

Mendocino

So closely does the town of Mendocino and this stretch of coastline resemble New England that much of the television show *Murder She Wrote* was filmed here.

Settled by Maine loggers in the middle 19th century, the town remained rough-and-tumble until the 1930s. The town languished for decades, only to be reborn as first an art colony and eventually a tourist destination. Couples come here for the galleries, the restaurants, and the romantic B&Bs. Families come to explore the beaches, to fish and whale-watch, to canoe up the rivers, and to hike in the forest parks.

The streets of Mendocino are crowded with country gardens that overflow picket fences, plus small shops, art galleries in historic buildings, and a few restaurants and inns. (Most of these are B&Bs that are inappropriate for children; plenty of family-oriented lodgings are found within a few miles north and south of town.)

Hundreds of California gray whales parade off the Mendocino coast on their 12,000-mile round-trip from the Arctic Circle to Baja, California. You can see them up close from whale-watching boats and from the bluffs around town—binoculars help—from late November through January and then again in March. Other good whale-watching sites are at Jug Handle State Reserve and Russian Gulch State Park.

Mendocino Headlands State Park (all ages)
Heeser Drive and Main Street, Mendocino; (707) 937-5804.

Wrapped around three sides of town, magnificent grassy headlands float high above swaying kelp beds in the sea, which boils through rocky arches and dark grottoes. With small children firmly in hand—there are no fences or railings—walk along cliff tops and through meadows that in spring are abloom with wildflowers. Looking back at white storefronts, Victorian homes, and the distinctive water towers of town, you can easily imagine the days when horse-drawn carriages parked in front of the Mendocino Hotel and ladies with parasols swept along the boardwalks in their long gowns. Restrooms and a picnic area are on the north end of the park, along Heeser Drive.

Big River Beach and State Park (all ages)
Off Highway 1 on the south side of Mendocino; (707) 937-5397. **Free.**

A new state park combines a gorgeous beach and a river lined with pristine forest and wildlife habitat. Where the deep Big River Valley meets the sea, a sandy, driftwoody beach and tide pools lie below the south cliff of Mendocino where you may see harbor seals, river otters, and great blue herons. Access the beach by a steep stairway from the headlands trail or from a small parking area off the highway, just south of town.

Kayaking and canoeing are popular on the river (see Catch a Canoe, below). And you can hike on forest trails—the old logging roads—into Jackson Demonstration State Forest and Mendocino Woodlands State Park on the north and to Van Damme State Park to the south. Flowers, blackberries, and legions of birds are among the glories to be found.

Catch a Canoe and Bicycles, Too! (ages 5 and up)
Stanford Inn by the Sea, Highway 1 and Comptche-Ukiah Road, Mendocino; (707) 937-0273; www.catchacanoe.com. Rentals $$–$$$$ per hour; day rates available.

Paddle canoes or kayaks from the mouth of the Big River, 7 or 8 miles upstream on an estuary—the longest unchanged and undeveloped estuary in Northern California—stopping for a picnic at a tiny beach or a meadow. The river is lined with fir and redwood groves, wildflowers, and wild rhododendrons. You will undoubtedly see ospreys, wood ducks, and blue herons; probably deer; and maybe even a small black bear. Time your canoeing expedition to paddle up the river when the tide is coming in, and be on the return trip as the tide goes out. The rental company can advise you on this, and they also rent mountain bikes, outriggers and other types of boats, and auto racks.

Shops for Kids in Mendocino

- **Bookwinkle's Children's Books,** Gallery Bookshop, Main and Kasten Streets; (707) 937-BOOK; www.gallerybooks.com. Kids get lost in their big corner of the bookstore, while parents browse in a huge selection of books about the coast and choose best sellers for a day at the beach. You will find wonderful cards, music, and magazines, too.

- **Out of This World,** 45100 Main St.; (707) 937-3335. A zillion science and nature-oriented toys and kits, binoculars, telescopes, robots, and puzzles. From here, look at the crashing surf from a lineup of telescopes.

- **Village Toy Store,** 10450 Lansing St.; (707) 937-4633; www.mendotoystore .com. Owned by former schoolteachers Bill and Susie Carr, the shop specializes in old-fashioned toys like blocks; Lincoln Logs; Tinker Toys; Brio; dolls; puppets; classic books, trains, and puzzles; plus lots of things-to-do kits and a huge inventory of kites.

- **Lark In The Morning Musique Shoppe,** 45011 Ukiah St.; (707) 937-5275; www.larkinthemorning.com. Ethnic musical instruments, including harps, African percussion instruments, guitars, whistles, drums, bagpipes, and instruments for youngsters. Books, recordings, videos, and more, too.

Ford House (all ages)

735 Main St., Mendocino; (707) 937-5397. Open 11 a.m. to 4 p.m. year-round. Free.

A visitor center for Mendocino Headlands State Park, a museum, and a good place to get a perspective on how the town is laid out. A scale model of Mendocino in the 1890s shows the dozens of tall wooden water towers that existed then. More than 30 of the towers, some double- and triple-deckers, remain in the skyline today. Here you can purchase guidebooks and history books, tide tables, and maps. The picnic tables in the meadow out back are delightful perches from which to watch the whales, which cruise by in the wintertime, close to the shoreline.

A Whale Festival is held here in March, with special exhibits, guided whale walks and cruises, whale-size hot dogs, an art and crafts fair, and a concert. Children's activities are scheduled at Point Cabrillo Lighthouse.

Kelley House Museum (all ages)

Across the street from Ford House on Main Street, Mendocino; (707) 927-5791. Free.

Set back from the street, next to a huge water tower and a duck pond surrounded by an old garden. Among the historical photos in the house are those of burly loggers hand-sawing ancient redwoods. Lumber for shipbuilding and for construction of the gold rush city of San Francisco brought easterners here in the mid-1800s. It took them 6 months by ship to reach this wilderness of mighty river valley and seacoast, inhabited only by Indians and fur trappers.

Van Damme State Park (all ages)

Three miles south of Mendocino, on Highway 1; (707) 937-5804. $ day use; $–$$$ camping.

Accessible right off the highway, the park has a popular beach and campground, plus hiking trails. The weird and wonderful Pygmy Forest, a National Natural Landmark, is seen on a 0.3-mile easy trail through a lush fern canyon and spooky woods of dwarf cypress, rhododendron, and other bonsai-like plants and trees. A 50-year-old cypress may be only 8 inches tall and have a trunk less than an inch in diameter. To reach the Discovery Trail and 10 miles of other trails, stop at the ranger station or take Little River Airport Road off Highway 1 and go 2.7 miles to the Pygmy Forest parking lot. A paved road is used by joggers and bicyclists, while the beach, right on Highway 1, is popular with abalone divers. Seventy-four developed campsites and sites for RVs up to 35 feet long. A few hike-in campsites are accessed by a 2-mile scenic trail. A sea kayak concession is right at the beach. Free Wi-Fi.

Stanford Inn by the Sea

Highway 1 and Comptche-Ukiah Road; (800) 331-8884; www.stanfordinn.com. $$$–$$$$.

On a hillside above the river near Mendocino lies a luxurious 26-room country inn surrounded by fabulous gardens. Llamas and horses graze in the meadows. Each spacious room and suite has a fireplace or wood-burning stove, sitting area, down comforters, and a private deck from which to watch the sun set over the sea. There are 2-bedroom suites, and some rooms have sofa beds, twin daybeds, and/or 2 queens. Wine and a bountiful breakfast are included. There is a spa, a sauna, and an Olympic-size swimming pool enclosed in a greenhouse crowded with tropical plants. Big River Nurseries is also located on the grounds of the inn, and it's fun to browse the rows of organic plants, veggies, and herbs. There is also a terrific vegetarian restaurant on-site.

Russian Gulch State Park (all ages)

Two miles north of Mendocino, on Highway 1; (707) 937-5804. Parking $$; camping $.

Sea caves, a waterfall, and a beach popular for rock fishing, scuba diving, and swimming in the chilly waters. From the headlands in the park, you can see the Devil's Punch Bowl, a 200-foot-long tunnel with a blowhole. Inland, the park includes 3 miles of Russian Gulch Creek Canyon and 12 miles of paved and unpaved mountain biking, hiking, and horseback-riding trails in dense forest and stream canyons. A small campground here is quite lovely, and a special equestrian campground offers riding trails into Jackson State Forest.

Jug Handle State Reserve (all ages)

Three miles north of Mendocino, on Highway 1; (707) 937-5804.

This 700-acre oceanside park is notable for an "ecological staircase" of marine terraces rising from sea level to 500 feet. Each terrace is 100,000 years older than the one below, affording a unique opportunity to see geologic evolution. The plants and trees change from terrace to terrace, too, from wildflowers and grasses to wind-strafed spruce, second-growth redwoods, and pygmy forests of cypress and pine.

Point Arena Pier (all ages)

From Highway 1 between Gualala and Elk, go west on Port Road.

A nice stop on the way up the coast, the fishing pier juts 330 feet out into the sea from the edge of a cove, where fishing, crabbing, and whale-watching are the main activities. In the rocks at the base of the cliffs, you can explore tide pools. A cliff-top trail leads to Schooner Gulch State Beach.

The original wooden fishing pier at Point Arena was dramatically smashed to pieces in a storm in 1983, along with all the buildings in the cove. In a cafe on the pier—the Galley at Point Arena—are photos of the rip-roarin' storm. The cafe serves chowder, snapper sandwiches, homemade pies, and crab in season. Adjacent to the pier are a few shops and other cafes.

Gualala Point Regional Beach Park (all ages)

42401 Hwy. 1, Gualala; (707) 785-2377. Parking $$.

A mile-long, driftwood-strewn beach and grasslands, habitat for birdlife, including great blue herons, pygmy owls, and seabirds. Camp here and hike on a coastside trail to the Sea Ranch. Stop in the visitor center to see displays of early California, Native American, and logging history, and to get trail maps. Rent canoes or kayaks to explore the Gualala River (www.adventurerents.com). In town, get home-style Italian dinners and fried chicken in the historic Gualala Hotel.

Point Arena Lighthouse (all ages)

Lighthouse Road off Highway 1, 2 miles north of Point Arena; (707) 882-2777. Free; suggested donation $–$$.

Erected in 1870, then reerected after the 1906 San Francisco earthquake, the 115-foot lighthouse is one of the best locations on the coast for gray whale–watching. Scramble around in the lighthouse and visit the museum of maritime artifacts below; tours are conducted from 10 a.m. to 3:30 p.m. daily. Black oystercatchers and cormorants wheel over the offshore rocks, and sea lions and harbor seals are often seen in the waters just south of the point. The four 3-bedroom Point Arena Coast Guard Houses here are available to rent ($$$$). Neat and clean, with kitchens, TV, and fireplaces, they're perfect for a family (877-725-4448).

Adjacent to the lighthouse is a beautiful 1,800-acre property, recently donated to the public, called Stornetta Public Lands (707-468-4000). You can wander for 2 miles on cliff tops and in meadows above the coastline to see ocean views, blowholes, and a 50-foot-tall waterfall that plunges into the ocean; and explore the estuary of the Garcia River and an adjacent beach. This is not the place to bring very young children due to rough areas and the occasional sinkhole; it's safe enough for older kids.

Where to Eat

Bay View Cafe. 45040 Main St., Mendocino; (707) 937-4197. Breakfast, lunch, and dinner, indoors or on the deck upstairs in a water tower with a knockout sea view. Good, simple fare, such as burgers, salads, pasta, and steak. $–$$

Mendo Burgers. 10483 Lansing St., Mendocino; (707) 937-1111. Beef, turkey, chicken, fish, and veggie burgers; cool 1950s decor; dine indoors or out. $

Mendocino Bakery and Cafe. 10483 Lansing St., Mendocino; (707) 937-6141. Breakfast and lunch are fun on the small deck. Kids like the pizza, bagels, and muffins; parents like the espresso drinks. You can get an early, simple dinner here, too, with Italian, Asian, and American dishes on the menu. $–$$

Mousse Cafe. Corner of Kasten and Ukiah Streets, Mendocino; (707) 937-4323. In a cottage garden, the cafe has a sophisticated menu with things that children like to eat. People sit here all afternoon, having tea and munching chunks of Blackout Cake and bread pudding. Lunch and dinner daily; Sunday brunch. $$

The Ravens. At the Stanford Inn, Comptche–Ukiah Road at Highway 1, just south of Mendocino; (707) 937-5615. The only fine restaurant on the Mendocino coast serving only vegetarian food: soups, pizza, pasta, grilled veggies; breakfast and dinner. Come early to browse the extensive organic vegetable and flower gardens. $$

Tote Fete. 10450 Lansing St., Mendocino; (707) 937-3383. California cuisine to go: apricot chicken salad, homemade meat loaf, calzones, focaccia sandwiches, dynamite desserts. Go around the corner to the Tote Fete Bakery for cake by the slice, doughnuts, and pastries. $$

Where to Stay

Inn at Schoolhouse Creek. 7051 Hwy. 1, Little River; (800) 731-5525; www.school housecreek.com. Lodge rooms, suites, and quaint cottages with kitchens, fireplaces, ocean-view decks, spa tubs, and feather beds, all including a sumptuous buffet breakfast and evening snacks. This is a family friendly place with access to the beach at Buckhorn Cove, lovely gardens, and forest glens. You can sit a spell by the fireplace in the parlor; browse the library of videos, books, games, and puzzles; hike in a fern canyon; or swing in a hammock. Kids get juice and cookies and special attention, pails for beach combing, and Matchbox cars. $$$

Little River Inn. 7751 Hwy. 1, Little River; (888) 466-5683; www.littleriverinn.com. A white wedding cake of a circa-1850 house anchors a beautiful country resort overlooking the sea, with an excellent restaurant, a fun 9-hole golf course, and tennis. Some of the spacious and comfortable rooms, each with ocean view and a deck, have 2 queens or doubles. You can walk from here to the beach and the Pygmy Forest at Van Damme State Park; Mendocino is 10 minutes away. The golf course is short, relatively easy, and inexpensive—perfect for beginners. $$$

Sea Rock Bed and Breakfast Inn. 11101 Lansing St., 0.5 mile south of Mendocino; (707) 937-0926; www.searock.com. One- and two-bedroom garden cottages with ocean views, Franklin stoves, feather beds, hearty continental breakfast served in an ocean-view dining room, some kitchens. Children are welcome with supervision. No pets. $$

Seafoam Lodge. 6751 Hwy. 1, Little River, 10 minutes south of Mendocino; (707) 937-1827 or (800) 606-1827; www.seafoamlodge .com. Families and pets are welcome at this inn, located on a private cove. Ocean-view units, continental breakfast in your room, some kitchens, decks, refrigerators. $$

For More Information

Fort Bragg/Mendocino Coast Chamber of Commerce. 332 North Main St., Fort Bragg; (707) 961-6300 or (800) 726-2780; www.mendocinocoast.com.

Mendocino Area State Parks. (707) 937-5804; www.mendoparks.org. Information about camping, day use, and interpretive programs. For campsite reservations call (800) 444-PARK.

Mendocino Coast Reservations. 1000 Main St., Mendocino; (707) 937-5033; www .mendocinovacations.com. In the Mendocino/ Fort Bragg area, rental cottages and homes, some family- and pet-friendly, some with hot tubs, fireplaces, and ocean views. $–$$$$

Bodega Bay

The warmest and some of the most beautiful Northern California beaches are found near the fishing village of Bodega Bay. The climate is mild, even in winter. Dense fog occurs only about 20 days annually.

Weathered clapboard houses, a handful of seafood restaurants, and a few shops and motels are scattered around the edges of a large, protected harbor where pleasure boats from all over the world come to anchor away from the open sea. Although the town was

Sonoma Coast **Beaches**

- **Doran Beach Regional Park,** south end of the bay off Highway 1 on Doran Park Road; (707) 785-3540; www.sonoma-county.org/parks. A popular 2-mile-long, day-use beach for swimming, surfing, kite flying, clamming, and kayaking, with breezy RV and tent campsites, restrooms, and showers. Get information and maps for county parks at the office here.

- **Bodega Dunes,** on the north end of town off Westside Road, accessed on Bay Flat Road; (707) 875-3483. Huge sand dunes, some as high as 150 feet. There is a 5-mile riding and hiking loop through the dunes and a hiking-only trail to Bodega Head. Thousands of monarch butterflies flock to a grove of cypress and eucalyptus trees adjacent to the dunes every October through February. Restrooms; RV and tent campsites. Campfire and Junior Ranger programs are held in the summer. A wheelchair-accessible boardwalk leads to the dunes. To protect the endangered snowy plover, no dogs or fires are allowed on the beach.

- **Salmon Creek Beach,** off Highway 1, 2 miles north of Bodega Bay; (707) 875-3540. Two miles of wide, sandy beach edged with grassy dunes. A creek and shallow lagoon (nice for swimming) are inhabited by throngs of seabirds. Restrooms.

- **Portuguese Beach,** between Salmon Creek and Wright's Beach on Highway 1. Best beach for rock and surf fishing.

- **Wright's Beach,** 6 miles north of Bodega Bay; (707) 875-3483. With a large parking area at beach level, it has the easiest access for all ages and abilities. Thirty campsites.

- **Shell Beach,** between Wright's Beach and Goat Rock, on Highway 1. A small, pretty beach with great tide pools; the best of the Sonoma beaches for shelling. Restrooms. From here, the Kortum Trail winds nearly 5 miles, an easy path through wildflowery meadows and gullies along the headlands, north to Goat Rock.

- **Goat Rock,** 2 miles south of Jenner on Highway 1; (707) 875-3483. Although a dangerous place to swim, this beach is popular for beachcombing, shore fishing, and freshwater fishing at the mouth of the Russian River. Seals like it, too; a large herd is often seen sunbathing and surfing where the river joins the sea. In spring they give birth to their pups here. This is protected territory for the seals, and visitors are advised to stay at a safe distance. More than 200 species of seabirds and shorebirds can be seen—great blue herons, white and brown pelicans, gulls, ospreys, and even peregrine falcons.

founded in the 1870s, most of the buildings of architectural interest are circa-1910 California Craftsman–style bungalows.

Whale-watching cruises and deep-sea fishing-party boats leave from the wharf, home base for about 300 fishing vessels. Clamming in the tidal mudflats and windsurfing in the harbor waters are also popular activities. The combination of freshwater wetlands and salt marshes attracts a great variety of shorebirds and waterfowl, plus pond turtles, harbor seals, and sea lions. On the north end of town, turn left onto Eastshore Road, then right onto Westshore Road, circling the bay. Boats are lined up here at Spud Point Marina, and there's a long fishing pier where you can try your luck. At Westside Park, you can picnic, dig for clams and bait, and launch a boat.

Almost a dozen Sonoma Coast beaches run from Bodega Bay 16 miles north to Jenner, and each has its own treasures to discover. This stretch of coastline is dramatic with sea stacks, sheer cliffs, rugged rocky coves, and vast wildflowery meadows—a spectacular drive. In April at Westside Park on the edge of the bay, the Bodega Bay Fishermen's Festival attracts crowds for the blessing of the fishing fleet, a decorated boat parade, a big outdoor fair with food and entertainment, a lamb and oyster barbecue, and arts and crafts.

Bodega Head (ages 5 and up)
On the west side of the harbor entrance; parking at the end of Westside Road; (707) 875-3483.

A vast promontory overlooking the open sea. Rangers and docent volunteers are on hand during whale-watching months to lead narrated walks on the 1.4-mile bluff trail. This is a bracing and beautiful walk at any time of the year, a trek accompanied by pelicans, oystercatchers, and sometimes even deer. Part of the narrow trail traces the very edge of the high cliffs; hold hands with your kids at all times as steep drop-offs are unguarded. Footpaths connect to 5 miles of hiking and horseback-riding trails in grassy dunes north of here.

UC Davis Marine Laboratory (all ages)
2099 Westside Rd., Bodega Bay; (707) 875-2211; www. bml.ucdavis.edu. Free drop-in tours Friday from 2 to 4 p.m. Call ahead to tour other days.

Half a mile of coastline and surrounding marine habitat is protected and studied by the university. Volunteers conduct fascinating tours for research projects such as aqua farming, global warming, species science, and more. Aquariums hold local fishes and invertebrates, a kelp forest, and tide-pool creatures. The young student guides are great with kids.

Chanslor Guest Ranch (ages 4 and up)
2660 Hwy. 1, on the north end of Bodega Bay; (707) 875-3333. Horseback rides $$$–$$$$; pony rides $$$.

Guided horseback rides on the beaches, along the bluffs, and through wetlands, plus hay wagon and barbecue rides. Special rides for kids ages 4 and up on gentle horses, ponies, or donkeys.

Pomo/Miwok Trail (ages 6 and up)
Across Highway 1 from Shell Beach; (707) 875-3540.

Up and over the hills to a small redwood forest, this is a moderately strenuous walk that takes about an hour and passes through meadows, over creeks, and under shade trees, with coastal views all the way. At the top hikers are rewarded with a redwood grove and creek, a perfect picnic spot. The path goes on from here to the Russian River and the Pomo/Miwok Campground.

Vista Trail (all ages)
Located 4.8 miles north of Jenner, off Highway 1; (707) 875-3483.

A wheelchair-accessible, 1-mile loop in a meadow on a bluff, this trail offers wide ocean views and picnic tables.

Fort Ross State Historic Park (all ages)
19005 Hwy. 1, 11 miles north of Jenner; (707) 847-3286. Parking $; camping $.

The Russians arrived here in 1812 to harvest otter and seal pelts and to grow produce for their northern outposts. Their small settlement of hand-hewn log barracks, blockhouses, and homes, together with a jewel of a Russian Orthodox church, was protected with high bastions and a bristling line of cannons, just in case the Spanish decided to pay a call. Several of the buildings and the church remain in a magical greensward above the sea. Inside the restored buildings are perfectly preserved rifles, pistols, tools, furniture, and old photos. At the excellent visitor center are exhibits, films, and guidebooks. A delightful protected beach hides below the fort. Twenty coastal canyon campsites are open March through November; picnic areas, hiking trails, restrooms. In July, Living History Day features costumed docents, historic reenactments, demonstrations, and special events.

Salt Point State Park (all ages)
Located 15 miles north of Jenner, on both sides of Highway 1; (707) 847-3221 or (707) 865-2391. Day-use fee $$.

Comprising 6,000 acres and 7 miles of coastline, the park has long, sandy beaches, rich tide pools, rugged cliffs, sunny meadows, and hiking and biking trails. The dense forestlands of Salt Point are inhabited by gnarly pygmy pines and cypress, their ghostly gray, mossy trunks tickled by maidenhair ferns. For tide pooling take the Gerstle Cove Campground turnoff and follow the road to Gerstle Cove parking. No collecting is allowed.

Sea Ranch Lodge
60 Sea Walk Dr., off Highway 1, 20 miles north of Jenner in Sea Ranch; (707) 785-2371 or (800) 732-7262; www.searanchlodge.com. $$$–$$$$.

Nestled in grassy meadows on headlands above the ocean, a small lodge, a restaurant, and nearby rentable homes are headquarters for a coastal getaway. Whether or not you stay at the lodge, you can access several beaches (Shell Beach, Pebble Beach, and Black Point Beach are the best) and walk easy paths on the bluffs. Walk or bike on quiet, paved

Bodega Bay **Shops**

Candy and Kites. 1425 Hwy. 1; (707) 875-3777; www.candyandkites.com. A must-stop before you hit the sand, this store features a huge and colorful variety of kites and games for the beach, plus air toys, books, saltwater taffy, and chocolates. Kite festivals in Bodega Bay take place in April and July.

Bodega Bay Gifts. Ocean View Center, 2001 Hwy. 1; (707) 875-2449. Giant inventory of T-shirts, sweats, shells and shell jewelry, games, local art, and stuff.

Bodega Bay Surf Shack. Pelican Plaza; (707) 875-3944; www.bodegabaysurf .com. Headquarters for rentals, maps, and advice on biking, beachcombing, kayaking, surfing, and windsurfing. Lessons and guided tours are available; beachwear and gear is for sale. Visit the website for fascinating satellite reports, maps, and forecasts about waves and weather.

Patrick's Salt Water Taffy. 915 Hwy. 1; (707) 875-9816. Look for the pink-and-white-striped little building on the bay side of the road. Bins and bags of a million kinds of taffy.

Second Wind. 1805 Hwy. 1, on the north end of town; (707) 875-9463. A large kite and wind toy shop, also selling toys, saltwater taffy, and retro candy.

country roads on the east side of the Highway 1. A relatively easy 18-hole, links-style golf course is laid on the bluffs, in meadows and forests.

From the Sea Ranch restaurant, you can easily see whales in the wintertime. The food is good—sandwiches, salads, homemade soups, fresh fish, for lunch and dinner. The lounge bar has a big fireplace. Twenty upscale rooms with king or queen beds have ocean views; one room has a fireplace and a hot tub (but no view). A new, larger lodge has been designed and will be under construction soon.

Stillwater Cove Regional Park (all ages)
Sixteen miles north of Jenner on Highway 1; (707) 847-3245.

A favorite surf-fishing spot, with small boat access and picnic area with a great ocean view. Five miles of hiking trails in the redwoods, a wheelchair-accessible trail, and a campground. Head down from the campground to the pretty little cove. Restrooms, showers. An easy half-mile trail leads to the historic 1-room Fort Ross Schoolhouse.

Where to Eat

Claudio's Trattoria. 1400 Hwy. 1, on the north end of Bodega Bay in Pelican Plaza; (707) 875-2933; www.claudiostrattoria.com. Great sea views from a sunny deck and a sunroom, stick-to-the-ribs traditional Italian food for dinner, and weekend lunches. $–$$$

Mom's Apple Pie. 4550 Gravenstein Hwy. North, Sebastopol; (707) 823-8330; www .momsapplepieusa.com. On the way to Bodega Bay, this shop has fabulous, luscious pies by Betty Carr, famous for apricot, blackberry, rhubarb, wild blueberry, chocolate cream, and more. Take out or eat in the simple cafe. For lunch, sandwiches, soups, and salads, too. $

Sandpiper Dockside Cafe. 1410 Bay Flat Rd., Bodega Bay; (707) 875-2278. The area's best-kept secret, this little place is hidden below the main road, featuring homemade everything: eggs with home fries, huevos rancheros, or crab omelets for breakfast; fresh seafood, burgers, cioppino, clam chowder, and more comfort food for lunch and dinner. $–$$

Seaweed Café. 1580 Eastshore Rd., Bodega Bay; (707) 875-2700; www.seaweedcafe.com. Serves upscale, organic "slow food" California cuisine, most of the ingredients from artisanal producers within 30 miles. Dinner Thursday through Sunday, and Sunday brunch. Sea views, fireplace, white tablecloths, wonderful seafood (Jean Michel Cousteau loves it . . .). Although the ambience is warm and friendly and the food is spectacular, picky young eaters may not take to the sophisticated menu. $$–$$$

Spud Point Crab Company. 1860 Westshore Rd., Bodega Bay; (707) 875-9472; www .spudpointcrab.com. Breakfast sandwiches, and for lunch, tri-tip and crab and shrimp sandwiches, chowder, chili, and hot dogs. Sit at an outdoor table to watch boating activity at the docks. Home-smoked salmon, and fresh crab and fish from the Anello family boats. $–$$

The Tides Wharf and Restaurant. 835 Hwy. 1, Bodega Bay; (707) 875-2751. On the wharf, with views of the bay and the boat action; a sunny cafe deck for light meals, snacks, and drinks; a souvenir shop; a gourmet food emporium and oyster bar; and a large, attractive restaurant serving great seasonal fresh seafood, from cracked Dungeness crab to cioppino, a huge variety of fish, and seafood salads. Every table has a view, and the seals have a view of you. Open for three meals a day. $–$$

Union Hotel. 3731 Main St., Occidental; (707) 874-3555. Famous for decades for supercolossal, multicourse, family-style Italian dinners; very popular on Sunday afternoons and holidays. Choices include homemade ravioli, fried chicken, veal, antipasto, minestrone, salads, and more—much more. Occidental makes a nice stop on the way to or from Bodega. Take the Bohemian Highway through Freestone for about 20 minutes on a winding mountain road to this tiny village and enjoy its restaurants, galleries, and shops. Dinner guests are welcome to park RVs here overnight. $–$$

Wild Flour Bread. Six miles west of Sebastopol off Highway 12, 140 Bohemian Hwy., Freestone; (707) 874-2938. A roadside stop for legendary sticky buns, artisanal breads, pizza, and other treats made from organic grains and seeds, and baked in a eucalyptus-fired oven. They hand-knead everything in front of your eyes, and the baking goes on all day. Open weekdays. $

Where to Stay

Bodega Bay Lodge. 103 Hwy. 1, on the south side of Bodega Bay; (707) 875-3525 or (800) 875-1007; www.bodegabaylodge .com. Perched above the bay and bird-filled marshes, all rooms and luxury suites have sea views, terraces or decks, cozy comforters, Jacuzzi tubs, and robes; some have fireplaces. In the lobby are a giant stone fireplace and two 500-gallon aquariums filled with tropical fish. Fresh, contemporary decor, swimming pool, spa, sauna, fitness center, complimentary bikes, golf packages. $$$$

Bodega Coast Inn and Suites. 521 Hwy. 1, Bodega Bay; (707) 875-2217; www.bodega coastinn.com. Each motel-style room and suite has an ocean view, balcony, and refrigerator; some have fireplaces and spas; one is a 2-bedroom with kitchenette. $$–$$$

Fort Ross Lodge. 20705 Hwy. 1, Jenner; (707) 847-3333; www.fortrosslodge.com. Comfortable ocean-view rooms and suites, some with fireplaces and spas, microwaves, refrigerators, TV/VCR. Barbecues on your private patio; a convenience store across the road. $$$–$$$$

Jenner Inn & Cottages. 10400 Hwy. 1, Jenner; (800) 732-2377; www.jennerinn.com. No TV, just fabulous views of the Russian River estuary where it enters the Pacific Ocean. Twenty-one spacious, nicely appointed, comfortable rooms and cottages are scattered in small buildings along the waterfront. Most have access to hot tubs and sauna, some have private decks—each one is different. Guests gather in the cozy lodge by the fireplace to enjoy the library, Wi-Fi and parlor games. On-site, the Jenner Inn Cafe & Wine Bar serves California cuisine and local seafood, poultry, and organic produce. $$$

Mar Vista Cottages at Anchor Bay. 35101 Hwy. 1, Gualala; (707) 884-3522 or (877) 855-3522; www.marvistamendocino .com. Pick produce, gather eggs and honey, and cook in your own equipped kitchen in one of a dozen sweet, simple, comfortable, vintage cottages, 1- and 2-bedrooms with

living rooms, fireplaces or woodstoves, some with ocean views; no TV, radio, or phone. Japanese soaking tub outdoors, barbecues, secret beach across the road. Kids love the bunnies, the chickens, the pygmy goats, and the dogs; you can bring your dog for a small fee (no puppies). $$$–$$$$

Pomo/Miwok Campground. Where the river meets the sea at Bridgehaven, 10 minutes off Highway 1; (800) 444-7275. There are 40 walk-in tent sites in a dense redwood forest at the end of a paved road (a beautiful road for biking and walking). A few sites are near the parking lot; it's a 5- to 15-minute walk to the others. If you arrive with no reservation, check the bulletin board to find available sites. Fire rings, picnic tables, and portable potties. $

For More Information

Bodega Bay Chamber of Commerce. 575 Hwy. 1, Bodega Bay; (707) 875-3866; www.bodegabay.com.

California Welcome Center. 9 4th St., Santa Rosa (take the downtown exit west); (707) 577-8674 or (800) 404-7673; www.visit santarosa.com. Brochures, maps, and advice for travel throughout the North Coast and the Wine Country.

Department of Parks and Recreation, Russian River District. P.O. Box 123, Duncans Mills 95430; (707) 865-2391. Information on private campgrounds.

Sonoma Coast Visitor Center. 850 Hwy. 1, next to Texaco, Bodega Bay; (707) 875-3866; www.visitsonomacoast.com.

Vacation Homes. (707) 875-4000, (707) 875-3942, or (707) 875-3000. From cabins to spacious vacation home rentals, from Bodega Bay to Timber Cove and beyond. $–$$$$

Wine Country

Due north across the Golden Gate, rugged mountain ranges and rich agricultural valleys shelter lakes, rivers, and a scattering of small, historic towns. Country pleasures are what families seek in Sonoma, Lake, and Napa Counties—everything from boating and fishing to biking and hiking, camping, and vestiges of California's early days.

The 1700s come alive in the small mission town of Sonoma, which contains the largest original Spanish plaza in the state. A few minutes away, in the Valley of the Moon, is a state park with riding trails and a delightfully spooky ruin in a redwood forest.

Kids like watching hot-air balloons and glider planes in the Napa Valley, and parents are surprised to find that there's a lot to do and see besides wineries. The waters of Lake Berryessa attract vacationers for summer waterskiing and swimming and for year-round trout and bass fishing.

Primary destinations are the oceanarium and wildlife theme park Six Flags Discovery Kingdom in Vallejo and Safari West near Calistoga, a preserve for African plains animals. Flowing from the valleys to the sea in western Sonoma County, the Russian River offers fishing holes and campgrounds, redwood groves and sandy beaches. Families that love to fish and water-ski also head north to Clear Lake. The smooth green flanks of 4,200-foot Mount Konocti, a dormant volcano, loom dramatically above the placid blue waters, which hold more fish per acre than any other lake in the country.

Lakeport

The largest town on the shores of Clear Lake, Lakeport features a few historic buildings and an old-fashioned band shell and playground in a grassy lakefront park. Several smaller towns and small resorts are scattered around the lake. When school's out, families begin arriving with their boats, camping gear, fishing rods, and water sports equipment. The largest natural lake in the state and rated the number-one bass lake in the western United

WINE COUNTRY

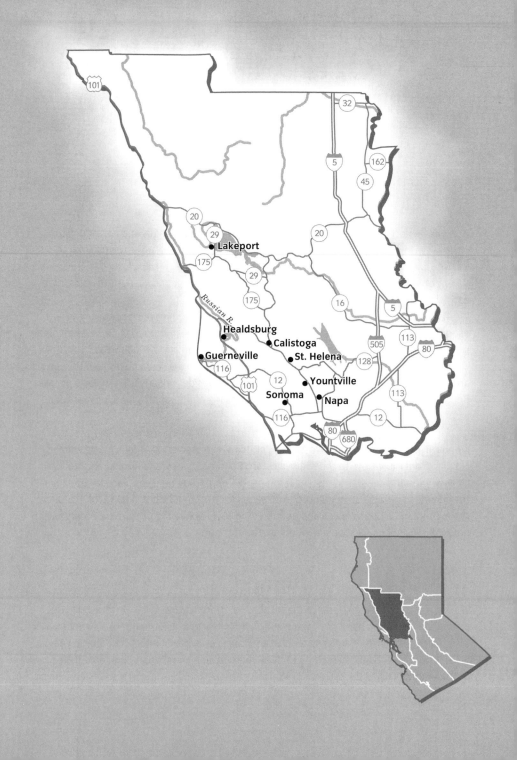

States, Clear Lake is ringed with family-oriented resorts, marinas, and campgrounds. The 2-lane highway from the Napa Valley to Lakeport is about 30 miles of curves; take advantage of the many pullouts for great views of jagged ridges, meandering valleys, and fall color.

Pomo Indian tribal heritage is prominent throughout the county at the museum, at Anderson Marsh State Park, in the crafts and art found in retail shops, and at annual Native American events.

Winters are mild here, a good time for fishing expeditions, rockhounding, and bird watching. You are likely to see bald eagles, and you can't miss the tremendous number of waterfowl and other migrating birds from Alaska and Canada that come to spend the season.

Lake County Museum (all ages)
255 North Main, Lakeport; (707) 263-4555. Free.

In a beautiful 1877 building that served as a school for more than 50 years, a big collection of stone tools, arrowheads, pioneer costumes and exhibits, and antique firearms, as well as a shop selling jewelry made by local Native Americans. The highlights of the collection are the superb Pomo Indian baskets.

Clear Lake State Park (all ages)
5300 Soda Bay Rd., Kelseyville; (707) 279-4293 (campground reservations: 800-444-7275). Some parking $$; some parking free; camping $.

Here you can camp beside the lake; fish for bass, catfish, crappie, and perch; swim; and bird-watch. Interpretive displays on local history and the natural environment and wildlife are at the visitor center. Behind the center look for great blue herons on the banks of Kelsey Creek; the large nests in the treetops are heron rookeries. A 700-gallon aquarium

Lake County **Discovery Trails**

The rolling countryside around Clear Lake and other parts of the county is as green as Ireland in spring and winter; wildflowery, dry, and hot in the summer and fall. Sixteen routes for biking and walking—county roads, city streets, state highways, and dirt roads—are mapped and described in detail, from strenuous to easy, in a booklet available at the visitor center or by mail; you will also find the routes on the website (875 Lakeport Blvd., Lakeport; 707-263-9644; www.lakecounty.com). The Highland Springs Reservoir Picnic Area and Trail just south of Lakeport offers easy to moderate paths for walking, horseback riding, and biking in oak woodlands and alongside wetlands and the lake. You can picnic here, play Frisbee golf, and engage in nonmotorized boating and fishing (707-263-2341).

shows Clear Lake fish and aquatic life. On Cole Creek are shady picnic sites, barbecues, and a swimming beach with lifeguards. Among miles of hiking trails, the short Indian Nature Trail showcases flora related to local tribes.

Clarke's Collectibles and Lunchbox Museum (all ages)

3674 East Hwy. 20, Nice; (707) 274-9952; www.retrodeb.com. **Free.**

In a former firehouse, a shop and museum showcasing more than 100,000 collectible items, including games, Star Wars memorabilia, dolls, toys, vintage and retro collectibles, an incredible display of 700-plus lunchboxes, and a big collection of Ponytail boxes. Also here are working animatronic pieces from the old Playland by the Sea in San Francisco. Call for hours and days.

Anderson Marsh State Historic Park (all ages)

Highway 53, between the towns of Lower Lake and Clearlake; (707) 994-0688. Parking $.

Herons, pelicans, ducks, grebes, coots, cormorants, bald eagles, and other species of waterfowl are seen regularly here. The sight of a bald eagle fishing for its dinner is a moment to remember. Bird watching is best in early spring and early in the morning when the birds are feeding. Numerous ancient Native American sites date from 8000 BC, when the shores and swamps surrounding Clear Lake were almost exactly as they are today. In the historic Anderson Ranch House are a small museum and a visitor center. To get very close to the wetlands wildlife, hike through the Redbud Audubon Society's McVicar Preserve within the state park, or rent a boat or canoe at Garner's Resort (707-994-6267) or Shaw's Shady Acres (707-994-2236), nearby.

Konocti Harbor Resort and Spa (all ages)

8727 Soda Bay Rd., Kelseyville; (800) 660-LAKE; www.konoctiharbor.com. $$–$$$$.

In the shadow of Mount Konocti, this sprawling lakeside resort and marina has 2 large swimming pools with lifeguards, lighted tennis courts, minigolf, playgrounds, a video games arcade, volleyball, and a lot more. The staffed Kids' Club provides child care and activities all summer and during concert evenings. If your family wants to stay put and enjoy the lake, this is the place. Older children particularly enjoy it, as there are kids to meet, beach volleyball, pool tables, and video games, plus Jet Skis, pedal boats, kayaks, and fishing poles to rent. Also here is a complete health spa, with exercise classes, a lap pool, and body and beauty treatments. An 80-passenger paddlewheeler excursion boat is docked at the marina. Live, top-name entertainment occurs year-round in 1,000- and 5,000-seat venues—mostly country western, with some (vintage) rock stars. The facility offers a wide variety of accommodations, including motel rooms, beach cottages, condo units, and family rate packages. The atmosphere is family-oriented and casual. Restaurants serve hearty American fare ($$).

On the Waterfront (all ages)

60 3rd St., Lakeport; (707) 263-6789.

Parasailing, plus rentals for Jet Skis, pedal boats, ski boats, and fishing and "patio boats"—an easy-to-handle sort of a barge, just the thing for families. Purchase beachwear and water-ski accessories here, too.

Outrageous Waters Park and Fun Center (ages 4 and up)
Highway 53 at Highway/Dam Road, Clearlake; (707) 995-4817. $$$; over 55 $; kids 3 and under **free.**

Four scary water slides are thrilling and cooling on a summer's day. Little kids will like the "Lazy River" and a huge kids' pool with waterfalls. A mini–Grand Prix racetrack, batting cages, and arcade games are available. Minimum height for slides is 48 inches.

Real Goods (all ages)

13371 Hwy. 101, Hopland; (707) 744-2100; www.realgoods.com.

A destination in itself, Real Goods is an unusual retail showplace of renewable energy products—solar, recycled, biodegradable, nontoxic, energy-efficient items for sustainable living, including toys, clothing, and books. Even the building itself demonstrates "green" concepts; the north and east walls of the main building were constructed of straw bales. Just exploring the surrounding landscaping is an educational experience. Outdoors are water features in which kids can play, and you can walk around and rest on the banks of a shady little lake.

Lake Mendocino (all ages)
1160 Lake Mendocino Dr.; 3 miles north of Ukiah, take Lake Mendocino Drive east off Highway 101; (707) 462-7581 or (707) 485-1427; www.lakemendocino.com.

Camping, picnic sites, boat launching, swimming beach, fishing, walking trails, sailing, personal watercraft, and pleasure boating. The visitor center has Pomo Indian culture exhibits.

City of Ten Thousand Buddhas (all ages)
2001 Talmage Rd., Talmage; (707) 462-0939; www.cttbusa.org.

A unique sightseeing stop to make if you are traveling from Lake County to the coast. Stop in at the administration building for a map and wander the grounds to see fascinating decorated Asian-style buildings. Ten thousand golden Buddhas and a Buddha with a thousand hands and a thousand eyes are the top attractions. You can have lunch in the vegetarian restaurant and enjoy the sights and sounds of monks going about their ceremonies and other activities.

Vichy Hot Springs (all ages)

2605 Vichy Springs Rd., Ukiah; (707) 462-9515; www.vichysprings.com. $$$–$$$$.

Since 1854, a family-oriented country resort famous for natural, warm, carbonated water springs that fill a large swimming pool and several tubs. Simple, spacious rooms and cottages are nicely decorated with Waverly floral prints; some have full kitchens, 1 or 2 bedrooms, and verandas overlooking sweeping lawns, meadows, and gardens. You can explore the ranch, mountain bike, and hike to 40-foot Chemisal Falls. There is a year-round stream and lovely wildflowers. Buffet breakfast is included. Ask about day use. You can hike on 700 acres of countryside.

Grace Hudson Sun House (all ages)
431 South Main St., Ukiah; (707) 467-2836; www.gracehudsonmuseum.org. Free.

An impressive complex housing Native American baskets, artifacts, and paintings, this is a light, colorful place that children enjoy. The late Grace Hudson painted the faces and the domestic life of native Pomo Indians, while her ethnologist husband assembled the extraordinary collection, one of the most important in the Northern Hemisphere. Open to inspection, their home is a wonderful redwood Craftsman-style bungalow. A tree-shaded park with picnic tables surrounds the museum buildings. My granddaughters have found Native American–oriented toys, books, and games in the gift shop.

Montgomery Woods State Reserve (all ages)
Fourteen miles west of Ukiah on Orr Springs Road; (707) 937-5804; www.parks.ca.gov. Free.

One of the least-visited state parks, this one shelters a miraculous virgin forest of redwood trees, including the Mendocino Tree, which, at 367½ feet, now holds the title of the world's tallest living thing. An easy loop trail of about 3 miles follows Montgomery Creek past 6-foot-tall woodwardia ferns, wild iris, columbine, and more gorgeous greenery to five redwood groves that have never been logged. The Mendocino Tree stands, without a marker to distinguish it, among two dozen or so redwoods that tower 350 feet and higher. The steep, winding road to the reserve is not at all appropriate for RVs.

Where to Eat

Blue Wing Saloon and Café. 9520 Main St., Upper Lake; (707) 275-2233; www.blue wingsaloon.com. A beautiful reproduction of a watering hole and stagecoach stop of the 1800s, Blue Wing has California comfort food and microbrews on the menu in a colorful, casual, Old West environment. Lunch, dinner, and Sunday brunch. $–$$$

Boneyard BBQ. 13441 Hwy. 101, Brutocao Schoolhouse Plaza, Hopland; (707) 744-2020. Barbecued ribs and chicken, baked beans, burgers, sandwiches, hot wings, fish-and-chips. Lunch and dinner. $–$$

Main Street Cafe. 14084 Lakeshore Dr., Clearlake; (707) 995-6450. Indoors or outdoors, the locals' favorite for down-home cooking. Children like the burgers and sandwiches. $

Park Place. 50 3rd St., Lakeport; (707) 263-0444. In a comfy booth, or on the deck with lake views, everyone goes for the homemade pasta, Nancy's amazing vegetable soup, fresh fish, and steak. Veggies come from a local patch, and the blackberries in the sorbet are picked in the owner's backyard. You can motor here in your boat and take a snooze in the park across the street. Open all day for breakfast, lunch, and dinner. $–$$

Where to Stay

Bell Haven Resort. 3415 White Oak Way, Kelseyville; (707) 279-4329; www.bellhaven .com. On Clear Lake's Soda Bay, a nice beach, a fishing and swimming pier, private docks, kayaks, and cabins with kitchens. $–$$

B. J. Wall's Lakeside RV and Campground. 2570 Lakeshore Blvd., Nice; (707) 274-3315. On Clear Lake, full hookups, campsites, shade trees, private beach, boat dock, showers, laundry. Walk to nearby restaurant and boat rentals. $

El Grande Inn. 15135 Lakeshore Dr., Clearlake; (707) 994-2000. On the lake, 45 very nice rooms and suites, plus a pool, sauna, garden courtyard, and restaurant. $–$$

Featherbed Railroad Company. 2870 Lakeshore Blvd., Nice; (800) 966-6322; www .featherbedrailroad.com. Nine irresistible renovated cabooses are a sweet surprise overlooking the lake. The Rosebud Caboose has bunk beds for 2 kids, and there is a small swimming pool. A hearty breakfast is served in the ranch house or on the front porch. In a parklike setting, the resort also has a private beach and pier, boat dock, boat ramp, and restaurant; boat and Jet Ski rentals nearby. $$

For More Information

Lake County Visitor Center. 6110 East Hwy. 20, Lucerne; (707) 274-5652 or (800) LAKESIDE; www.lakecounty.com.

California State Park Campground Reservations. (800) 444-7275.

Lakeport Regional Chamber of Commerce. 875 Lakeport Blvd., Lakeport; (800) 525-3743; www.lakeportchamber.com.

Calistoga

More than a century ago, people came to this little tree-shaded Victorian spa town in horse-drawn carriages to "take the waters." Steam rises from 200-degree mineral springs at a dozen or so health resorts—this is the place for rest and rejuvenation, for massages and mud baths. Children are not likely to go for a massage or for wine tasting at the many wineries in the area. They will love the town's museum, a unique wildlife preserve, and biking down Mount St. Helena. Except for the busy few blocks of the main street, Lincoln Avenue, this is the quiet side of Napa Valley, making biking and hiking particularly serene. This is a walking town, a compact grid of streets that look suspended in time. Stroll up and down the streets perpendicular to Lincoln, on the west side, and look for the sweet gazebo and playground in creekside Pioneer Park on Cedar Street.

Sharpsteen Museum (all ages)

1311 Washington St., Calistoga; (707) 942-5911; www.sharpsteen-museum.org. Free.

Kids love the unstuffy atmosphere of this place, which was built and donated by a 30-year veteran of the Disney studios. His Disney memorabilia are on display, along with an elaborate diorama re-creating the 1800s resort town, plus a big collection of old photos; a stagecoach; a Victorian dollhouse; a barn and farming equipment; a cottage of the original hot springs resort; a general store; and a blacksmith shop.

Indian Springs Hot Springs Spa and Resort

1712 Lincoln Ave., Calistoga; (707) 942-4913; www.indianspringscalistoga.com. Day use $$–$$$; accommodations $$$$.

Founded in 1865, Indian Springs is one of the oldest spa resorts in town, and it still has an old-fashioned air about it. Filled with mineral water from three natural geysers, the Olympic-size pool is heated to 92 degrees in summer and 101 degrees in winter. Horseshoes and a clay (!) tennis court, bicycles and bike surreys, croquet, hammocks, and Weber grills are available here. From a studio cottage to a large house, accommodations are simple and comfortable, including fireplaces, robes, and air-conditioning.

Old Faithful Geyser (all ages)

A mile north of Calistoga, on Tubbs Lane; (707) 942-6463; www.oldfaithfulgeyser.com. Adults $$; kids 6 to 12 $; under 6 free.

One of only three regularly erupting geysers in the world. Every 40 minutes or so, a column of 350-degree water and steam roars more than 60 feet into the air. That's it.

Safari West (ages 3 and up)

3115 Porter Creek Rd., Santa Rosa, 10 minutes east of Calistoga; (707) 579-2551; www.safari west.com. Call for reservations and schedule. $$$$.

Giraffes in Wine Country? Yes. At the far northern end of the valley, on open grasslands and rolling hills, sits a wildlife preserve with more than 400 exotic animals and birds, as well as African plains animals, including zebras, elands, giraffes, impalas, cheetahs, and rare endangered antelopes. Private half-day, narrated tours are conducted in safari vehicles. You can stay overnight here in a nice tent cabin outfitted with 2 double beds; breakfast is included, and African food is available for dinner in the Savannah Café, where you can sit with staff members.

It's hot and dry here in summer and early fall, so be prepared with hats and sunscreen. I don't recommend bringing toddlers along unless you know they can handle a 3-hour, sometimes bumpy ride. The last time we went to Safari West, we saw a newborn zebra and a baby wildebeest, and we loved it when the herd of Watusi cattle came pounding down the road and crowded up against the truck. What shoulders!

Robert Louis Stevenson State Park (all ages)

Seven miles north of Calistoga, on Highway 29; (707) 942-4575. Free.

On the wooded slopes of Mount St. Helena, take forest trails for easy walks or embark on the steep, 5-mile scramble to the 4,343-foot summit. Mountain bikers use the fire road, which starts about 0.25 mile north of the parking lot. Spyglass Hill in Robert Louis Stevenson's *Treasure Island* is based on the landscape of Mount St. Helena; see a museum devoted to Stevenson's life and works at the library in St. Helena (707-963-3757). No dogs are allowed in the park, and there is no water.

Petrified Forest (all ages)

4100 Petrified Forest Rd., 5 miles west of Calistoga; (707) 942-6667; www.petrifiedforest .org. Adults $$; kids 4 to 17 $; younger kids **free.**

For an unusual 1-hour side trip, walk on an easy, 0.25-mile path through a redwood forest turned to stone 6 million years ago by a volcanic eruption, a site you're not likely to see elsewhere. One-hundred-foot tree trunks are swirled in opalescent purple and pink. The gift shop sells colorful polished stones, semiprecious gems, and fossils. Wheelchair access is marginal but doable; pets are okay.

Where to Eat

Buster's Southern Barbecue. At Highway 29 and Lincoln Avenue, Calistoga; (707) 942-5605. A true hole-in-the-wall and a dynamite find if you like barbecue. Pork loin, ribs, and other meats cooked outdoors, served at picnic tables with slaw and baked beans, as sandwiches or platters; servings are quite large. Unless you like your sauce extra-hot, ask for mild. $

Calistoga Inn. 1250 Lincoln Ave., Calistoga; (707) 942-4101. In a charming, circa-1880 building with a splendid outdoor dining terrace on the Napa River, the inn serves inventive sandwiches, meal-size salads, lots of appetizers to share, and grilled meats, as well as microbrews from the on-site brewery. $–$$

Pacifico Restaurante Mexicano. 1237 Lincoln Ave., Calistoga; (707) 942-4400. Warm, bright colors and a casual, kid-friendly atmosphere are the backdrop for fine Mexican food at breakfast, lunch, and dinner. Ask for *pico de gallo* to go with your warm tortilla chips. Try the blue-corn buttermilk pancakes, fresh enchiladas, and chiles rellenos. $–$$

Where to Stay

Carlin Country Cottages. 1623 Lake St., Calistoga; (707) 942-9102 or (800) 734-4624; www.carlincottages.com. Nice, simple cottages in a wide courtyard, with Shaker-style furnishings. Some cottages have Jacuzzi tubs;

some have 1 or 2 separate bedrooms with kitchens. Spring-fed swimming pool. $$–$$$

Comfort Inn. 1865 Lincoln Ave., Calistoga; (707) 942-9400. Half of the 55 rather basic rooms have 2 queen beds; **free** breakfast with homemade waffles. Likely the best value in the upper valley. Warm, natural, mineral-water pool and Jacuzzi; sauna and steam for adults. Upper balconies are best for view and a glass of wine while the kids watch 86 cable channels. Walk to town. $–$$

Solage Calistoga. 755 Silverado Trail, Calistoga; (866) 942-7442; www.solagecalistoga .com. Within short biking distance to town, a new, upscale, contemporary-design cottage-style property with a 130-foot swimming pool, children's pool, and playground; full-service spa and mud treatment venues. Pets are VIPs, too. Some suites and studios have 2 queens, fireplace, and private patio. In-room "games menu" offers popular board games, and cruiser bikes are **free** to use. The stylish Solbar restaurant and lounge serves all meals and will produce a picnic. Guests here have the use of spas, restaurants, recreational venues, and hiking trails at nearby luxury resorts Auberge du Soleil and Calistoga Ranch. $$$$

Stevenson Manor Inn. 1830 Lincoln Ave., Calistoga; (707) 942-1112. A small, very nice Best Western motel on the main street. Rooms have 2 doubles, **free** Wi-Fi, microwave, refrigerator; some with fireplace. Continental breakfast included; small swimming pool, sauna, steam. Walk to the park, restaurants, shopping. $$$–$$$$

For More Information

Calistoga Visitors Bureau. 1458 Lincoln Ave., Calistoga; (707) 942-6333; www.calis togafun.com.

St. Helena

Families like the little town of St. Helena for its tree-shaded old-fashioned neighborhoods, for postcard-perfect Main Street lined with 19th-century stone buildings—each with a quaint shop or cafe inside—and for the biking and walking trails in the surrounding countryside and the nearby state park. Kids who like to cook will enjoy visiting the Culinary Institute of America at Greystone and the West Coast annex of a famous gourmet store, Dean and DeLuca. It's best to park your car and walk around.

Dean and DeLuca

601 Hwy. 29, just south of St. Helena; (707) 967-9980; www.deandeluca.com.

Huge gourmet market, wine shop, produce mart, and deli—a welcome offshoot of the famous New York store. You'll find here an incredible variety of cheeses and meats, rotisserie chicken, and wonderful salads and entrees to go, plus packaged gourmet foodstuffs of all kinds. I like the big glass jars of exotic dried mushrooms and marinating olives, and the amazing array of vinegars and oils to taste, from fig balsamic vinegar to olive oil pressed in the most isolated, obscure orchard in Tuscany. You can enjoy your sandwiches, fresh fruit smoothies, and espresso drinks in the back on the sunny patio.

Bothé-Napa Valley State Park (all ages)

3801 Hwy. 29 at Larkmead Lane, St. Helena; (707) 942-4575 (campground reservations: 800-444-7275). **Free;** camping $.

Wilderness trails in a pine and redwood forest, plus a sycamore-shaded campground in Ritchie Creek Canyon. Surprising in a state park is the small swimming pool here, with a lifeguard, open June through Labor Day. Day-trippers picnic on the grass along the creek. It's a short walk from here into Bale Grist Mill State Park, a wooded glade with a 36-foot grinding wheel powered by a rushing creek. Costumed docents grind grain on the millstones and make bread during Old Mill Days in October and frequently on summer weekends. The 50-site campground has hot showers and laundry tubs.

Napa Valley Trail Rides offers 1- and 2-hour, easy, slow, guided horseback rides in the park along Ritchie Creek and up on the ridges overlooking the valley (707-996-8566).

Culinary Institute of America
at Greystone (CIA) (all ages)

2555 Main St., just past Beringer Winery on Highway 29, St. Helena; (707) 967-1010; www
.ciachef.edu. Museum and grounds are free. Kitchen tours and demonstrations $; call
ahead for tours and for lunch and dinner reservations.

A massive landmark guarded by towering palms, Greystone was built in 1889 with 22-inch-
thick, hand-cut volcanic stone blocks. Today it's one of the nation's most prestigious culinary
colleges, the Culinary Institute of America at Greystone (CIA). Plan at least an hour to wander
around, see the food and wine museum, and browse the school store—a blockbuster of
a gourmet emporium, where CIA logo attire and 1,500 cookbook titles are just part of an
unbelievable inventory of tools and gifts in an environment reminiscent of southern Europe.

The attractive, noisy restaurant and outdoor terrace, which overlook an ancient oak
forest and rolling vineyards, are pricey for families, and the food often fails to measure up
to top valley restaurants. Graduate chefs are on view, preparing Spanish tapas and Mediterranean cuisine. A drink and snack on the terrace is a pleasant experience.

Kids enjoy the medieval castle look of the interior. Restless youngsters, accompanied, of course, can run around on the beautiful grounds; paths wind through aromatic

Shopping with the Kids in **Napa Valley**

Hurd Beeswax Candle Factory. 1255 Lincoln Ave., Calistoga; (707) 942-7410;
www.hurdbeeswaxcandles.com. Watch fanciful and weird candles being
made by hand. The large shop flickers with hundreds of unusual candles,
including storybook characters, gnomes, and seasonal figures.

Freckles Children's Boutique. 1309 Main St., St. Helena; (707) 963-1201. For
babies and children up to 6, pricey, fabulous clothing, gifts, and toys.

The Learning Faire. 1343 Main St., Napa; (707) 253-1024; www.learningfaire
.com. A huge selection of educational toys, games, books, arts and crafts,
things to do in the car, and teaching supplies.

Fideaux. 1312 Main St., St. Helena; (707) 967-9935. Don't forget Muffie and
Spot. Pick up a lavish cat bed, a handmade dog collar, chew toys, gourmet
biscuits, a rubber frog, a life jacket or a saddlebag, and fab futons.

V Marketplace 1870. 6525 Washington St., Yountville; (707) 944-2451; www
.vmarketplace.com. An old stone winery building filled with shops and galleries is a good place to rest or run around—a nice lawn in back is bordered by
trees and benches. Don't miss Cups and Cones, the ice-cream and sweet shop,
and Hansel and Gretel for baby and kids' clothing.

herb gardens. Take budding chefs on the teaching kitchen tour in the upper reaches of the building.

Where to Eat

Gillwoods. 1313 Main St., St. Helena (and Napa Town Center); (707) 963-1788; www.gill woodscafe.com. Home-style American food: tuna sandwiches, grilled cheese, homemade soup, burgers, fried chicken, chili, ribs, meat loaf, apple pie. Breakfast, lunch, and dinner. $–$$

Model Bakery. 1357 Main St., St. Helena (and Oxbow Market, Napa); (707) 963-8192. A circa-1920 brick oven turns out sourdough and rustic breads, pizzettas, fruit tarts, and amazing desserts. The simple cafe serves wonderful soups, salads, and sandwiches for here or to take out. $

Pizzeria Tra Vigne. 1016 Main St., St. Helena; (707) 967-9999; www.travignerestaurant .com. An offshoot of the ultra-gorgeous main restaurant, this charming pizza house has booths, TVs, and a billiard table to keep families happy while they wait for luscious, brick-oven baked, Cal-Ital pizzas. Besides traditional favorites, you can order the Benito (fennel sausage, hot coppa salami, smoked pork), the Ducati (roasted onions, broccoli rabe, smoked mozzarella, and chicken and apple sausage), and the Clam Pie (garlic paste and fresh-chopped clams), or just create your own. $–$$$

Taylor's Refresher. 933 Main St. on the south end of St. Helena (and Oxbow Market, Napa); (707) 963-3486. For more than five decades, this roadside stop with picnic tables has been serving burgers and dogs, fish-and-chips, garlic fries, and Mexican food, plus Double Rainbow ice cream in fabulous shakes, floats, and malts. $

V. Sattui Winery. 111 White Lane, 11.2 miles south of St. Helena on Highway 29; (707) 963-7774. A pretty, shady picnic grove around a stone-walled 1885 winery. The gourmet deli sells literally hundreds of varieties of cheeses and meats, fresh breads, juices, and drinks. One disadvantage is the sight of the busy highway. Don't be concerned if you miss the wine tasting here; there are better choices for wine. $

Where to Stay

El Bonita. 195 Main St., just south of St. Helena on Highway 29; (707) 963-3216 or (800) 541-3284; www.elbonita.com. Hidden behind the original 1930s art deco motel are newer 2-story motel units with private balconies looking into the trees and over the gardens. Large, 2-room suites have microkitchens. Small pool, sauna, continental breakfast. $$–$$$

Harvest Inn. 1 Main St., just south of St. Helena on Highway 29; (707) 963-9463. Somewhat pricey, but with great advantages: lush, rambling English gardens; a labyrinth of shady pathways, lawns, and bowers; and 2 nice pool terraces. If I had babies or toddlers, I would definitely choose this place and spend time walking, playing on the lawns, and lolling in the pools. Some suites have antiques, four-posters, fireplaces, and eclectic collections of elaborate furnishings; other rooms are simpler and more appropriate for a child or two. An expanded continental breakfast is served in a beautiful "great room." $$–$$$

Meadowood Resort. 900 Meadowood Lane, St. Helena; (800) 458-8080; www .meadowood.com. Tucked away in a magical redwood forest, plush accommodations and a unique summer program of half-day, week-long sessions or drop-in days for children of resort guests: croquet, golf, tennis, music, hiking, arts and crafts, swimming, and more fun activities are scheduled. While kids are busy, parents can luxuriate in the full-service spa; go wine tasting and shopping in St. Helena and Calistoga; play golf on the 9-hole course, ramble the walking trail, or learn to play croquet on the tournament green. Cottages, suites, and lodges, some with sofa beds, whirlpool or soaking tubs, stone fireplaces, private decks and terraces; understated, luxurious decor. Top-rated restaurant overlooking sweeping lawns, gardens, and forest. $$$$

For More Information

St. Helena Chamber of Commerce. 1010 Main St., St. Helena; (707) 963-4456; www .sthelena.com.

Wine Country Reservations. (707) 257-7757.

Yountville

Yountville is a tiny Wine Country burg whose few streets are lined with vintage cottages in overgrown country gardens. Washington Street, the main drag, holds a blizzard of shops, restaurants, and inns. A nice half-day excursion here will include a little shop and gallery browsing, a walk on an idyllic country road, a picnic and playtime at a great playground, and exploration of a fascinating old cemetery.

Yountville Park and Pioneer Cemetery (all ages)
At the north end of town, on Washington Street.

An oak-shaded grassy commons, with a great children's playground and picnic tables. Next to the park is a wonderful cemetery with fascinating tombstones from the 1800s, including the graves of George Yount, founder of the town, and early pioneers from around the world. While living temporarily in New England in 1997, I became fond of cemeteries whose stones tell haunting stories, from shipwrecks to fires and storms. My granddaughter and I strolled around the Yountville graveyard, a pretty, tree-studded place, discussing burials and cremations. Now she is the family expert on what happens to people when they die.

Yount Mill Road Walk (all ages)
East of the playground on the north end of Yountville (park where the houses end).

An easy, 3-mile round-trip walk or bike ride, north to Highway 29 and back. Running along a tributary of the Napa River, the road is quiet, shady, and bedecked with lovely views of the mountains and vineyards. Watch for a plaque about George Calvert Yount, the first white settler in the valley. Yount wrangled from Mexico the huge land grant of Rancho Caymus in the 1850s—composing much of the heart of the valley, including Yountville—and built grist- and sawmills on the river. You will see the remains of one of his large wooden barns.

Wine Country **Biking**

Biking is big in Napa Valley. The advantages here are gorgeous scenery; miles of easy, flat routes; easy access to rest stops, food, and restaurants; and sightseeing attractions along the way. You can bike your brains out and still be within a few minutes of civilization. The mostly flat Silverado Trail, running 35 miles along the east side of the valley, is a main biker's route. Crisscrossing the valley between Highway 29 and the Silverado Trail are myriad leafy country roads. Bike shops will give you maps. Some bike shops will deliver rental bikes to your hotel and pick you up at the end of your ride in the valley.

The Napa Valley Museum (all ages)

55 Presidents Circle, Yountville; (707) 944-0500; www.napavalleymuseum.org. $; younger than 7 free.

Among old oaks and a redwood grove by a creek, an architectural surprise: a museum of contemporary art and the history of the valley, with indoor and outdoor exhibits and garden terraces to roam.

The museum is on the beautiful grounds of the Veterans Home of California, where you can take a walk under magnificent, century-old trees and lounge on the sweeping lawns. Adjacent is the Yountville Golf Club, a pretty 9-holer with a spectacular driving range and a casual indoor-outdoor cafe; this is a good place for beginning golfers (707-944-1992).

Napa River Ecological Reserve (all ages)

Yountville Cross Road at the Napa River; (707) 944-0500. Free.

A short walk beside the river, under oaks and sycamores, with oceans of wildflowers in the spring and butterflies; watch out for poison oak. You can wade and fish here and play on the sandy riverbank.

Where to Eat

Compadre's. 6539 Washington St., Yountville; (707) 944-2406. Mexican food and a lively atmosphere, on delightful, palm- and oak-shaded patios. $$

Gordon's Cafe and Wine Bar. 6770 Washington St., at the north end of Yountville near the park; (707) 944-8246. In a former stagecoach stop, the best place in town for California cuisine picnic fare to go and casual,

quick meals served at individual tables or the communal table. A small, noisy, popular, and fun cafe and deli. Breakfast (cinnamon buns, yes!) and lunch every day; prix fixe dinner on Friday. $$

La Luna Market and Taqueria. 1153 Rutherford Rd., Rutherford, between Yountville and St. Helena; (707) 963-3211. In a back corner of a wonderful Mexican market, authentic

Mexican tacos and burritos to go, in a valley where Mexican Americans know how to cook. The burritos weigh a pound or more. $

Mrs. McDonald's. 3392 Solano Ave., Napa; (707) 224-5668. Biscuits baked in tin cans, zillions of egg dishes, traditional American comfort food; very popular with families for breakfast and lunch. $–$$

Pacific Blues Cafe. 6525 Washington St., Yountville; (707) 944-4455; www.pacificblues cafe.com. Indoors or on the deck, a cafe serving breakfast burritos, biscuits and gravy, and hearty traditional breakfasts; for lunch and dinner, it's gourmet burgers and sandwiches, veggie specialties, fresh seafood, lots of appetizers, homemade soups, big salads, and microbrews on tap. A thoughtful kids' menu features grilled cheese, pizza, plain pasta, and more. $–$$$

Rutherford Grill. 1880 Rutherford Rd., Rutherford, on Highway 29 (watch for the two huge palms); (707) 962-1782. No reservations. Go for the smoky baby back ribs, for mountains of feathery onion rings, inventive pastas, grilled and spit-roasted poultry and meats, garlic mashed potatoes, and jalapeño corn bread. Big booths inside; umbrella tables and a wine bar outside. This is a popular, fun place, and you may have to wait on weekends. It has the advantage of being pleasantly noisy inside, so kids go unnoticed. $$–$$$

For More Information

Yountville Chamber of Commerce. 6484 Washington St., Suite F, Yountville; (707) 944-0904; www.yountville.com.

Napa

For 35 miles, from Napa north to Calistoga, the Napa Valley is crisscrossed by quiet country roads where families discover places to bike and hike, play on the riverbanks, shop, and sightsee. Some of the popular family attractions are state and regional parks, a geyser and a petrified forest, and two wildlife parks.

In the town of Napa, charming Victorian neighborhoods are bounded by Franklin, Division, Elm, and Riverside Streets. Extensive new development has transformed the downtown waterfront with upscale shopping, restaurants, and luxury hotels. You can rent kayaks and paddle the Napa River below downtown and south toward San Francisco Bay. Riverbank scenery is scant, the river is anything but pristine, and it's windy the farther south you go.

Six Flags Discovery Kingdom (all ages)

At Highways 80 and 37, 1001 Fairgrounds Dr., Vallejo; (707) 643-6722; www.sixflags.com /discovery. $$$$; kids 2 years and under free; ask about family pricing. Check the website calendar for off-season, weekday closures.

What I like best about this oceanarium, wildlife, and amusement park is the chance to get close to animals and marine life. My granddaughter Melati knows what a giraffe's blue tongue looks and feels like, because she fed one leaves and apples. She played tug-of-war with an elephant and hugged a chimpanzee.

With roller coasters, dozens of rides, live shows, and 30-plus animal attractions with more than 1,700 animals, it is a challenge to get everything into one day. Among the highlights are a white Bengal and a Siberian tiger, the killer whale and dolphin shows, and interaction with seals, sea lions, walruses, sharks, and otters. Reptiles are on display, from snapping turtles to Gila monsters, lizards, alligators, and snakes.

Some of the outrageous rides are the Boomerang, the Cobra and the Kong roller coasters. The Medusa is supposed to be the tallest, fastest, longest, and most technologically-advanced roller coaster in Northern California, taking passengers on 3,500 feet of twisted track with 7 inversions. Your skateboarders will defy gravity on the new Tony Hawk's Big Spin, where riders move at 35 miles an hour through banked turns, quick hairpin curves, and steep drops, all while spinning in circles.

Rides for younger children are the Ferris wheel, Monkey Business teacups, and the Shoreline Express railway. Little ones also love the new Thomas Town, and the butterfly garden where more than 300 winged beauties flit before their eyes. There are jungleland rides, a tree house to climb, a hot-air balloon gondola ride, Jeep tours, a river ride, a splash zone, exotic birds, an elephant, and more. Snow and ice are brought in for Christmastime skating, sledding, and a festival of lights.

Cafes and food booths offer some healthy, if pricey, choices. To avoid lines, arrive early and have lunch early; your own food is not allowed. Rent a dolphin stroller for kids 4 and younger, as you will be walking your feet off! A carefree way to reach the park from the Bay Area is by ferry from San Francisco (707-643-3779). Ask about ferry packages and special-event days.

This amusement park has been the subject of controversy in recent years concerning the treatment of its animals—specifically the exposure to noise (from the rides) and the size and type of enclosures.

Skyline Wilderness Park (all ages)

2201 Imola Ave., on the east side of Napa; (707) 252-0481. Parking $; camping $.

A regional park with hilly woodlands and meadows for hiking, horseback riding, picnicking, and RV and tent camping. Find the waterfalls for a summer splash. Picnic and fish on the shores of Lake Marie, a 2.5-mile walk from the parking lot.

Lake Berryessa (all ages)

Seventeen miles east of Napa, at Highways 128 and 21; (707) 966-2111; www.usbr.gov/mp /berryessa.

One of the state's most popular recreation lakes, with 165 miles of hilly, oak-covered shoreline. On the west shore, Knoxville Road gives access to marinas, park headquarters, a resort, beaches, and campgrounds. Oak Shores Park day-use area ($) has the best beach and picnic sites, with lifeguards on weekends. Spring is ideal for bass fishing; fall, for trout. Marinas rent fishing, patio, and ski boats and other watercraft. This is a mild environment in which to learn windsurfing.

Napa Valley Wine Train (ages 3 and up)
1275 McKinstry St., off Soscol, Napa; (707) 253-2111 or (800) 427-4124; www.winetrain.com. $$$$.

Elegant, restored Pullman railroad dining and observation cars take passengers on a relaxing ride up the valley, a 3-hour chug from Napa to St. Helena and back, with a gourmet lunch or dinner included—a pricey and rather confining experience for youngsters, although a la carte snacks and meals are offered in a separate deli car, and there are Family Fun Excursions when children 3 to 12 ride **free**; a supervisory staff keeps the kids happy with games, movies, and food while parents enjoy a quiet gourmet meal.

Oxbow Public Market (all ages)
Next to COPIA, 610 1st St., Napa; (707) 226-6529; www.oxbowpublicmarket.com.

A whopping big addition to this foodie's town are more than two dozen local purveyors of yummies clustered together in a huge, contempo-industrial building, from artisanal baked goods to wine, Hog Island oysters, farmhouse cheeses, Fatted Calf charcuterie, and fresh-roasted coffees. Get burgers, shakes, and sandwiches at Taylor's Refresher, nosh at one of the many cafe tables, and walk around with a Three Twins Organic Ice Cream cone while you pick up items for home or for picnic: homemade salami, Model Bakery cookies and scones, fresh teas from China, gifts, and cookbooks. Seasonal farm stands make up a daily outdoor market, and one of the world's greatest, the Napa Farmers' Market, is held in the parking lot on Saturday and Tuesday mornings.

di Rosa Preserve (all ages)
5200 Carneros Hwy. 121, Napa; (707) 226-5991; www.dirosapreserve.org. $$ adults; **free** for ages 11 and under; **free** for all on Wednesday.

Not your grandfather's art gallery, this is the most significant collection of Bay Area art in the world, 2,200 works by more than 900 artists on over 200 acres in the idyllic Carneros wine growing area. Besides viewing some of the most amusing, flamboyant, and startling art you'll ever see (such as autos hanging from trees, wildly decorated skateboards, the "rhinocar," and more eye-popping sights), the family will enjoy the lovely grounds and the lake. The kids, no matter what age, will not be bored. Call ahead for tour information, and for dates—various Sundays—of ArtisTree, where families can create art blindfolded, backwards, and with no hands, focusing on the fun process of making art.

Where to Eat

Alexis Baking Company. 1517 3rd St., Napa; (707) 258-1827. Where the locals go for breakfast and coffee breaks, Sunday brunch, and lunch. Homemade pastries and desserts are remarkable. $$

BarbersQ. 3900 D Bel Aire Plaza, Napa; (707) 224-6600; www.barbersq.com. Just off Highway 29, near Whole Foods, Target, and a great bookstore, BarbersQ has Memphis-style barbecue pork sandwiches and ribs, plus fried shrimp, homemade chicken soup, hot fudge sundaes, hot apple pie, and more, in an upscale, casual, fun environment. $–$$

Downtown Joe's American Grill and Brewhouse. 902 Main St., Napa; (707) 258-2337. Breakfast, lunch, or dinner on the patio overlooking the Napa River, adjacent to a small, grassy park where little ones can run while waiting for their dinners. Salads, sandwiches, pastas, pizza, and a microbrewery. $$

Gillwood's Bakery and Cafe. 1320 Town Center, Napa; (707) 253-0409. Luscious pastries and desserts; great old-fashioned breakfast, lunch, and dinner. $–$$

Pasta Prego. 3206 Jefferson St. in the Grapeyard Center, Napa; (707) 224-9011. A friendly trattoria frequented by winery families. Served here are northern Italian food, seafood, pasta, and grilled fresh fish. For the most fun sit at the counter and watch the cooks. Lunch and dinner; indoors or on the tiny patio. $$–$$$

Soda Canyon Store. 4006 Silverado Trail, Napa; (707) 252-0285. At Soda Canyon Road just north of Napa, a great place to stop for a quick picnic or to pick up yummy provisions for lunch or snacks on the road. Locals start the day with breakfast burritos, smoothies, pastries, and espresso drinks. Gourmet deli sandwiches, cheeses, homemade salads, a nice selection of local wines, and packaged condiments that make nice gifts. $

Villa Corona. 3614 Bel Aire Plaza, Napa, and 1138 Main St., St. Helena; (707) 257-8685. A small place with great, inexpensive Mexican food to have here or take out. $

Where to Stay

Embassy Suites Napa Valley. 1075 California Blvd., adjacent to Highway 29, Napa; (707) 253-9540; www.embassysuites.com. Upscale Mediterranean-style hotel, with spacious suites, with a king or 2 doubles, refrigerator, microwave, coffeemaker, iron, 2 TVs,

wet bar, and a separate living area with sofa bed. Conveniently located at the highway. Complimentary full breakfast and 2 hours of cocktails and snacks in the pleasant cafe by the lovely gardens. Indoor and outdoor pools, sauna, complimentary passes to nearby health club. Guest laundry. $$$–$$$$

Hawthorn Inn and Suites. 314 Soscol Ave., Napa; (707) 226-1878 or (800) 527-1133; www.napavalleyinns.com. Sixty large rooms and suites in a property on a very busy road; nothing within walking distance, yet a good value with excellent amenities for families. Some rooms with 2 queens, refrigerator, microwave, iron, wet bar, Internet; some have a sofa, good-size table, or a large desk. Complete hot breakfast buffet is **free;** small indoor pool and hot tub, workout equipment. $$$

For More Information

Napa Valley Conference and Visitors Bureau. 1310 Napa Town Center, Napa; (707) 226-7459; www.napavalley.com.

Napa Valley Reservations. 1819 Tanen St., Napa, on the north end of town just off the highway; (707) 252-1985 or (800) 251-6272; www.napavalleyreservations.com.

Sonoma

On the west side of the Mayacamas Mountains, Sonoma Valley comprises a patchwork of vineyards and farmlands, with a fascinating early California history, best displayed in the town of Sonoma, which was laid out by a Mexican general in 1834. The site of many annual fiestas, parades, and art, wine, and food events, Sonoma Plaza is surrounded by the past, including a small California mission, a military compound from the days of the Mexican conquest, thick-walled adobe and Victorian homes, and a blizzard of upscale shops and restaurants. The plaza is popular for picnicking under the trees and for the two playgrounds. You can feed the ducks and, sometimes, pet the two-humped camel who comes to visit. April through October, the Tuesday night farmers' market is a big family event, usually with live entertainment.

Sonoma Mission and Sonoma Barracks (all ages)

1st and Spain Streets, Sonoma; (707) 938-1519. Adults $; free for kids under 16. The home is part of the state park property, so one admission ticket is good at the mission, the barracks compound, and the Vallejo home.

The commandant who held sway in the Sonoma area when Mexico owned California, Gen. Mariano Vallejo built a barracks compound for his soldiers, and it is now a state park and a museum on the plaza. The museum is an easy walk-through for children, offering re-created rooms and costumes of the early days. In May a special Children's Day is held at the mission. The last of the California missions built, this one has a beautiful small chapel and museum.

General M. G. Vallejo Home (all ages)

About 0.5 mile northwest of the plaza off Spain Street, Sonoma; (707) 938-1519. Adults $; free for kids under 16. The home is part of the state park property, so one admission ticket ($) is good at the mission, the barracks compound, and the Vallejo home.

Accessible by the walking path and by car, this beautiful yellow-and-white "Yankee-style" Gothic Revival house was shipped around the Horn and erected in 1851 by Mexican General Vallejo. Called Lachryma Montis, meaning "Tears of the Mountain," the house is shaded by huge magnolias and twined with rambling yellow roses.

My granddaughters love to wander through, looking at the original and period furnishings, and daydream about the days when Vallejo and his several daughters lived here before the turn of the 20th century. There are tintypes of the daughters, their hair below their waists, wearing long, elaborate dresses, black stockings, and high-button shoes. Their bedrooms are as they were, with a tiny dollhouse, a miniature stove, tin bathtubs, lace coverlets, and cut velvet couches. The general's son had his own private pad, where his rifle, a narrow bed, and keepsakes are carefully preserved.

Sonoma Walking/Biking Path (all ages)

Fifty yards north of East Spain Street, Sonoma. From 4th Street East, west to Sonoma Highway 12; (707) 996-1090.

A paved path for walking, biking, and in-line skating winds 1.5 miles from one end of Sonoma to the other, passing through parks and playing fields and ending on the west side at a big park with a playground. A block from Sonoma Plaza on the walking path, Depot Park has a playground, barbecues, and picnic tables under the trees: a good choice when the plaza is crowded. My granddaughter Laurel learned to in-line skate on the trail, and her little sister, Melati, pedaled shakily along on her first "big girl's" bike ride.

Sonoma Overlook Trail (all ages)

At the north end of 1st Street West, Sonoma (on the right past the police station, park next to the cemetery); (707) 996-1090.

Wide views of the Sonoma Valley are dazzling from the upper meadows of this 3-mile loop of trails on wooded hillsides. Blue lupine and flax, wild roses, and California poppies are rampant; buckeye, live oak, and manzanita trees create shady hideaways. After a hard rain, you may need to ford a small creek.

Depot Park Museum (all ages)

270 1st St. West, on the Sonoma Walking/Biking Path, Sonoma; (707) 938-1762. Open afternoons (hours vary) Wed through Sun. Free.

If you get hooked on local history, make a stop here to see a restored stationmaster's office, re-creations of Victorian households, and photos of early Sonomans. Gift shop.

Sonoma Traintown (ages 2 to 8)

20264 Broadway, 1 mile south of the plaza, Sonoma; (707) 938-3912; www.traintown.com. Open daily in summer; weekends the rest of the year. Adults and children $.

Younger children love this: an open-air steam train ride through a redwood forest to a tiny farm that has a petting zoo; also, a Ferris wheel, a vintage carousel, Dragon Coaster, and Chattanooga Choo Choo Chairs, plus a snack shop. For lunch or dinner go next door to Pizza Capri.

Sebastiani Trolley Ride and a Secret Picnic Site (all ages)

Sonoma Plaza, Sonoma; (707) 938-5532. Free.

On a replica of a San Francisco cable car, ride from Sonoma Plaza around town to and from Sebastiani Cellars, a few blocks away. Pick up picnic provisions, hop on the trolley, hop off at the winery, and walk 1 block to behind the winery to shaded picnic tables next to a vineyard with dazzling vineyard and hillside views. For an easy 20-minute stroll, walk north from the picnic area a few hundred yards and take the first left turn (Gehricke Road) past the vineyards; take the first left, turn left again, turn left yet again, and you're back where you started.

Shops for Kids in Sonoma

The streets and alleys surrounding the plaza are lined with upscale boutique shops, primarily of interest to adults. A handful of shops are fun for kids.

- **Baksheesh,** 423 1st St. West, (707) 939-2847; www.vom.com/baksheesh. Head for the back room of this emporium of handcrafted gifts from the developing world to find toys and books for kids.

- **Half Pint,** 450 1st St. East on the plaza; (707) 938-1722. Have your credit cards tuned up for these trendy and fanciful kids' clothes, hats, and shoes, including unique imports; and a few toys, too. For babies through about age 8.

- **Fine Line Art Supply,** in the shopping center at the corner of 5th Street West and West Napa; (707) 935-3199; www.finelineartsupply.com. Art kits, unique coloring books, and painting and craft-making supplies for children.

- **Tiddle E. Winks,** 115 East Napa St.; (707) 939-6933. Retro collectibles and memorabilia like lunch boxes; old-time candy, saltwater taffy; and replica toys from throughout the 20th century.

- **Sonoma Barracks Shop,** 1st and Spain Streets; (707) 938-1519. The museum shop is a great place to find educational books, toys, paper dolls, and coloring books relating to California history.

- **Three Dog Bakery,** 526 Broadway; (707) 933-9780. Very fun, whether you have a pet or not. An amazing array of baked goods that tourists often mistake for human food, and lots of fabulous toys, clothing, collars, and gifts for dogs and cats and their people.

- **Sonoma Rock & Mineral Gallery,** 414 1st St. East, in the alley; (707) 996-7200. Kids love rock shops. This one is crammed with fabulous colorful rocks and spectacular mineral specimens, carvings, beads, and quartz, with some bins of inexpensive stones and several huge, sparkling geodes.

Jack London State Park (all ages)

2400 London Ranch Rd., off Arnold Drive, Glen Ellen; (707) 938-5216; www.parks.ca.gov. Day-use fee per auto $.

The Valley of the Moon is named for famous (some say infamous) resident Jack London, author of the classic adventure tales *Call of the Wild* and *The Sea Wolf.* London's globe-trotting life early in the 20th century is portrayed in photos and haunting artifacts in a wonderful Craftsman-style lodge, the "House of Happy Walls." Once London's ranch, the park comprises 800 acres of trails, crisscrossed by creeks winding through magnificent groves of oaks, madrones, fir, redwoods, and fern grottoes. You can picnic here in a wildflowery meadow and see the ruins of Wolf House, London's eccentric stone mansion, found at the end of a 0.5-mile path through the trees (handicapped accessible by golf cart). Only walls and chimneys remain of the elaborate home that burned to the ground a few days before London and his wife, Charmian, could move in. Newly opened is the charming, completely restored cottage where the author lived and worked, full of memorabilia and photos. Intrepid hikers enjoy the steeper trails on the hillsides on the west side of the upper parking lot and are rewarded with wide-open views of the valley. The easy 2-mile round-trip Lake Trail goes through the forest to a lake, where you can picnic under the trees. You can ride your own horses in the park; for guided horseback riding call (707) 996-8566.

Benziger Family Winery (all ages)

1883 London Ranch Rd., Glen Ellen; (707) 935-3000 or (800) 989-8890; www.benziger.com.

Located here are beautiful valley oaks and gardens, an art gallery, shady picnic grounds, and a tasting room. This is the only winery in the valley to offer a motorized tram tour of the vineyards, and children are welcome. Call ahead for reservations.

Sugarloaf Ridge State Park (all ages)

Adobe Canyon Road off Highway 12, just north of Kenwood; (707) 833-5712 (campground reservations: 800-444-7275); www.parks.sonoma.net. Day-use fee $; camping $.

A 3,000-acre green and golden jewel of hillsides, redwood groves, creeks, wildflower-strewn meadows, and views. Take a short walk or a strenuous hike, picnic in the pines, park your RV overnight, or camp out in your tent.

Sonoma Valley Regional Park (all ages)

Across the road from the Garden Court Cafe, Highway 12 between Arnold Drive and Madrone Road, near Glen Ellen; (707) 539-8092. Parking fee $.

A mostly flat, paved path winding about 1 mile one-way through an oak forest, with a pretty creek along the way. You can bike and picnic; dogs must be leashed. There is a dog park here, too. My little granddaughter and her buddies like to pick up sticks and branches, drag them along on the walk, and build a fort on a fallen tree trunk.

Annadel State Park (all ages)

Just east of Santa Rosa off Highway 12, end of Channel Drive; (707) 539-3911. Day-use $.

My children grew up hiking the trails of Annadel, a 5,000-acre paradise of streams, meadows, rolling foothills and canyons, and woodlands thick with oak, fir, and redwood. Biologists say this is the best example of northern oak woodland in existence. You can hike, horseback ride, bike; fish for bass and bluegill in Lake Ilsanjo—a 2.5-mile hike from the parking lot—and eat at picnic tables at the lake. Wildflowers explode from March through early summer; it can be hot and dry in late summer and early fall. Bring your own water.

Cornerstone Gardens (all ages)
23570 Hwy. 121, near Sonoma; (707) 933-3010; www.cornerstonegardens.com.

Watch for a bright blue tree dressed in blue balls to find a new complex of arty boutiques, a deli, a fascinating salvage emporium, and a unique group of gallery-style gardens created by prominent designers. The Blue Tree Café offers light breakfast, pastries and espresso drinks, soups, salads, and sandwiches, to eat here or take out. Although older kids may be bored, little ones can cruise around outside while parents shop and browse.

Where to Eat

Basque Boulangerie Cafe. 60 1st St. on the plaza, Sonoma; (707) 935-7687. French and Basque-style salads, pastries, muffins, cakes, and tarts; home-baked breads and rolls; espresso drinks. Sit at the counter in the tiny cafe or at a sidewalk table. Open from breakfast through late afternoon, it's pricey for families. $

Breakaway Cafe. 19101 Hwy. 12, in the Albertson's shopping plaza, Sonoma; (707) 996-5949. The best family place in town, with big booths, a toy corner, and all-American food, such as pork chops and mashed potatoes, roast chicken, burgers, salads, comforting soups, huge omelets, veggie specials, smoothies, and a kids' menu. They know kids here, and they like them. Breakfast, lunch, and dinner. $–$$

Deuce. 691 Broadway, Sonoma; (707) 933-3823. Some of the best California cuisine in the Wine Country on a shady patio, just a couple of blocks from the plaza. The owners have young twin girls and are happy to see babies and families. $$–$$$

Juanita Juanita. 19114 Arnold Dr., on the west side of town, Sonoma; (707) 935-3981. Absolutely the best Mexican food in the valley, in a tiny, friendly place frequented by local families; sit on the patio in the summertime. Kids have decorated the walls. $

Mary's Pizza Shack. 452 West Spain St., Sonoma; (707) 938-8300. On the plaza, really good pizza. Ask for pizza sticks while you wait. $

Red Grape. 529 1st St. West, Sonoma; (707) 996-4103; www.theredgrape.com. Our favorite pizza place on the planet, specializing in "New Haven" style, thin-crust pies with traditional and exotic toppings; plus pasta and salads. The light, airy restaurant and shady patio bustle with families and tourists, just a half block from the plaza. Does a pizza place take reservations? This one does. $–$$

Rin's. 139 East Napa St., Sonoma; (707) 938-1462. Indoors or on the patio, enjoy excellent Thai food. If your kids are not familiar with Asian food, start with chicken satay (they love the peanut sauce) and fried or plain rice. Kids

Winery Fun for Kids

A winery tour may last an hour or more, and youngsters can get restless. Choose your wineries well!

- **Chateau Montelena,** 1429 Tubbs Lane, Calistoga; (707) 942-5105. Exotic ducks and swans glide around two red-lacquered gazebos in a small lake. Young children love to stand on the bridges and toss feed to attract the ducks and the koi fish. On the winery grounds a few picnic tables beneath weeping willows are within sight of the mossy, crenellated castle of French limestone where the wine is made.

- **Kaz Winery,** 3 Adobe Canyon Rd., Kenwood; (877) 833-2536; www.kaz winery.com. Kids and dogs are welcome at this small family-run winery, which is based in a barn. Play-Doh, fruit juice, and dog biscuits are complimentary, and you can picnic by the koi pond. The owner/winemaker is often on-site, regaling visitors with his tall tales, and other family members hold forth at times, too.

- **St. Supéry Winery and Wine Discovery Center,** 8440 St. Helena Hwy., at Rutherford; (707) 963-4507. Besides lawns and picnic sites here, there is a lot to see that may be interesting to school-age children. A Victorian farmhouse, a wine-growing demonstration area, and relief maps of the valley are here, too. You can easily leave the winery tour at any time; it's fun to walk on catwalks above the giant storage tanks.

- **Rutherford Hill Winery,** 200 Rutherford Hill Rd., off the Silverado Trail, Rutherford; (707) 963-7194. Cool, delightfully spooky underground caves are fun to see on a 35-minute tour. You can buy juices and picnic goodies here to enjoy at tables under the oaks or in the olive grove with wide valley views.

- **Sterling Vineyards,** 1100 Dunaweal Lane, Calistoga; (707) 942-3359. Tram tickets: all ages over 10 $$; kids 10 and under free. Take a thrilling, 4-minute gondola ride to a sky-high terrace for bird's-eye views. The winery tour is self-guided, and there are outdoor tables up here for picnicking—with your own provisions, or you can buy simple deli items on-site. Children are given an activity bag with juice, raisins, crayons, cards to color, and stickers!

are warmly welcomed in this casual place. Big advantage: The restaurant is open all day long. $–$$

Sonoma Cheese Factory and Deli. 2 West Spain St., Sonoma; (707) 996-1931. Cheeses and deli foods to go, or eat here at picnic tables. The disadvantage is that this is the place where the tour buses stop, and it thus is often impossibly crowded. $

Sunflower Café. 421 1st St. West, Sonoma; (707) 996-6645. New owners have freshened up this small cafe on the plaza, and now it's especially nice for snacks or lunch in the garden patio. Order healthy breakfast items, sandwiches, salads, smoothies, and soups to enjoy at a sidewalk or patio table, or to take away to a picnic table in the plaza; coffee drinks, ice cream and shakes, wine, and beer, too, and Wi-Fi. $

Where to Stay

El Pueblo Inn. 896 West Napa St., Sonoma; (800) 900-8844; www.elpuebloinn.com. In a super-convenient location on Highway 12, a recently renovated motel with heated pool, courtyard garden, and rooftop Jacuzzi; some rooms have fireplaces, minifridges, and 2 queen beds. Complimentary continental breakfast; rental bicycles available. $$–$$$$

Flamingo Resort and Spa. 2777 4th St., Santa Rosa; (800) 848-8300; www.flamingo resort.com. Within a half hour of Sonoma, just 5 minutes from Highway 101 and a huge, very nice shopping center, the recently renovated, long-established, low-rise hotel is in walking distance to restaurants and shops. Kids love the giant swimming pool terrace (one of the largest hotel pools in the state) and acres of lawns. Parents love the fabulous full-service health club/spa with a heated lap pool and tennis courts, and the child care facility. Ask for a poolside patio room with sofa bed that opens onto the pool terrace. Small fridges, coffeemakers, and guest laundry. $$–$$$$

Sonoma Valley Inn. 550 2nd St. West, Sonoma; (707) 938-9200 or (800) 334-5784; www.sonomavalleyinn.com. Nice rooms around a courtyard with pool; some rooms with fireplace and microwave. Guest laundry. Across the street from a shopping center. $$–$$$

For More Information

Sonoma Valley Visitors Bureau. In the plaza, 4532 1st St. East, Sonoma; (707) 996-1090; www.sonomavalley.com.

Sonoma Reservations. (800) 576-6662. Motels, inns, spas, condos, homes.

Healdsburg

The small town of Healdsburg sleeps peacefully under a canopy of trees. On most summer weekends, band and jazz concerts and outdoor festivals are held in the classic Spanish-style town plaza, which is ringed with cafes and shops. The farmers' market fills the plaza on Tuesday evenings and Saturday mornings, spring through fall; bring a picnic blanket and enjoy the live music. On the west side of town, the Dry Creek Valley is prime biking and wine-tasting territory. For an easy, scenic 20-mile loop on gently rolling hills, start at the town plaza, head south to Mill Street, cross under the highway, and join Dry Creek Road heading north. Endless vineyards and rows of low, forested mountains remain in view throughout the ride; picnic sites are available at wineries along the way.

Healdsburg Museum (all ages)

221 Matheson St., Healdsburg; (707) 431-3325. Free.

In the beautiful Carnegie Library building, circa 1910, are displays of Pomo Indian basketry, artifacts from the Mexican rancho and pioneer eras, great old photos, and a fun shop with educational toys and books for kids.

Jimtown Store (all ages)

6706 Hwy. 128, Healdsburg; (707) 433-1212; www.jimtown.com.

Just out of town on a lovely country road, a charming, circa-1860 country store like no other. On the patio out back, dig into chili, grilled cheese and deli sandwiches, and chocolate cake; try the homemade scones and pastries on weekend mornings. You can order picnic lunches ahead, too. Give the kids a few dollars and let them browse the shelves of old-fashioned toys and penny candy, while you look at antiques and collectibles.

Mrs. Grossman's (ages 5 to 12)

3810 Cypress Dr., Petaluma; (800) 429-4549; www.mrsgrossmans.com. Admission to the visitor center and museum is free; tours Mon through Fri (for ages 5 and up) $; call for reservations and directions.

The largest sticker company in the country, Mrs. Grossman's makes absolutely wonderful stickers, hundreds of different designs for every season, every holiday, every sport. An

Healdsburg Area Parks

All of these parks are within a few minutes of Healdsburg. Information: (707) 565-2041; www.sonoma-county.org/parks. Parking $.

Riverfront Regional Park. 7821 Eastside Rd., Windsor. A shady redwood picnic grove anchors this new park. Two miles of flat walking trails around two small lakes open to fishing and nonmotorized boating; restrooms. Leashed dogs okay.

Shiloh Regional Park. 5750 Faught Rd., Santa Rosa. This park has 850 acres of natural woodlands; 3 miles of trails for hiking, biking, and horseback riding; restrooms; and barbecues. No dogs, except leashed in picnic area.

Foothill Regional Park. 1351 Arata Lane, Windsor. Moderate hiking/walking trails in a lovely oak forest; three small lakes for fishing from the banks; horseback riding. Restrooms, no dogs.

Healdsburg Veterans Memorial Beach. 13839 Old Redwood Hwy., Healdsburg. A popular swimming spot with a sandy beach, picnic areas, and lifeguards during the summer. Leashed dogs in picnic area, not on the beach or in the river.

hour in length, tours include a fun, 20-minute video, a 30-minute walking tour of the factory in action, **free** stickers, and a mini-seminar on sticker projects. On-site are a sticker museum and a great big sticker and accessories store, with a workshop where you can make your own creations. Bring snacks or a picnic if you wish to eat indoors or on the patio; there are vending machines here.

Sonoma County Farm Trails (all ages)

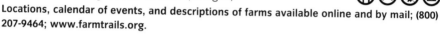

Locations, calendar of events, and descriptions of farms available online and by mail; (800) 207-9464; www.farmtrails.org.

More than 200 farms in the county are open to the public, and you can watch cheese and olive oil being made, wool loomed and woven, and encounter miniature horses, llamas, goats, and piglets. You and the kids can find the perfect pumpkin and pick fruit, learn about beekeeping, fish for trout, cut a Christmas tree, and much more. On the calendar of events is the annual "Weekend Along the Farm Trails" in September, when the farms hold fall harvest open houses with special educational activities. Families are welcome to walk in the fields and pick produce, and get up close and personal with farm animals and with the farmers. Many farms offer tastings of their crops fresh off the vine, prepared in family recipes or preserved in a jar.

Charles M. Schulz Museum (all ages)

2301 Hardies Lane, Santa Rosa; (707) 579-4452; www.schulzmuseum.org. Ages 4 and up $$; under 4 **free.**

Snoopy, Woodstock, Charlie Brown, Lucy, and their buddies live here now, since their creator, "Sparky" Schulz, passed away. The beautiful museum showcases Peanuts cartoons and those of other famous artists; Schulz's studio and his tools and memorabilia are on display; and there is much to see, indoors and on the patio. My grandkids Wyatt and Rachel spent an hour or so in the Education Room using the cartooning instruction books, activity sheets, and art supplies provided. They loved the **free** movies. Check the website for the schedule of all the Peanuts movies and TV programs, classes, and special events.

You can get snacks and light meals next door at Snoopy's Redwood Empire Ice Arena, while watching the action on the rink.

Lake Sonoma (all ages)

North end of Dry Creek Road, Healdsburg; (707) 433-9483 or (707) 433-2200; www.lake sonoma.com.

The Warm Springs Dam created a large, many-fingered lake where water sports and fishing are popular all year in this mild climate; winter and spring are best for exploring and camping, when the meadows are green and full of wildflowers. Launch a boat or rent one, go kayaking, take a hike, have a picnic, go fishing, swim, or camp out. Exhibits at the visitor center showcase local history and wildlife, and there is a fish hatchery to see. Bass, perch, catfish, sunfish, and bluegill fishing is good, and there are many sites for RVs and tents, and oak-studded picnic grounds. At the Lake Sonoma Marina are a boat ramp; a full-service marina; a patio; waterskiing, sailing, and fishing; boat and kayak rentals; and a small store (707-433-2200).

Pacific Coast Air Museum (all ages)

Airport Boulevard off Highway 101, between Healdsburg and Santa Rosa; (707) 575-7900; www.pacificcoastairmuseum.org. Requested donation $; under 12 free.

Nearly three dozen antique, World War II, and early-1950s military and historically significant planes, including "Top Gun" F-14 Tomcat and F-16 Vipers, are here. A big air show in August brings in more rare planes for dazzling performances, and a monthly "Climb Aboard Day" is exciting for budding pilots. My grandson Wyatt likes the guns on the fighter planes.

Where to Eat

Bear Republic. 345 Healdsburg Ave., Healdsburg; (707) 433-2337; www.bearrepublic.com. A hearty brewpub menu featuring burgers (including veggie), lots of appetizers, garlic cheese fries, salads, chili, soup, and homemade breads. Although a brewpub, this noisy, fun, casual place with an outdoor patio is very popular with families; try the homemade sodas. Just a few steps away from the town fountain, where toddlers can romp. $–$$

Costeaux French Bakery and Cafe. A block from the plaza, 417 Healdsburg Ave., Healdsburg; (707) 433-1913. Award-winning breads and pastries, scrumptious sandwiches, and picnic items to stay or to go; breakfast and lunch at a few indoor and sidewalk tables. Look for the red '53 Ford outside. $

Dry Creek General Store. 3495 Dry Creek Rd., Healdsburg; (707) 433-4171; www.dcgstore.com. Buy sandwiches and picnic goodies to eat here, or bring them along in your bike baskets for a picnic by the side of the road. With new owners, prices and quality have gone up. A tiny cocktail bar here, too, popular with locals. $

El Farolito. 128 Plaza St., Healdsburg; (707) 433-2807. In a town with a large Mexican population, really good Mexican food. $

Flying Goat Coffee Roastery Cafe. 324 Center St., Healdsburg; (707) 433-9081. Hang out with the locals and read the paper; have a Goat Bar (chocolate, oats, nuts) or some coffee cake. Simple bistro food. $

Hamburger Ranch & Pasta Farm. 31195 North Redwood Hwy., Cloverdale; (707) 894-5616. Harleys may be lined up in the parking lot on weekends at a rustic roadhouse that has satisfied local ranchers, loggers, and travelers for more than 50 years. The outdoor barbecue pit produces luscious beef burgers, turkey burgers, and chicken, and pasta, too. Don't fail to stop here on your way north. $–$$

Oakville Grocery. 124 Matheson St., on the square, Healdsburg; (707) 433-3200. An outdoor fireplace makes the terrace a cozy spot for pizza from the brick oven, rotisserie chicken, sandwiches, and wonderful pastries. The pricey, gourmet grocery sells top-quality seasonal local produce and local cheeses, charcuterie, and wines. $

Where to Stay

Alexander Valley Campground. Alexander Valley Road near the Healdsburg Bridge, Healdsburg; (707) 431-1453. A large tent and RV campground on the riverbank, with swimming beaches and canoe rentals. $

Camellia Inn. 211 North St., Healdsburg; (707) 433-8182 or (800) 727-8182; www .camelliainn.com. Near the plaza, romantic bed-and-breakfast rooms in a Victorian house, plus a family suite with trundle bed in an adjoining room; beautiful swimming pool, lovely gardens. Full breakfast in the rather formal dining room. Also a 2-bedroom apartment suite downtown with kitchen, living/dining room. Unusual for a B&B, they welcome well-behaved children. Ask about restaurant and attraction discounts; pet boarding nearby. $$$$

Vineyard Valley Inn. 178 Dry Creek Rd., Healdsburg; (800) 499-0103. Simple hotel with sauna and whirlpool, coffee shop, **free** continental breakfast. $

For More Information

Healdsburg Visitors Bureau. 217 Healdsburg Ave., Healdsburg; (707) 433-6935; www .healdsburg.com. Ask for the **free** tree booklet for a self-guided tour of fabulous big old trees on the plaza and side streets, including a dawn redwood, palms, oaks, magnolias, and more.

Russian River/Guerneville

Anchored by the town of Guerneville, the Russian River Valley cradles the river as it flows through forest canyons and past sandy beaches and vineyards. The river is generally slow-moving and calm, with quiet coves and sandy beaches along the way. Canoeing, kayaking, and tubing are popular activities; try them on the scenic, 10-mile stretch from Forestville to Guerneville, where there are nice beaches and stopping points for fishing and picnicking. Osprey, blue herons, deer, turtles, and more wildlife will accompany your trek.

A laid-back summer vacation town since the mid-1800s, Guerneville is draped lazily along the bank of the Russian River. The town is primarily souvenir shops, a few galleries and casual cafes, and a supermarket or two where you can stock up on provisions for camping and day trips on the coast, on the beaches, and in the redwood park. Sandy riverside beaches are easily accessible around Guerneville. Johnson's Beach is a good choice because of the lifeguards and roped-off children's swimming and wading area; rentals of canoes, kayaks, paddleboats, tubes, umbrellas, and beach chairs; and the snack bar. You can also launch your own watercraft here. Steelhead Beach at 9000 River Rd. in Forestville has shaded picnic tables and Porta Potties; no lifeguard.

When you stop in Guerneville for meals and at the beaches, do not be surprised to see quite a few gay men and lesbians. The town has been a gay weekend and vacation destination for years.

Duncans Mills (all ages)

Five miles west of Guerneville on Highway 116; (707) 865-9080; www.duncansmills.net.

A charming Victorian-era village on the river with an old-fashioned general store, cafes, and boutique shops. Children can run around and take a short walk on the quiet country road that runs alongside the village. Take a look at the only remaining North Pacific Coast Railroad station. The General Store stocks fishing gear, groceries, deli items and antiques, while Gold Coast Coffee & Bakery offers baked goods fresh from their wood-fired brick oven. American comfort food and seafood are popular at Cape Fear Cafe, a great spot for Sunday brunch. You can rent canoes and kayaks here and paddle around in the river nearby or head right out to the coast (Russian River Outfitters).

Armstrong Grove Redwoods State Reserve (all ages)

In Guerneville, go north off Main Street on Armstrong Woods Road; 2.2 miles to the park entrance; (707) 869-2015. Day-use fee $.

Easy, flat forest trails wind through magnificent stands of old-growth redwoods, some more than 300 feet tall. Picnic sites are cool and shady on the warmest summer days. Available are wheelchair access, a Braille trail, restrooms, a visitor center, no-reservation campsites, and mountain-biking and equestrian trails. Park just outside the park entrance and walk in for **free,** joining right up with the 1.5-mile Pioneer Nature Trail. Accessed from the park entrance is the Armstrong Woods Pack Station (horseback-riding day trips, www.redwoodhorses.com).

Austin Creek State Recreation Area (all ages)

Accessed through the Armstrong Redwood Reserve entrance; (707) 869-2015. Parking $.

A haven of 5,000 relatively undeveloped acres of grasslands and hills, river glens and can-yons, open forests, a hike-in campground, 20 miles of trails, and a horse camp (carry your own water). You'll find wildflowers in the spring, good birding, and bluegill and black bass fishing in Redwood Lake. Hot and dry in the summer, gloriously green in the winter and spring, the preserve is abundant with wildlife, from great blue herons, woodpeckers, and ravens to deer, fox, and, occasionally, bobcats.

Bullfrog Campground here is accessed by a steep, narrow, 2.5-mile road that can-not be negotiated by RVs more than 20 feet long. Reservations by phone are advised, but you can also drop in and check the bulletin board at the campground for open sites (707-869-2015).

Armstrong Woods Pack Station (ages 10 and up)

Armstrong Grove; (707) 887-2939; www.redwoodhorses.com. $$$$.

Even beginning riders will enjoy the lunch ride, which meanders gently out of the red-wood forest through wildlife habitats to ridgetops overlooking the Russian River Valley. On top of the world with a 360-degree view of five counties, enjoy a a gourmet lunch laid out on white tablecloths in a wildflower-strewn meadow. You can also ride your own horses on the guided pack trips and bring your own food. Children under 10 require guide's permission; riders must be in good physical condition and able to mount without assistance.

Johnson's Beach & Resort (all ages)

16241 1st St., Guerneville; (707) 869-2022; www.johnsonsbeach.com. Open daily from mid-May to early Oct, 10 a.m. to 6 p.m. Free.

Running the **Russian**

Canoeing or kayaking the Russian River is a must-do for many visitors—May through October are the best months. Most rental companies will supply all equipment and shuttle you back to the starting point. Bring plenty of water and a change of clothes for the return ride, secure your car keys with a safety pin in your pocket, wear hats and rubber-soled shoes (to protect against sharp rocks), and beware of sunburn on the tops of your legs. If you bring an ice chest, also bring bungee cords to secure it to the canoe. No pets or glass containers.

- **Burke's Canoe Trips,** Mirabel Road at 8600 River Rd., Forestville; (707) 887-1222; www.burkescanoetrips.com. Shuttle service and canoe rentals for 10-mile trips to a private beach. Campground with hot showers. $45 per canoe.

- **Gold Coast Coffee and Kayaks,** 23515 Steelhead Blvd., next to the Blue Heron, Duncans Mills; (707) 865-1441. Sit-on-top kayaks and all equipment for self-guided paddles. Coffee drinks and snacks, too. From $10 per hour.

- **Russian River Adventures,** 20 Healdsburg Ave., Healdsburg; (707) 433-5599; www.rradventures.info. Paddle an inflated SOAR canoe on a quiet section of river; the 3-hour trip begins at the Memorial Beach Dam. $45 per adult; ages 2 to 12, $22. If you wish, a naturalist guide will take your kids while you wine-taste ($120 per day). Leashed dogs okay.

- **River's Edge Kayak & Canoe Trips,** 13840 Old Redwood Hwy., Healdsburg; (707) 433-7247 or (800) 345-0869; www.riversedgekayakandcanoe.com. Oldest established operator in the area; shuttle to several put-in spots. $80 per person full day; hourly rates and family packages available.

Families flock to this wide, sandy beach below town to swim in the Russian River (lifeguards on duty). There is a roped-off swimming area for small kids, and visitors can rent canoes, kayaks, paddleboats, umbrellas, inner tubes, and beach chairs. You can also launch your own watercraft here.

Kozlowski Farms (all ages)

5566 Hwy. 116 North, just outside of Forestville; (707) 887-1587; www.kozlowskifarms.com.

For more than six decades, a family-run farm and open-air produce market famous for fresh berries, vinegars, sauces and jams, lots of Wine Country gift items, more than a dozen kinds of homemade pies, and other bakery goods. Stop here for yummies to take home and on picnics; you can picnic here, too, with a vineyard view.

Where to Eat

Big Bertha's Burgers. 16357 Main St., Guerneville; (707) 869-2239. Casual truck-stop decor at this locals' favorite for big burgers; plain or with fancy toppings like goat cheese and portobello mushrooms. $

Coffee Bazaar. 14045 Armstrong Woods Rd., Guerneville; (707) 869-9706. Snacks, lunches, and great ice cream, near the entrance to the state park. Sit outside in the summertime. Browse the used bookstore next door. $

Main Street Station. 16280 Main St., Guerneville; (707) 869-0501. Good for a lunch stop while driving to the coast; hearty Italian meatball sandwiches and sausage sandwiches, country-style pizza, salads, smoothies, and great desserts. $–$$

Roasters Espresso Bar. On Highway 116 in the middle of a one-horse town, Forestville; (707) 887-1632; www.roastersespressobar .com. Award-winning, home-roasted, organic coffee. Stop here on the way to the coast for pastries, cold drinks, artwork, and **free** Wi-Fi. $

Where to Stay

Casini Ranch Family Campground. 22855 Moscow Rd., Duncans Mills; (707) 451-8400, (800) 451-8400; www.casiniranch.com. On the Russian River, adjacent to a small village of shops and restaurants, the campground is 20 minutes from the Sonoma Coast. More than 200 RV and tent camping sites, some on the river. It's just a few steps to good fishing. Grocery, laundromat, showers, boat rental, outdoor movies, beach bonfires, hayrides; pets okay. $

Creekside Inn & Resort. 16180 Neeley Rd., Guerneville; (707) 869-3623; www.creek sideinn.com. About 30 country-cozy cottages of various sizes with kitchens, some with fireplaces, hot tubs. Modular cottages with private decks are based on environmentally sustainable design. Swimming pool. $$–$$$$

Hilton Family Campground. 10750 River Rd., Forestville; (707) 887-9206; www.hilton parkcampground.com. Within walking distance to Korbel Winery and restaurants, and 4 miles to Armstrong Woods, the campground has laundry, hot showers, firewood, and video games. You can see each campsite and cottage on the website. Reserve in advance; it's popular. $

For More Information

Russian River Chamber of Commerce. 16200 1st St., Guerneville; (800) 253-8800; www.russianriver.com.

Redwood Empire Association and North Coast Visitors Bureau. 2802 Leavenworth, San Francisco; (415) 394-5991; www.redwoodempire.com. Comprehensive brochures and other materials covering all of the Wine Country, the North Coast, and Redwood Country.

Sonoma County Tourism Bureau/California Welcome Center. 9 4th St. (take the downtown exit west), Santa Rosa; (800) 404-7673; www.visitcwc.com. Brochures, maps, and advice for travel throughout the North Coast and the Wine Country.

Russian River Travel. (707) 869-9000; www.russianrivertravel.com. Visitor information, lodging and vacation home rentals, parks, maps, mileage, and more for all the towns in the region.

High Sierra North

A sapphire gem sparkling across the California and Nevada borders, Lake Tahoe lies above 6,000 feet in the icy embrace of the Sierra Nevada Range. In a dreamlike setting of snow-frosted peaks and evergreen forests, the lake is "clear enough to see the scales on a cutthroat trout at 80 feet," as Mark Twain put it. Families return year after year to the summer vacation towns, campgrounds, and ski resorts of the Tahoe region.

The choice of summer sightseeing and recreation is phenomenal: hiking and mountain biking on forest trails; fishing, swimming, and boating; exploring old logging towns. Some families head for state park campgrounds in the woods or on the lakeshore. Others rent a cabin at the beach, or they stay at a big resort with a pool and lots of organized activities.

Get an overview of the dazzling mountain landscape by taking the family on a slow cruise on one of the big paddlewheeler tour boats, across the lake to Emerald Bay. You'll see row after row of jagged granite peaks reflected in the deep blue water: 1,600 feet deep, and cold, very cold. Legends tell of Indian chiefs in full regalia and women in Victorian garb floating motionless and frozen at the bottom of the lake. Children love to hear the old Tahoe stories, especially tales of Tahoe Tessie, the Loch Ness–style monster whose spiny back is occasionally seen rippling above the surface. Watch for Tessie!

The sun shines an average of 274 days a year. Soft spring days are clear and wildflowery; fall is brisk, with aspen colors glittering through the pines. Winter days are lively at 16 alpine ski resorts and as many cross-country ski areas. More ski resorts are concentrated here than anywhere else in North America.

The 72-mile-long Tahoe lakeshore is roughly divided into the South Shore, the West Shore, and the North Shore, each with unique attractions. Anchored by Tahoe City, the West Shore has an "Old Tahoe" feel, with log cabins from the 1920s and 1930s and old-fashioned cottage-style resorts. The Truckee River is a good reason to headquarter on the West Shore. You can spend a day rafting—it's exciting but not at all dangerous—and hike and bike on a paved trail that runs along the river and the lakeshore.

HIGH SIERRA NORTH

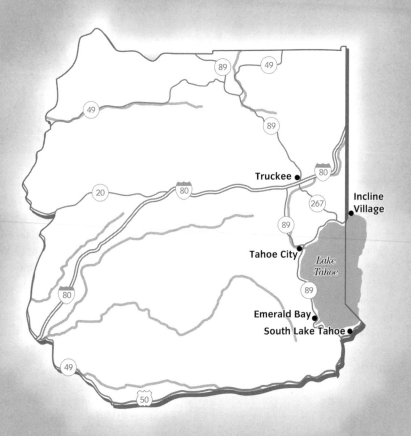

Truckee •

Incline
Village •

267

89

Tahoe City •

*Lake
Tahoe*

89

Emerald Bay •

South Lake Tahoe •

The North Shore is primarily the Incline Village area, the least developed and quietest part of the lake. On the South Shore, the only real city on the lake, South Lake Tahoe, is famous for casinos, although families head for the historic sights and a chain of beautiful beaches. Outdoor fun is nearby in the Tahoe and El Dorado National Forests and in Desolation Wilderness.

First-timers are tempted to take the 72-mile scenic shoreline drive around the lake (www.mostbeautifuldrive.com). As spectacular and enjoyable as that may be for adults, it's too curvy and too long a trek for most kids. Also, weekends and high summer season are crowded with traffic.

TAKING CARE

It's wise to remember that Lake Tahoe is at a high elevation—6,227 feet at the lakeshore. For the first day or two of your visit, everyone in the family, and particularly the children, may feel more tired than usual. If someone feels nauseated for no apparent reason, it is likely to be altitude sickness; extra rest and limited physical activities are the cures. If you are not experienced skiers or hikers, you will do well to plan an easy first day. If someone in the family continues to feel sick, sleepy, and disoriented, discuss it with a doctor; the only way to get over persistent altitude sickness is to descend to a lower altitude.

High altitude also means greater risk of sunburn, especially in winter. Use sunscreen every day, no matter how cold it feels outdoors.

During the summer and on winter weekends, avoid driving to Tahoe on Friday afternoons or returning on Sunday afternoons, to elude heavy traffic. A snowstorm can transform Highways 50 and 80 into parking lots for hours. Every month of the year, check the weather and road conditions, and keep a bag of jackets, blankets, and dry provisions in the car year-round.

South Lake Tahoe

Between Lake Tahoe and a magnificent wall of Sierra Nevada peaks, the city of South Lake Tahoe appears at first glance to be a canyon of neon, casinos, and hotels. Get off the main highway that bisects town, however, and you will see why families spend their vacations here. Beautiful beaches and family-oriented resorts are located all along the lakeshore. From here it's a short drive to a tremendous variety of outdoor recreation and sightseeing destinations in the Tahoe Basin.

Three public beaches in town—El Dorado, Regan, and Connelly—have extensive facilities, including playing fields and swimming pools. At Nevada Beach and Zephyr Cove, you can rent every imaginable type of water sports equipment and take lessons; take a boat tour of the lake, try parasailing, go fishing, or just lie in the sun (camping here, too).

The Stateline Transit Center is a hub for shuttles, buses, and trolleys that access the entire lake (www.laketahoetransit.com). Park your car and take the Nifty 50 trolley all over the place, stopping at resorts, hotels, beaches, lake cruises, shopping, Camp Richardson, and more, with connections to Emerald Bay and the West Shore; look for the computerized kiosks ($3 all day; www.bluego.org). Paralleling the highway and bordered by tall pines, Linear Park, a paved walking and biking trail, is a welcome addition.

Highlights of your visit to South Lake Tahoe might be a sleigh ride behind a team of beautiful blond Belgian horses or a summer sail across the lake on a huge catamaran. Watch for road signs announcing snow-play areas, public beaches, and trailheads. A mile from Stateline at Ski Run Boulevard at Ski Run Marina, kids can fly high on a giant trampoline, and you can rent canoes and kayaks.

Cruises

- **MS *Dixie II* Paddlewheeler,** 5 miles north of South Lake Tahoe on Highway 50, Zephyr Cove; (530) 543-6191; www.laketahoecruises.com. Several Emerald Bay cruises a day. In the wintertime, the *Dixie* becomes a ski shuttle, taking skiers from South Lake Tahoe to ski resorts on the West Shore. The largest cruiser on the lake, the paddlewheeler was a cotton barge on the Mississippi in 1927, then a floating casino at Tahoe, when it sank and was raised and converted into a tour boat. Adults $$$$; children $$.

- ***Tahoe Gal* Paddlewheeler,** 850 North Lake Blvd., Lighthouse Mall, Tahoe City; (530) 583-0141 or (800) 218-2464; www.tahoegal.com. May through Oct, breakfast, lunch, shoreline, and evening cruises. Adults $$$; children $$.

- ***Tahoe Queen* Paddlewheeler,** 900 Ski Run Blvd., South Lake Tahoe; (800) 238-2463; www.laketahoecruises.com. This huge, beautiful paddlewheeler makes dinner cruises to Emerald Bay, and shorter Mark Twain lunch cruises. Ask about the Family Fun Cruise with Tahoe Tessie. Off-season family discounts. Besides summertime cruises, you can ride the *Queen* in the winter to Tahoe City and meet shuttle buses for major ski resorts; there is a big breakfast buffet in the morning and live music and food on the afternoon return cruise. Adults $$$$; children $$.

- ***Woodwind II* Sailing Cruises,** Zephyr Cove Marina, South Lake Tahoe; (775) 588-3000; www.sailwoodwind.com. This 50-passenger, 55-foot trimaran with a glass bottom and indoor/outdoor seating is a comfortable boat but a breezy experience, so it's probably not a good choice for toddlers. You can also book cruises on a classic 40-foot powerboat and a gorgeous 80-foot motor yacht, and on the *Woodwind I* out of Camp Richardson on the south end of the lake. Adults $$$$; children 3 to 12 $$$; website discounts.

Heavenly Village (all ages)

1001 Heavenly Village Way, South Lake Tahoe; (775) 265-2087; www.theshopsatheavenly .com.

Replacing circa-1960 motels and junky shops on Highway 50/Lake Tahoe Boulevard, this expansive new tourism development sports two massive Marriott hotels, a lighted, outdoor ice-skating rink, an eight-screen movieplex, minigolf, shopping, an ice-cream parlor, and restaurants, all connected by pleasant pedestrian walkways. Teens in particular,love the laser tag, the games arcade, Cold Stone Creamery, and Nestle Toll House Café. Parents like the open-air cafes, shops, Rocky Mountain Chocolate Factory, outdoor fireplaces, and live music and events.

Heavenly Gondola (all ages)

Off Highway 50 on the east end of Ski Run boulevard, South Lake Tahoe; (775) 586-7700; www.skiheavenly.com. Age 5 to adult $$$$; kids 4 and under free.

An 8-passenger gondola whisks you 2.4 miles up the mountain to an observation deck at 9,123 feet, with views of the Carson Valley to the east, Desolation Wilderness to the west, and the entire lake, a must-do for first-timers to Tahoe. At the top, peer through high-powered telescopes, take a hike, and have a picnic. High-altitude dining is fun at the Adventure Peak Grill, the Umbrella Bar, and at Café Blue on the observation deck (you can bring your own picnic, too).

In the wintertime, families love Adventure Peak Snow Park up here, where you can go tubing, sledding, cross-country skiing, and snowshoeing; rental equipment available. In the summer take a daytime or full-moon hike, and try out the climbing wall.

New on the mountaintop, the year-round Heavenly Flyer is the longest zipline in the lower 48 states, a thrilling 3,100-foot-long zoom with 525 feet of descent ($$$$; minimum 75 pounds and 52 inches height).

Heavenly Mountain Resort (all ages)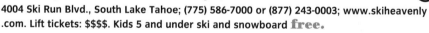

4004 Ski Run Blvd., South Lake Tahoe; (775) 586-7000 or (877) 243-0003; www.skiheavenly .com. Lift tickets: $$$$. Kids 5 and under ski and snowboard free.

One of the largest ski resorts in the western states, Heavenly Mountain has an annual average of 360 inches of snow, covering more than 90 ski runs. On the summit you have the phenomenal experience of feeling like you are skiing right into the lake. If your legs can take it, start from the top of Sky Express and ski 5 miles nonstop downhill.

Heavenly is beloved by beginners and intermediates, who head for the High Roller terrain park and superpipes and the Nightlife Terrain Park, open until 9 p.m. on weekends. Beginning boarders are comfortable at the Low Roller park. The new high-speed Olympic Express quad chair zips skiers to Olympic Downhill, 3 new trails, and to Nevada Woods for the best tree skiing.

One of the most family oriented of all Tahoe resorts, Heavenly has 3 children's ski centers offering lessons, equipment, lunch, and supervision for ages 4 to 13. For little ones who are not sure they want to ski, check out the one-hour, Ski/Play program in the Enchanted Forest for ages 3 and 4, and the Half-and-Half ski and play days. Child care is available for all ages from 6 months and up, and you can even reserve a nanny to accompany your child in any group program.

Sugar Bowl Ski Area (all ages)

750 Mule Ears Court, Norden; (530) 426-9000 (snow phone 530-426-1111); www.sugarbowl
.com. Kids 5 and under ski **free.**

On the slopes of 8,383-foot Mount Judah, Sugar Bowl's express lifts and multimillion-dollar expansion of trails and facilities make this one of the best medium-size ski resorts at the lake. Among recent additions is the Den, a huge children's learning center; a Flying Carpet lift to expanded terrain for beginning skiers and boarders; the SnowBomb Terrain Park; a family play park for beginners and younger kids, with a moving carpet; and expanded child-care programs both in the village and in the Mountain Sports Learning Center. There's also a new backcountry adventure center and the new summit chair. With little kids, take the gondola from the village parking lot to the lifts, day care, and lessons areas. Kids' learning programs are Sugar Bears for ages 3 to 5, Base Camp for ages 4 to 6, and Summit Camp for ages 7 to 12. **Free** lessons and rentals on "general admission" days with the purchase of an all-mountain lift ticket or for seasonal pass holders. You can stay right here at the Inn at Sugar Bowl in family units; ask about winter and summer packages (530-426-6742).

Upper Truckee River Marsh (all ages)

(530) 542-5580.

Take an idyllic, 4-mile, self-guided kayak paddle on the Upper Truckee River, starting at the Highway 50 Bridge to the lake and down to Ski Run Beach. The river meanders quietly through meadows and forest, and you will likely see waterfowl and beautiful marshlands with water lilies and other aquatic plants. Rent kayaks and canoes at SunSports at the Ski Run Marina.

Emerald Bay

West from South Lake Tahoe on Highway 89, also called Emerald Bay Road, around the south end of the lake are a number of sightseeing, cultural, and recreation destinations. Emerald Bay is the most photographed place at Tahoe, a scintillating piece of water surrounded by dense pine forests and decorated with an island that is topped by a teahouse.

Built in 1928, Vikingsholm, the treasure of Emerald Bay, is a cross between an 11th-century castle and an ancient church. Reached by a steep, downhill, 1-mile paved trail (or by tour boat), the 38-room mansion is considered the finest example of Scandinavian architecture in North America. The **free** ranger's tour of the fancifully furnished estate is well worth an hour of your time. This is a beautiful spot to have a picnic, swim and sunbathe, and take a short hike before you take your time climbing back up to Highway 89.

Snow-Play Areas

You can rent sleds, tubes, saucers, and, in some cases, mini-snowmobiles and other snow toys at these snow-play areas. Some have lifts and refreshment stands; some disallow kids under 4; and some disallow bringing your own equipment. Most areas charge a fee ($–$$).

- **Boreal Ski Area,** Highway 80 at Castle Peak exit on Donner Summit; (530) 426-3666. Groomed sledding and tubing lanes at Playland Park, mini-snow-mobiles to rent, restrooms; no personal sleds permitted. Sledders must be 42 inches tall.

- **Granlibakken Ski Area,** 667 Lakeshore Dr., just south of Tahoe City; (530) 581-7333. Groomed sledding hill for saucers.

- **Donner Memorial State Park,** Donner Lake exit off Highway 80; (530) 582-7892. Bring your own saucers for **free** play on a tame slope.

- **Mount Rose Ski Tahoe,** on Ski Way off Highway 28 at the south end of Incline Village; (702) 832-1177. Supervised, groomed hill for ages 3 to 6.

- **North Tahoe Regional Park,** National Avenue off Highway 28, Tahoe Vista; (530) 546-5043. Groomed runs, restrooms, bonfire, snacks.

- **Northstar-at-Tahoe,** Highway 267 at Northstar Drive; (530) 562-2267. Tubing hill at midmountain accessed by tow; no saucers or sleds permitted. Night play with entertainment, bungee trampoline, snow toys.

- **Spooner Summit,** Highway 28 at Highway 50, 9 miles south of Incline Village. Some steep areas; bring your own equipment. **Free.**

- **Tahoe City Snow Play Area,** Highway 89, 0.8 mile south of the Tahoe City "Y." Gentle slope; bring your own equipment. **Free.**

- **Soda Springs,** 1 mile east of Highway 80 at Soda Springs exit; (530) 426-3901. Elaborate tubing runs with lifts and groomed play areas for sledding. Mini-snowmobile rentals for kids ages 6 to 12. Planet Snow Kids for kids 8 and under, with moving carpets, snowboarding and tubing, and tube carousels; **free** sleigh rides.

- **Squaw Valley,** 5 miles north of Tahoe City off Highway 89; (530) 581-7246. At the top of the cable car at High Camp, a tubing venue with lift.

- **Tahoe Donner at Trout Creek,** off Highway 80 at Truckee-Donner exit; (530) 587-9400. Wide, groomed, supervised sledding hill. **Free** for ages 3 and under. Deli nearby.

From the highway it's an easy 2-mile loop hike to Eagle Falls and Eagle Lake, which are surrounded by the sheer walls of Desolation Wilderness, a glorious outback of rugged alpine territory crisscrossed by trails and dotted with hundreds of lakes. Desolation Wilderness is best in the off-season, as easy accessibility makes it extremely popular for hiking and backpacking in high season. For an 11.4-mile loop day trip, take the Glen Alpine trailhead at the end of Fallen Leaf Lake Road and hike to Lake Aloha.

Near Emerald Bay, Baldwin, Pope, and Kiva Beaches are accessible by bus from South Lake Tahoe. The popular Emerald Bay State Park Campground has 100 tent and RV sites and boat-in campsites (closed from mid-September until mid-June).

US Forest Service Lake Tahoe Visitor Center (all ages)

Four miles north of the "Y" on Highway 89, Emerald Bay Road, Baldwin Beach; (530) 573-2600. Open 8:30 a.m. to 8:30 p.m. during summer.

Here are exhibits of geology, animal habitats, and history. You can get maps and advice as to trail conditions and campground availability and sign up for a ranger-led interpretive walk. A **free** children's program called Woodsy Rangers is presented each day, and families gather for narrated campfires in August.

A 4-hour, 5-mile, rather strenuous loop hike from here to the summit of Mount Tallac rewards trekkers with magnificent views at 9,700 feet. For casual strollers and those in wheelchairs, the Rainbow Trail is a paved path wandering past signs that explain the natural habitat; over 100 species of wildflowers bloom alongside the trail. The Stream Profile Chamber is a cross section of a real stream habitat filled with rushing water, fish, rocks, plants, and other wildlife. Children can get a peek at the underwater world of a mountain stream through floor-to-ceiling viewing windows and in 12-foot-high murals. In the fall, thousands of visitors come to watch brilliant red spawning salmon wiggle their way from Lake Tahoe up Taylor Creek.

Camp Richardson Resort (all ages)

Five miles south of the "Y," Emerald Bay Road, South Lake Tahoe; (530) 541-1801; www .camprichardson.com. Camping $; other accommodations $–$$$$.

A favorite family summer vacation resort for decades, with small, simple rooms in a cavernous main lodge and cottages to rent. Summer and winter activity camps are offered for kids ages 5 to 13. There is a marina, a sandy beach (with beach volleyball), riding stables, restaurants, a 300-unit campground, a "trading post," and a general store. The camp makes a convenient headquarters from which to set off on horseback or on foot into Desolation Wilderness. Paddleboats, Jet Skis, and other water toys are rented at the marina. Cross-country ski and snowshoe trails are open in the winter, with rentals, lessons, and tours.

Morning or afternoon guided horseback rides from Camp Richardson to Fallen Leaf Lake are a thrill for youngsters and the whole family. They take about 3 hours, include either breakfast or dinner, and are very popular, so reserve ahead. Children must be at least 6 years old; guided rides for children only are also available.

Fallen Leaf Lake is accessible by road off Highway 89 and makes a wonderful day trip from Camp Richardson. You can hike around the lake, swim, picnic or barbecue, and launch a boat.

Tallac Historic Site (all ages)

Five miles south of the "Y" at Camp Richardson, Highway 89; (530) 542-4166.

The rich and famous kicked up their heels in the 1920s at this beautiful lakeside compound of formerly private estates, an old casino, the Valhalla Boathouse, working forge and black-smith shops, and a hotel. The buildings are restored and open for tours, and many musical and art events are held here in the summer. Ages 6 to 12 can participate in the Living History for Kids program. Also here is Kiva Beach, **free** and open to the public, where you will find picnic sites in the shade, and shallow waters; leashed dogs are allowed.

Kayak Tahoe (ages 4 and up)

Timber Cove Marina at South Lake Tahoe; Carnelian Bay; and Commons Beach in Tahoe City; (530) 544-2100; www.kayaktahoe.com. Day tours, camping trips, lessons, rentals.

Rent kayaks here or take a guided kayak tour. Today's new kayaks are lighter and easier to use than those you may remember from years past. Smaller children can ride with parents on most boats, and children from about 7 years old can manage easily by themselves.

D. L. Bliss State Park (all ages)

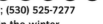

Seventeen miles south of Tahoe City on Highway 89 near Emerald Bay; (530) 525-7277 (campground reservations: 800-444-7275); www.parks.ca.gov. Closed in the winter.

Six miles of sandy and rocky beaches bordering glorious Emerald Bay, with miles of nature trails, fishing, picnic sites, a pretty campground, restrooms, and hot showers. Take a short jaunt on the self-guided Balancing Rock Nature Trail to see a rock weighing 130 tons, teetering on a narrow base.

Tahoe Amusement Park (all ages)

2401 Lake Tahoe Blvd., South Lake Tahoe; (530) 541-1300. An old-fashioned family amusement park open from May to Oct. Free admission; buy ride tickets.

Younger kids, primarily, will like the trolley, Tilt-A-Whirl, carousel, kiddie coaster, a mini-train, and more mild rides, while kids age 10 and up will go for the go-karts.

Sorensen's Resort (all ages)

14255 Hwy. 88, Hope Valley; (530) 694-2203 or (800) 423-9949; www.sorensensresort.com. Lodging $$$–$$$$, 2-night minimum; restaurant $$–$$$.

In a pine and aspen grove on the West Fork of the Carson River, 30 miles from South Lake Tahoe, Sorensen's Resort was a rest stop for emigrants in the 1800s. Rustic log cabins here have homespun country decor, brass beds, woodstoves, and some kitchens. At night, lights twinkle around the cabin doors, and wood smoke is in the air. This is a popular place for families, and reservations need to be made weeks or even months in advance.

You can sit in a rocker on your cabin porch while the kids fish in the small stocked pond for trout. An old logging road adjacent to the resort leads right into the Toiyabe National Forest. Ask about the guided hike on the Emigrant Trail. Worn smooth by pioneers on their way west, it's a fascinating route, with evidence of how wagons and animals were hauled up and down steep grades and cliffsides.

The fishing is great on the Carson, which winds through the valley beyond the resort. You can buy guidebooks and fishing licenses here and get advice on where to catch the big ones. Fishing and cross-country ski instruction and rentals are available. The resort offers special events and classes during the year, from llama treks to fly fishing, star watches, birding, hikes, and more. At the nearby Hope Valley Outdoor Center, you can rent winter and summer sports equipment of all kinds and sign up for hikes, kayak trips, and ski tours; 60 miles of ski/snowshoe trails are **free** (530-694-2266; www.hopevalley outdoors.com).

Cozy with a wood-burning stove, Sorensen's Country Cafe serves hearty breakfasts, lunches, and dinners, indoors by the fireplace and outside under the trees. Sit with others at a big wooden table and tuck into beef stew, fresh fish, homemade bread, and fruit cobbler. Breakfast is all-you-can-eat waffles or bacon and eggs. A drive to Sorensen's just for a meal makes a nice getaway from South Lake Tahoe.

Kirkwood Mountain Resort (all ages)

601 Kirkwood Rd., Highway 88, at Carson Pass; (209) 258-6000 or (800) 967-7500; www.kirk wood.com. Lift tickets: ages 13 and up $$$$; 6 to 12 $$$; 5 and under $$.

A year-round destination at 7,800 feet in elevation, Kirkwood is headquarters for fly fishing, cross-country and downhill skiing, and high-altitude hiking and backpacking. On hundreds of acres of alpine meadows, Nordic skiing is perfection—it's one of the nation's top beginner areas, with gentle terrain and gradual fall line. The Mighty Mountain Ski Center offers child care, lessons, and a kids-only lift. Kamp Kirkwood entertains nonskiing kids, and there is an evening program for 6- to 12-year-olds. A Children's Center is located at the Timber Creek Lodge, near a terrain garden and a beginner and intermediate chair. Children have their own cross-country trail—Kiddie Kilometer—with life-size cutouts of forest animals. There are also a new high-speed quad to the top of the beginner area, a new learn-to-ride snowboard center, women's clinics, and newly expanded terrain parks for all skill and age levels.

Five miles from the resort, the Cross Country and Snowshoe Center offers 50 miles of skating and double-track trails. Take Juniper and Outpost Trails to a warming hut and outstanding views of Caples Lake and snowy peaks (209-258-7248).

Come summer, meadows turn to waves of wildflowers. Biking, hiking, and lake and stream fishing are popular here and at nearby Caples Lake. You can stay in a lodge room, or rent a condo or a house. Among a wide variety of accommodations, Mountain Club is a deluxe condo hotel with 1- and 2-bedroom units with lofts. Recent developments are a beautiful outdoor ice skating rink, a fitness and swim complex, snazzy boutique shops, a freestyle terrain park and halfpipe, an expanded tubing hill with a lift, and Bub's Sports Bar & Grill, with TVs and electronic games for kids.

Where to Eat

Beacon Bar and Grill. Highway 89 at Camp Richardson, South Lake Tahoe; (530) 541-0630; www.camprich.com. At the beach for lunch or dinner, try the signature clam chowder, gourmet burgers, sandwiches, salads, pasta, fish, and steaks. Light breakfast at the Camp General Store; frozen treats at the ice-cream parlor. $–$$

Blue Angel Café. 1132 Ski Run Blvd., near Heavenly; (530) 544-6544; www.theblueangel cafe.com. On the way to Heavenly Mountain Resort, enjoy breakfast, lunch, and dinner in a casual alpine environment. Hang out by the stone fireplace while waiting for hearty gourmet cuisine. $–$$

The Cantina. 765 Emerald Bay Rd., South Lake Tahoe; (530) 544-1233. Voted best Mexican food on the South Shore, with outdoor dining and a lively atmosphere. Try Blue Corn Salmon, Texas Crab Cakes, or the Smoked Chicken Polenta. $–$$

Ernie's. Near the "Y," 1146 Emerald Bay Rd., South Lake Tahoe; (530) 541-2161. Casual atmosphere; American breakfasts and lunches. $

Hot Pepper Grill. 3490 Lake Tahoe Blvd., South Lake Tahoe; (530) 542-1015. Wonderful tacos and fresh Mexican food, for here or to go. $

The Red Hut. 2749 Hwy. 50, 3.5 miles south of Stateline, South Lake Tahoe; (530) 541-9024. Decked out in retro red-vinyl stools and booths, the Hut has been famous since 1959 for huge waffles (try the coconut waffle sandwich), biscuits and gravy, omelets, homemade soup, grilled cheese, and more comfort food. A second Red Hut is at 227 Kingsbury Grade (775-588-7588). $–$$

Strawberry Lodge. Highway 50, Kyburz; (530) 659-7200. Good, simple American food and soda fountain specialties in a restored 1940s lodge. Stop here on the way in and out of South Lake Tahoe. $–$$

Womack's Texas Bar BQ. 4041 Hwy. 50, South Lake Tahoe; (530) 544-2268. A cozy little spot for nearly three decades serving what could be the best barbecue outside of Texas: baby back ribs, Louisiana gumbo, red beans and rice, peach cobbler, and sweet potato pie; kids' portions. $–$$$

Where to Stay

Embassy Suites Lake Tahoe Hotel and Ski Resort. 4130 Lake Tahoe Blvd., South Lake Tahoe; (800) 362-2779; www.embassy suites.com. Upscale, contemporary mountain-lodge style, 400 two-room suites that are bargains for families: 2 double beds, a sofa bed, 2 TVs, and a microwave. Indoor pool and spa, sundeck, workout room; seasonal packages; **free** shuttle to the airport and the Heavenly Valley ski area and to casinos. Room rate includes full breakfast and an early-evening party of snacks, drinks, and alcoholic beverages. The Tahoe Kid's Camp for small groups of kids ages 6 to 13 is based here, where day and evening sessions are comprised of educational hikes, outdoor play, swimming, movies, and various fun activities (www.tahoekids.com). $$$$

Fireside Lodge. 515 Emerald Bay Rd., South Lake Tahoe; (530) 544-5515 or (800) 692-2246; www.tahoefiresidelodge.com. The last lodge to be found on the way to Emerald Bay, with National Forest trails and public access beaches nearby; old-Tahoe-style, log-cabin suites with gas fireplaces and kitchenettes.

Complimentary bicycles, float tubes, and kayaks; complimentary expanded continental breakfast; picnic and barbecue areas; log swings; 2 queen-size bed suites. $$$

Forest Suites Resort. 1 Lake Pkwy., South Lake Tahoe; (800) 822-5950; www.forest suites.com. This resort, completely renovated throughout, has 1- and 2-bedroom suites with kitchens and living rooms, and it is located on 5 acres of forest at the base of the high-speed gondola at Heavenly Mountain Resort. Also adjacent to Harrah's Casino. Two swimming pools, health club, game room, complimentary breakfast, and transportation to ski areas and casinos. $$$

Lake Tahoe Accommodations. 2048 Dunlap Dr., South Lake Tahoe; (530) 544-3234 or (800) 544-3234. Condo and home rentals. $–$$$

Lakeland Village. 3535 Lake Tahoe Blvd., South Lake Tahoe; (530) 544-1685 or (800) 822-5969; www.lakeland-village.com. Spread out along the lake in 19 acres of pines, with a private, sandy beach, 2 heated swimming pools, a wading pool, and tennis courts. Condo or lodge units, some with fireplaces and kitchens. Convenient shuttle buses connect the resort with nearby ski areas and downtown. $$–$$$

Rustic Cottages. 7449 North Lake Blvd., Tahoe Vista; (888) 778-7842; www.rustic cottages.com. Guests return year after year to cottages across the street from a public beach, with fireplaces, kitchenettes, microwaves, refrigerators, and decks. Huge DVD library, bikes, croquet and horseshoes, sleds, snow saucers, snowshoes, and barbecues. Continental breakfast and chocolate chip cookies are complimentary; dogs are okay. For this location and amenities, these small, fresh, and clean cottages are a steal. $$–$$$

Tahoe Keys Resort. 999 Tahoe Keys Blvd., South Lake Tahoe; (530) 544-5397. Homes and condos for rent; indoor and outdoor swimming pools, health club, bicycles, outdoor games, playground, private beach, ski shuttles, powerboat rentals, parasailing, Jet Skis, boat launching—in other words, vacation central. $$–$$$

For More Information

California State Campgrounds Reservations. P.O. Box 942896, Sacramento 94296-0001; (916) 653-6995 or (800) 777-0369; www.cal-parks.ca.gov.

Ski Lake Tahoe. P.O. Box 10797, South Lake Tahoe 96158; (530) 541-2462 or (800) 588-SNOW; www.skilaketahoe.com. Represents several major ski resorts; ask about packages and family discounts.

Road Conditions and Ski Reports. California: (916) 445-1534 or (800) 427-7623; Nevada: (877) 687-6237.

Lake Tahoe Visitors Authority. 1156 Ski Run Blvd., South Lake Tahoe; (800) AT-TAHOE; www.bluelaketahoe.com. Use this number to book reservations, get tickets to events, obtain airline tickets, and hear about weather and road conditions.

Tahoe City/West Shore

Summers have that "vacation in the mountains" feeling on the West Shore of Lake Tahoe, when families return to their cabins at the beach and to favorite campgrounds and cottage resorts in the pines. The small town of Tahoe City, whose main street is right on the lakeshore, is headquarters for restaurants and shopping. Two of the largest ski resorts are nearby: Squaw Valley USA—site of the 1960 Winter Olympics—and Alpine Meadows. Both resorts have condos and houses to rent.

On the south end of town at the junction of Highways 89 and 28, you can't miss Fanny Bridge. Here, where the Truckee joins the lake, people are always lined up, leaning over to watch and feed the fish in the trout ladder—a line of fannies, hence the name Fanny Bridge. Bring bread or fish food for a fun half hour. Nearby, the Gate-keeper's Museum showcases hundreds of Native American baskets (530-583-1762; www .northtahoemuseums.org).

The largest winter carnival in the western states, Snowfest takes place in March and is based in Tahoe City, Truckee, and at ski resorts. Fireworks and a torchlight parade at Squaw Valley start off a weekend of parades, ice carving, ice-cream eating, and live com-edy and musical performances. More than 100 events include the Great Ski Race, a 30K Nordic event between Tahoe City and Truckee; a Snow Dog contest; celebrity races; and the Snowboard Spectacular. It's wall-to-wall people and lots of fun. Many children's events are scheduled, such as the dress-up-your-dog and snow sculpture contests.

Truckee River (all ages)
One of the loveliest places to walk, in-line skate, and bike a good distance is the paved Truckee River Bike Path, which winds 4.5 miles, one-way, along the river into Tahoe City, then heads south along the lakeshore for 9 more miles through forested neighborhoods

Easy Bike Paths at Tahoe

Tahoe Trailways Bike Paths: Head out in three directions from Tahoe City: 8 miles on a mostly level route to Squaw Valley, following the Truckee River. A 9-mile ride to Sugar Pine Point State Park along the West Shore, with some moderate grades and highway crossings; and a 2.5-mile path to Dollar Point following Highway 28, which passes Lake Forest Beach and Tahoe State Park.

Truckee River Legacy Trail: Short, scenic, easy path along the Truckee River from Truckee River Regional Park to River View Sports Park.

South Lake Tahoe Bike Path: Ten miles, from El Dorado Beach through a forest and along streams to connect with the Pope-Baldwin Bike Path.

Pope-Baldwin Bike Path: A gentle 3.4-mile trail passing the Taylor Creek Visi-tor Center, Camp Richardson, Tallac Historic site, and 2 beaches.

Lakeshore Drive Bike Path: Along the lakeshore in Incline Village, 2.5 miles beside a sidewalk, past dazzling mansions and gardens, and private beaches. This is a lovely walking route, too.

and parks. Much of the path is flat enough for baby strollers and wheelchairs. This is a beautiful path in fall, when the days are crisp and aspens turn gold. In the low-water days of late summer and fall, the river slides quietly along; in winter and spring it boils and crashes past ice-decorated trees and snowy islands.

Rafting the Truckee is a "must" on at least one of your Tahoe trips. It's a Class 1 river, meaning it's quite safe most of the year. Even if you've never rafted before, after a short lesson you can easily manage. If you have children under 5, be sure to call ahead to ask if the rafting company allows younger kids.

You rent 6-person rafts and life jackets and paddle merrily along downriver about 5 miles, stopping along the way to play and swim if you wish and maybe to picnic on a sand spit. Some people bring their fishing rods along. Paddling without stopping, it takes about 2 hours to reach your destination, which is River Ranch, where a shuttle bus takes you back to your car. Rentals are $30 per person, $20 for ages 6 to 12, at the Truckee River Rafting Center (530-583-RAFT) on the south end of Tahoe City.

Blackwood Canyon (all ages)

Off Highway 89, 9.5 miles south of Tahoe City, just north of Tahoe Pines; (530) 573-2600 or (916) 573-2600.

This is one of the most accessible yet least-known wilderness areas at Tahoe. The road into the canyon is perfect for easy walks, in-line skating, and biking. The paved road is the only development and has almost no traffic, making a good add-on to the shoreline bike path. On the leafy banks of Blackwood Creek and in the forests and meadows here are idyllic picnic spots. You can hike on the flat valley floor or drive up the road to the steep trails of 8,000-foot Barker Pass, hooking up with the Pacific Crest Trail. Cross-country skiing is blissful on the road and in the meadows, and there is a snowmobile route.

Sunnyside Restaurant and Lodge

1850 West Lake Blvd., 2 miles south of Tahoe City; (530) 583-7200; www.sunnysideresort.com. $–$$$.

With one of the most breathtaking blue-water and high-mountain views on the lake, the deck at Sunnyside is the place to be on a summer afternoon. Boats of every description come and go in the marina, french-fried zucchini and onion rings are tops, and once you and the kids get settled outside on the deck, you'll find it hard to move from the spot. Kids can run around a bit, staying away from the boats.

Here you can rent Jet Skis, sailboats, and power boats and take a sailing lesson. Winter evenings are warm and friendly in the lounge in front of a giant river rock fireplace. Sunnyside's lodge rooms are small and very nice, though rather pricey and not set up for families.

Homewood Mountain Resort (ages 3 and up)

5145 West Lake Blvd., 5 miles south of Tahoe City, Homewood; (530) 525-2992 (snow phone: 530-525-2900); www.skihomewood.com. Lift tickets: ages 5 and up $$$$; 4 and under ski **free.**

One of the most accessible and most reasonably priced ski areas for children and beginning skiers, Ski Homewood offers 9 lifts and terrain parks on a small mountain with big views of Lake Tahoe. GPS tracking for kids. Snow Rangers Academy for ages 4 to 6, with colorful snow critters, tubing carousel, indoor games, climbing wall and all-day supervision; and Mountain Rangers for ages 7 to 12. The old Quad Chair has been replaced with the Homewood Express, cutting the ride to 5 minutes. Call ahead to book the Homewood shuttle from sites on the West Shore.

Chambers Landing (all ages)

One mile south of Homewood, on Highway 89; (530) 525-7672. Day-use fee $. Restrooms; no lifeguard.

A good place to plunk down on the beach for the day is at Chambers Landing, which has a short pier with a bar at the end where locals hang out. On one side of the pier is a private beach for people staying in the Chambers Landing condos and on the other side is a public beach, one of the nicest on the West Shore. It's a good beach for small children, because there are enough boating and water sports activities to keep them interested in the passing scene, yet not so many people that you feel overwhelmed. The upscale restaurant here has a glass-enclosed, heated terrace.

Tahoe Maritime Museum (all ages)

5205 West Lake Blvd., Homewood; (530) 525-9253; www.tahoemaritimemuseum.org. $; under 12 **free.** Call about hours and guided tours.

In a gorgeous new building reminiscent of an old boathouse, a showcase of more than two dozen classic Tahoe wooden boats (including the famous Shanghai, a late-1890s wooden boat that was recovered from the depths of Lake Tahoe), artifacts, photos, outboard motors, antique fishing gear, Aquaplanes, and water skis. Children can participate in hands-on knot tying, boat building, and arts and crafts.

Sugar Pine Point State Park (all ages)

Five miles south of Tahoe City on Highway 89; (530) 525-7982. The facility has 175 campground sites (reservations: 800-444-7275). Parking fee $$; camping $.

This is a place to spend a whole day, tour a vintage mansion, walk in the woods, swim and sunbathe, and picnic and play at the lakeside.

One of the grande dames of Tahoe, a spectacular 3-story, 12,000-square-foot Queen Anne–style summer home, the Ehrman Mansion, once a privately owned estate, is now owned by the National Park Service. The mansion is surrounded by sweeping lawns shaded by tall pines. Rangers give daily **free** tours of the house and the charming boathouse, while they impart stories of halcyon old days on the lake. Even little kids enjoy the tour because the house is full of interesting stuff, and you clamber up wooden staircases, looking into family bedrooms. After the tour wander around the grounds, spread a blanket on the beach, or take a walk on flat, easy trails along the lakeshore. Stop in at the Nature Center to see wildlife, flora, and ecology displays. A longer hike is accessible from the large campground across the road.

In the wintertime, rangers lead **free** ski, skating, winter survival skills, avalanche awareness, and Animals in Winter seminars. From here you can cross-country ski or snow-shoe on 14 kilometers (close to 9 miles) of marked and skier-tamped trails.

Meeks Bay Resort and Marina (all ages)
Ten miles south of Tahoe City, Highway 89; (530) 525-7242 or (530) 573-2600. Camping $.

Owned by the US Forest Service, Meeks Bay is a popular Jet Ski and water-ski beach. This is a good place for beachy activities such as rowing, canoeing, paddleboating (all rentable), swimming in the designated area, and hanging out in the sun, though all the motors create plenty of noise during summer. My granddaughters and I have canoed from here around the coves and shorelines on either side of the bay. In just a few minutes, you are away from the fracas on the beach. Just watch the boat traffic when you are paddling in and out of the bay. A little cafe here serves snacks and burgers, and there is a 150-unit campground and a few cottages.

Carnelian Bay (all ages)
Between Tahoe City and Tahoe Vista on the West Shore; (530)-581-6900; www.gotahoe north.com.

On the quiet side of the lake, a great wetlands boardwalk traces the lakeshore, accessing good-size picnic grounds and a rocky beach where sunsets are legendary—shoreline water is shallow, so little kids can wade. Carnelian Beach is next to Gar Woods (see "Where to Eat") and across the street from the Magic Carpet minigolf course. Also adjacent is the Sierra Boat Company, one of the top boat builders in the country, showcasing used and new "woodies," the classic wooden beauties that you will see cruising the lake and tied up at the Gar Woods marina. Well over 100 antique boats are on display here at the annual Tahoe Wooden Boat Week in August. Just a block uphill, Carnelian Woods vacation rental townhomes are reasonably priced and popular (800-208-2463 or 888-486-3143; www.carnelianwoods.com).

Squaw Valley USA (all ages)
Between Tahoe City and Truckee on Highway 89, Olympic Valley; (888) 766-9321 (snow phone: 530-583-6955); www.squaw.com. Lift tickets: ages 13 and up $$$$; ages 12 and under $.

A huge summer and winter recreation area, Squaw Valley is spectacular in every season. Waves of wildflowers—or snowfields—roll across open meadows below a jagged circle of snowcapped peaks. Lodges, hotels, rental condos, and homes are scattered in forested areas.

To get an overall view of the valley, take the 150-passenger aerial cable car to the High Camp complex, a thrilling, 2,000-foot ascent to an 8,250-foot summit. Up here on the top of the world, you can ice-skate, hike, mountain bike, swim, picnic, play volleyball and tennis, bungee jump, or just blink in amazement at the surrounding mountains. Look for the indoor climbing wall where the cable car departs.

The Village at Squaw Valley is a complex of multistory condos, nearly four dozen shops, and more than 50 restaurants clustered around plazas, right at the foot of the mountains (888-805-5022; www.thevillageatsquaw.com). Scattered throughout the plaza are lounge chairs, umbrella tables, benches, and boulders from which to people-watch, doze, eat and drink, and listen to live music. Watch an outdoor movie, water your dog, and let the kids bounce on the bungee trampolines. Wandering around, you will find Starbucks, which has indoor/outdoor fireplaces; a candle-making shop; a chocolate factory; a fun cat and dog store; smoothies and great bagels at Mountain Nectar; and live entertainment and special events every summer weekend. You can park your car and get to nearby Truckee and to destinations around the lake by **free** shuttle bus.

A nice 4-mile hike from the floor of Squaw Valley is the Shirley Lakes trail, starting behind the Olympic Village Inn. Younger children like it because they can stop to wade or swim in the creek, roll around in grassy meadows, or take naps under the pines.

One of the world's largest and best ski mountains—actually five peaks—Squaw Valley USA Ski Resort, where the 1960 Winter Olympics were held, has 34 lifts accessing more than 4,000 acres of skiable terrain. Among new additions are a trenched superpipe equipped with lights, the only night-access superpipe in the Tahoe basin; plus full-moon snowshoe tours and new guided backcountry tours for intermediate/advanced skiers and boarders. The Squaw Valley Nordic Center consists of 18 kilometers (11 miles) of groomed track and wilderness trails, plus a telemark downhill area accessed by lifts.

For 2- to 12-year-olds, Children's Center is a separate venue offering special amenities, from ski rentals and lessons to meals (530-452-7166). The staff is so friendly and caring that kids want to stay all day. Beginners have their own mostly flat learning area with a neato "people-mover" that they step onto, and a little ski lift. A bright, spacious, licensed day-care facility cares for toddlers with meals, music, games, snow play, and quiet time. New for kids is the Snow Play Zone in the Papoose learning area, and a beginner terrain park with mini-halfpipe.

Save money on lift tickets and lessons by asking about frequent-skier programs, multiday tickets, college days, and lodging packages. There are snowboard clinics, women's clinics, Snow Sliders for ages 4 to 12, and Mountain Buddies, a supervised camp-style program.

As soon as the snow melts, the High Camp tram starts transporting mountain bikers and their bikes to the Squaw Valley USA Mountain Bike Park. Because of the phenomenal access to alpine-level trails, mountain biking is wildly popular at Tahoe. Annual biking events at Squaw include the Fat Tire Fest in August and the Downhill Mania and American MB Championship, both in September.

Alpine Meadows Ski Area (all ages)

Six miles northwest of Tahoe City on Highway 89, P.O. Box 5279, Tahoe City 96145; (800) 441-4423; snow phone: (530) 583-4232; www.skialpine.com. Lift tickets: ages 13 and up

$$$$; ages 7 to 12 $$$; 6 and under $$. Stay and Ski packages at nearby condos save families money (800-949-3296). Free shuttle buses connect skiers with lodgings on the West and North Shores.

Priding itself on the longest ski season, Alpine is known for its laid-back, casual atmosphere. Intermediate and advanced ski runs have scary names like Chute That Seldom Slides, Promised Land, and Our Father.

Kids are VIPs at Kid's Camp (ages 3 to 6), Children's School (7 to 12) and in Learn to Ride clinics. On the Sun Kid beginner surface lift, children just step onto a slow conveyor belt with their equipment on, avoiding the sometimes intimidating chairlift until they are ready for it. Designed for little shredders, the Tiegel Terrain Park features are modified versions of the main park, with rollers, banked turns and quarterpipes, mini tabletops, and a Tuga Tunnel, accessed by a Poma surface lift right at the base lodge. Programs for all ages are offered for racing, snowboarding, telemark, freestyle, and just plain skiing. There's GPS tracking on kids.

Several places to eat, from panini sandwiches at the Last Chair to cookies at Treats and hearty winter dishes at Meadows Café.

Where to Eat

Evergreen. 475 North Lake Blvd., Tahoe City; (530) 581-1401; www.evergreentahoe.com. From an umbrella table, watch the passing scene on the main street across from the beach and enjoy some of the best food at the lake. The chef-owner comes from a CIA background and top-rated restaurants, while his charming wife, Heather, runs the friendly, casual, welcoming place. They focus on locally sourced, fresh, seasonal, sustainable ingredients. Kids love their own menu—pasta with butter or red sauce, hot dogs, chicken tenders and burgers; parents are into the Dungeness crab cakes, Angus beef steaks, house-made pasta, artisanal cheeses, and daily specials. Locals love it, so make reservations. $$

Fire Sign Cafe. 1785 West Lake Blvd., Tahoe City; (530) 583-0871. Home-style cooking, huge portions, cozy country atmosphere; breakfast and lunch. Voted "best breakfast" by locals. $–$$

Fireside Pizza Company. Village at Squaw Valley; (530) 584-6150; www.firesidepizza.com. Sit outside by firelight or inside at a place voted Best Family Dining. Parents like the spicy appetizers and gourmet pizzas (try the pear and Gorgonzola or portobello with goat cheese). On the Campfire Kids Menu are plain, kid-size pizzas with just cheese or pepperoni; PB&J; or pasta with just cheese. $–$$

Gar Woods Grill and Pier. 5000 North Lake Blvd., Carnelian Bay; (530) 546-3366; www.garwoods.com. Indoors or on the glassed-in deck, year-round, this is a wonderful spot for a long lunch, Sunday brunch, or sunset dinner. While watching boating activity on the lake and Tahoe's famous vintage wooden speedboats cruise in and out of the marina, restless kids can play around on the small pier and the pathways along the water below the deck; those about 5 and under will need supervision. Sunday brunch at Gar Woods on a sunny day—it doesn't get any better. Carnelian Beach is adjacent. Reservations recommended. $$–$$$

Mamasake. Village at Squaw Valley, (530) 584-0110; www.mamasake.com. Snowboarders go nuts over the wall-size screen showing eye-popping movies of extreme boarders.

The sushi is expensive and really good, and there are some nonsushi menu choices like New York bagel roll, salad roll, Heads Will Roll, and more fun food. $–$$$

Old Post Office Coffee Shop. 5245 North Lake Blvd., Carnelian Bay; (530) 546-3205. Families wait on the porch for their turn at monster-size, all-American breakfasts and lunches. No reservations. $–$$

River Ranch Lodge. Highway 89 at Alpine Meadows Road, Tahoe City; (530) 583-4264; www.riverranchlodge.com. A small, charming hotel with a very popular indoor/outdoor restaurant and bar, River Ranch is on the south end of the Truckee Bike Path. The river-rafting trips end here, and rafters invariably hang out for a while in the sun, eating burgers and salads and watching other rafters and bikers arrive. $$–$$$ (lodging $–$$$)

Rosie's Cafe. 571 North Lake Blvd., Tahoe City; (530) 583-8504; www.rosiescafe.com. For nearly five decades, ski bums and locals, families, and summer vacationers have flocked here for burgers and sandwiches, Philly cheesesteaks, prime rib, Mexican specialties, and more rib-sticking comfort food. Breakfast and dinner here, too; happy hour appetizers by the fireplace. Take a look around at the museum-like display of vintage Tahoe artifacts. $–$$

Where to Stay

Chinquapin Resort. 3600 North Lake Blvd., 3 miles north of Tahoe City; (800) 732-6721. Spacious 1- to 4-bedroom town houses and condos with wonderful lake views. Fireplaces, fully equipped kitchens, pool, and tennis courts. $$$

Cottage Inn. 1690 West Lake Blvd., 2 miles south of Tahoe City; (530) 581-4073. Fifteen mountain-style cottages with Scandinavian decor, fireplaces, hearty **free** breakfasts, sauna, private beach, and dozens of carved

wooden bears. Ask for a unit away from the road. This is a popular place. $$$–$$$$

Granlibakken Resort. P.O. Box 6329, Tahoe City 96145 (located just north of Tahoe City); (800) 543-3221; www.granlibakken.com. A perfect headquarters for families in either summer or winter, this 160-room condominium resort has a beginner ski and snowboard hill, Nordic skiing, developed snow-play area, tennis, and a big swimming pool and hot tub. Some units have fireplaces, kitchens, lofts, and decks or patios. The complimentary hot breakfast is huge! In advance, call about ski-and-stay packages to get passes to seven ski resorts. $–$$

Mourelatos Lakeshore Resort. 6834 North Lake Blvd., Tahoe Vista; (800) TAHOE-81; www.mlrtahoe.com. Right on the beach, with just about every amenity a family could want. Private sandy beach, fire pit, beach chairs, umbrellas, BBQs, picnic tables, hot tub, ping-pong, volleyball, badminton, bocce, DVDs, Wi-Fi; on-site ice-cream shop, and right across the road, biking and walking paths to North Tahoe Regional Park. Water toys, boats and Jet Skis available. Restaurants within walking distance, too. Thirty-two three-diamond-rated suites with fridges, microwaves, wet bars, coffeemakers—most with lake views. Some with gas fireplace, equipped kitchen, Jacuzzi, king with sofa bed, or 2 queens. $$$–$$$$

Squaw Valley Lodge. 201 Squaw Peak Rd., Olympic Valley; (530) 583-5500 or (800) 922-9970; www.squawvalleylodge.com. A sprawling, all-suite lodge with 1 or 2 bedrooms and lofts, equipped kitchens, and luxurious amenities such as down comforters. Enjoy the tennis courts and big pool, and use of a nearby health club. Ski right out the door to the lifts! $$–$$$

Tahoe Taverns. 300 West Lake Blvd., near Fanny Bridge in Tahoe City; (530) 583-3704. Large complex of nice condos in a pine grove, on the waterfront; pool, lawns, quiet, ultra-convenient location. $$$–$$$$

The Village at Squaw Valley. Between Tahoe City and Truckee off Highway 89, Olympic Valley; (866) 818-6963; www.thevil lageatsquaw.com. A complex of new 1-, 2-, and 3-bedroom condos in multistory build- ings that are upscale and loaded with ameni- ties for families, from a little kids' playroom and a big-screen media room (both in the South building) to outdoor hot tubs, 5 fitness centers, and laundry rooms. Most units have mountain views; all have simple contempo- rary decor, daily maid service, fireplaces, sofa beds in the living rooms, 2 or more TVs and DVDs (movies are **free**), ski lockers, underground parking, and private balconies.

They are compact or spacious, depending on the number of bedrooms. Kitchens are completely outfitted. Avoid units directly above the main plaza and across from the cable car; live music and noisy people can be annoying. Also, be aware that there is no air-conditioning. Ask about ski and summer packages. $$$$

For More Information

North Lake Tahoe Visitor Center. 380 North Lake Blvd., Tahoe City; (800) 824-6348; www.nltra.org.

Truckee-Donner Chamber of Commerce/ California Welcome Center. 10065 Don- ner Pass Rd., Truckee; (530) 587-2757; www .truckee.com.

Incline Village/North Shore

A small community on steep, forested hillsides above the North Shore of Lake Tahoe, Incline Village has three private beaches with breathtaking views. Lots of outdoor recre- ation is within a few minutes' drive. If you have small children, you'll like the quiet, family residential atmosphere here. With the kids in tow, you can get in beach time and take walks around town, visit a Western theme park nearby, and plan a few half-day outings to easily accessible mountain meadows, lakes, and streams.

Incline's private beaches and a beautiful recreation center with a pool, playground, and tennis courts are available only to those who rent, own, or stay at selected hotel and motel accommodations in Incline. Renting a condo or house is the way to stay here, and it can be as cost-effective as a resort or a motel. When you make your arrangements for accommodations, be sure to ask about getting an IVGID card, which will admit you and the family to the beaches and the rec center.

A paved sidewalk on Lakeshore Drive runs along the lake for several miles, past the beaches and lovely homes—perfect for jogging, baby carriage–pushing, walking, and bik- ing. Giant sugar-pine cones are scattered liberally about, free for the taking. The gardens and the architecture are interesting sights in themselves.

There are **free** concerts around the north and western part of the lake nearly every day of the week in the summertime. Sundays rock out at Tahoe City's Commons Beach. It's Blues Tuesdays at the Village at Squaw Valley, and live music every Wednesday at Truckee Regional Park. The Village at Northstar puts on live events every Thursday, while Kings Beach rings with live music on Fridays and Tahoe City on Saturdays at Heritage Plaza. See the calendar of events at www.gotahoenorth.com.

Incline Village Recreation Center (all ages)
980 Incline Way, Incline Village; (775) 832-1300; www.YourTahoePlace.com. $$–$$$

The fabulous rec center is open to the pubic with daily, weekly, and monthly passes. Fitness and weight rooms (on-site assistance weekdays), basketball, 8-lane heated swimming pool, and snack bar. Yoga, Pilates, and aerobics classes daily. Licensed child care for infants to 10 years of age.

Tahoe Environmental Research Center (all ages)
291 Country Club Dr., Incline Village, NV; (775) 881-7560; terc.ucdavis.edu. **Free.**

Step aboard a scale model of the research vessel that scientists use to study lake water quality. See scientists at work, look through microscopes, watch videos, dive underwater and into the earth with a 3-D virtual reality flight, watch a multimedia display about the Hubble Space program. Open most afternoons. An annex of this facilitly, the Eriksson Education Center and fish hatchery is at 2400 Lake Forest Rd., about 1.25 miles northeast of Tahoe City (call for tour information: 775-881-7566).

North Tahoe Regional Park (all ages)
National Avenue off Highway 28, Tahoe Vista; (530) 546-5043.

Across the road from the beach, a place to let the kids go. Lighted tennis courts, ball fields, basketball, sand volleyball, playground, disc golf, para course, walking and bike trails, picnic tables, restrooms. Snowmobile track and cross-country ski trails.

Spooner Lake (all ages)
Highway 28, 12 miles south of Incline Village; (888) 858-8844; www.spoonerlake.com.

Amid pine and aspen forests crisscrossed by easy hiking trails, you can have picnic in a meadow and fish for trout in the small lake. In winter, Spooner Lake becomes a small cross-country ski and snowshoe area; rent equipment here and cruise the groomed trails, or bring snow saucers and slide around.

Here is the trailhead for a moderately strenuous, uphill, 10-mile hiking and mountain-biking trail to Marlette Lake (rent bikes here; 775-749-5349; www.theflumetrail.com). Spectacular views of the lake and surrounding mountains are the reward at the top, especially in fall when the aspens are blazing yellow. You can see vestiges of a huge system of wooden flumes that were built in the mid-1800s to move water from the lake to the booming silver-mining towns of Virginia City and Carson City, on the eastern side of the mountains.

Mount Rose (all ages)
Seven miles northeast of Incline Village on Highway 431. Hiking trails and undeveloped cross-country ski trails and sledding hills. No restrooms. Roadside parking.

Above Incline Village at 10,800 feet, Mount Rose is the highest peak in the area. From the scenic overlook on Highway 431, almost the entire 22-mile-long lake gleams below, rimmed by the Sierras on the west and the Carson Range on the east. Seven miles beyond the lookout point, on the east side of the road, Tahoe Meadows is a scattering of glorious alpine meadows where you can enjoy cross-country skiing and summertime hiking, easy or strenuous. Tahoe Meadows Whole Access Trail is a wide, 1.3-mile loop designed for those in wheelchairs and baby strollers.

The 12-mile loop hike to the summit of Mount Rose starts on an old Jeep road, near the cinder-block building close to the highway on the west side. Even if you can't make it to the top for the view that awaits, you might want to start up this trail; there is a pond with a frog chorus in residence and wildflowers galore. At the top you'll see the whole lake basin and the Carson Valley sweeping away into the distance—and even Lassen Peak, in Lassen National Park, on a clear day. Just beyond Tahoe Meadows, Mount Rose Campground is nice and cool in midsummer and often has tent and RV sites available when campgrounds near the lake are full (775-882-2766). Stop here for fresh water and restrooms. You can walk from the campground to the top of the mountain and the Tahoe Meadows trail system.

Old Brockway Golf Course (all ages)
7900 North Lake Blvd., Kings Beach; (530) 546-9909; www.oldbrockway.com.

At the intersection of Highway 89 and the lake, this lovely, old golf course is perfect for beginners and families, as most of the fairways are wide, and there are kids' tees and a nonintimidating atmosphere. Towering evergreens and wildflowers make for a pleasant rounds. If you're a low handicapper, drive from the back tees and expect a slow round in high season and on weekends. Cross-country skiing here in the wintertime, too, and, a casual, pretty darned good cafe with a lakeview deck.

Truckee (all ages)
Highway 80 at Highway 267; (530) 587-2757; www.truckee.com.

A popular stop on the way to the West Shore, the tiny town of Truckee was a rollicking railroading, logging, and ice-harvesting headquarters in the 1800s. The picturesque main street, Donner Pass Road, is lined with Western wear and outdoor equipment stores, restaurants, and saloons in brick and stone false-front buildings facing the railroad tracks and the 1869 depot where Amtrak trains blast into town daily.

Although most of the shops have gone considerably upscale and pricey in the last few years, an Old West ambience and a few old-timey stores remain. Kids like the Variety Company, an old-fashioned general store selling zillions of little cars and trucks, penny candy, and toys; give the kids $5 each and let them loose! A model train chugs around Truckee Train and Toy, ground zero for all kinds of toy trains and specialty dolls and toys. At Bud's Sporting Goods and Fountain, you can sit on a stool at the mirrored soda fountain and have a Cherry Coke or an ice-cream soda, while Dad shops for fishing gear.

The historic Union Pacific/Amtrak Depot houses the visitor center, where you can browse a huge array of brochures and maps and get sightseeing and outdoor recreation advice for the North Tahoe area; look at great photos of early days; check your e-mail; and ask about annual events. In May the town steps back in time with gunslingers trodding the boardwalks, gold panning, strolling musicians, and storytelling. Truckee Railroad Days

North Tahoe **Beaches**

- **Burnt Cedar Beach,** 300 Lakeshore Dr., Incline Village; (702) 831-1310. A big heated pool with a lifeguard makes this a unique Tahoe beach, plus a playground, lawns shaded by tall sugar pines, and a small, sandy beach with shallow water for wading and deeper water for swimming. Kids fish for crawdads in the rocks. Buy lunch at the snack bar or bring a picnic; nice picnic tables and barbecues open to IVGID cardholders only. $.

- **Ski Beach and Incline Beach,** 500 Lakeshore Dr., Incline Village; (702) 831-1310. Ski Beach, open to guests at Hyatt Regency Lake Tahoe, and adjacent Incline Beach, open to IVGID cardholders, are busier than Burnt Cedar but are more fun for older children and long enough for a half-hour stroll. Lifeguards are here in the summer; boat and water-toy rentals. $.

- **Sand Harbor State Park,** Highway 28, 3 miles south of Incline Village; (702) 831-0494. $$ parking. One of the most beautiful beach parks at the lake, with giant boulders, boat launching sites, pine groves, and white-sand beaches with lifeguards. Jet Ski rentals are popular. Families return every year in July and August to the Music and Shakespeare Festival in the outdoor amphitheater overlooking the lake (530-583-9048). Bring the kids, a picnic, and blankets, and lie stargazing while you listen to one of the bard's comedies or a reggae, Dixieland, or country western concert. You may notice clusters of parked cars between Incline and Sand Harbor on the lakeshore highway. There are a number of small beaches and fishing spots along this shoreline, including a nude beach, so don't say I didn't warn you! $.

- **Kings Beach State Recreation Area,** 12 miles northeast of Tahoe City, Highway 28; (530) 546-7248. Wildly popular, a long, sandy beach buzzing with summertime activity: volleyball, boat rentals, Jet Skis, paddleboats, playground, basketball court, picnic tables and barbecues, restrooms. $.

features antique trains, handcar rides, a parade, exhibitors, and vendors, and the Railroad Regulators reenact scenes from the Wild West.

A half mile south of Truckee on Highway 267, stop in at the Truckee River Regional Park for ice skating in the wintertime (rentals, snack bar, lessons, evening bonfire, and overhead lights); in the summer for the picnic grounds, disc golf, skate park, nature trails, basketball and volleyball courts, and more (530-583-7720).

For a break on the way to Tahoe, stop at the Donner Summit Roadside Rest Area on Highway 80 and take the easy, short, self-guided nature trail that begins and ends at the rest stop. The easy path is posted with signs about how glacial action carved and polished the area (530-587-3558).

Tahoe Donner Cross County (all ages)
11509 Northwoods Blvd., Truckee; (530) 587-9484; www.tdxc.com. $$$, ages 12 and under and 70 and older are **free.**

More than 100 kilometers of groomed striding, skating, and snowshoeing trails in a lovely pine and aspen forest, on the gentle rolling hills and flat meadows of the Euer Valley. Tiny Tracks Ski School caters to ages 5 through 9, with equipment, instruction, snack, lunch, snow play, and constant supervision. Cozy fireplace and cafe in the day lodge. Snacks and lunches at the Cookhouse, a 3.5K ski from the lodge. 2.5K lighted loop for night skiing, too.

Tahoe Rim Trail (all ages)
(775) 298-0012; www.tahoerimtrail.org.

From 12 trailheads around the lake, connect with the 165-mile, relatively level hiking, equestrian, and mountain biking path that follows the ridgetops of the Lake Tahoe Basin, at elevations between 6,300 and 10,000 feet, passing through six counties and incorporating about 50 miles of the Pacific Crest Trail. Panoramic lake views, gorgeous forests, stunning lakes, and wildflowery meadows are among the rewards. One relatively easy segment starts at the west end of the Truckee River access parking lot on Highway 89, 0.25 mile south of the intersection of Highway 28 in Tahoe City. The first 2.5 miles meander through fir and pines to Paige Meadows. The website gives you very detailed descriptions of day hikes appropriate for all skill levels and for the various parts of the lake.

Truckee Railroad Museum (all ages)
10075 Donner Pass Rd., Truckee; truckeerailroadmuseum.com. **Free.**

Brand-new, in a red caboose next to the Southern Pacific Railroad depot smack in the middle of downtown, displays of models, historic photographs, and artifacts heralding the area's rich railroad heritage. An impressive array of rolling stock, too.

Donner Lake Rim Trail (all ages)
(530) 587-3558 or (530) 582-4711.

Hikers, mountain bikers, equestrians, and photographers are loving this new trail that circles the lake. Access the trail at Donner Memorial State Park, or take the Boreal exit off I-80 at Donner Summit and go east a 0.25 mile to the Pacific Crest Trail parking lot. The trail is still in development, and there are more trailheads.

Five Favorite Things to Do at **Lake Tahoe**

- **Rafting on the Truckee.** The 5-mile stretch of rambling, rolling Truckee River between Tahoe City and River Ranch is a hoot, whether you're 2 or 92. The water moves fast enough to be exciting and slow enough for stops along the way to fish and swim, explore sandbars, hide in shady pine glades, and lie in the sun listening to wild ducks and mountain breezes in the willows.

- **Cruise to Emerald Bay.** A slow cruise on a big paddlewheeler across one of the world's largest, deepest, clearest, and most spectacular alpine lakes. Among the sights are parasailors, windsurfers, antique power boats and sailboats, quiet stretches along a shoreline dotted with log cabins, and the looming circle of snow-capped peaks. The destination, Emerald Bay, is the most photographed sight at Lake Tahoe, a Shangri-la of a place with a teahouse on a tiny island, a quiet cove lined with beautiful beaches and forests, and a dreamlike Viking's castle.

- **Sugar Pine Point.** In a state park on the lakeshore stands a turn-of-the-20th-century mansion filled with the trappings of a wealthy family whose Tahoe summers are now faint memories. Today's families laze on the vast stretch of lawn under tall sugar pines, walk the wooded trails, and lie about on the small beach and boat dock.

- **Cross-Country Skiing in Hope Valley.** Just stop on the side of the road, put on your skis, and head across a snowy meadow, where an icy river runs through an aspen grove and jagged white mountain peaks rise straight up from the valley floor. At 7,000 feet, the largely undeveloped valley is carpeted with wildflowers in the summer and endless reaches of snow in the winter—60 miles of marked cross-country trails.

- **Mountain Biking/Hiking at Northstar.** In the summertime, ski lifts carry bikers and bikes to a mountaintop 100-mile network of trails in a pine forest, with dizzying views of the lake and the surrounding peaks. Beginners take the easy route to picnic at a small lake and cruise slowly down. Hot-doggers find plenty of steep and rugged terrain. Guided hikes and kids 12 and under are free. New is the Bike Academy, offering private lessons and clinics (530-562-2268).

Northstar-at-Tahoe (all ages)

Highway 267 between Truckee and Lake Tahoe; (530) 562-1010 or (800) 466-6784; www .northstarattahoe.com. Lodging $$$–$$$$

One of the largest resorts at the lake, Northstar is a self-contained family-oriented complex laid out in a spectacular mountain and forest setting. Golf course, equestrian trails and stables, mountain biking and hiking trails, 35 or so shops and restaurants, and a plethora of high-rise condos, older lodge rooms, and homes to rent. **Free** on weekends are outdoor concerts, festivals, ski lessons, and ice skating (if you bring your own skates).

A recent expansion and renovation included new restaurants with outdoor seating, a year-round ice-skating rink, outdoor fire pits and lounging areas, chic shops, art galleries, and apparel stores—the atmosphere and the prices have gone upscale. Just opened, a Ritz-Carlton hotel at the top of the mountain.

In the summer, chairlifts take hikers and bikers up to beautiful mountaintop trails, and there is a busy schedule of activities and events all year. At the Recreation Center, older kids head for the teen center and the workout rooms. Parents love the lap pool. Little kids can play in the wading pool and the shallow end of the main pool, under the watchful eye of a lifeguard. The Rec Center is available to guests at the older condos and homes; the new condos have a separate pool and recreation facilities.

Skiing is great for families, with many intermediate and beginning downhill and boarding runs; all trails funnel back to the main area, making meet-up easy. Six boarding

Shops at Northstar

- **Ambassador Toys.** (520) 562-2600; www.ambassadortoys.com. Global cultures are showcased in educational toys, books, games, crafts and collectibles.

- **Butterbox.** (530) 562-3650. Snowboards and snowboard apparel, flip-flops, bikinis, board shorts, and tank tops.

- **Mine.** (530) 562-3640. A children's store for ski and snowboard apparel to size 14, shoes, gifts, books, toys, games, puzzles. Ask about the monthly kids' activities.

- **Freckles.** (530) 562-8723. Upscale clothing, toys, books and accessories from newborns to age 14. Voted "Best Children's Clothing Store" in North Lake Tahoe.

- **All Fired Up.** (530) 562-1995; www.allfireduptahoe.com. Choose from hundreds of pottery pieces to paint with washable, nontoxic paints. Your child's creation will be ready to take home or ship the next day.

Adventure Parks, each with a theme and skill level, are scattered across the mountain. Minor's Camp cares for kids 2 to 6, with ski lessons optional. Ask about the Mommy, Daddy, and Me program, the Parent Predicament sharing ticket, and the gondola ticket that gets you to the tubing area and the Nordic and snowshoe center. New is the Burton Progression snowboard park designed for new boarders, a less-intimidating alternative to the 17-foot superpipe. At the Action Zone, the excellent tubing area has a lift; no sleds or saucers. Try the bungee trampolines and the snow toys. Every Friday and Saturday evening during the winter season, the Village at Northstar offers Parents Night Out: child care and entertainment for ages 4 to 12; $49 per child.

Donner Lake (all ages)

Between Soda Springs and Truckee off Highway 80; (530) 582-7892.

Families who want a quiet, old-fashioned vacation in the mountains love Donner. On the 7.5 mile shoreline, you can camp, launch a boat, rent a cabin, fish, hike, ski, and enjoy the crystal-clear, blue waters. There are nearly 30 public piers on the north side for fishing and boating. Shoreline Park offers bank fishing and a pier, boat launching, picnic sites, and swimming. A swimming area is supervised by lifeguards on West End Beach, which also has a snack bar, picnic areas with barbecues, kayak and paddleboat rentals, and a tennis court.

Above the lake on Highway 80, the Emigrant Gap viewpoint on Donner Summit, at 7,135 feet, is a must stop. Your family will get a dramatic geology lesson when you look out over hundreds of miles of high country to see the tremendous tilted block of the Sierras sloping toward the west. Glacial canyons are gouged out of the granite, and the Yuba and Bear Rivers have cut their own valleys.

Donner Memorial State Park (all ages)

Three miles west of Truckee, off Highway 80; (530) 582-7892.

Stop on the way to Tahoe to get a history lesson and enjoy walking paths and picnic groves beneath towering evergreens, cool and shady at 5,950 feet in elevation. From here you can access a relatively easy portion of the Donner Lake Rim Trail, a 23-mile-long, sometimes steep trail crossing ridges and granite knobs; it connects with the Pacific Crest Trail. The Emigrant Trail Museum depicts stories of the Donner Party, a group of pioneer families who were trapped here during the violent winter of 1846–47. A monument rests on a stone base 22 feet high—the snow level of that fateful winter. In the museum are artifacts and displays on the building of the railroad through the Sierras in the 1800s. In the distance, you can see train tracks, mostly covered with snow buildings, running along the rugged mountainsides above Donner Lake; the tracks are still in use by Amtrak today. The museum features exhibits about Native American and railroad history. There is also a gift shop and a visitor center.

Rangers guide interpretive walks throughout the summer, explaining local flora and fauna and the history of the Donner Party. In the wintertime, rangers lead **free** snowshoe history hikes and introductions to cross-country skiing. It's **free** to cross-country ski on a 3-mile loop.

Inexpensive **Ski Areas**

Low prices for lift tickets, lessons, and other expenses make these long-established ski resorts family favorites. Expert skiers and boarders will likely be bored; new skiers and children and adults looking to take it easy will love these shorter, less-intimidating ski slopes. Kids' learn-to-ski programs are top-notch.

- **Tahoe Donner.** Donner State Park exit off Highway 80, (530) 587-9444; www.skitahoedonner.com. Downhill skiing on 14 runs; 110 kilometers of cross-country trails with warming huts. Kids under 6 ski **free.** Nearby snow-play area and lodge restaurant. The website has a great, detailed introduction and tips for parents and first-time skiers.

- **Soda Springs.** One mile east of Highway 80 at Soda Springs exit; (530) 426-3901; www.skisodasprings.com. Oriented toward young children, with the tubing runs alongside the ski runs; mini-snowmobiles, too. For $10, children 10 and under can try out ski or snowboard equipment, access the easy slopes on the moving carpet, and play on the tube carousel; and the Kids X boarding park is a great place to learn.

- **Donner Ski Ranch.** 19320 Donner Pass Rd., on Old Highway 40, Norden; (530) 426-3635; www.donnerskiranch.com. Dozens of uncrowded runs; kids 5 and under are **free;** ages 6 to 12 are $10. Ask about value days.

- **Sierra-at-Tahoe.** From South Lake Tahoe, 12 miles up Highway 50 west over Echo Summit; (530) 659-7453; www.sierratahoe.com. Wild Mountain Ski and Snowboard camp for ages 4 to 12; day care; kids 4 and under ski **free.** Good snow between 6,600- and 8,800-foot elevation; snow play on-site and a tubing hill. At the Telemark and Backcountry Center, ask about the guided snowshoe tours, easy enough for kids ages 7 and up. You will find boarding terrain off every lift, from a 17-foot halfpipe to 50 tabletops and dozens of rails. At midmountain, you can rent snow bikes and scooters. The Family Private Lesson offers personalized instruction for all levels of ability, all at the same time!

Diamond Peak (all ages)

1210 Ski Way, on Highway 431 above Incline Village; (775) 832-1177; www.diamondpeak .com. Lift tickets: $$$$; kids 7 to 14 $$$; kids 6 and under and adults over 80 **free.**

With mostly intermediate and beginners slopes and short distance to the North Shore, families like this medium-size ski resort. Bee Ferrato Child Ski Center for ages 3 to 7 offers private and group lessons, separate lift, and one instructor to five children; **free** lift tickets with lesson. The Diamond Pete program includes indoor supervision, lessons, lunch, and rentals. The lodge was recently renovated and snowmaking has been expanded.

This full-service ski resort has spectacular lake and mountain views, the highest base elevation at Tahoe, downhill and cross-country skiing, snowboarding, restaurants, ski school, equipment rental, and child care. Intermediates and beginners are happy here; expert skiers love the 200 acres of chutes and the double black diamond runs, some pitching 55 degrees. Snow conditions are less dependable than at higher-elevation resorts, but when the snow is primo, this is a good choice for families who prefer uncrowded ski runs and a casual, family-oriented atmosphere. Ask about "Learn to Ski and Ride" discounts, twilight tickets, and family rates. Among numerous annual events, Elvis Day Saturday in January is fun, when Elvis will likely issue your lift ticket, fit your skis, and teach you how to ski.

Boreal Ski Area (all ages)

Highway 80 at Donner Summit; (530) 426-3666; www.rideboreal.com. Lift tickets: adults $$$$; ages 5 to 12 $$; 4 and under are free.

A reasonably priced, nonintimidating choice for new skiers and boarders, Boreal focuses on families, with a variety of terrain features for kids, a family terrain zone, parent-shared passes, and packages and discounts. The Kids Club package for ages 4 to 10 includes an all-day pass, equipment rental, lesson, supervision from 10 a.m. to 3 p.m., lunch, and snack, from $70. Night skiing is popular at Boreal, especially with teenagers, who like the illuminated terrain park with its 450-foot-long superpipe, 100 rails, tabletop jumps, and rolls. Rent sleds and tubes and whiz down the groomed lanes at the Playland sledding area. Admission is free at Boreal's Western American Ski Sport Museum, where ski history from the 1850s to the present is depicted in photos, displays, and vintage movies.

Royal Gorge USA (ages 7 and up)

Off Highway 80, Soda Springs; (530) 426-3871 or (800) 500-3871; www.royalgorge.com. Trail passes: adults $$$$; children $$$; ages 10 and under and ages 75 and older are free.

Royal Gorge is the largest Nordic ski resort in the nation and has been voted the best in North America. The network of groomed trails is so vast and so varied that you definitely need to carry the trail map—all the better to locate the 10 cozy warming huts and the 4 cafes, which make comforting destinations during a day of skiing or snowshoeing. You can rent everything here, including pulk sleds for small children, so you can pull them behind you. Accommodations in the Wilderness Lodge and in the cabins include meals and trail passes. You can also stay at Sugar Bowl or at nearby, cozy Rainbow Lodge (www.rainbow lodge.com) and connect directly to Royal Gorge trails; free shuttle bus to and from Sugar Bowl.

This is an especially good place to introduce children to the sport, as they offer a Kid's Camp for 6 to 12 year olds, group and private lessons for all ages, and 4 surface lifts to make it easy for beginners. At Summit Station is the cozy Family Center, with a fireplace, beanbags, benches, and tables, all overlooking the main trailhead.

Where to Eat

Austin's. 120 Country Club Dr., Incline Village; (775) 832-7728. Voted Best Family Restaurant by the locals, this casual, friendly place serves hearty, Texas-style food three meals a day. Bring your appetite for Mountain Man Omelet, pork chops and steak sandwiches, buttermilk fries, and chicken-fried steak. Don't miss the homemade pie. $$

Azzara's. 930 Tahoe Blvd., in the Raley's Center, Incline Village; (702) 831-0346. For more than 50 years, everything Italian, such as Sicilian artichokes, saltimbocca, cannelloni, osso bucco, and pizza, seafood, and pasta. Reservations are definitely required for dinner at this popular place. $$–$$$

Blue Onion Café. 7900 North Lake Blvd. at Highway 267, at the Old Brockway Golf Course, Kings Beach; (530) 546-3913; www .blueonion.com. On the sunny deck, surrounded by greenery and with a lake view, enjoy breakfast and lunch daily, and dinner in the summertime. Casual and friendly, with an extensive comfort-food menu. $–$$

Hacienda de la Sierra. 931 Tahoe Blvd., across from Raley's, Incline Village; (702) 831-8300; www.haciendatahoe.com. Voted the best Mexican restaurant by locals; warm, colorful atmosphere, booths indoors or tables on the deck. Fajitas, huge burritos, combo platters. $–$$

Steamer's Beachside Bar and Oven. 8290 North Lake Blvd., Kings Beach; (530) 546-2218. One of the most popular pizza restaurants on the North Shore, with a great outdoor patio on the lakeside, and indoor seating by the windows for when the weather turns cool. If your family likes calzones and pizza, they'll love Steamer's; dig into the $2 tacos. The kids can run around on the beach while they wait for lunch or dinner. $

Where to Stay

Donner Lake Village Resort. 15695 Donner Pass Rd., Truckee; (530) 587-6081; www.donnerlakevillage.com. Moderately priced, comfortable accommodations, from lodgettes sleeping 4 to town houses sleeping 6. Right on the lake with great views, a private marina, and boat rentals. $$–$$$

Hyatt Regency Lake Tahoe. Lakeshore and Country Club Drive, Incline Village; (702) 832-1234; www.laketahoe.hyatt.com. Highrise hotel and 24 two-bedroom luxury lakeside cottages, recently remodeled, in their own compound surrounded by lawns. Camp Hyatt day and evening child care. $$$–$$$$

Ice Lakes Lodge. 1111 Soda Springs Rd., Soda Springs; (530) 426-7660; www.icelakes lodge.com. A few minutes from Sugar Bowl and Royal Gorge, at Donner Summit right on a beautiful lake, a very nice, rustic, 23-room lodge open year-round. Ground-floor rooms have small patios; upstairs, some have decks; some rooms have 2 queen beds. Hearty American food and kids' menu in the casual restaurant, with views of Serene Lakes and Castle Peak. Box lunches are available; **free** continental breakfast. Linger on the sofa in front of the massive stone fireplace. Hiking, biking, fishing, and canoeing in the summer;

cross-country skiing and snow play in the wintertime. $$–$$$

Parkside Inn at Incline. 1003 Tahoe Blvd., Incline Village; (702) 444-6758; www.innat incline.com. Recently freshened-up motel units in a forest setting; small indoor pool, sauna, spa. Continental breakfast, some kitchenettes, small lounge with fireplace. $$$

Truckee Tahoe Inn. 11331 Hwy. 267, between Truckee and Northstar; (530) 587-4525; www.bestwesterntahoe.com. Reasonably priced motel with simple, fresh rooms and suites with sofa beds and complimentary continental breakfast, sauna, and spa. Ask about ski packages and off-season rates. $–$$

Vacation Station Lake Tahoe. 110 Country Club Dr., P.O. Box 7180, Incline Village, NV 89451; (800) 841-7443; www.vacation station.com. Agency for rental of homes and condos.

For More Information

Incline Village Crystal Bay Visitors Center. 969 Tahoe Blvd., Incline Village; (775) 831-4440; www.gotahoe.com.

Incline Village Parks and Recreation. 980 Incline Way, Incline Village; (775) 832-1310; www.ivgid.org. Recreation center, tennis, classes, sports programs, swimming pools, beach.

Truckee Ranger Station. 10811 Stockrest Springs Rd., Truckee; (530) 587-3558. In a new, eco-friendly location, lots of books; hiking, biking, and driving maps; and good advice about about trails, campgrounds, and points of interest in the Tahoe National Forest.

Shasta Cascade

W here the Sierra Nevada Range ends and the Cascade Range begins, two colossal glaciated volcanoes are visible for hundreds of miles. Dormant 14,162-foot Mount Shasta and still-active 10,457-foot Lassen Peak loom like misty ice gods above the forested recreation lands of northernmost California.

Families who crave recreation in the great outdoors, high-country scenery, and sightseeing in historic towns can spend a lifetime of vacations in the Shasta Cascade area. Roughly the size of Ohio, the region contains seven national forests, eight national and state parks, five mighty rivers, and hundreds of lakes.

Fishing is legendary on the McCloud, Sacramento, Klamath, Salmon, and Scott Rivers. Lush woodlands along the riverbanks are precious ribbons of wilderness that shelter birds, waterfowl, and other wildlife in great numbers.

One of the largest recreational lakes in the country, Lake Shasta is encircled by 370 miles of wooded shoreline that spreads out into four main arms fed by three rivers and a creek. Houseboating is one of the most popular ways for families to vacation on the lake.

On the fringes of the wild, dark forests of the Trinity Alps are sprinkled a handful of tiny towns favored by antiques hunters and trout fishers. The forty-niners, pioneers, and Chinese immigrants in the area left a rich cultural heritage that can be seen in the charming old buildings and museums of Weaverville.

A unique geophysical crossroads, mountainous Lassen Volcanic National Park boils and bubbles with mudpots and sulfury hot springs. On the slopes of both Lassen Peak and Mount Shasta are developed areas for downhill and Nordic skiing, as well as snow play.

Anchoring Highway 5, the main route to the Northwest, the city of Redding is the jumping-off point for adventures in the Shasta Cascade. A wide variety of motels, restaurants, recreation opportunities, and fishing outfitters, plus easy access to the Sacramento River, make this an important stop.

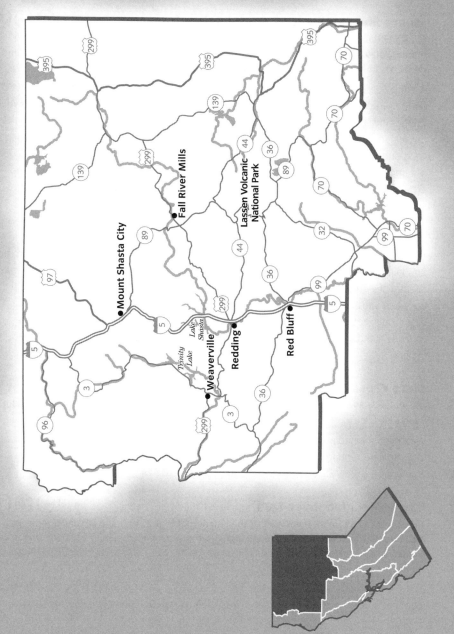

SHASTA CASCADE

Mount Shasta City

At the foot of Mount Shasta, the laid-back small town of Mount Shasta City is where many families headquarter, heading out every day to explore the national forests in the summertime and to ski when the snow falls.

Mount Shasta Bike, Board, and Ski Park (all ages)

Located 10 miles east of Mount Shasta City, at 104 Siskiyou Ave.; (530) 926-8600 (snow phone: 530-926-8686); www.skipark.com. Lift tickets: adults $$$$; ages 8 to 12 $$$; 7 and under $$. In the summer lift fees are $$ for adults and free for kids under 12.

A good-size winter resort, with mostly intermediate and beginner downhill runs at 5,000 feet, a ski school, Nordic and night skiing, and a nice day lodge with a restaurant. Powder Pups is the supervised ski program for kids ages 4 to 7; across the road from the ski park, Snowman's Hill is a snow-play area. At the Nordic skiing center are 16 miles of groomed trails and skating lanes, with a lodge, a warming hut, and shuttle service. The advantage of family skiing here is the reasonable cost, child-oriented staff, the lack of lift lines and crowds, and a carefree drive on Highway 5, which is seldom encumbered with enough snow to require chains.

In summer take the 20-minute round-trip up the chairlift for the view of a lifetime. Hike around up here, picnic, and take the lift back down. Or bring your mountain bikes up (or rent them here) and pedal the excellent trails, ending up back at the lodge. In the summer and fall, the wildflowers in the meadows on top and at the base of the mountain are truly spectacular. There are frequent concerts and festivals in the beautiful outdoor amphitheater, and you can buy hot food to eat on the sunny deck or cold picnic fare to carry back to your blanket. In response to the climbing craze, a 24-foot tower has climbing routes for ages 4 and up. There is also a free multimedia exhibit about the formation of Mount Shasta.

More Cross-Country Skiing (all ages)

Off Highway 89 beyond Mount Shasta Ski Park in the Shasta-Trinity National Forest; (530) 926-4511. Free.

Watch for signs to Bunny Flat and Sand Flat, marked cross-country trails for beginners and intermediates and maintained by the US Forest Service. Restrooms and parking are available only at Bunny Flat, which is also a snow-play area.

Upper McCloud River Trail (all ages)

Take Highway 89 for 15 miles east of the junction of Highways 5 and 89, and 5 miles east of McCloud; at the Fowlers Campground sign, go south 0.6 mile to Lower Falls Day Use Area. The trailhead is below the Lower Falls stairway. (530) 964-2184; www.fs.fed.us/r5/shasta trinity.

Perfect for a family ramble along the river, accessed at several points along the McCloud River Loop Road, this is a rather easy, absolutely gorgeous hike where you see three

Thar She **Blows**

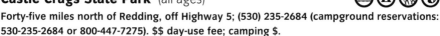

At 14,162 feet, Mount Shasta is the fourth-highest peak in the continental United States and the largest volcano by volume—80 cubic miles.

Shasta is near the southern end of the Cascade Range, which begins with the active volcano Lassen Peak and runs north to British Columbia, with volcanoes about every 50 miles—quite a sight from a plane. The Cascades are part of the notorious "Ring of Fire" that surrounds the Pacific Ocean.

The last recorded eruption of Mount Shasta was in 1786.

spectacular waterfalls, forests, and rock formations. It starts at Lower Falls Day Use Area and winds about 12 miles along the river to Cattle Camp Campground. Good fishing, too.

Castle Crags State Park (all ages)

Forty-five miles north of Redding, off Highway 5; (530) 235-2684 (campground reservations: 530-235-2684 or 800-447-7275). $$ day-use fee; camping $.

A fortress of 6,000-foot granite pillars and monster boulders, with 2 miles of the Sacramento River gleaming below and good trout fishing in the streams. At this spectacular park you can swim, hike, rock climb, and camp in one of 76 developed sites. Get maps at the park office and amble up the sun-dappled Indian Creek Nature Trail, a 1-mile loop. The Crags Trail to Castle Dome is 5.5 strenuous miles up and into the Castle Crags Wilderness, connecting with the Pacific Crest Trail. People often stop at the park just to fill up jugs with natural soda water. The road is plowed all winter for ice fishing on Castle Lake.

Lake Siskiyou Camp Resort (all ages)

Three miles from Mount Shasta City, take Hatchery Road to a left onto Old Stage Road, then turn right at W. A. Barr Road; (530) 926-2618; www.lakesis.com. Day-use fee $; camping $.

One of the prettiest multiuse camping and RV facilities in the state, the resort is located at a large reservoir in a fresh, clean, pine-scented setting. You can rent a fully equipped trailer on-site or bring your own tent or RV. Day-trippers are welcome to lounge on the 1,000-foot-long sandy beach, swim, or launch a fishing boat. Available to rent are water toys, kayaks, canoes, paddleboats, sailboats, and fishing equipment. Also here are a store, a snack bar, outdoor movies, and a playground. Check out the gift shop and general store, and upgrades all around the grounds. A 7-mile walking and biking trail circles the lake.

At the end of W. A. Barr Road, Gumboot Lake is a tiny, shallow bit of icy water stocked with trout, surrounded by meadows, mountains, and forests. Bring a picnic, an inflatable raft, or a canoe.

Castle Lake (all ages)

Passing the Lake Siskiyou Camp Resort entrance on W. A. Barr Road, go left on Castle Lake Road, 7 miles to the parking area; (530) 926-4511.

This is one of the most easily accessible alpine lakes in Northern California. The parking lot is a few yards from the lakeshore, and within a short easy stroll, you can be in an idyllic, seemingly isolated wilderness setting. Walk in either direction along the lakeshore through beautiful forest, putter around in the creek, fish in the lake, launch your skiff or kayak, or have a picnic. The water here is wonderfully pure and clear, and the fishing and (chilly) swimming are great. For a 3-mile-round-trip, moderately strenuous hike, take the trail to the left of the lake near the stream, along the lakeside, and up above the lake to 5,900 feet. Bear to the right up 100 feet more to Heart Lake, a small lake that warms up in summer and is popular for swimming. One of the best photo ops of Mount Shasta is on Castle Lake Road, about 0.5 mile before the parking lot.

McCloud Railway (all ages)

Main Street, McCloud; (800) 733-2141; www.shastasunset.com. Adults $$$; ages 8 and under $$.

During the summer on weekends, an hour's delightful ride in open-air cars pulled by historic steam locomotives affords views of alpine forests and Mount Shasta.

McCloud River Mercantile Company (all ages)

241 Main St., McCloud; (530) 964-2846; www.mccloudmercantile.com/mercantile.htm.

While on McCloud's Old West Main Street, stop in at this irresistibly quirky emporium, where Dr. Hunter's foot crème, badger shaving brushes, Pendleton blankets, and vintage toys, games, and dollhouses are on display. How about a bright red enamelware teapot, an oil lamp, or a Timeworks old-time clock? Here also is an absolutely lovely, upscale hotel, the McCloud River Mercantile Hotel, where family rooms are appealing.

Where to Eat

Casa Ramos. 1126 South Mount Shasta Blvd., Mount Shasta; (530) 926-0250; www.casaramos.net. A family favorite for Mexican food made by a Mexico City family, so popular they have opened Casa Ramos restaurants in Red Bluff, Redding, Chico, and other locations, and Tecate Grill in Redding. The servings are massive. $–$$

Lily's. 1013 South Mount Shasta Blvd., Mount Shasta City; (530) 926-3372; www.lilysrestaurant.com. Hearty breakfast, lunch, dinner, and weekend brunch on the deck surrounded by a lovely garden, from Mexican

food to steaks, pasta, and veggies. This is a very popular place. $–$$

Michael's. 313 North Mount Shasta Blvd., Mount Shasta City; (530) 926-5288. Italian specialties and continental dishes including homemade pasta, soups, sandwiches, burgers. Lunch and dinner. $–$$

Where to Stay

Durango RV Resort. 810 Main St., Red Bluff; (530) 732-1616; www.durangorvresorts.com. Pull-through RV spaces, some on the riverfront, from 75 to 90 feet in a new,

175-unit resort with Wi-Fi, 2 large clubhouses with pools and saunas, shuttle to stores and restaurants, vehicle wash area, 45 acres of private walking trails, and an outdoor recreation area. $

Mount Shasta KOA Campground. 900 North Mount Shasta Blvd., Mount Shasta City; (530) 926-4029; www.mtshastakoa.com. A grassy, gardeny place with RV and tent sites, animal corrals, camping cabins, a store, a swimming pool, and a playground. $

Mount Shasta Ranch. 1008 W. A. Barr Rd., five minutes from Lake Siskiyou, Mount Shasta City; (530) 926-3870; www.stayin shasta.com. In a beautiful country setting, a B&B with spacious rooms, suites, and a carriage house; a gigantic common living room and game room; and a full breakfast. Children are quite welcome in the carriage house. $$

Mount Shasta Resort. 1000 Siskiyou Lake Blvd., Mount Shasta City; (530) 926-3030 or (800) 958-3363; www.mountshastaresort .com. In a pretty wooded setting near walking trails and lakes, beautiful 1- and 2-bedroom chalets with fireplaces, sofa beds, fully equipped kitchens, spacious living rooms, and decks. The golf course here is spectacular and challenging; spend an hour on the practice range with budding golfers. There is a comfortable restaurant with views of the mountains, plus a snack bar with outdoor tables. Ask about ski and golf packages. $$–$$$.

Railroad Park Resort. 100 Railroad Park Rd., Dunsmuir; (530) 235-4440; www.rrpark .com. One of the best places in the region for families to stay. Stop here for a meal and take a look at the collection of old railcars and railroading paraphernalia. Accommodations include an RV park, a campground, cabins, and motel rooms in restored freight cars and cabooses; the boxcar has a kitchen. Swimming pool. $$

Strawberry Valley Inn. 1142 South Mount Shasta Blvd., Mount Shasta; (916) 926-2052. Lovely landscaped grounds and shade trees make this reasonably priced motel a winner; some rooms have 2 beds, and there are 2-room suites. A huge breakfast buffet is served on a sunny patio or by the fireplace. $–$$

Tree House Best Western. 111 Morgan Way, at Highway 5 and Lake Street, Mount Shasta City; (530) 926-3101; www.bestwest ern.com. Large, nicely landscaped motel, with some 2-bedroom units and refrigerators, Wi-Fi; includes breakfast. Large heated indoor pool; casual restaurant with fireplace. $$

For More Information

Shasta Cascade Wonderland Association. 1699 Hwy. 273, Anderson; (530) 365-7500 or (800) 474-2782; www.shastacascade .com.

Mount Shasta Visitor Bureau. 300 Pine St., Mount Shasta City; (800) 926-4865; www .mtshastachamber.com. Two blocks east of the Highway 5 central exit at Lake and Pine Streets.

US Forest Service. 204 West Alma, Mount Shasta City; (530) 926-4511; www.recreation .gov.

Lake Shasta

They call it California's Water Wonderland, a huge warm-water lake at the confluence of several major rivers. The surface waters reach 80 degrees in summer, perfect for swimming and waterskiing. Attracting avid anglers are 16 species of fish, from bass to trout, sturgeon, salmon, and channel catfish.

With a filigreed shoreline of 370 miles, Shasta is very popular for all kinds of water sports and houseboating. Houseboats range from 15 to more than 65 feet long and sleep from 4 to 22 people. These boats are easy to navigate, even for first-timers. You can get air-conditioning, TV, and washers and dryers, among other amenities. Rentals at the dozen or so houseboat marinas on Lake Shasta cost $1,000 per week and up. The houseboats come completely equipped except for linens and food. You motor slowly along, exploring hidden inlets, fishing, and stopping at beaches and marinas. (See "Houseboating Tips for Families" in The Big Valley chapter.)

Four national forests are located in the Shasta region, and some operate developed and boat-in campgrounds at the lake. More than two dozen private campgrounds and marinas are scattered along the river arms of the lake, primarily on the Sacramento near Lakehead and on the McCloud. You can sleep overnight in a boat anywhere on the lake. There are even floating restrooms!

Hike Lake Shasta (all ages)

Hiking around the lake can be a hot, dry experience in summer, but trails are green and gorgeous all other times of year. From Packer's Bay Road take Waters Gulch Trail through an oak forest (about 3 miles) up to great views of the Sacramento arm of the lake. Eastside Trail, also at Packer's Bay, is a 0.5-mile, easy walk to swimming and fishing spots. From the Bailey Cove parking lot, a trail runs for almost 3 miles through a pretty, wooded area with lake views, and you can swim at several places along the way.

Lake Shasta Caverns (ages 7 and up)
Fifteen miles north of Redding off Highway 5, take the O'Brien/Caverns exit; (530) 238-2341; www.lakeshastacaverns.com. Ages 3 and up $$$.

One of the most dramatic natural wonders in the western states, the caverns constitute a fantasy of multicolored columns, 20-foot-high stone draperies, stalactites and stalagmites, brilliant crystals, and unusual limestone and marble formations, all subtly lit for maximum effect. A 15-minute boat ride ferries you across the lake to a wooded island, where you go by bus 800 feet up a steep road through aromatic bay, oak, and manzanita. Groups of about 20 people are guided up and down hundreds of stone steps through a series of giant chambers. The atmosphere is damp and drippy and a constant 58 degrees, which is refreshing in the summer, when outside temperatures can reach more than 100. For many people this is a highlight of their Shasta trip, a once-in-a-lifetime adventure; for toddlers and for people who have a hard time walking, it may not be doable.

Shasta Dam (all ages)

Off Highway 5, just north of Redding, on Shasta Dam Boulevard; (530) 275-4463; www .shastalake.com/shastadam. Free.

Walk out on the rim of the second-tallest concrete dam in the United States. Take a look at historic photos and watch a short film in the visitor center. The free guided tour into the dam involves an elevator ride that kids under age 8 may find scary. When high water is released through the spillway, the noise can be extremely loud; earplugs are recommended. Call ahead to check on this, and to get the tour schedule, which changes seasonally. You are welcome to enjoy the tree-shaded picnic lawns overlooking the lake.

Shasta Houseboating Resorts (all ages)

Of the several lakeshore resorts that offer rentals of patio boats, ski boats, fishing skiffs, and houseboats, Bridge Bay Resort is the first large one you come to, 12 miles north of Redding (10300 Bridge Bay; 530-275-3021 or 800-752-9669; www.sevencrown.com). Under a big bridge over the lake, this is a full-service marina with cabins, a motel, and a restaurant. The houseboat rental company here, Seven Crown Resorts, is one of the largest and oldest of its kind. They also have operations at Digger Bay on Lake Shasta, in the California Delta, and in other states.

At another large, full-service resort, Jones Valley Resorts, you can rent a variety of houseboats, including *The Titan,* a towering, three-decked, 65-foot cruiser with 6 staterooms, 3 baths, and an expansive main salon, sleeping 22 people. This massive vessel comes with a gourmet galley, a state-of-the-art entertainment center, and a crow's nest upper pavilion with a second galley, TV, and hot tub for eight; there's also a 3-story water slide (Oasis Road exit off Highway 5 and two other sites on Lake Shasta; 877-474-2782; www.shastalakeresorts.com).

The houseboat marinas often have general stores selling groceries, fuel, water toys, and fishing equipment. Jones Valley even has a floating recreation center on the dock complete with basketball, pool table, table tennis, foosball, and shuffleboard. See more about houseboating in The Big Valley chapter.

Holiday Harbor Resort and Marina (all ages)

20061 Shasta Caverns Rd., O'Brien; (530) 238-2382 or (800) 776-2628; www.lakeshasta.com.

The largest boat and water recreation rental center on the lake. Houseboats, patio boats with restrooms and barbecues, ski boats, wakeboards, inner tubes, and a wild and crazy variety of water play equipment. Also a motel, RV hookups, a playground, and a grocery.

Hedge Creek Falls Park (all ages)

Dunsmuir Avenue at Mott Road, Dunsmuir; (800) 474-2782.

From a nice picnic spot, take a 0.25-mile, steep hike down to a lovely fall spilling over a massive stone cliff festooned with ferns. Stand inside the big cave to peer out through the water curtain.

Blue Goose Excursion Train (all ages)

Yreka Depot, Yreka; (530) 842-4146. $$, kids under 3 are free.

Take a 3-hour trip on the historic short-line Yreka Western Railroad from Yreka to Montague. A 1915 Baldwin engine pulls cars over the river through beautiful ranchlands of the Shasta Valley with views of Mount Shasta. You get time in the quaint burg of Montague to have lunch, shop, and take a horse-drawn wagon ride, then return to the Yreka Depot, where model trains and railroad memorabilia are on display.

Where to Eat

Tail of the Whale. Twelve miles north of Redding, at the Bridge Bay exit off Highway 5; (530) 275-3021. Dependable American food in a setting overlooking an arm of the lake and Bridge Bay Resort; seafood, prime rib, Cajun shrimp; a hearty, all-American menu. $

Where to Stay

Antlers Resort and Marina. 20679 Antlers Rd., Lakehead; (530) 238-2553; www .shastalakevacations.com. Another source for houseboat rentals, cabins, and water sports equipment; campground, grocery. $$–$$$

Lakehead Campground & RV Park. Just off Highway 5, exit 702; (530) 238-8450; www .lakeheadcampgroundandrv.com. A short walk from Shasta Lake and restaurants, shaded camp sites with fire pits; RV sites with full hookups. New cabin tents are cozy with beds, electricity, picnic tables and BBQs, sleeping 4 to 6 people. Free Wi-Fi, rec room, volleyball, horseshoes, laundry, convenience store. Lots to keep kids occupied here. $

Lakeshore Villa RV Park. 20672 Lakeshore Dr., Lakehead; (530) 238-8688. Rent a cabin, houseboat, ski boat, or fishing boat. Enjoy the pool, or just have lunch and watch the action. $

Shasta Lake Motel. 20714 Lakeshore Dr., Lakehead; (530) 238-2545; www.shastalake motel.com. Within walking distance of the lake, a longtime favorite for families seeking a value-oriented, nice, clean, small motel. Simple, knotty-pine-paneled guest rooms; some with extra beds, minifridges and microwaves, and/ or kitchenettes. Lawns, barbecues, large swimming pool, nearby groceries, and restaurant. $

For More Information

Shasta Cascade Wonderland Association. 1619 Hwy. 273, Anderson; (530) 365-7500 or (800) 474-2782; www.shastacascade .com.

Shasta Lake Visitor Information Center. 14250 Holiday Rd., 10 miles north of Redding on Highway 5; (530) 275-1589. Maps, brochures, campground reservations, advice, and information on the Whiskeytown-Shasta-Trinity National Recreation Area and the Shasta-Trinity National Forest. Here also is a gift shop, a children's hands-on learning corner, and an interpretive center focusing on Native American and regional history. The Shasta Lake Ranger Station is located here, too.

Lassen Volcanic National Park

The largest plug dome volcano in the world, 10,457-foot Lassen Peak last blew its top in 1915. Hot springs, boiling mudpots, and sulfury steam vents remind us that sometime in the next few hundred years, a drive through Lassen Volcanic National Park may not be a good idea. For now, it's one of the wonders of the world.

You can drive through the park in half a day, including stops along the 35-mile route up and over the 8,000-foot summit, viewing the snow-covered peaks and crystalline lakes from a distance. Better yet, settle into a campground for a week of fishing on a few of the 50 lakes and hiking on some of the 150 miles of interconnecting wilderness trails. Several lakes allow nonpowered boating. Seventeen miles of the Pacific Crest Trail twist through aromatic conifer forests, magnificent stands of aspens and cottonwoods, and wildflower-washed meadows.

In the fall, the entire mountain and lake region seems to burst into flame—the aspen, birch, and oaks are spun gold; eastern maples, chokecherry, and dogwood (and poison oak!) turn red along the highways and hiking trails, and are reflected in the many mountain lakes. In winter cross-country skiers, snowshoers, and snow campers take off into the spectacular backcountry. The snow may fly as early as September and as late as May (be advised to carry chains). Campgrounds are all located above 5,650 feet and are open from Memorial Day to the end of September, depending on road and snow conditions.

Anglers from all over the world come to the Lassen area for wild trout fishing in the cold, clear waters of Hat Creek and the Fall and McCloud Rivers on the north side of the park. Nonfishing members of the family will enjoy wildlife viewing in the Hat Creek area, where osprey, bald eagles, elk, and a variety of waterfowl are commonly seen.

Visitor Center

The main park headquarters is at 38050 Hwy. 36, just east of Mineral, near the park; (530) 595-4444; www.nps.gov/lavo. $$ per car.

At one of the three park entrances, stop here for the Lassen Park road guide and the current schedule of naturalist-led tours and kids' story hours. More than 60 points of interest and trails are indicated in the guide and are numbered to correspond to road signs. The park road winds around three sides of the park, past woodlands, meadows, streams, and lakes. Among the spectacular sights is Bumpass Hell near the southwest park entrance, where you walk on boardwalks over hot springs, steam vents, mudpots, and other eerie manifestations of Earth's hot insides. The Devastated Area Interpretive Trail, one of several that are wheelchair accessible, is a 0.25-mile path through a lush forest of lodgepole pines and aspens, breathtaking in the fall. To get to the beautiful 30-foot cascade of Kings Creek Falls, meander 1.5 miles, one-way, through meadows and forests.

From late June through August, kids ages 7 to 12 can participate in the park's Junior Ranger and Junior Firefighter programs, which involve completing an activity book and earning a certificate. For kids under 7, ask about Chipmunk Club activity cards and stickers. A wide variety of **free** ranger-led programs and guided walks are scheduled during the summer, for all ages; check the park newspaper on the website for time and place of events, plus maps, campground information, and what's new.

The old Southwest Information Station at the southwest entrance has been replaced by the elaborate, big, new Kohn Yah-mah-nee Visitor Facility, complete with a large gift shop and nice restaurant, exhibits, films, and interpretive programs.

Lava Beds National Monument

Get started on exploring the spectacular, unusual geologic and historic sites at Lava Beds by spending time at the new visitor center, where exhibits and videos explain what you will see. You can borrow lanterns and helmets here for self-guided and ranger-led tours of the lava tubes—there are more than 400 of them (I recommend only guided tours, for safety's sake). A popular lighted cave, Mushpot has a mile of fascinating catacombs, and Skull Cave is a 750-foot-tall chamber with ice floors. Although most of the sights are underground, you can also see a lot on walking trails. The Schonchin Butte 0.75-mile trail leads to a panoramic view from the fire lookout, which is staffed from June to September; ask the rangers about the Junior Fire Lookout badge. There are Modoc Indian War battlefields, spatter cones, craters, lava flows, petroglyphs, and more wild and crazy sights. The monument is 8 miles from Tulelake off Highway 139; (530) 667-2282; www.nps.gov/labe.

Manzanita Lake (all ages)

In the national park near the north entrance, Highway 89 at Highway 44; (530) 335-7557.

A postcard-perfect, evergreen-surrounded lake at 5,890 feet in elevation with dazzling views of the mountain. The visitor center here offers exhibits, maps, permits, books, brochures, and ranger-led interpretive programs. Rangers give talks about wildlife in the park amphitheater. Take the easy, 1.5-mile hike around the lake by yourselves or on a ranger's tour. Nonmotorized boating, camping, and trout fishing are the main activities here. Campsites are pretty and private. In fall Canada geese and wood ducks arrive in great numbers. Open in summer, the Camper Store sells food and supplies, and offers laundry facilities and showers.

Lassen Park Ski Area (all ages)

Located 3 miles southwest of Chester on Highway 36, just inside the southwest park entrance, and at the north entrance on Highway 44; (530) 595-4444.

The entire main road through the park is available for cross-country skiing, with unending views of snowbound mountains, valleys, and lakes. Equipment can be rented for sledding, snowshoeing, snowboarding, and downhill and cross-country skiing. The small downhill skiing hill has 4 runs, all beginning and intermediate, with a warming hut. Ski lessons are **free** on Saturday, and a **free** 2-hour, guided snowshoe hike is offered twice on Saturday and Sunday, too, for ages 8 and up; snowshoes are **free.** There are 7 miles of groomed ski trails near Manzanita Lake, with no attendant facilities.

Butte Lake (all ages)

From Old Station go 10.5 miles east on Highway 44, go south on Butte Lake Road, and drive 7 miles on a rough dirt road; (530) 595-4444.

A beautiful campground sits at lakeside at 6,049 feet in elevation, surrounded by ponderosa pines and rugged volcanic outcroppings. Motorized boats are not allowed, and the fishing is phenomenal. Interesting cinder cones and other volcanic formations, plus two more lakes nearby and backcountry trails, make this a great destination. Always call ahead about accessibility of the campground.

Lake Almanor (all ages)

Some 40 miles southeast of Lassen Peak, off Highway 89 near Chester; (530) 258-2141.

At this pine-fringed, 13-mile-long lake at 4,500 feet, the snowy peak of Lassen and surrounding mountains are mirrored in clear, calm waters. Families who like to swim, boat, fish, and water-ski enjoy the sandy beaches, small lodges, and campgrounds on the western shore; summer lake surface temperatures reach 75 degrees. The Lake Almanor Recreation Trail, an easy, flat, 9.6-mile paved route for biking, walking, and cross-country skiing, follows the west shore of the lake.

The small town of Chester caters to vacationers with simple, '50s-style lakeside resorts, motels, B&Bs, houseboats, and campgrounds.

Wild Horse Sanctuary (ages 14 and up)

Thirty miles east of Red Bluff at Highways 44 and A6, Shingletown; (530) 335-2241; www .wildhorsesanctuary.org. $$$$.

On this perfectly beautiful 5,000-acre ranch, your family will have the experience of a lifetime tracking wild mustangs on a 2- or 3-day horseback ride in the foothills of Lassen Peak, through a landscape of oaks and pines, bubbling streams, and lava-rock-strewn, wildflowery meadows; a swim in spring-fed swimming hole makes a refreshing rest stop.

Vibrating with spirit, muscle, and shiny coats, the horses are a spectacular sight. Nervous when they see riders, they hang around for a few minutes, watching, sometimes as close as 40 or 50 feet—while riders snap photos like mad—then they gallop off. Wild turkeys, deer, bald eagles, coyotes, foxes, owls, burros, and bobcats are also commonly sighted. The original band of 80 horses has been joined by those rescued from federal lands, wild mustangs from Nevada's Shoshone Indian Nation and Virginia Range, a small herd of Santa Cruz Island horses from Channel Islands National Park, and individual stars such as Phantom, the magnificent wild stallion from western Nevada.

Some riding experience makes this more enjoyable, although it is not required. For children under 14, get approval in advance. The pace is leisurely as the group proceeds slowly through brush, over creeks and gullies, and across meadows. You stay overnight at a rustic camp by a small vernal lake, in basic frontier-style cabins. Hearty meals are prepared while guests rest, swim, help groom and feed the horses, and explore.

Snowmobiling in Lassen National Forest

In the national forest are 6 designated trail areas for snowmobiling, each with parking and **free** admission; for information call (530) 335-7575.

- **Ashpan:** 9 miles southwest of the junction of Highways 44 and 89; 39 miles of trails; warming hut.

- **Swain Mountain:** 9 miles north of the junction of Highways A21 and 36; 47 miles of trails.

- **Jonesville:** 2 miles east of Cherry Hill Campground on Butte Meadows; 43 miles of trails.

- **Fredonyer:** 10 miles west of Susanville; 80 miles of trails.

- **Morgan Summit:** 5 miles east of Mineral on Highway 36; 77 miles of trails; warming hut.

- **Bogard Rest Stop:** 30 miles west of Susanville on Highway 44; 75 miles of trails.

Where to Eat

Creekside Grill. 278 Main St., Chester; (530) 258-1966. In a charming country setting by a creek, with a fireplace and an outdoor dining deck, the grill's fine chef produces sophisticated California cuisine and comfort food, too. $–$$

Peninsula Station Bar and Grill. 401 Peninsula Dr., Lake Almanor; (530) 596-3538. Fresh trout and reasonably priced, excellent meals with good selections for children. $–$$

Stover's St. Bernard Lodge. Mill Creek, 10 miles west of Chester; (530) 258-3382. Knotty pine walls, stained glass, and antiques in a casual dining room; hearty American food, such as huge hamburgers, fresh fish, steak, and fried chicken. Take a walk around the trout pond. $–$$

Where to Stay

Bailey Creek Cottages. 433 Durkin Dr., Lake Almanor; (530) 259-7829; www

.baileycreek.com. Right on a highly rated public golf course, nice 1- and 2-room suites with stone fireplaces, private decks, kitchens or kitchenettes, king beds or 2 twins, and sofa beds. $$$–$$$$

Childs Meadow Resort. 41500 Hwy. 36E, Mill Creek; (530) 595-3383 or (888) 595-3383; www.childsmeadowresort.com. Between Susanville and Red Bluff, a quiet year-round resort in a picturesque meadow at the foot of the Cascades, 5 miles from the southwest entrance to Lassen National Park. Nothing fancy, a fresh, clean motel with cabins, a store and cafe, and nearby hiking, fishing, biking, Nordic skiing, and snowmobiling; RV sites too. $–$$$

Drakesbad Guest Ranch. End of Warner Valley Road, Lassen Volcanic National Park; mailing address: Drawer K, Chester 96020; (530) 529-1512, (866) 999-0914; www.drakesbad .com. Secluded within the southeastern corner of the national park, a century-old hot springs resort in spectacular scenic surroundings at

5,700 feet. The old-fashioned Western ranch experience brings families back year after year—it's the kind of place where you can just let the kids go to participate in the many activities: trail rides, a little kids' program, hikes, crafts, swimming, badminton, horseshoes, table tennis, volleyball, and fishing. Rustic, comfortable lodge rooms, cabins, and bungalows, with kerosene lamps for light (cabins and bungalows have no electricity). Make reservations months in advance; for high-season weekends and holidays, a year ahead. $$–$$$

Lake Almanor Resort. 325 Peninsula Dr., Lake Almanor; (530) 596-4530; www.lake almanorresorts.com. A multifaceted, lively, nice lakefront resort on the north shore, with boat dock and fully equipped cabins and lodge units, and tent and RV sites. A 3-bedroom, 1-bath lakeside house has a sleeping porch, boat slip, and washer and dryer. The marina and playground areas are busy in summertime, and you can rent boats and kayaks, and lounge and swim at the lawn/beach area. $$–$$$

Spanish Springs Guest Ranch. 512450 Hwy. 395, North Ravendale; P.O. Box 70, Ravendale 96123; (530) 234-2050. Family ranch vacations, cattle drives, buckaroo camp, horseback riding on a big working cattle ranch. Accommodations vary, from a log cabin to a vintage ranch house. The fishing for trout is easy in stocked ponds. Family-style, hearty meals are served in the ranch house. $$–$$$

For More Information

Chester/Lake Almanor Chamber of Commerce. 529 Main St., Chester; (530) 258-2426; www.chester-lakealmanor.com. Go online to request the *Plumas County Visitors Guide* and to check out seasonal events.

Fall River Valley Chamber of Commerce. P.O. Box 475, Fall River Mills 96056; (530) 336-5840; www.fallrivervalleycc.org.

Campgrounds. (877) 444-6777; www.recre ation.gov.

Redding

A regional hub at the junction of Highways 5, 299, and 44, with attractive motels, as well as fishing and camping outfitters, Redding is also a refuge for the last mature riparian woodland left in the state. The Sacramento River runs along the edge of town, bordered by a great walking path. Most of the attractions of the Shasta Cascade are within a short drive of Redding.

East of Redding, in the southeastern corner of the Klamath National Forest, McArthur–Burney Falls Memorial State Park in the McCloud River Valley offers waterfalls, swimming holes, great fishing, and campgrounds. Within the park, Lake Britton is one of several lakes in the area, a trout-fishing mecca for trophy-size brown, rainbow, and eastern brook trout.

Turtle Bay Exploration Park (all ages)

800 Auditorium Dr., near the intersection of Highways 299 and 273, Redding; (530) 243-8850; www.turtlebay.org. Ages 16 and up $$$; ages 4 to 15 $$; under 4 are admitted free.

On a bend of the Sacramento River, indoor and outdoor activities and exhibits focus on the Sacramento River watershed, natural sciences and resources, art, culture, and human history. Follow Paul Bunyan's huge footprints to hands-on interpretive sites like the Giant Tree Maze, a fish ladder, and a miniature Shasta Dam. Climb the fire lookout tower and play on child-size earth-moving equipment, and on the Spar Swings and the Log Slide. Wander in the butterfly house. Explore the Redding Museum of Art and History; take a look at owls, hawks, bees, turtles, and beetles at the Carter House Natural Science Museum. Stroll or ride a Segway on paved walking trails through oak savanna and wetlands, to see otter ponds, a raptor exhibit, and botanic gardens in the Redding Arboretum by the river. There is so much to see here: a fabulous collection of Ansel Adams photographs; an elaborate, leafless replica of an oak tree, its roots extending beneath a see-through glass floor; a Wintu Indian bark house; a river seen from beneath the surface; and touchable pelts of native animals. A teenage staff of docents makes science and history fun.

Linking the park with a national recreation trail and a 200-acre arboretum on the other side of the river is the spectacular Sundial Bridge, said to be the world's tallest sundial, designed by Spanish architect Santiago Calatrava. A dazzling white, 710-foot-long icon with a translucent glass walking surface, the soaring bridge spans the river without footings in the water, so as not to impact Chinook salmon spawning grounds.

Sacramento River Trail (all ages)

In Redding, drive north on Market Street to Riverside Drive on the south side of the Sacramento River, and go west to the parking lot where the trail begins at Caldwell Park; (800) 874-7562. Free.

A tree-shaded, 16.7-mile paved path along the riverbanks from Redding to Shasta Lake. The southern portion covers 2.5 fairly flat miles. On the north side of the footbridge over the Keswick Dam, the trail continues 1.4 miles over steeper terrain with a break through a residential area, then goes on for 0.8 mile and exits on Lake Redding Drive, near Caldwell Park and the original entrance. Most riders take the 7-mile loop from the spectacular Calatrava Sundial Bridge past the 1915 open-spandrel-arched Diestelhorst Bridge, and back.

The Fly Shop

Off Highway 5, on the south end of Redding; 4140 Churn Creek Rd.; (530) 222-3555; www .theflyshop.com.

Look for a weathered gray building with a big fish visible from the highway. Available here are equipment, tours, and advice on which fish are biting, where to catch 'em, and water conditions. This is said to be the largest fly-fishing shop in the country. A popular summer fly-fishing camp for boys and girls, ages 10 to 15, is offered through the shop's own Antelope Creek Lodge near the town of Weed. Campers learn fly casting, safe wading, and about lures and bugs. In the evenings, they tie flies, hear camp stories, and make s'mores by the campfire. The property has a lovely stream and two lakes, and nice walled tents.

Waterworks Park (ages 4 and up)

151 North Boulder Dr., Redding; (530) 246-9550; www.waterworkspark.com. $$–$$$.

Ride a giant water slide and tube the 400-foot Raging River. Little kids like the watery playground designed just for them, while teens head straight for the beach volleyball.

Park Marina Raft Rental (ages 4 and up)

2515 Park Marina Dr., Redding; (530) 246-8388. $$$$.

Everything you need to raft the Sacramento River, including life jackets. In 3 or 4 hours, rafters and canoers float south down the Sacramento River from Redding to Anderson River Park. Beneath overhanging sycamores, cottonwoods, oaks, and willows, you can slide quietly along or stop to fish the salmon-spawning riffles. Raft-rental companies pick you up at the park and shuttle you back to Redding.

Redding Big League Sports Complex (all ages)

Take Highways 678/44 exit east nearly 4 miles to Old Oregon Trail, and go north 1.3 miles to the entrance on Viking Way; (530) 225-4485 or (530) 223-1177; www.bigleaguedreams .com. $.

Fenway Park, Wrigley Field, and Yankee Stadium are replicated in ¾-scale, and batting cages, an indoor multisport field house, sand volleyball courts, playgrounds, a family restaurant, and walking trails are among the facilities at this sports center.

McArthur–Burney Falls Memorial State Park (all ages)

Eleven miles northeast of Burney, off Highway 89; (530) 335-2777. $$.

In the Shasta-Trinity National Forest, the big attraction here is two million gallons of water a day tumbling over a misty, fern-draped, 129-foot cliff. Take a short hike down into the forest gorge to the base of the fall, where wild tiger lilies, maples, dogwoods, black oaks, and pines decorate the streamside. The walk is about a half hour for the fit and fast, an hour for amblers and photographers, and 2 hours for walkers who take side trails. Good trout fishing can be had in the deep pool at the base of the falls and in the 2-mile stream above and below. Pleasant hikes in and near the park in evergreen forests include a 1.5-mile flat route to Lake Britton Dam, then 3 miles farther to Rock Creek.

Lake Britton (all ages)

In McArthur–Burney Falls Memorial State Park, off Highway 89; (530) 335-2777 (campground reservations: 800-444-7275). Camping $.

Located here are 18 miles of shoreline amid evergreen forests near the Pit River. Camping and RV sites are not too private but are nice in the off-season. Accessible by boat (rentals here), with a terrific swimming hole at its foot, Clark Creek Falls is a jet of frigid water crashing into the lake. Crappie, bass, and catfish bite all season.

Ide Adobe State Historic Park (all ages)

21659 Adobe Rd., 2 miles south of Red Buff; (530) 529-8599. $ per car.

On the way to the Shasta region, a lovely rest stop on the river. The park is cool and shady, with giant oaks, lawns, picnic tables, historical displays, an old adobe home, and a small visitor center. You can fish here, but swimming in the fast current is not advisable. Crafts demonstrations are presented most summer weekends.

Where to Eat

Buz's Crab Stand, Seafood Restaurant, Market & Deli. 2159 East St., Redding; (530) 243-2120; www.buzscrab.com. A fun, casual setting for chowder, fish-and-chips, salmon burgers and crab cakes, cioppino, and myriad seafood dishes, salads, and sandwiches. Purchase fresh fish, condiments, and fixings to take away. $

Jack's Grill. 1743 California St., Redding; (530) 241-9705; www.jacksgrillredding.com. In a casual, noisy, hometown atmosphere, enjoy 16-ounce steaks, deep-fried prawns, and big plates of good old American food. Dinner only. $

Wild Bill's Rib-Steakhouse and Saloon. 500 Riverside Way, Red Bluff; (530) 529-9453. A casual place with a deck on the river; steaks, pasta, and fish. $

Where to Stay

Fairfield Inn and Suites. 5164 Caterpillar Rd., Redding; (530) 243-3200; www.marriott .com. Seventy-two brand-new, three-dia-mond-rated rooms and suites. Studio suites have 2 TVs, sleeper sofas, entertainment centers, mini refrigerators and microwaves; **free** continental breakfast, Wi-Fi, laundry room, small outdoor pool. $$$

Hampton Inn and Suites. 2160 Larkspur Lane, 1 block east of Hilltop Drive, Redding; (530) 224-1001; www.hamptoninn.com. Within walking distance of shopping and restaurants, near Turtle Bay Park. Both 1 and 2 bed rooms and larger suites, some with whirlpool tubs. Swimming pool, guest laundry, **free** breakfast, TV, video games. Suites have kitchenettes and sleeper sofas. $$–$$$

Hilltop Inn. 2300 Hilltop Dr., Redding; (530) 221-6100; www.thehilltopinn.com. A large, very nice motel with simple, spacious rooms with refrigerators and DVD/VCRs. Swimming pools, a wading pool, and **free** continental breakfast. Two reasonably priced restaurants. $$

Red Lion Motor Inn. 1830 Hilltop Dr., Redding; (530) 221-8700; www.redlion.rdln.com. A big garden court with a swimming pool, a wading pool, a putting green, and lots of trees. Rooms are large and very nice. Coffee shop and a terrific bar and grill are on-site; room service. Pets allowed with advance notice. $$

River Inn. 1835 Park Marina Dr., Redding; (530) 241-9500. At the edge of town on a small lake, with mountain views, nice motel rooms, a pool, barbecue, and a boat launch into the Sacramento River. Within walking distance to Turtle Bay. $–$$

For More Information

Redding Convention and Visitors Bureau. 7777 Auditorium Dr., Redding; (800) 874-7562; www.visitredding.com.

Fall River Valley Chamber of Commerce. P.O. Box 475, Fall River Mills 96056; (530) 336-5840; www.fallrivervalleycc.org.

California Welcome Center. Nine miles south of Redding at Shasta Outlets, Anderson; (800) 474-2782; www.shastacascade .com. **Free** maps, brochures, advice, a book and gift store, and historic displays.

Weaverville/Trinity

Glaciers chiseled the jagged peaks of the Trinity Alps eons ago, then melted away, leaving more than 50 sparkling alpine lakes among the brooding conifers of the Trinity Alps Wilderness, part of the Shasta-Trinity National Forest. Black bears, mountain lions, Roosevelt elk, mink, river otters, eagles, and spotted owls inhabit the upper reaches of one of the wildest and least visited national forests in the country.

Thousands of feet below snowy peaks, Trinity Lake snakes several miles through a rugged valley, where a few small summer resorts and villages attract families who like the quiet side of the Shasta Cascade region. More than two dozen US Forest Service campgrounds are scattered on the west side of the lake. Call (530) 623-2121 for information.

Sometimes a stretch of calm water, sometimes rapids raging in a gorge, the Trinity River leaps with salmon and steelhead, yielding fish of 10 pounds or more. Wildflowers run riot in the spring, and fall foliage is brilliant all along the river.

Surrounded by a dramatic mountain backdrop, Weaverville's original structures were destroyed by fire and replaced in the mid-1800s by brick buildings with wooden overhangs and exterior spiral staircases. A circa-1900 bandstand and the second-oldest courthouse in California contribute to an Old West atmosphere.

A gorgeous driving tour is the 140-mile-long Trinity Scenic Byway from Redding to Arcata along the river canyon and through the national forests on the southern border of the Trinity Alps. Pick up a self-guiding brochure at the chamber of commerce in Weaverville so as not to miss the nice places to stop and swim, fish, camp, and take it easy; this is a curvy, curvy road, not recommended in the wintertime—spring through fall is best. Look for the foot-long cones of the gray pine on the roadside.

Joss House State Historic Park (all ages)
Oregon and Main Streets, Weaverville; (530) 623-5284. $.

Remnants of the gold rush remain at the colorful Joss House, the "Temple Amongst the Forest Beneath the Clouds," built in forty-niner days for the Taoist worship of those Chinese who built the California railroads and sought gold on the river. Carved altars, tapestries, and elaborate artifacts are restored to their former glory. Shady picnic sites lie beside a creek in the park.

Jake Jackson Museum and
Trinity County Historical Park (all ages)
508 Main St., Weaverville; (530) 623-5211. Free.

Gold rush and pioneer days are re-created in a stamp mill, a miner's cabin, a blacksmith shop, and other displays.

Trinity Lake (all ages)
Accessed off Highway 3 between Weaverville and Coffee Creek; main campground and resort area is 10 to 15 miles north of Weaverville; (530) 623-2131 or (530) 623-6101.

More than 1,507 miles of rugged shoreline and hundreds of coves seem to absorb and hide houseboats, water-skiers, Jet Skis, and fishing boats. The west side is dotted with campgrounds, resorts, and boat launch ramps, while the east side, with somewhat restricted auto access, is largely undeveloped. Try your luck at fishing for trophy-size largemouth bass, trout, kokanee salmon, and catfish. Headquarters for houseboat, fishing boat, and watercraft rentals is the Trinity Lake Resorts marina (north on Highway 3, 15 miles to Cedar Stock Road). Here also are rental cabins, a casual restaurant, and general store (800-255-5561).

South Fork Trinity River National Recreation Trail (all ages)

Maps and information: Shasta-Trinity National Forest, 3644 Avtech Pkwy., Redding; (530) 226-2500; www.fs.fed.us/r5/shastatrinity.

The beautiful trail follows the South Fork Trinity River for 21 miles, from Scott Flat Campground near Forest Glen to Wildwood Road, and for 4 miles from a trailhead near Hyampom to Forest Glen.

Wilderness & Fishing **Expeditions**

- **Bigfoot Rafting Company,** Willow Creek; (530) 629-2263 or (800) 722-2223; www.bigfootrafting.com. The largest and most experienced river outfitter in the Klamath-Trinity region. Of special interest for younger children is their Tish Tang Gorge run on the Trinity River, complete with vertical canyon walls and beautiful forests, turtles, ducks, otter, and beaver; great for swimming.

- **Turtle River Rafting Company,** P.O. Box 313, Mount Shasta 96067; (530) 926-3223; www.turtleriver.com. Guided raft trips on the Klamath, Rogue, Trinity, and Sacramento Rivers.

- **Trinity River Rafting,** Coffee Creek Ranch, Big Bar; (530) 623-3033; www.trinityriverrafting.com. White-water rafting on the Trinity and other rivers, guided and self-guided. Raft and kayak rentals.

- **Trinity Trail Rides,** Coffee Creek Ranch, Trinity Center; (530) 266-3343. Horseback pack trips into the Trinity Alps.

- **Backpacking Shasta-Trinity National Forest,** Mount Shasta Ranger District office, 204 West Alma, Mount Shasta City; (530) 926-4511. Get wilderness permits, advice, and maps here for exceptional backpacking in the national forest and on the Pacific Crest Trail, which is accessed west of town at Parks Creek, South Fork Road, and Whalen Road, and at Castle Crags State Park.

Lewiston (all ages)
Twenty-nine miles west of Redding off Highway 299; (530) 623-2131 or (530) 623-6101.

A half hour from Weaverville, and so tiny that you can see all of it in a glance, the country village of Lewiston is strung out prettily along the rushing Trinity River. A 1903 landmark is the Old Lewiston Bridge, one of the last 1-lane bridges still in use. Buildings from the 1860s are on the National Register of Historic Places. Several antiques shops have literally thousands of square feet of collectibles of all descriptions.

Cold, constantly moving water flows into Lewiston Lake from Trinity Lake, an ideal situation for large rainbow, brook, and brown trout. Salmon and steelhead show up below the Lewiston Dam, below the bridge, and in the smaller streams.

Coffee Creek Guest Ranch (all ages)
Coffee Creek Road, HC2 Box 4940, Trinity Center 96091; (530) 266-3343 or (800) 624-4480; www.coffeecreekranch.com. Lodging (including meals, sports, and activities) $$$–$$$$; packages available.

Not much changed since the 1920s, this is a great place for families. Offered are rustic housekeeping cabins and weekly activities such as square dancing, trail rides, bonfires, movies, tennis, tubing, badminton, and more. Situated on 127 acres, with Coffee Creek rushing through, the resort is within 2 miles of trailheads into the Trinity Alps Wilderness Area. You can have three hearty, family-style meals a day here. There is a heated swimming pool, a rifle range and trapshoot, fly fishing in Coffee Creek for rainbow and German brown trout, guided hikes, and archery. Also available are babysitting for ages 3 and under, supervised play and organized games and activities for ages 3 to 17, and even overnight camping and riding lessons. This is summer camp for everyone in the family! Bring your cowboy hats and your fishing poles. Open in the wintertime, too—dogsled and sleigh rides!

Scott Museum (all ages)
Airport Road, Trinity Center; (530) 266-3367. Free.

Indian artifacts, covered wagons, stagecoaches, and artifacts from old pioneer and gold rush days.

Whiskeytown Lake (all ages)
Eight miles west of Redding; (530) 246-1225; www.nps.gov/whis. $.

A National Recreation area with 70 miles of hiking and riding trails. Popular for windsurfing and sailing, kayaking, fishing, and swimming. Check into stand-up paddle boarding at Brandy Creek Beach—on this flat water, it's easy for all ages (530-244-1129). Ask the park rangers at the visitor center about spectacular 220-foot Whiskeytown Falls, and three more waterfalls. Lovely picnic spot at Crystal Creek Falls; more shaded picnic areas with tables, grills, and restrooms at Brandy Creek, Oak Bottom, and Whiskey Creek boat launch.

Where to Eat

Allan's Oak Pit Bar-B-Q. 1324 Nugget Lane off Main, at the edge of Weaverville; (530) 623-2182. Barbecued chicken, beef, and pork dinners, plus sandwiches. $–$$

Lewiston Hotel. Deadwood Road, Lewiston; (530) 778-3823. On the river since 1862 when it was a stagecoach stop, the fun and funky hotel has a very casual restaurant with a deck above the river. Prime rib, burgers, kids' menu; all-you-can-eat spaghetti on Wednesday nights. $–$$

Pacific Brewery. Across from the Joss House, 401 Main St., Weaverville; (530) 623-3000. Hearty American fare in a circa-1850 brick building. Breakfast, lunch, and dinner. $–$$

Strawhouse Café. Highway 299, Big Flat; (800) 902-3276; www.strawhouseresorts .com. A beautiful straw bale structure with a deck over the Trinity River, just the spot to sit under an umbrella and watch kayakers and swimmers as you dig into lox and bagels, quiche, and traditional items for breakfast; tri-tip and grilled chicken sandwiches for lunch; and barbecued and roasted meats, pasta, and fish for dinner. There are fresh baked goods, brownies, and homemade pies all the time. $–$$$

Where to Stay

Lakeview Terrace Resort. Trinity Dam Boulevard off Highway 3, HC 01 Box 250, Lewiston 96052; (530) 778-3803; www.lake viewterraceresort.com. On Lewiston Lake, simple, clean 1- to 5-bedroom cabins about 20 to 30 yards apart under the trees, completely equipped, and, thankfully, with no TVs or phones. There is also an RV site with lake views, hot showers, and laundry facilities; pets okay. You can rent 14-foot fishing boats and patio boats holding up to eight people. $$–$$$

Ripple Creek Cabins. Off Highway 3, north of Coffee Creek; (530) 266-3505. Old-fashioned housekeeping cabins on the Trinity River, with a nearby swimming hole and trails leading to alpine lakes. Borrow inner tubes and bikes here. No TV or phones, except at the office. Well-behaved pets okay. Open in the wintertime for cross-country skiing. $

Strawhouse Cottages. Highway 299, Big Flat; (800) 902-3276; www.strawhouse resorts.com. On the banks of the Trinity River, lovely cottages sleeping up to 6, with living/ dining areas, equipped kitchens, and large, furnished decks with river or park views. You can barbecue or cook here or order from the restaurant, which is excellent. Well-behaved pets are welcome for a fee. Fishing guides and equipment are available on-site. $$–$$$

Weaverville Victorian Inn. 1709 Main, Weaverville; (530) 623-4432. A nice place for families, offering spacious motel rooms, a swimming pool, a woodsy setting, and guest laundry facilities. $–$$

Wyntoon Resort. Highway 3 just north of Trinity Center, P.O. Box 70, Trinity Center 96091; (530) 266-3337. RV, trailer, and tent campgrounds on 90 wooded acres; a marina; boat, water sports, and bike rentals. $

For More Information

Trinity County Chamber of Commerce. 317 Main St., Weaverville; (530) 623-6101 or (800) 421-7259; www.trinitycounty.com.

Shasta Trinity National Forest. 3644 Avtech Parkway, Redding; (530) 226-2500.

Redwood Country

The largest and oldest trees in the world live in a narrow band along the Northern California coastline and a few miles inland, with magnificent groves clustered in the "Redwood Empire" of Northern California. Walking beneath a 300-foot redwood forest canopy among these silent giants from the age of the dinosaurs will be an unforgettable experience for your family, ranking right up there with Yosemite and the Grand Canyon. The deepest, oldest groves have a truly prehistoric look: In fact, *The Lost World: Jurassic Park* was shot in Humboldt County redwood parks.

Beaches, birding, camping, fishing, and country pleasures are more reasons to spend vacations in Humboldt County. Ferndale, Eureka, and Arcata are charming, walkable "all-American" towns, each chockablock with Victorian buildings. And there is much new in the way of family friendly restaurants, shops, museums, and outdoor recreation.

Ferndale

Five miles off Highway 101 in idyllic dairylands, the village of Ferndale is two long streets of more than 200 glorious Victorian buildings. The entire tiny town is a State Historic Landmark. Pick up a walking tour map at most businesses in town. It will take a couple of hours to stroll Main Street, take pictures of the old buildings, and browse in the shops. Save a roll of film for the Gingerbread Mansion on Berding Street, a masterpiece of Victorian architecture.

On the edge of the Eel River Delta, a resting point on the Pacific Flyway, Ferndale is within minutes of great birding and some nice walks. Running 5 miles west out of town, Centerville Road leads to the beach, where a wide variety of birdlife and animals can be seen on walks north and south—swans, geese, sandpipers, pelicans, cormorants, seals, and whales.

On the east side of town are country lanes leading to the Eel River Estuary, where there are great routes for walking and biking. You can launch canoes and kayaks here in

REDWOOD COUNTRY

quiet waters or take a guided boat tour of the estuary (Eel River Delta Tours; 707-786-4187). More than 150 feathered species live in or pass through these wetlands, including loons, cormorants, harriers, and egrets. Where the Eel meets the sea, watch for sea lions, seals, and river otters.

Ferndale Museum (all ages)

Corner of Shaw and 3rd Streets, across from Main Street, Ferndale; (707) 786-4466; www .ferndale-museum.org. $.

A small but mighty exhibit of Ferndale history and the agriculture of the "Cream City," with period rooms, an operating seismograph, and a blacksmith shop.

Kinetic Sculpture Museum (all ages)

580 Main St., in the Ferndale Art and Cultural Center, Ferndale; (707) 845-1717. Free.

Here, in one of the strangest museums in the world, are some of the wild and weird, handmade, people-powered machines that travel over land, mud, and water in the World Championship Great Arcata to Ferndale Cross-County Kinetic Sculpture Race held annually in May. Called the "triathlon of the art world," this three-day event is great fun to watch, as the fantastical contrivances are driven, dragged, and floated over roads, sand dunes, Humboldt Bay, and the Eel River! Among the machines in past races were "Nightmare of the Iguana" and "Tyrannosaurus Rust," which was powered by cavemen!

Fun Shops in Ferndale

- **Sweetness and Light,** 554 Main St., Ferndale; (707) 786-4403; www .sweetnessandlight.com. Moo Bars (homemade marshmallow topped with almonds and caramel, smothered in chocolate), opera creams, fudges, brittles, caramel, truffles, and more fresh handmade candies; watch them being made in copper kettles.

- **Golden Gait Mercantile,** 421 Main St.; (707) 786-4891. Time is suspended in the 1850s with barrels of penny candy, big-wheeled coffee grinders, and glass cases lined with old-fashioned restoratives and hair pomades. Remember Burma Shave?

- **Dave's Saddlery,** 491 Main St.; (707) 786-4004. Cowboy boots, beaded hatbands, hand-tooled saddles, silver buckles, Ferndale T-shirts.

- **Fernbridge Antique Mall,** 597 Fernbridge Dr.; (707) 725-8820. On the way into town, watch for a large, light green building with striped awnings and a red door, a veritable bazaar of 40 dealers selling everything from estate jewelry to Victorian furniture.

Avenue of the Giants (all ages)

Off both sides of Highway 101 just north of Garberville; (707) 946-2311.

The highlight of your visit is likely to be the sight of the 2,000-year-old coastal redwoods in the Eel River Valley. A 30-mile scenic drive called the Avenue of the Giants, within Humboldt Redwoods State Park, is well marked, with turnouts and parking areas accessing short loop trails into the forest. Begin your tour at the visitor center, 2 miles south of Weott, where a movie, exhibits, and trail maps will help get you oriented (restrooms here, too). Ask for advice on the length and type of walks and drives you can take. At the south end of the avenue, accessed via the Phillipsville exit off the highway, you will find small grocery stores.

Humboldt Redwoods State Park (all ages)

Off Highway 101; visitor center 2 miles south of Weott on the Avenue of the Giants; (707) 946-2409; www.humboldtredwoods.org. Day-use fee $$ per car.

The largest and one of the least visited state parks, in part because it encompasses several small towns, the park is divided by the highway and has no main entrance. Most visitors do not realize that most of the park lies to the west and is reached by leaving the Avenue of the Giants and taking Mattole Road.

Not to be missed is the Rockefeller Forest in the Big Trees area, a 5-mile drive in on Mattole-Honeydew Road. Since the former champion sequoia Dyerville Giant, 362 inches in diameter, fell in rain-saturated ground in spring 1991, the new champ is a 363-inches-in-diameter behemoth in the Rockefeller Forest. Tiptoeing along boardwalks and spongy pathways in the damp, cool stillness at the foot of these magical giants, you'll hear only the bustle of chipmunks. A short trail leads to a sandy riverbank for sunbathing, wading, picnicking, and fishing.

A hundred miles of trails in the park are frequented by hikers, backpackers, mountain bikers, and horseback riders. Meanderings will turn up old homesteaders' cabins and several campgrounds, some for RVs and others consisting of simple sites in the backcountry. Apple blossoms bloom in orchards planted by early settlers. In fall big-leaf maples, alders, and buckeyes turn red and gold. Sighted in the farthest reaches of the park are bobcats, black-tailed deer, foxes, ring-tailed cats, and even black bears.

Having survived eons of ice ages and climate changes, only fragments of the original redwood forests now survive their greatest threat—logging companies. From the late 19th century to today, the virgin stands have been largely decimated, primarily by clearcutting, which destroys not only the trees but many of the creeks, rivers, and hillsides as well as wildlife habitats. Established in 1918 for the purpose of rescuing the Eel River Valley from the lumbermen, the Save-the-Redwoods League is credited with the establishment of the California parks that shelter most of the old-growth redwoods remaining in the world.

At the visitor center are a museum and exhibits, a native plant garden, a slide show, and a bookstore. Guided walks and talks are available.

Children's Redwood Forest (all ages)

One mile north from Myers Flat on the Avenue of the Giants to Williams Grove; (707) 946-2409; www.humboldtredwoods.org. Day-use fee $$ per car.

Following a major fire in 2003, this forest trail is a lovely, mostly flat, 0.75-mile round-trip loop beneath an old growth canopy. Cross the seasonal bridge over the Eel River to the trailhead. Check in at the Humboldt Redwoods State Park visitor center for weekly guided walks on this trail.

Benbow Lake State Recreation Area (all ages)

Two miles south of Garberville on Highway 101; (707) 923-3238.

Hundreds of acres of forestland and Benbow Lake, where you can fish, swim, and rent a canoe or paddleboat. Hiking trails, picnic grounds, and a campground are along a mile of the Eel River. A tourist attraction here is the four-diamond-rated, historic Tudor-style Benbow Inn, which has an excellent restaurant overlooking the lake. Call ahead about ranger-led interpretive canoe tours.

Where to Eat

Candy Stick Fountain and Grill. 351 Main St., Ferndale; (707) 786-9373. Sit on a red vinyl stool, have a shake or an ice cream soda, and pick up a game of pool or watch video games. Open for lunch and dinner—burgers, comfort food. $

Curley's Grill. 400 Ocean Ave., Ferndale; (707) 786-9696. California cuisine, homemade soup and focaccia, local fresh fish, grilled sandwiches, and more; served indoors in an old-fashioned dining room or on the patio. Lunch and dinner. $–$$

Loleta Cheese Factory. 252 Loleta Dr., Loleta; (800) 995-0453. Between Ferndale and Eureka. Yummy cheeses, deli items, and sandwiches to take out or eat here on the patio. Surrounding are great country roads for biking. $

No Brand Burger Stand. 1400 Main St., Ferndale; (707) 786-9474. Homemade burgers, fries, and shakes to go. $

For More Information

Victorian Village of Ferndale. 248 Francis St., Ferndale; (707) 786-4477; www.victorianferndale.org/chamber.

Eureka

The hub of Redwood Country, Eureka is homeport to more than 500 fishing boats in Humboldt Bay. The town's founding coincided with the birth of Victorian architecture, and blocks and blocks of elaborate 1850–1904 houses remain. A stunning example is the William Carson Mansion at 2nd and M Streets, a mixture of several styles that took 100 workers more than two years to build. The house is said to be the most photographed

Victorian home in America. You don't need to drag the kids on a sightseeing tour of the Victorians, because these structures are everywhere you look.

A new boardwalk runs along the bay front from G to C Streets, and a large area of downtown is packed with galleries, shops, coffeehouses, and restaurants in restored vintage buildings.

Use Eureka as your base for exploring the redwood parks. If your family likes to fish, head for the Mad, the Van Duzen, the Eel, and other rivers. At one time named the Best Small Art Town in America, Eureka is a uniquely creative community, as demonstrated in many art-, music-, and culture-related events, festivals, and galleries. Take note of the flamboyant murals around town—ask for a mural walk map at the visitors bureau. Another good brochure to pick up, entitled *Redwood Coast Heritage Trails,* lays out several easy walks with architecture, history, and Native American themes. Younger children will enjoy the Maritime Heritage walk along the waterfront.

Humboldt Bay Maritime Museum (all ages)
1577 Cookhouse Rd., next to the Samoa Cookhouse; (707) 444-9440. Free.

The museum has displays and artifacts of nautical relics, old navigation equipment, early radar, lighthouse lenses, fragments of wrecked ships, and the like.

Indian West Emporium
326 2nd St., Eureka; (707) 442-3042.

Native American art and artifacts, Western memorabilia, and vintage clothing. Kids are not always happy to shop and browse in art galleries, but this shop and the Many Hands Gallery at 2nd and 7th Streets are chock-full of cool things of interest to youngsters.

Clarke Memorial Museum (all ages)
3rd and E Streets, Eureka; (707) 443-1947. Free.

This 1920s Italian Renaissance former bank with a glazed terra-cotta exterior houses an extraordinary collection of Indian basketry and ceremonial regalia, antique weapons, maritime artifacts, and photos of early Humboldt days.

Geppetto's
416 2nd St., Eureka; (707) 443-6255.

A toy store offering costumes, dolls, games, hundreds of stuffed bears, puppets, tin toys, paper dolls, games, magic tricks and joke items, books, stickers, and more!

Moon's Play and Learn
440 F St., Eureka; (707) 442-5761.

In the largest toy store north of the Bay Area, you'll find brightly colored kites, windsocks and wind toys, puzzles, craft kits, science and nature items, books, and kinetic yard art kits.

Easy **Wildlife Walks**

- **Eureka Waterfront.** A paved waterfront path offers beautiful views of the bay and boats.

- **Sequoia Park.** Park near the Duck Pond. Take a 1-mile loop trail in redwood and alder groves.

- **Woodley Island.** Take Highway 255/R Street across the Samoa Bridge, and park at the Samoa Cookhouse or along the road. From here you can walk or bike along the edge of Humboldt Bay, 6 miles north to Arcata. The birdlife is extraordinary, from marbled godwits to curlews, dowitchers, falcons, and many more.

- **Humboldt Bay National Wildlife Refuge.** 1020 Ranch Rd., Loleta, just south of Eureka; (707) 733-5406. Take the Hookton Road exit from Highway 101 and follow it 1.2 miles to the Hookton Slough trailhead, a 1.5-mile path along the south edge of Humboldt Bay. Thousands of birds and ducks migrate through these beautiful grasslands, freshwater marshes, and mudflats, including 25,000 black brants, which fly from their nesting grounds in the Arctic to Baja. Look for herons, owls, ospreys, mallards, egrets, terns, and more. Restrooms.

- **Russ Park.** On the south end of Main in Ferndale. Three miles of pleasant, wildflowery trails and good birding in a 110-acre, closed-canopy spruce and redwood forest. Restrooms.

- **Ferndale Bottoms.** On the east side of Ferndale. The bottoms are great for walking and biking; a network of country lanes between lovely meadows leads to the Eel River Estuary. You can launch a canoe or kayak at the end of Morgan Slough Road or take a guided boat tour of the estuary (Eel River Delta Tours; 707-786-4187). Loons, cormorants, harriers, egrets, and over 150 feathered species live in or pass through these wetlands. Where the Eel meets the sea, watch for sea lions, seals, and river otters.

- **Loleta Bottoms.** From Loleta drive (or bike) west on Cannibal Island Road to Crab Park, at the mouth of an arm of the Eel River. You can scramble around the edge of the estuary and walk back east on the quiet road, watching for plovers, tundra swans, and curlews. Go right on Cock Robin Island Road, where mudflats attract masses of shorebirds. Continue back to your car or on toward Loleta, where the Loleta Cheese Factory is a good place to stop for sandwiches, snacks, and cheese tasting (fabulous organic cheese).

Sequoia Park (all ages)
Glatt and W Streets, downtown Eureka; (707) 441-4227.

Fifty-two delightfully green acres of virgin redwoods are home to a little zoo, a playground, formal gardens, walking paths, and a duck pond. There are interactive displays in the Secrets of the Garden exhibit, and the Wells Fargo Kids Koop and barnyard is where kids can milk a goat and drive a tractor. The zoo's most famous resident, Bill the chimpanzee, is one of the oldest chimps in an American zoo and an artist; see his works in the gift shop.

Humboats Kayak Adventures (all ages)
At the foot of F Street, Eureka; (707) 443-5157. $$$–$$$$.

Rent boats here or arrange to take a guided tour of Humboldt Bay: sea kayaks, sailboats, water-taxi rides.

Blue Ox Millworks Historical Park (all ages)
At the foot of X Street, Eureka; (800) 248-4259; www.blueoxmill.com. Adults $$, ages 6 to 12 $, 5 and under free.

A museum-like sawmill and job shop that makes custom trim for Victorian buildings, using the same machines that created the originals. Take a self-guided tour on catwalks overlooking the artisans and watch them turn columns, carve rosettes, and form wooden gutters and gewgaws, or call ahead to ask about scheduled tours. Surrounded by an enchanting wetlands wildlife sanctuary, the Blue Ox has set up a re-creation of a loggers' camp, a school, a bird-viewing station, and other attractions.

Woodley Island (all ages)
Cross the Samoa Bridge on Highway 255 (R Street) from Eureka; (707) 443-0801.

A marina, a paved footpath, a waterfront cafe, a souvenir shop, the Table Bluff Lighthouse, and the Samoa Cookhouse and museum. Look for the dramatic statue of a fisherman and his boat, honoring those "whom the sea sustained and those it claimed." You can rent kayaks here ($$$) for paddling along the edge of the bay (707-443-5157).

Samoa Cookhouse (all ages)
Across the Samoa Bridge from downtown Eureka, on Samoa Boulevard; (707) 442-1659; www.samoacookhouse.net.

Built on Woodley Island in 1885, this is the last surviving lumber camp cookhouse in the West. Giant American breakfasts are served from 6 a.m., including biscuits with sausage gravy, platters of pancakes, and scrambled eggs. Lunch and dinner are served family-style at long oilcloth-covered tables with charmingly mismatched chairs. Huge loaves of bread, cauldrons of soup, big bowls of salad and vegetables, baked ham, and roast beef are followed by wedges of homemade pie. Prices are quite reasonable, and kids 4 and under eat free.

Even if you don't eat here, stop in to see the free museum of logging equipment, artifacts, and fantastic photos of early days. A short walk from the restaurant is a quiet bayside village and a nice playground.

M.V. *Madaket* (all ages)
At the foot of C Street, Eureka; (707) 445-1910. $$–$$$.

Cruise the bay on a fantastic wooden steam-driven ferry built in the 1920s, an exciting way to get a new perspective on the harbor and the shoreline. The historical and natural sights are explained as you pass oyster farms, fishing and pleasure craft, the third-largest colony of harbor seals in the West, and zillions of fresh- and saltwater birds.

Big Lagoon County Park (all ages)
Off Highway 101, 34 miles north of Eureka; (707) 445-7652.

A 3-mile-long, protected lagoon, popular for beachcombing, swimming, sailing, windsurfing, kayaking, parasailing, and boating. Campsites in a Sitka spruce forest on the lagoon and the shore. Dogs welcome, no reservations required; no showers or hookups.

Where to Eat

Cafe Marina. Woodley Island, Eureka; (707) 443-2233; www.samoacookhouse.net. Overlooking the docks of Humboldt Bay on a deck with umbrella tables, enjoy fresh seafood and typical American diner fare. Breakfast, lunch, and dinner. $–$$

Cafe Waterfront Oyster Bar and Grill. Corner of 1st and 7th Streets, Eureka; (707) 443-9190. Enjoy Eureka's famous seafood and sea views—fish burgers, clams, and oysters in a casual Victorian setting. Breakfast, lunch, and dinner. $–$$

OH's Townhouse. 206 West 6th St., Eureka; (707) 443-4652. Family owned for 40 years, a casual place with oilcloth-covered tables, and a meat and seafood market. A big menu of fresh, fresh fish, a variety of great steaks, and Cajun-style prime rib. $$–$$$

Ramone's Bakery and Cafe. 209 E St., Eureka, and at several more locations in the

About **Redwoods**

- A coastal redwood can live to be more than 2,000 years old.
- The tallest living things on Earth, some redwoods grow to exceed 300 feet in height.
- The world's tallest tree is a coastal redwood in Redwood National Park, at 367.8 feet.
- Redwoods's ecosystems contain up to 10 times the living matter of tropical forest ecosystems.
- Humboldt Redwoods State Park shelters the largest remaining stand of ancient redwoods in the world.
- Winter rainfall in the northern redwoods can reach 100 inches a year.

area; (707) 445-2923. Where the locals go for cappuccino, killer bagels, breakfast and lunch, homemade soups, salads, sandwiches. $–$$

Sea Grill. 316 E St., Eureka; (707) 443-7187. Consistently voted Best Seafood Restaurant in the county for many years, and a noisy, popular place. Come early to avoid the crowds and enjoy choosing from a huge seafood menu; reservations are usually necessary. Lunch and dinner. $$–$$$

Where to Stay

Dean Creek Resorts. 4112 Redwood Dr., Redway; (877) 923-2555; www.deancreek resort.com. On the Eel River 3 miles from Avenue of the Giants, grassy, tree-shaded RV sites with full hookups, including TV, water and electric, barbecues, and fire rings; motel rooms; and new cabins with bathrooms, small kitchens, and TV, sleeping 4. Convenience store, swimming pool, sauna, playground; fishing nearby. $–$$

Eureka Inn. 518 7th St., Eureka; (707) 442-6441 or (800) 862-4906. A fabulous English Tudor–style, half-timbered hotel built in the 1920s, with a huge fireplace in the lobby, a comfy dinner house, a casual cafe, and a poolside dining area, all serving great American food and fresh seafood. Christmastime is festive; a towering, glittering tree is the backdrop

for nightly live entertainment. The staff is particularly friendly, and families feel welcome here. Rooms vary in size and amenities. $$$

Giant Redwoods RV and Camp. 455 Boy Scout Camp Rd., Myers Flat; (707) 943-3198. Twenty-three acres of riverfront on the Avenue of the Giants, a quiet family camp with full hookups and tent sites. $

Red Lion Inn. 1929 4th St., Eureka; (707) 445-0844 or (800) 547-8010; www.redlion .rdln.com. A large, family friendly motel, with a pool, a restaurant, and family suites. $$–$$$

Thunderbird Inn and Suites. 232 West 5th St., Eureka; (800) 521-6996. Featuring a heated pool, a recreation and games area, guest laundry facilities, some refrigerators, some 2-bedroom units, barbecues, and restaurants. $$

For More Information

Eureka/Humboldt County Convention and Visitors Bureau. 1034 2nd St., Eureka; (707) 443-5097 or (800) 346-3482; www.red woodvisitor.org. Call for a copy of *Destination Redwood Coast.*

Redwood Empire Association. 1925 13th Ave., Oakland; (510) 536-8828; www.redwood empire.com.

Arcata

Seven miles north of Eureka by way of scenic Highway 255 bordering Humboldt Bay, Arcata is an old loggers' town and the home of Humboldt State University. The town is headquarters for visitors to Redwood National Park, several miles to the north.

Just north, the coastal village of Trinidad on Trinidad Bay offers a pier, beaches, fishing access, a few shops, and a handful of terrific restaurants. Trinidad State Park and Patrick's Point State Park are nearby. Maps, brochures, and advice for travelers to the north coast are available at the California Welcome Center near the interchange of Highways 101 and 299; pick up souvenirs and artful items made by local artisans here, too.

Arcata Marsh and Wildlife Sanctuary (all ages)
569 South G St., Arcata; (707) 826-2359; arcatamarshfriends.org. Free guided walks are scheduled on Saturday, rain or shine.

Spend a couple of hours here on 4.5 miles of quiet footpaths in a stunning bayside setting, with freshwater ponds, a salt marsh, tidal mudflats, and winding water channels alive with birds and ducks. This is also a good place to jog or have a picnic; leashed dogs are allowed. You would never guess this is a wastewater reclamation project, and, in fact, a model for the nation. Stop at the interpretive center here for maps and information about birding walks throughout the region, and ask about guided walks at the marsh. In March the annual spring migration bird festival, called Godwit Days, is a big event, bringing birders from across the country (800-908-WING). For daily bird sightings call (707) 822-LOON.

Humboldt State University (HSU) Natural History Museum and Store (all ages)
1315 G St., Arcata; (707) 826-4479. Free.

Kids can touch a dinosaur tail, million-year-old fossils, and the inhabitants of a tide pool; see live native animals, such as bugs, toads, frogs, and bees; identify seashells; and learn about the natural history of the region. When you're in Trinidad, just up the highway (directions at http://sorrel.humboldt.edu/~natmus; 707-826-3689), visit the Humboldt State University Marine Lab and Aquarium, where you'll find touch tanks and ocean exhibits.

Redwood Park and Forest (all ages)
14th Street and Union, Arcata; (707) 822-7091. Free

A playground, lawns and picnic areas are pleasant retreats in Redwood Park. Within the park, the 600-acre Community Forest is a shady, green place to wander. To get to the Historic Logging Trail, take Nature Trail #1 on the west side of the parking lot to see logging sites and equipment from a century ago. A new 11.5-mile bike and walking path threads 790 acres of woodlands, including a few old-growth sequoias, and many second-growth trees.

Humboldt Lagoons State Park (all ages)
Thirty miles north of Eureka on Highway 101, Orick; (707) 488-2171. Free; camping $.

It's a 0.75-mile paddle or row to a 6-site boat-in campground at Ryan's Cove, located on a mysterious 520-acre lagoon. There is much wildlife to see, including Roosevelt elk. On the edge is a 3-mile, very quiet beach, plus access to the Coastal Trail. For day-use and environmental campsites, enter the park (by car) at Milepost 114.5.

Patrick's Point State Park (all ages)
Five miles north of Trinidad, on Highway 101; (707) 677-3570; www.parks.ca.gov. Parking $$; camping $.

Forest trails, picnic sites, a sandy beach, and world-class sea views from a vast headland. More than a hundred campsites; restrooms, showers; RVs to 31 feet.

Fishing in Redwood Country

This is prime ocean- and river-fishing country. For first-timers and beginning fisherpersons, stick to the riverbanks and the piers or go on a guided expedition with a company that provides equipment, transportation, and advice. For fishing conditions call the North Coast Fishphone, (707) 444-8041; or Eel River Headquarters, (707) 946-2311. For surf and rock fishing, lingcod, and salmon, try the K Street and F Street piers in Eureka; South jetty, 11 miles south of Eureka; or North jetty, 6 miles from the west end of Samoa Bridge.

- Clamming on beaches near Eureka and Arcata.

- King and silver salmon, as well as steelhead, on the Eel, the Mad, the Van Duzen, the Little River, and Redwood Creek, all near Eureka, and on the Klamath, farther north.

- Twenty lakes in Humboldt County are stocked with trout.

- **Celtic Charter Service.** Woodley Island Marina; (707) 442-7580. A 50-foot twin-diesel sportfishing boat takes families on salmon- and rock-cod-fishing and whale-watching expeditions.

- **Eureka Fly Shop.** 505 H St., Eureka; (707) 444-2000. Everything for fly fishing.

Clam Beach County Park (all ages)
Off Highway 101, 7.5 miles north of Arcata; (707) 445-7652.

A long stretch of shoreline for beachcombing, clamming, fishing, picnicking, and surfing. Vehicles, bonfires, and horses are okay, keeping in mind the posted information about the nesting of the snowy plover, an endangered shorebird.

Redwood National Park (all ages)
Visitor center between the park entrance and the town of Orick; (707) 488-3461; www.nps .gov/redw.

Twenty-two miles north of Arcata and stretching for more than 40 miles, Redwood National Park is a World Heritage Site encompassing three state parks: Prairie Creek, Del Norte, and Jedediah Smith. There are more than 300 developed campsites in the three state parks within the national park, as well as shoreline trails and beaches, swimming in the Smith River and Redwood Creek, and ranger-guided tours. You will need a **free** permit to drive the steep, 17-mile road to Tall Trees Grove, where a 3-mile-round-trip walking trail leads to some of the world's tallest trees.

The first mile or so of the easy, flat Redwood Creek Trail along the creek is okay for strollers. In late summer and fall, kids can wade in the streambed; with older kids, wear your tennis shoes and walk up the creek, looking for swimming holes and sandbars.

Redwood Trails Horseback Rides offers rides in the park ($$$$). Kids must be 5 years and up for the regular horseback rides (half hour, 1 hour, 3 hours, or 6 hours); pony rides ($$$) for kids 2 and up (707-488-3895).

Hammond Coastal Trail (all ages)

Two miles north of Arcata on Highway 101, take the Giuntoli Lane exit, go west on Janes Road, and follow signs to Mad River Beach. From the north, take the Clam Beach exit and watch for the trail; (707) 445-7651; www.redwoods.info.

Residents call this the best place to walk, jog, or bike in the county. Five miles of wide, smooth pathway are popular for strollers and in-line skaters, too. Beaches, bluffs, streamsides, and views of the river and the Pacific. Restrooms, picnic spots, and playgrounds at Hiller Park in McKinleyville.

Prairie Creek Redwoods State Park (all ages)

Six miles north of Orick, take the Elk Prairie Parkway exit off Highway 101. For park information call (707) 465-7354; www.parks.ca.gov. Some trails are wheelchair accessible. Parking $$; camping $.

A World Heritage Site featuring 12,000 acres of magnificent coastal redwoods, 70 miles of mountain-biking and hiking trails, herds of Roosevelt elk, a museum, 5-mile-long Gold Bluffs Beach, gorgeous campgrounds, and fabulous Fern Canyon, where lush ferns cover 50-foot rock walls. The visitor center is particularly interesting, with a museum, a natural history bookstore, displays of animals that live in the area—gray fox, great horned owl, elk, mountain beaver, raccoon, black bear—and a touch table and nature books.

For a drive-through, take the Newton B. Drury Parkway through the redwoods, past walls of ferns and magnificent trees. Many trails are accessed at the turnouts. Part of *The Lost World: Jurassic Park* was filmed here. If I were to camp and stay at only one redwood park, this would be the one, because of the almost surreal beauty and the variety of environments and wildlife. Best weather is fall and spring—both winter and summer can be cool and damp.

The Gold Bluffs Beach Campground is in the dunes of a stunning 10-mile beach, with tent and RV sites (to 24 feet long); no reservations required; restrooms, solar showers; leashed pets allowed. Exposed to wind, rain, and fog, sites are between the ocean and a forested bluff.

Where to Eat

Bon Boniere Ice Cream. 215 F St. in the Jacoby Storehouse, Arcata; (707) 822-6388.

Since 1898 this company has been famous for making ice cream, caramel popcorn, and other sweets. It also has soup, salad, and sandwiches. Another location is in Old Town Eureka on F Street. $–$$

Plaza Grill. 791 8th St., Arcata; (707) 826-2345. On the third floor of historic Jacoby's Storehouse, on the town plaza, a casual cafe with a beautiful long bar, a fireplace, and town views. Families love the burgers, sandwiches, fish platters, and the kids' menu. $–$$

Wildflower Cafe and Bakery. 1604 G St., Arcata; (707) 822-0360. Yummy muffins and pastries to go, and vegetarian cuisine for breakfast, lunch, and dinner. Homemade soup, Mexican and Chinese food, hearty daily specials like quiche and stroganoff. $

Where to Stay

Best Western Humboldt Bay Inn. 232 West 5th St., at Highway 101,Eureka; (800) 521-6996; www.humboldtbayinn.com. Indoor/outdoor heated pool, arcade games, pool table, coin laundry, double queen and double-double rooms with armchairs; some king rooms have sofa beds and recliners, flat-screen TVs, and robes. **Free** continental breakfast; casual coffee shop; **free** limousine ride to town. Ask for a room on the parking lot to avoid abundant highway noise. $$–$$$

Elk Meadow Village Vacation Homes. 1 Valley Green Camp Dr., Orick; (707) 845-7668; www.redwoodadventures.com. Remodeled loggers' cabins, the only lodgings within Redwood National Park. Three bedrooms, 2 baths, equipped kitchen, laundry room. See wildlife from your window and enjoy a private park on Prairie Creek. You can order food, beverages, and sporting good rentals

in advance. The operators are experienced naturalists and experts who conduct guided tours, horseback rides, and fishing trips, and rent bikes and kayaks for exploration of Redwood National Park. $$$$

Mad River Rapid RV Park. 3501 Janes Rd., Arcata; (707) 822-7275. Landscaped sites with all amenities; game room, pool, tennis; part of the Mad River Quality Inn resort. $

Redwood National Park Hostel. 14480 Hwy. 101, Klamath; (707) 482-8265; www.redwoodhostel.org. Voted one of the two best Hostelling International hostels in the world (by users of HIHostels.com), tied with a Japanese hostel for first place for 2007–2008, based on friendliness of staff, efficiency of service, level of comfort, cleanliness, security, and location. Housed in a 1907 pioneer homestead overlooking the ocean. $

Hampton Inn and Suites Arcata. 4750 Valley West Blvd., Arcata; (707) 822-5896; www.hamptoninn.hilton.com. Brand-new 82-room inn offering **free** hot breakfast, Wi-Fi, flat-screen HDTV, laundry room, indoor pool, and fitness room. Some spacious king rooms have sofa beds, desks, coffeemakers, and small refrigerators. $$–$$$

For More Information

Trinidad Chamber of Commerce. Main Street and Patrick Point Drive, Trindad; (707) 441-9827; www.trinidadcalif.com.

California Welcome Center. 1635 Heindon Rd., near the interchange of Highways 101 and 299, Arcata; (707) 822-3619; www.visitcwc.com. Maps, brochures, and travel magazines for the north coast; souvenirs and gifts from local artisans.

Index